REVISED EDITION

Racial Attitudes in America

Trends and Interpretations

Howard Schuman

Charlotte Steeh

Lawrence Bobo

Maria Krysan

D1173445

Harvard University Press
Cambridge, Massachusetts
London, England · *1997*

Library of Congress Cataloging-in-Publication Data

Racial attitudes in America : trends and interpretations / Howard Schuman . . .
    [et al.].—Rev. ed.
        p.   cm.
    Includes bibliographical references and index.
    ISBN 0-674-74568-X (cloth : alk. paper).—
    ISBN 0-674-74569-8 (paper : alk. paper)
        1. United States—Race relations—Public opinion—History—20th century.
    2. Social surveys—United States—History—20th century.
    3. Public opinion—United States—History—20th century.
    I. Schuman, Howard.
    E185.615.R2136   1997
    305.896′073—dc21   97-27071

Racial Attitudes in America

Contents

Preface to the Revised Edition

The primary purpose of our second edition, as of our first, is to present and interpret changes in American racial attitudes since the early 1940s. Our book is not an argument for a single point of view on the nature of racial attitudes, let alone of race in America. Although we do not hesitate to offer interpretations when they seem useful, we try to present the evidence in a way that allows readers to make their own judgments and arrive at their own conclusions. In addition, we attempt to place trends in the context of a broader recognition of the problems of interpreting attitudes and attitude change, and of the different theoretical perspectives that have been offered by others.

The present edition is a complete revision of the 1985 edition. Although a number of sentences and occasionally whole paragraphs are unchanged, this is only where they seem to us as accurate today as when originally written. Much of the book has been rewritten, and there are substantial additions, not only because of new data available in the decade since the first edition, but also because of new thinking about earlier interpretations. For the benefit of readers of the 1985 edition, we list here the major additions and changes, though there are many other minor ones throughout the book.

Chapter 1 has a new theoretical introduction discussing the relations among attitudes, norms, behavior, and inner convictions. In addition, the historical account has been brought into 1997 and in some places deepened as well.

Chapter 2 includes a more extended discussion of the problems caused by race-of-interviewer effects, especially for data on black Americans; a consideration of the differences presented by telephone data, which are now added in Chapters 3 and 5; and a report of recent research on the issue of social desirability in survey responses.

Chapter 3 now includes trend data for questions concerning white explanations of black socioeconomic disadvantage; questions about perceptions of discrimination; and questions about two forms of affirmative action. In addition, the distinction between principle and implementation questions has been reconceptualized, as has the difference between implementation and affirmative action. Additional time points for some previous questions have also led to modifications in conclusions about change. Although here as elsewhere in the book we rely mainly on survey data gathered by others, in a few cases we have carried out our own replications in order to extend a time series that lacked a recent time point.

Chapter 4 is an entirely new chapter, providing a considerable expansion of a previously limited analysis of intercohort and intracohort effects. In addition, the different relations to racial attitudes of education and income are explored, and associations of gender and racial attitudes are documented. The analysis in this chapter uses regression to introduce a greater degree of statistical control than in other chapters, but an effort has been made to present the main results in a way that is accessible to readers less interested in technical aspects of the work. Here as in the other chapters, we rely heavily on graphs that can show the main relationships visually.

Chapter 5 includes the new questions about explanations for black disadvantage, the extent of discrimination, and affirmative action, and emphasizes mainly comparisons with white attitudes on the same issues. Again, the importance of race-of-interviewer effects is stressed: such effects are especially important with black respondents because so many are interviewed by whites. Social class differences in black perceptions of discrimination are also presented and discussed.

Chapter 6 considers more recent writings by authors discussed in the 1985 edition, plus some entirely new authors, though no attempt is made to cover what is a large and growing literature. Two survey-based experiments of our own are presented, one attempting to clarify attitudes toward affirmative action, the other about the nature of objections to government intrusion.

Chapter 7 includes experimental data that indicate the extent to which norms regarding government enforcement have implications beyond issues of black-white integration, and also show how such norms differ from personal preferences. The complexity of the forces acting on racial attitudes and behavior is emphasized. This largely rewritten chapter is not a summary of the book; for that purpose, see the summaries of the main chapters.

We should note that as in the earlier edition, the data and interpretations in this book are much more extensive on white than on black attitudes, though we attempt some consideration of the latter also. For reasons explained in Chapter 2, data from the major national surveys are notably less adequate and probably less valid for black than for white Americans. This is a problem we could not overcome in the present book, but fortunately there are now some large-scale surveys of African Americans; when these are repeated over time in the future, a good deal can be learned that can only be dimly seen with data available to us at present. We also do not in this book attempt to deal with attitudes toward rapidly growing parts of the U.S. population that are neither black nor white, a challenge that will need to be taken up in the future. It will not be easy, because ethnic classification in surveys has been much more in flux with Hispanics and some other groups than with African Americans.

As with the first edition, the order of authorship does not adequately indicate contributions to the revised edition. Charlotte Steeh took primary responsibility for preparing the new chapter on cohort effects, and she also contributed additions to the historical account in Chapter 1. Lawrence Bobo had commitments that prevented his active involvement in the present edition beyond critical reading, suggestions on drafts, and additions to the historical chapter, but his substantial contributions to the earlier edition carry forward into this one. Maria Krysan joins us for the first time in this edition, and her involvement has been essential to its preparation. She took responsibility for making almost all the data available for our new analysis and for solving many problems in the use and interpretation of the data. Her own research figures importantly in Chapter 2, which she also helped revise more generally, and she contributed valuable advice on drafts of other chapters as well. The book could not have been completed without her involvement from beginning to end. Howard Schuman retains overall responsibility for the volume, including both its general orientation and its final form, and he must continue to be regarded as accountable for whatever limitations or misinterpretations it may contain.

Most of an earlier draft of this revision benefited significantly from an early critical reading by James A. Davis, and two of the main chapters received a similar critical review by Marylee C. Taylor. Willard L. Rodgers provided important help on the statistical analysis for Chapter 4. Howard Schuman received frequent advice on computing from his son Marc Schuman, the more necessary as much of the book involved collaboration via the Internet among four authors located in different parts of the country. At Harvard University Press, Michael Aronson served as the senior acquisitions editor for this edition, as for the previous edition, with the involvement also of the assistant editor Jeff Kehoe. Our manuscript editor, Christine Thorsteinsson, recommended additions, deletions, and other changes that greatly improved the clarity and pace of the book at many points. We are grateful to each of these individuals for their help in making this a better book.

As we were completing the book in early 1997, it looked as though most of our trends would end in 1994. Through the cooperation of Marilyn Potter at the Roper Center, however, we were able to draw on the 1996 General Social Survey as soon as it was released, and the Gallup Organization (with the special help of Sheila M. Kearney and Jacob Ludwig) provided us with early results from their large 1997 poll on racial attitudes. Finally, data from the 1996 National Election Study reached us just as the book was being copyedited, enabling us to keep most of our analysis completely up to date in terms of time points. Since it is rare for the kinds of trends we are concerned with to change reliably in a matter of just two or three years, this is more a psychological advantage than a matter of real substance. We think it quite likely that the present edition will remain "current" into the twenty-first century.

A small grant from the National Science Foundation (SBR 9310794) facilitated various steps involved in secondary analysis of archival data. Finally, we thank the several survey organizations that provided the data on which the book is based. This includes especially those associated with the University of Michigan Survey Research Center's Monthly Survey, which allowed the needed time and setting for our own experiments and replications.

Howard Schuman

Preface to the 1985 Edition

Survey organizations began asking Americans about their attitudes toward racial issues in the 1940s. In this book we trace the changes in such attitudes over the past four decades indicated by national survey data, discuss interpretations of these changes that have been offered by various analysts, and present our own conclusions.

Although some of the trends we describe have been reported elsewhere, this is the first attempt to draw on all available trend data for both whites and blacks. We combine findings from the three major survey organizations that have collected such data over time: Gallup, the National Opinion Research Center (NORC), and the Institute for Social Research (ISR). This breadth makes possible comparisons that turn out to be illuminating. We also report several original experiments in supplementary surveys that throw light on issues raised by the main sources of data.

Trends in racial attitudes are a significant part of the larger picture of race in America, but they are obviously not the whole picture. In Chapter 1 we briefly sketch some historical elements that are useful to keep in mind as background, though this book cannot begin to cover the economic, political, legal, and other factors that contribute to the complexity of black-white relations in the United States. We certainly do not believe that American race relations should be studied only in attitudinal terms, but we do think that a knowledge of changes in black and white attitudes (and in the social norms that attitudes reflect) is important to an understanding of the changing meaning of race in this country from the 1940s to the present.

The order of authorship on the title page does not adequately describe contributions to this book. Lawrence Bobo, a graduate student when the study began, took an increasingly important role as the research progressed. He contributed in significant ways to the conceptual framework of the analysis, drafted Chapter 1, designed and drafted Appendix B on statistical testing, and provided crucial help in many other ways. Charlotte Steeh was responsible for locating, obtaining, and organizing most of the data we use; for drafting sections of Chapters 2 and 3 on sampling and cohort effects, as well as Appendix A; and for many other important steps in the design and execution of the study. Howard Schuman initiated the project and drafted most of Chapters 2–6; although drafts of all chapters went through joint revision, he is ultimately responsible for any limitations in the book.

Acknowledgment is due to Ronald Humphrey and Jacqueline Scott for their helpful research assistance; to Margaret Grillot and Nancy Crosbie for careful typing of several versions of the manuscript; and to Camille Smith, whose intelligent and thorough editing improved the book substantially.

The initial review process employed by the Social Science Research Council was extensive and intensive. We benefited greatly from suggestions from James A. Davis and John Modell, the editors of the series Social Trends in the United States, from Robert Pearson of SSRC, and from Troy Duster, Reynolds Farley, Andrew M. Greeley, Paul Sheatsley, D. Garth Taylor, J. Mills Thornton III, Robin M. Williams, Jr., and William L. Yancey. Patrick Bova located and provided early NORC questionnaires, and Tom W. Smith answered numerous questions about recent NORC data.

A Guggenheim Fellowship allowed time for Howard Schuman to begin the project and develop its overall design. The collection and analysis of the data were supported by an NIMH Grant (MH 34116), with some supplementary help from the Social Science Research Council. The experiments on question form, wording, and context were part of methodological research supported by the National Science Foundation (SES-8016136). For all of these sources of support over several years we are most grateful, and of course none of the individuals and organizations that offered support is responsible for the specific conclusions we reach in the pages that follow.

Racial Attitudes in America

1

Theoretical and Historical Perspectives

This is a book about racial attitudes. Although the term "attitude" is widely used in both speech and writing, there is often some uncertainty about how seriously attitudes should be regarded, especially attitudes reported by sample surveys. Thus it is useful to begin by clarifying what we mean when we refer to attitudes, and then to consider briefly the relation of the attitude concept to three other important terms: norms, behavior, and inner convictions.[1]

Theoretical Considerations

The Attitude Concept

In most social science writing, the term "attitude" refers to a favorable or unfavorable evaluation of an object. The object may be a person, a group, a policy, an idea, or indeed anything at all that can be evaluated. Many of the questions that we discuss in later pages fit well this definition of an attitude. For example, in Chapter 3 we consider responses to the question, "Do you approve or disapprove of marriage between whites and nonwhites?" Approval and disapproval are essentially synonyms for favorable and unfavorable evaluations of the object, which in this case is racial intermarriage.

Sometimes an evaluative question is phrased in a more indirect fashion, yet could easily be rephrased to use words like "approve or disapprove" or "favor or oppose." This is the case for the question, "Do you think white students and black students should go to the same schools or to separate schools?" Here respondents are clearly being asked to provide an evaluation of school integration.

Most of the questions we will consider in this book fit closely the evaluative form just illustrated, but some do depart from it more noticeably and seem to inquire about beliefs rather than about attitudes in a purely evaluative sense. For example: "On the average, blacks have worse jobs, income, and housing than white people. Do you think these differences are mainly due to discrimination?" Here the question asks whether the respondent believes in the pervasive effects of racial discrimination. Yet in common parlance such inquiries are usually referred to as attitude questions also. Moreover, this and other belief questions that we analyze all have obvious evaluative implications. If the answer is "yes" to the inquiry about the pervasiveness of discrimination, this suggests that whites are responsible for black disadvantage and that steps might well be favored to prevent discrimination or even to compensate blacks for the unfair treatment they receive. If the answer is "no," the implication is that no such steps are needed and that probably some limitations of blacks themselves, not the practices of whites, are responsible for black disadvantage.

In this book we use the term "attitude" in a broad sense to include not only direct evaluations but also beliefs that are evaluative in implication. This is not a very controversial approach to take in applied research. What is more controversial is the assumption that attitudes play an important role in relations between blacks and whites. We address this issue by considering the connection of attitudes to three other concepts that are of obvious importance.

Attitudes and Norms

A frequent concern raised about racial attitudes is that they may represent little more than the superficial verbalization of socially approved norms. If it has become less acceptable over the past half century for whites to express negative attitudes toward blacks, then are we measuring how whites actually feel, or are we instead measuring how whites think they should report feeling, especially in the interview situation? The term "social desirability" is often used to characterize answers to survey questions that conform to current norms, rather than to what people truly feel. In Chapter 2 we present several kinds of evidence indicating that at least some responses to attitude questions do appear to vary depending on the nature of the interview situation. In one case, attitudes shift in relation to the degree of privacy provided to respondents, with some white attitudes becoming more negative toward blacks when the survey setting is more private. In another case, the assumptions that respondents make about an interviewer's attitudes appear to influence the respondents' own expression of attitudes.

The issue is more complex than this line of thinking suggests, however. It is useful to recognize that attitudes themselves can be distinguished as primarily normative in origin or primarily a matter of personal preference. For example, what to order from a restaurant menu can be considered largely a matter of personal taste, and each person is free to make his or her own choices within a wide range. But it would be naive to think that the transformation of white racial attitudes over the last half century has occurred simply because a great many Americans have each altered their personal views. Up until at least the 1940s, segregation, discrimination, and openly verbalized prejudice toward minorities of all kinds were entirely acceptable throughout much of the United States. But today very few people would express open support for any of these. Norms calling for equal treatment regardless of race are now highly salient in America, not only in much of the legal structure, but in more intangible ways as well. In this sense, certain of the trends that we report in Chapter 3 for attitude questions can be regarded as revealing substantial changes in American norms.[2]

Thus our book might well be called *Racial Norms in America: Trends and Interpretations*. This would not make the book any less significant. On the contrary, tracing such a momentous change in norms is a very important effort. The elimination of hotel advertisements stating "Only White Christians Welcome" and the inclusion in job advertisements of "Equal Opportunity Employer" are not trivial signs of a cultural transformation. Even if we do not entirely understand what has led to the changes or what their effects are, the trends say something quite meaningful about American life. But beyond that larger transformation, norms have real force, else why should a respondent care what an interviewer thinks? It is exactly the power of norms that is revealed when we say that a person gives a different answer because he or she is in the presence of an interviewer, especially since the same pressure is likely to occur in a number of other social situations.

Indeed, that norms are powerful is the paradoxical implication of certain social psychological experiments that were carried out to demonstrate just the opposite. For example, Gaertner and Dovidio (1986) show the importance of covert prejudice by drawing on Latane and Darley's (1970) classic finding that people are less likely to help in an emergency when other potential helpers are available than when they are alone. Gaertner and Dovidio "predicted that the belief that other bystanders are present would have a greater inhibiting effect on the subject's response when the emergency involved a black victim than when it involved a white victim. Failure to help a black person in this situation could be justified or rationalized by the belief that the victim is being helped by someone else. Bystanders believing themselves to be the sole witness, however, were not expected to discriminate against black victims relative to white victims . . . [because when a bystander is] alone, the failure to help a black victim could be more readily attributed to bigoted intent" (1986:77). Although the experiment is presented to show the hypocrisy that lurks behind a liberal front, it also points to the power of the norm of equal treatment to influence behavior when the norm is made salient (the "alone condition"). If the white subjects show their "true feelings" when normative forces are removed, then the condition that produces a different behavior when norms of equal treatment are brought to the fore tells us that norms are really quite important in shaping actions.

Still, there is the question of the degree to which norms are "internalized" and become personal attitudes, so that they operate even when interviewers or other observers are not present. There is good reason to think that this varies greatly across individuals, with some having made the norm an integral part of their personality and thus attempting to live in accord with it all of the time. For others, the norm functions more as an external constraint, shaping their behavior to the extent that they feel observed by those assumed to uphold the norm. But even for the latter people, we can see the norm as meaningful, since it does influence the way they act in certain public situations. It is by no means unimportant, for example, that many people try to use nonracist or nonsexist language because of external normative constraint, even if this does not reflect their inner preferences. In addition, widely supported social norms are available to be called on in critical situations, as the extremely negative nature of the charge of "racism"—whether deserved or undeserved—indicates.[3]

From a larger standpoint, if there were not important changes in racial attitudes more generally, why should respondents assume interviewers to be so different in their expectations in the 1980s than in the 1940s? Norms do not exist in thin air, and in the absence of legal or other coercion they must receive some support from personal attitudes. Just as many attitudes are shaped by social norms, so individual attitudes support social norms by being called forth when there is a violation of the norm. The circularity of this statement is no accident: a norm can be thought of as a kind of collective attitude or evaluation, and its efficacy depends on its receiving sufficient support in the form of individual attitudes toward those who violate the norm. When attitudes at the individual level no longer support a norm—for example, when attitudes toward a presidential candidate are no longer affected by his having been divorced—then the norm itself is well on its way to disappearing.

Attitudes and Behavior

Sometimes a person hearing or reading about attitudes challenges their importance on the grounds that we should really be interested in behavior outside the survey situation. In examining this issue it is necessary to keep in mind that although we often speak of responses in surveys as "attitudes," this is a shorthand form of expression. More precisely, an attitude is something social psychologists believe to underlie the responses expressed in actual surveys, rather than being the responses themselves, which are a form of verbal behavior. From this standpoint, it is important to acknowledge that attitudes are only one determinant of behavior, both within and outside the interview. Within the interview itself, as we have already noted, the respondents' assumptions about the interviewer and other aspects of the survey can sometimes influence their answers significantly. Outside the interview, it would be altogether naive to expect a rigid one-to-one correspondence between attitude responses from a survey and the ordinary behavior of the same individuals.

The looseness of the relation between attitude data and behavior does not mean that information about attitudes is not valuable. A moment's reflection will bring to mind examples of attitudes that are quite real and useful to know about, yet which for good reason do not manifest themselves at all in overt behavior. At the simplest individual level, one person may dislike another and yet behave in a polite and even friendly manner toward the other person, whether out of courtesy, convention, or a need to please someone more powerful. At a societal level, people living in a police state (or, in earlier times, in slavery) may have to behave in ways quite different from their own inclinations in order to survive. In such cases it would not make sense to disregard either the attitudes, assuming they could be identified, or the behavior in attempting to understand the present or to have some sense of what the future will be like.

Still, if attitudes and behaviors existed in entirely separate spheres, learning about attitudes would be of little practical value, whatever their interest from the standpoint of intellectual understanding. But careful reviews of a wide range of past studies (Schuman and Johnson 1976; Ajzen and Fishbein 1977; Eagly and Chaiken 1993), as well as specific experimental research (for example, Brannon et al. 1973; Weigel and Newman 1976; Fazio and Zanna 1981), make it clear that this is not the case. Attitudes and relevant behavior at the individual level are usually correlated to some extent, from small to fairly large, and there is increasing knowledge about the conditions under which the correlations will be higher or lower. Once the naive notion that there should be a rigid identity between expressed attitudes and behavior is rejected, then the degree of relation in any particular area of life becomes itself an important fact to understand.

More generally, attitudes frequently provide useful clues to behavior, even though they are not always direct and powerful determinants of behavior. For example, verbally expressed white opposition to school busing has always been very high. The hard facts of protest movements and violence, seemingly endless litigation and legislation, and significant white flight to suburban areas not touched by desegregation orders all attest to the broader relevance of these "softer" attitudinal indicators. There is, in fact, evidence that attitudes have considerable influence on participation in antibusing movements (Useem 1980; Begley and Alker 1982).

In this book we concentrate on national patterns of attitude change on the assumption that these patterns are relevant to understanding past, present, and potential behavior. Our analysis, however, is geared to identifying as well as we can the complexities that affect the degree to which attitudes are expressed in behavior, including response behavior during the interview itself. Thus we use experimentation to test how particular types of question wording and questionnaire context affect answers. We discuss the effects of the race of the interviewer and of the degree of privacy that a survey affords to respondents. Furthermore, we often compare answers to different questions in the interest of making sense not only of apparent inconsistencies in attitudes but also of the relation of the attitude data to larger social and political events and changes. Both in this chapter and in Chapter 7 we consider briefly the parallels between the kinds of national attitude trends we are reporting and other evidence of racial change over the same period. Throughout we try to keep in mind that attitudes are only one type of evidence about a society, and, like all evidence, must be weighed and evaluated rather than taken at face value.[4]

Inner Convictions

Although critics of the use of attitudes sometimes claim to look to overt behavior as the ultimate goal of knowledge, just as often the real goal is not so much behavior but rather the inner life of people—what they really think and feel (their true attitudes!) as opposed to what they say or do. After all, overt behavior is itself frequently less than completely sincere, whether in relatively innocuous ways, as when we are polite to someone we may dislike, or in more significant ways, as when a white president appoints an African American to a high government position for purely political purposes. Social behavior is controlled to a considerable extent by exactly the same norms that control the expression of attitudes in surveys, and one should not look to either for final evidence of what goes on in the hearts of men and women, white or black (for example, see our reference to Truman, p. 19).

Indeed, the question of what goes on in the hearts of individuals is something no survey or direct observation of behavior can be sure to uncover. Recent theoretical and experimental work in social psychology has emphasized the ambivalence of many white Americans toward blacks and toward racial issues (Katz, Wackenhut, and Hass 1986). One finds not a simple positive nor a simple negative stance, but a mixture of positive and negative attitudes. For example, there is some evidence that white Americans are more positive toward highly successful blacks than toward equally successful whites, but that the opposite holds when relatively unsuccessful blacks and unsuccessful whites are compared. This work is still at an early stage, but it provides a more complex view of white racial attitudes that is probably closer to the truth than arguments over degrees of overt and covert prejudice.

Our book assumes that change or lack of change in attitudes is a significant part of the larger picture of race in America, but it is obviously not the whole picture. In the balance of this chapter we briefly sketch some past events that are useful to keep in mind as background, though our book cannot begin to cover all of the economic, political, legal, and other factors that contribute to the complexity of black-white relations in the United States. We certainly do not believe that American race relations should be studied only in attitudinal terms, but we do think that knowledge of changes in white and black attitudes—and in the social norms that attitudes reflect—is important to an understanding of the meaning of race in this country from the 1940s to the present.

Historical Background

"The pervasive gap between our aims and what we actually do," stated President Truman's Committee on Civil Rights in 1947 (p. 129), "is a kind of moral dry rot which eats away at the emotional and rational bases of democratic beliefs." With these words and the moral undercurrent they epitomized, the committee's report, entitled *To Secure These Rights,* placed the rights and status of blacks and other American minorities high on the national agenda. Arguing that the treatment accorded blacks contravened the highest principles of American democracy, the committee called for the swift implementation of measures to ensure the physical safety of blacks, to protect their right to vote in the South, and to improve their job opportunities. Beyond these specific steps it made a bold call for the desegregation of American life more generally.

The tension created by the presence of a large and degraded black population in a nation founded on the assumption that "all men are created equal" had haunted American dialogue, ideas, and leaders for more than three hundred years. Thomas Jefferson, a preeminent figure in shaping American democracy in the eighteenth century, believed that a harmonious biracial society was inconceivable. "Deep rooted prejudices entertained by the whites," he wrote, and "ten thousand recollections, by the blacks, of the injuries they have sustained," combine to make equal, peaceful coexistence between blacks and whites impossible. Rather, Jefferson thought, the meeting of free blacks and whites would result in a conflict leading to "the extermination of the one or the other race" (1972:138).

Jefferson's apocalyptic outlook was echoed in the nineteenth century by Alexis de Tocqueville. Citing Jefferson to support his claims, Tocqueville argued that "Negroes and . . . whites must either wholly part or wholly mingle" (1945:388). The latter outcome, a mixing of the races in common society, was considered out of the question by both of these thinkers. Indeed, Tocqueville added, "I do not believe the white and black races will ever live in any country upon an equal footing" (1945:388–389).[5]

As the writings of Jefferson and Tocqueville suggest, racial imagery and attitudes have influenced Americans since the founding of the first colonial settlements. Winthrop Jordan makes this clear in *White Over Black: American Attitudes toward the Negro, 1550–1812*. Jordan's concern with attitudes about race prompted him to write: "If it were possible to poll the inhabitants of Jamestown, Virginia, concerning their reaction to those famous first 'twenty Negars' who arrived in 1619 I would be among the first at the foot of the gangplank, questionnaire in hand" (1968:viii).

Although we cannot attempt a comprehensive history of relations between blacks and whites from those earliest days, we will briefly review here the major events pertinent to racial change over the past half century. Such a review will make more understandable our later consideration of trends in racial attitudes. As important as are the thoughts and attitudes of whites and blacks, the historian Ronald Takaki is right to chastise researchers for tending to isolate racism as a history of attitudes (1979:xiii). Other economic, political, intellectual, and legal matters must not be forgotten as we present survey data.

The historical record suggests that the last sixty or so years can be broken into four clearly discernible periods: (1) a prelude to civil rights politics, which involved the discrediting of theories of biological racism, massive black out-migration from the South, and substantial black involvement in World War II; (2) the late 1950s and early 1960s, during which effective civil rights protest movements developed to emphasize black voting rights and racial equality before the law; (3) the period marked by the urban riots and the Vietnam War that saw public attention turn away from the active pursuit of racial equality, though conflicts and actions over the unfinished civil rights agenda continued to arise; and (4) the events of the last decade and a half, involving cultural, material, and political gains for African Americans and at the same time signs of civil rights retrenchment and deepening racial tensions. The actions of the U.S. president, Congress, and the

Supreme Court have been critical in defining the tenor of each period. The equivocal nature of very recent events clouds predictions about the course of future black and white relations.

Prelude to Civil Rights Politics, 1930–1954

Through the late nineteenth and early twentieth centuries, most whites, North and South, considered blacks to be their biological and social inferiors (Fredrickson 1971; Takaki 1979). The difference between this period and that of Jefferson and Tocqueville lay in the full development and flourishing of highly intellectualized theories of "biological racism." The proponents of segregation and white supremacy who ushered in the Jim Crow laws of the late 1880s and 1890s pegged their antiblack ideology on notions of Social Darwinism that were fashionable at the time. The *Plessy v. Ferguson* ruling of 1896, which proclaimed "separate but equal" facilities to be constitutional, was the political and intellectual capstone of this later era. Justice Brown, writing for the majority, said:

> Legislation is powerless to eradicate racial instincts or to abolish distinctions based upon physical differences, and the attempt to do so can only result in accentuating the difficulties of the present situation. If the civil and political rights of both races be equal one cannot be inferior to the other civilly or politically. If one race be inferior to the other socially, the Constitution of the United States cannot put them on the same plane. (163 U.S. 537, 16 S. Ct. 1138, 41 L. Ed. 256 [1896], pp. 550–551)

It is evident that the ideas and opinions of the day were significant forces in shaping the *Plessy* ruling. As one writer suggests, "the ruling was redolent with [then popular] sociological speculation, permeated with theories of social Darwinism, and carr[ied] overtones of white racial supremacy as scientific truth" (Harris 1960:98).[6]

Despite some erosion of faith in the applicability of Darwinism to human groups, in the 1930s and early 1940s many whites still believed that blacks were an inferior people. Data collected by the National Opinion Research Center (NORC), for example, indicate that more than half of the white population surveyed in 1942 assumed that blacks were less intelligent than whites. At the same time, 54 percent opposed the integration of public transportation, and 68 percent supported racially segregated schools. But a general shift in the thinking of American scientists and scholars had begun in the 1920s and accelerated in reaction to Nazi racism during the 1930s and 1940s. The new intellectual currents were quickly made applicable to the situation of blacks in America. Indeed, the late 1930s have been characterized as a period when

> the research of biologists, psychologists, and social scientists undermined the shibboleths long used to rationalize second-class citizenship for blacks. A new intellectual consensus emerged. It rejected the notion of innate black inferiority; it emphasized the damage done by racism; and it depicted prejudice as a sickness, afflicting both individuals and the very well-being of the nation. (Sitkoff 1978:190)

An example of this change can be found in research by the social psychologist Otto Klineberg. Klineberg dealt a serious blow to a key element of the "scientific" case for black inferiority by challenging the results of IQ tests administered by the army in World War I, which showed blacks scoring lower than whites. He demonstrated that such environmental factors as more education, higher socioeconomic status, and exposure to Northern culture improved blacks' scores markedly (see Sitkoff 1978).

The war against Hitler's Germany drove racist doctrines into further disrepute. "American war propaganda stressed above all else," wrote the historian C. Vann Woodward, "the abhorrence of the West for Hitler's brand of racism and its utter incompatibility with the democratic faith for which we fought" (1974:131). Thus both scholarly research and wartime propaganda began to lay a cultural basis for challenging racial discrimination and inequality in America.

One of the most significant pieces of scholarship to come out of this era was Gunnar Myrdal's monumental work *An American Dilemma: The Negro Problem and Modern Democracy* (1944). Myrdal addressed America's treatment of blacks as a significant moral issue and as a major challenge to the national democratic tradition. He pointed out a fundamental contradiction between America's highest values of "liberty, equality, justice, and fair opportunity for everybody," and the degraded position of blacks in society:

> The American Negro problem is a problem in the heart of the American. It is there that the interracial tension has its focus. It is

there that the decisive struggle goes on . . . The "American Dilemma," referred to in the title of this book, is the ever raging conflict between, on the one hand, the valuations preserved on the general plane which we shall call the "American Creed," where the American thinks, talks, and acts under the influence of high national and Christian precepts, and, on the other hand, the valuations on specific planes of individual and group living, where personal and local interests; economic, social, and sexual jealousies; considerations of community prestige and conformity; group prejudice against particular persons or types of people; and all sorts of miscellaneous wants, impulses, and habits dominate his outlook. (1944:xlii)

An American Dilemma not only furthered the trend toward racial equalitarianism in American ideas but also documented in remarkable breadth and detail the features of discrimination against blacks. A key facet of discrimination, then as now, was limited black access to jobs. As Myrdal noted, World War II was "of tremendous importance to the Negro in all respects," especially in terms of new job opportunities. The war, he suggested, would create for blacks a new "strategic position strengthened not only because of the desperate scarcity of labor but also because of the revitalization of the democratic Creed" (p. 409). At that time blacks were still excluded from work in many industries, and even when hired they were generally restricted to unskilled work. Nonetheless, World War II, like World War I before it, drew Southern blacks in record numbers to the industrial centers of the North. It is estimated that 1.5 million blacks left the South between 1940 and 1950 in response to the pull of wartime jobs and the push of growing mechanization in agriculture in the South (Farley 1968).

The wartime upturn in the economy did not, however, provide peaceful entrance into the job market for blacks. By one estimate, during the month of March 1943 alone, "102,000 man-days of war production time" were lost "through hate strikes directed against the employment or upgrading of black workers" (Newman et al. 1978:12). Walter White, then the executive secretary of the National Association for the Advancement of Colored People (NAACP), recalled one such striker as saying, "I'd rather see Hitler and Hirohito win the war than work beside a nigger on the assembly line" (see Wilkins 1982:182). The city of Detroit, the destination for many blacks seeking jobs, experienced violent racial disturbances in June 1943. During the rioting more than

$2 million in damage was done and 34 people (25 blacks and 9 whites) were killed (U.S. National Advisory Commission on Civil Disorders 1968:104).

Blacks in the 1940s were not without advocates who tried to secure and protect their rights. Under the threat of a massive "March on Washington" organized by the black labor leader A. Philip Randolph, in June 1941 President Roosevelt issued Executive Order 8802, which was intended to ban discrimination in all defense plants and branches of the federal government. This order also created the President's Committee on Fair Employment Practices, which later became the Fair Employment Practices Commission. The order was the most important federal effort since Reconstruction and provided a great symbolic victory, even though it lacked provisions for enforcement.

During the New Deal era and World War II blacks gained access to the ranks of several labor unions, in particular those of the newly formed Congress of Industrial Organizations (CIO). Prior to their acceptance by white labor organizations, blacks seeking jobs often were forced into the role of low-wage strikebreakers.[7] Even after blacks moved into the union rank and file, however, it was rare for them to rise to positions of much influence within unions. Segregation of work groups continued, and jobs with lower skill levels and limited chances for advancement were often reserved for blacks. Nonetheless, participation in previously all-white labor unions improved blacks' prospects for moving into the economic mainstream. In the words of the historians August Meier and Elliot Rudwick, "the CIO's contribution to the changing patterns of race relations has been incalculable. It made interracial trade unionism truly respectable." Moreover, by opening membership to blacks, the CIO began to engender in "black and white workers a sense of common interest, of solidarity, that transcended racial lines" (1976:262).[8]

The changing intellectual currents, shifts in the regional composition of the black population, and improving job prospects were all significant, but they were far from being fundamental transformations in the second-class status of black Americans. World War II was basically a Jim Crow war, with separate units, quarters, and duty assignments for black and white soldiers (see Bogart 1969; Dalfiume 1969). Not until July 1948, when President Truman, under pressure from A. Philip Randolph and the NAACP, issued Executive Order 9981, were segregation and discrimination in the military forbidden. Roy Wilkins, who would follow Walter White as NAACP executive secretary, recounts the cruel contradictions of American policies during the war:

> Negroes did not need us at the NAACP to tell them that it sounded pretty foolish to be against park benches marked JUDE in Berlin, but to be for park benches marked COLORED in Tallahassee, Florida. It was grim, not foolish, to have a young black man in uniform get an orientation in the morning on wiping out Nazi bigotry and that same evening be told he could buy a soft drink only in the "colored" post exchange. (1982:184–185)

The discriminatory treatment accorded black soldiers was a poignant display of the depth of the "American Dilemma," but the basic contradiction was apparent in many other domains as well. In 1940 black educational attainment was well below that of whites (Newman et al. 1978:70); the average black male had completed about seven years of schooling, as against approximately ten years for white males (Farley 1984:17). In 1947 the median income of black families was only 51 percent of that of white families (Newman et al. 1978:269). The occupational distributions of blacks and whites were also markedly disparate: in 1940, only 3 percent of employed black men worked in professional, managerial, or other technical jobs, as compared with 16 percent of white men; 41 percent of black men were involved in some farm-related occupation, as compared with only 21 percent of white men; fully 59 percent of black women in the labor force were employed as maids and domestics, more than five times the percentage (11 percent) of white women holding such jobs; and fewer than 6 percent of black women held professional or managerial positions, as compared with 19 percent of white women (U.S. Bureau of the Census 1969:116). The weight of these inequalities was, to some extent, reflected in life-expectancy figures: black life expectancy at birth in 1942 was 57 years, a full 10 years below that of whites (U.S. Bureau of the Census 1980:96–97).

These economic and other handicaps were supported by the segregation of schools, housing, and public accommodations. Racial segregation was a matter of law and preeminent social concern in the South, and often a matter of custom and social expectations in the North. One indicator of the pervasiveness of racial segregation can be drawn from "segregation indexes" based on Census housing data. A segregation index, used by Karl and Alma Taeuber, indicates the percentage of blacks "that would have to shift from one block to another to effect an unsegregated distribution" of homes (Taeuber and Taeuber 1965:30). In 1940 the average segregation index score for 107 cities in the United States, North and South, was 85.2 percent.[9] On average, a shift of well over four-fifths of the black population in these cities would have been required to eliminate residential segregation. In the Taeubers' words:

> No further analysis is necessary to reach some broad generalizations concerning segregation: In the urban United States, there is a very high degree of segregation of the residences of whites and Negroes. This is true for cities in all regions of the country and for all types of cities—large and small, industrial and commercial, metropolitan and suburban. It is true whether there are hundreds of thousands of Negro residents, or only a few thousand. Residential segregation prevails regardless of the relative economic status of the white and Negro residents. It occurs regardless of the character of local laws and policies, and regardless of the extent of other forms of segregation or discrimination. (1965:35–36)

The Black Ballot. Even though in the 1940s blacks seemed to be locked into a segregated and inferior social and economic status, several signs of progress were emerging, especially in politics. One of the portentous results of black out-migration from the South was the growing power of black ballots in the North. Each black person "going to the North meant another potential voter pressuring both parties for civil rights legislation" (Sitkoff 1971:605). These voters would come to rank among the most persistent and persuasive forces for black civil rights.

Politics and the ballot box were not entirely new to blacks even in the South. During the Reconstruction period and shortly thereafter, under the protective presence of federal troops, blacks began to participate in politics. In the years between the passage of the Military Reconstruction Acts of 1867 and the removal of all federal troops in 1876–1877, around 800 blacks in the South were elected to public office (U.S. Bureau of the Census 1979:155).

By the early 1900s, however, in the absence of federal scrutiny and protection, black disfranchisement had been effectively reinstated by Southern constitutional conventions and legislatures. For example, "two years before Louisiana revised its constitution in 1898, some

130,000 Negroes were registered to vote; in 1900, only 5,000 blacks remained on the rolls. In Virginia the effect of the constitutional provisions was to reduce the black electorate from 147,000 to 21,000" (Lawson 1976:14–15). Such racial discrimination in voting had been prohibited in principle by the Fifteenth Amendment to the U.S. Constitution, but Southern states enacted a number of ostensibly "colorblind" voting restrictions that actually kept blacks off the voting rolls. For example, Oklahoma adopted a permanent grandfather clause exempting all people eligible to vote prior to the Civil War and their descendants—that is, whites only—from the requirement that they be literate in order to register to vote (Lawson 1976:12, 18–19). Several other states, such as Louisiana and Alabama, adopted similar provisions on a temporary basis. Even when blacks managed to register, the imposition of poll taxes prevented many of them, along with large numbers of poor whites, from exercising their right to vote. Literacy and character tests, complex registration procedures, separate "white primaries" conducted by the state Democratic parties in the South, registrar malfeasance, and direct acts of intimidation were other tools used to stifle black suffrage.

These measures were so effective that Ralph Bunche, who had conducted research on black political participation for Myrdal, reported that "of a total Negro adult population of 3,651,256 in the 8 Deep Southern states (excluding Oklahoma) of Alabama, Georgia, Mississippi, Louisiana, Florida, Texas, South Carolina, and Arkansas . . . only 80,000 to 90,000 . . . voted in the general election of 1940" (Myrdal 1944:475). If the higher estimate of 90,000 is taken as accurate, then fewer than 3 percent of Southern black adults participated in electoral politics in 1940, far below what might have been expected in the absence of extensive disfranchisement and intimidation. Myrdal summarized the situation quite accurately: "The concern of the Southern Negroes is not how they shall use their votes but how to get their constitutional right to vote respected at all" (1944:512).

Among the best hopes for securing the right to vote was the growing potency of black ballots in the North. The influence of black votes upon Northern politicians and national politics first became apparent in the election of 1936 and gained even more prominence in the election of 1948. Blacks had voted disproportionately Republican in 1932, when Roosevelt was first elected to the presidency (see Myrdal 1944:493–495; Sitkoff 1978:95–96). By 1936, as New Deal programs began to ease black poverty, civil rights leaders exhorted black people to recall that the party of Lincoln was also the party of Hoover. They served notice to Democrats and Republicans alike that they would encourage the expanding ranks of black voters to support the party that took the strongest stand in favor of civil rights. Both parties responded by courting black votes as never before. The Republicans adopted a platform supporting anti-lynching legislation and opposing discrimination. Democrats, who for the first time had black delegates at their nominating convention, worked closely with civil rights activists to get out the black vote, and generally "emphasized the economic assistance given blacks by the Roosevelt administration" (Sitkoff 1978:94). In the end, blacks "abandoned the party of Lincoln and joined the party of Roosevelt" (Lawson 1976:21), and did so in such substantial numbers as to "persuade many a civil rights leader and white politician that the Negro vote had become a balance of power in national elections" (Sitkoff 1978:97).

By 1948 the influence of white liberals and civil rights activists in the Democratic party was substantial and had begun to rankle the party's Southern members. In February of that year, responding to the demands of black leaders and to the report of his Committee on Civil Rights, President Truman called for legislation "to abolish the poll tax, make lynching a federal crime, curtail discrimination in employment, and prohibit segregation in interstate commerce" (Sitkoff 1971:600). Southern politicians were outraged. They denounced these plans as the work of liberals out to "Harlemize" the nation, threatened to bolt the party, and buttressed their threats by convincing Southern contributors to cancel several hundred thousand dollars in pledges to the Democratic National Committee (Sitkoff 1971:601–603).

Truman had apparently underestimated the severity of the Southern response. During the next few months he attempted to placate Southern Democrats by distancing himself from his earlier proposals. These efforts were stymied, however, by a coalition of liberals, civil rights leaders, and labor leaders, who succeeded in having the party platform endorse the original proposals. The Democratic convention of 1948 erupted into applause when Mayor Hubert Humphrey of Minneapolis declared: "The time has arrived for the Democratic party to get out of the shadow of states' rights and walk into the bright sunshine of human rights" (quoted in Ashmore 1982:124). Southern discontent was increased further during the campaign when Truman issued Executive

Orders 9980 and 9981. The latter order, as mentioned earlier, desegregated the military, whereas the former created a Fair Employment Practices board within the Civil Service Commission to ensure fair treatment for blacks in federal employment (Newman et al. 1978:51).

The defiant splinter candidacy of "Dixiecrat" Strom Thurmond notwithstanding, the civil rights platform, both executive orders, and a last-minute appeal to black voters in the North helped to secure a victory for Truman in 1948. "Dewey would have won," according to Sitkoff, "if Truman had not polled a higher percentage of the Negro vote than Roosevelt had done in any of his four presidential victories"; in fact, "Truman's plurality of Negro votes in California, Illinois, and Ohio provided the margin of victory" (1971:613). Thus the election of 1948 placed civil rights high on the national agenda and helped force national leaders to address the pervasive gap between the American Creed and the position of blacks in society. As Roy Wilkins saw it: "The message was plain: white power in the South could be balanced by black power at the Northern polls. Civil rights were squarely at the heart of national politics—if we could keep them there" (1982:202).

Although the election of 1948 seemed to be a civil rights watershed, white public opinion at the time was mixed on the "Negro problem." The Gallup Poll asked a national sample of Americans about their attitudes toward anti-lynching legislation, the desegregation of public transportation, federal efforts to end job discrimination, abolition of the poll tax, and the Truman proposals as a whole. The poll, taken in March 1948, indicated that some 56 percent of those surveyed felt that the Truman proposals, taken as a whole, should not be passed (Gallup 1972:722–723). There were marked North-South differences on some of the more specific measures: more than 60 percent of Southern respondents but only 38 percent of Northern respondents were against allowing the federal government to intervene in lynchings; 84 percent of Southerners but only 36 percent of Northerners thought blacks should be "required to occupy a separate part of a train or bus when traveling from one state to another." On the question of federal action to end job discrimination, however, 68 percent in the South and 42 percent in the North, a plurality in both regions, thought the federal government "should do nothing." Abolition of the poll tax elicited more substantial support: 65 percent nationally and a plurality, 48 percent, in the South (Gallup 1972:748). In sum, white public opinion was far from unanimous on any aspect of the Truman proposals, even

on the poll tax, which also kept many whites from voting and constituted one of the most egregious restrictions of the basic rights of citizens
in a democracy.

Truman, president from 1945 to 1953, was a crucial figure in the
transition of the United States from a nation that took for granted
segregation and discrimination to a nation that claimed to believe and
act in terms of equal treatment for all, regardless of race or color. There
is no dispute about the importance of Truman's order desegregating
the armed forces, nor about the significance of other actions he took
that made civil rights an increasingly central issue in the 1950s. What
has been disputed is how much Truman acted on the basis of personal
convictions and how much he responded to immediate pressures out
of purely political concerns.

Truman himself grew up in rural Missouri at a time when segregation
was in place, terms like "Nigger" and "boy" were common in referring
to blacks, and any thought of questioning the traditional racial structure was far from the minds of most white people. Truman absorbed
this culture, and even continued into his later years to use occasional
racial epithets that would be condemned today. Yet from his earliest
years in politics he sought votes from blacks, and once in the Senate
he usually (though not always) supported measures to improve the
position of blacks in America. Once he became president, Truman took
actions and made statements that were far more liberal than those of
any previous president, though on occasion he soft-pedaled in order to
retain the support of powerful Southern white Democrats. Some writers see Truman's actions as guided largely by political considerations
and essentially a sign of the growing power of the black vote in
Northern cities (Berman 1970), whereas others believe that Truman
underwent a conversion in the early years of his presidency and became
what in the 1950s was a genuine liberal on racial issues (Leuchtenburg
1991). The fact that there can be considerable uncertainty on this score
even for a person whose words and actions were so public shows how
difficult it can be to distinguish clearly between inner convictions and
external pressures as determinants of racial behavior.

The Modern Civil Rights Movement, 1954–1965

The struggle to implement the types of changes advocated by Truman's
Committee on Civil Rights would be a long one. As the journalist Harry

Ashmore put it, "no one in Washington believed that there was any chance of getting the package through Congress without drastic revision. Its introduction was [largely] a symbolic gesture" (1982:121). Nonetheless, there were many who tried to capitalize on the gains made in 1948. Most important in these efforts would be several civil rights organizations, especially the NAACP.

Founded in 1909 by black leaders like W. E. B. Du Bois and progressive whites like Oswald Garrison Villard and Jane Addams (see Myrdal 1944:819–822; Meier and Rudwick 1976:227–228), the NAACP was dedicated from its inception to improving the legal and material status of black Americans, changing the attitudes of whites toward blacks, and furthering the cause of racial equality and integration. These ambitious goals, and they were certainly ambitious in the early 1900s and even in the 1940s, were the embodiment of civil rights militancy to white Americans at the time.

Supreme Court Decisions. An example of the significance of the linkage between the NAACP and the courts can be found in efforts to secure the ballot for Southern blacks. The NAACP scored its first victory in voting rights in 1915, when the grandfather clause was declared unconstitutional. It then sought other cases that might be used to test the constitutionality of voting hindrances aimed at blacks. In the 1940s, under the legal stewardship of Thurgood Marshall, the organization set out to eliminate white primaries. On April 3, 1944, in the case of *Smith v. Allwright,* the Supreme Court sided with the NAACP and ruled the white primary to be unconstitutional.

A decade later a similar but far more consequential victory was achieved in the area of school segregation. On May 17, 1954, Chief Justice Earl Warren read the text of the Court's decision in *Brown v. Board of Education of Topeka*. The direction of the ruling became evident when he read: "We come then to the question presented: Does segregation of children in public schools solely on the basis of race, even though the physical facilities and other 'tangible' factors may be equal, deprive the children of the minority group of equal education opportunities? We believe it does." In this short, unencumbered, and unprovocative paragraph, the *Plessy* doctrine of "separate but equal" had been overturned. Several paragraphs later Chief Justice Warren departed from his prepared manuscript with the addition of just one word: "We conclude—*unanimously*—that in the field of public education the doctrine of 'separate but equal' has no place. Separate educational facilities are inherently unequal" (see Kluger 1975:707). Jim Crow was now on the defensive. The largest legal step since Reconstruction had been taken toward closing the pervasive gap between the American Creed and the lives of black Americans.

Reactions to the *Brown* decision were quick in coming. Herman Talmadge, then the governor of Georgia, accused the justices of having "reduced the Constitution to a 'mere scrap of paper.'" Senator James O. Eastland of Mississippi vowed to fight the ruling, declaring that "the South . . . 'will not abide by or obey this legislative decision by a political court'" (Kluger 1975:710). But those at NAACP headquarters in New York sensed that a new era was beginning. Roy Wilkins described their feeling:

Later in the day Thurgood came back from Washington. I heard a commotion in the corridors outside my office—laughing and cheering—then the door flew open and Thurgood walked in and kissed me. Later that afternoon we held a press conference, and Walter [White] did the talking while Thurgood sat quietly in the background. I can still see him sitting there, smiling slightly. Plessy-Ferguson was through. An American Joshua in the person of Thurgood Marshall fit the battle of Jericho and the walls came tumbling down. (1982:213)

Thurgood Marshall would later comment on that day: "I was so happy I was numb." He was happy enough, indeed, to venture the prediction that racially segregated schools would be eliminated within five years (Kluger 1975:706).

Marshall's forecast regarding the implementation of school desegregation was as inaccurate as the Court's ruling was historic. The Court knew that making its ruling a part of daily practice would be no simple task. In the final paragraph of the opinion the justices called for more arguments on how a compliance decree should be drafted. To further the process of adjustment, the Court kept the *Brown* opinion itself short, clear, and understandable by a lay audience. There was an evident need to persuade as well as to adjudicate. "You know," said Justice Clark, "we don't have money at the Court for an army, and we can't take ads in the newspaper, and we don't want to go out on a picket line in our robes. We have to convince the nation by the force of our opinions" (Kluger 1975:706).

Public opinion on the ruling was sharply divided by region. In 1954 the Gallup Poll asked the following question: "The Supreme Court has ruled that racial segregation in the public schools is illegal. This means that all children, no matter what their race, must be allowed to go to the same school. Do you approve or disapprove of this decision?" Only 24 percent of Southern respondents, in contrast to 60 percent of Northern respondents, approved (A. W. Smith 1981:580).

A favorable climate of opinion in the North was not enough to implement the *Brown* decision. The job of forcing the hand of Southern politicians and citizens fell to black activists and whites sympathetic to their cause. A milestone event presented itself on December 1, 1955, when Mrs. Rosa Parks, a seamstress and secretary of the Montgomery NAACP, refused to give up her seat on a bus to a white passenger. The bus driver threatened to have her arrested for violating the local segregation ordinance, which required her to yield her seat when instructed to do so. Mrs. Parks replied, "Go on and have me arrested" (Sitkoff 1993:38). News of her arrest spread quickly through the black community. E. D. Nixon, a former president of the Alabama NAACP and the president of the Montgomery local of the Brotherhood of Sleeping Car Porters, was certain that the arrest would lead to a crucial test case of forced segregation in Alabama. He also believed that blacks could play a more direct role in winning their rights by boycotting the buses. One of the first men to whom Nixon took his plan was a local minister, Dr. Martin Luther King, Jr.

Nixon, King, and nearly 50 other prominent blacks organized a boycott to begin on December 5. Nearly 100 percent of the black bus ridership found other means of transportation that day. For 381 days thereafter, and in the face of constant intimidation, black citizens of Montgomery shared taxis, carpooled, rode mules, hitchhiked, and walked, in their collective determination to make Jim Crow yield. "Once a car-pool driver chanced on an old woman hobbling along with great difficulty, and he offered her a ride. She waved him on. 'I'm not walking for myself,' she said. 'I'm walking for my children and my grandchildren'" (Oates 1982:76).

In addition to demonstrating the passionate desire of Southern blacks for their full measure of human rights and the extent to which they would engage in mass protest to gain those rights, the Montgomery bus boycott propelled twenty-six-year-old Martin Luther King, Jr., the pastor of the small Dexter Avenue Baptist Church, to the forefront of the civil rights crusade. It was during the Montgomery protest that King's image as an American Gandhi proposing a strategy of nonviolent protest began to take shape.

King spoke on December 5, 1955, at the first mass meeting held to dramatize the bus boycott. He opened his largely extemporaneous address by pointing out that democracy was more than an abstract set of values recorded on paper, but rather concerned moral principles that had to be "transformed from thin paper to thick action" (Oates 1982:70). He talked of the human dimension of the pervasive gap between American principles and practices:

> There comes a time when people get tired. We are here this evening to say to those who have mistreated us so long that we are tired of being segregated and humiliated, tired of being kicked about by the brutal feet of oppression. We have no alternative but to protest. For many years we have shown amazing patience. We have sometimes given our white brothers the feeling that we liked the way we were being treated. But we come here tonight to be saved from that patience that makes us patient with anything less than freedom and justice. (Sitkoff 1993:45)

And he discussed how the struggle to close the gap must be carried out: "In our protest, there will be no cross burnings. No white person will be taken from his home by a hooded Negro mob and brutally murdered. There will be no threats and intimidation. We will be guided by the highest principles of law and order" (Oates 1982:71). When King finished, the massive crowd of listeners were clapping, yelling, and crying for joy. The struggle for black freedom had been elevated to a new stage, and a leader with a voice to move people to action had come forward.

Less than a year after the end of the successful bus boycott, a major civil rights confrontation occurred in Little Rock, Arkansas. In defiance of a federal court order and the plans of the local school board, Governor Orval Faubus ordered the National Guard to prevent nine black students from entering all-white Central High School. Faubus's actions precipitated a direct clash with federal authority and prompted President Eisenhower to federalize the Arkansas National Guard. The president dispatched a thousand troops to protect the handful of black students from angry white mobs and to ensure compliance with the court order. Before the troops arrived, crowds of whites milled outside the high school shouting slogans like "Two, four, six, eight, we ain't gonna integrate," and "Niggers keep away from our school. Go back to the jungle." In Eisenhower's words, failure to uphold the court order in the face of such incipient mob violence would have been "tantamount to acquiescence in anarchy and the dissolution of the union" (Sitkoff 1993:31).

Another situation in which an American president was forced to use federal troops to bring Southern whites into compliance with the law of the land took place in Oxford, Mississippi, when James Meredith attempted to become the first black student at the University of Mississippi. Meredith applied for admission to Ole Miss in January 1961, just days after John F. Kennedy was inaugurated as president. Meredith was initially refused admission, but with the assistance of attorneys from the NAACP won a federal court ruling that he had the legal right to enroll and attend classes. Mississippi Governor Ross Barnett called for resistance and "asked a statewide television audience to join in opposing the federal government's policy of racial genocide" (Brauer 1977:181). Again there were large white crowds chanting racial epithets. Violence broke out on September 30, 1962, the day before Meredith was to enroll. As a result, two people were killed and many others injured. Despite the efforts of U.S. Attorney General Robert Kennedy and President Kennedy himself, Governor Barnett continued to refuse to uphold the law and protect Meredith. Compliance in the end required several hundred federal marshals and troops.

Just hours before the violence in Oxford, President Kennedy addressed the nation about the developing crisis. He emphasized the need to uphold the law: "Americans are free to disagree with the law, but not to disobey it. For in a government of laws and not of men, no man, however prominent and powerful, and no mob, however unruly or boisterous, is entitled to defy a court of law." He pointed out that he had exhausted all means of upholding the law short of the use of federal troops:

> The enforcement of [the court's order] had become an obligation of the United States Government. Even though this government had not originally been a party to the case, my responsibility as President was therefore inescapable. I accept it. My obligation under the constitution and statutes of the United States was and is to implement the orders of the court with whatever means are necessary, and with as

little force and civil disorder as the circumstances permit. (*New York Times,* Oct. 1, 1962, p. 22)

Kennedy had earlier used federal marshals to suppress the "Freedom Rider" riots in Montgomery in 1961. He would be forced to consider the use of troops again in 1963, when two black students attempted to enroll at the University of Alabama.

New Leadership: A Second Reconstruction. The efforts of James Meredith and of the nine black students in Little Rock to desegregate historically white school campuses are noteworthy because federal troops were used to protect the rights of blacks. There were other incidents in which the federal government did not intervene to protect blacks because no explicit federal statute or court order had been violated. Two protests that eventually led to the passage of major legislation took place in Alabama: in Birmingham in 1963 and in Selma in 1965.

In April 1963, King and the Southern Christian Leadership Conference (SCLC) determined again to challenge openly white supremacy and segregation in the South. This time they chose Birmingham, which was often labeled the most segregated city in America. The segregation of public facilities such as restaurants and hotels, a key target of the Birmingham protest, did not violate federal law: that is, a hesitant but sympathetic Kennedy White House had no clear legal basis for intervention (Brauer 1977). Moreover, local authorities, under the leadership of Eugene T. "Bull" Connor, were absolutely committed to "keeping the niggers in their place" (Sitkoff 1993:121).

The protest began officially on April 2. King and his associates called for an economic boycott of local businesses and began sit-ins at segregated lunch counters. After several days of nonviolent demonstrations and hundreds of arrests, local officials secured a court injunction on April 10 banning the demonstrations. King, having backed down in the face of such an injunction during the abortive "Albany Movement" in Georgia the year before, chose to defy the court order and continue the protests. On April 12 he was arrested while leading a march on the Birmingham city hall. During this incarceration King wrote his famous "Letter from Birmingham Jail," an eloquent statement of why blacks had justifiably lost their patience with Southern unwillingness to end segregation and discrimination.[10]

Shortly after King was released from jail, the protests rose to a new level. More than a thousand black children, some as young as six years of age, joined the demonstrations on May 2. Scenes of black youngsters chanting "Freedom Now" as they were arrested by Bull Connor and his men were carried on the national television news. When another thousand children prepared to demonstrate the next day, Bull Connor responded with brute force. Before national and international television audiences, black children and women were attacked by police dogs, beaten by police officers, and blasted with water from high-pressure fire hoses. The viciousness of the attacks on the peaceful demonstrators horrified many whites, including President Kennedy. On May 4 Kennedy said that the scenes in Birmingham had made him "sick." He went on to say, "I can understand why the Negroes in Birmingham are tired of being asked to be patient" (Brauer 1977:238).

Kennedy faced growing political pressure to act. By no means was all of the pressure from internal and domestic sources. The international image of the United States as the world's leading democracy was already tarnished by continued racial discrimination during the years since World War II, and it was further damaged by the events in Birmingham and other parts of the South. Such pressures forced Kennedy to reexamine his own thinking on the role that the federal government should play in changing race relations. At about the same time, the Kennedy administration was trying to persuade Alabama Governor George Wallace to allow blacks to enroll at the University of Alabama. Kennedy hoped to be better prepared to prevent violence than he had been in Mississippi the year before, and thus to avert another showdown altogether. However, the prospects for peaceful desegregation of the university campus were not bright. In his inaugural address Wallace had pledged to "draw the line in the dust and toss the gauntlet before the feet of tyranny . . . Segregation now! Segregation tomorrow! Segregation forever!" (Sitkoff 1993:145).

Although Wallace ultimately settled for a symbolic act of defiance—standing in the schoolhouse door while actually capitulating to National Guardsmen sent to ensure the peaceful enrollment of the black students—the incidents at Ole Miss, at the University of Alabama, and in Birmingham combined to convince Kennedy that new federal legislation was needed. Just a few hours after the two black students enrolled at the University of Alabama, Kennedy made a major address to the nation. It carried the message that gaining full civil rights for blacks was a moral issue requiring new legislation. In the words of Carl

Brauer, the speech "marked the beginning of what can truly be called the Second Reconstruction, a coherent effort by all three branches of government to secure blacks their full rights" (1977:259–260). The issues, Kennedy said, were "as old as the scriptures and . . . as clear as the American Constitution."

> The heart of the question is whether all Americans are to be afforded equal rights and equal opportunities, whether we are going to treat our fellow Americans as we want to be treated. If an American, because his skin is dark, cannot eat lunch in a restaurant open to the public, if he cannot send his children to the best public school available, if he cannot vote for the public officials who represent him, if, in short, he cannot enjoy the full and free life which all of us want, then who among us would be content to have the color of his skin changed and stand in his place? Who among us would be content with the counsels of patience and delay? (Brauer 1977:260)

The Kennedy administration began work on what would become the landmark Civil Rights Act of 1964. The legislation addressed segregation in public facilities, discrimination in jobs, and school desegregation, and, most important, it set up mechanisms, including the withdrawal of federal funding, for direct federal action to ensure compliance.

The changes in Kennedy's thoughts and attitudes were probably indicative of the thoughts of many Northern whites who witnessed, through television and other media, the brutality of Bull Connor and other white supremacists. Many historical accounts of the period speak of the rethinking and searching of conscience that were prompted by the events of 1963. Public opinion data also suggest that such a rethinking was taking place. The data show that support for the 1964 Civil Rights Act grew substantially between the summer of 1963 and the time of its actual passage in July 1964. The Gallup Poll asked a national sample of whites how they would "feel about a law which would give all persons—Negroes as well as whites—the right to be served in public places such as hotels, restaurants, theaters, and similar establishments." In June 1963, 55 percent of Northern whites supported such legislation, as opposed to only 12 percent of Southern whites. By January 1964, after the peaceful and biracial March on Washington at which King delivered his "I have a dream" speech, and in the wake of continued civil rights protests and the assassination of

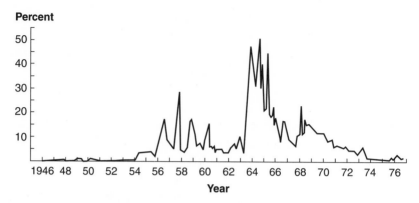

Figure 1.1. Percentage of Americans naming civil rights as the most important problem facing the country. From Tom W. Smith, "America's Most Important Problem," *Public Opinion Quarterly* (Summer 1980): 170–171. Copyright 1980 by the American Association for Public Opinion Research.

President Kennedy, white support had risen to 71 percent in the North and to 20 percent in the South (Gallup 1972:1827, 1863).[11]

The growing concern with civil rights could be seen in other ways as well. Figure 1.1 shows the percentage of respondents in Gallup surveys mentioning civil rights as the nation's "most important problem." As Smith (1980) wrote about these results, civil rights

> was virtually unrecognized as a problem area until 1956, when the civil rights movement [came to public attention] with the Montgomery bus boycott. Concern rose quickly until it peaked in the fall of 1957, during the Little Rock school desegregation battle. Smaller peaks occurred during the renewed Arkansas and Virginia school desegregation fights in the fall of 1959 and the lunch counter sit-ins in the spring of 1960. Worry then subsided rapidly until, from mid-1960 to early 1963, it rested at pre-Montgomery levels. A second take-off occurred in the fall of 1963 following a summer of intensified civil rights activity capped by Martin Luther King's "I have a dream" speech . . . at the [Lincoln Memorial] in August. From then through early 1965, civil rights remained at or near the top of the problem list. Pushed aside by Vietnam and other problems, civil rights concerns once again practically disappeared as a matter of "most important" concern. (pp. 170–171)

Perhaps the secondary peak in 1968 reflected the urban riots, the highly publicized Report of the National Advisory Commission on Civil Disorders, and the assassination of Martin Luther King, followed by further riots. In addition, some of the concern over the riots then appeared in a different type of response, which was categorized as "social control."

After Kennedy's assassination, Lyndon Johnson won a sweeping victory over Barry Goldwater, one of the few Northern senators to have voted against the 1964 Civil Rights Act. The outcome of the election appeared to provide convincing evidence of broad sympathy for civil rights among the American people. Less attention was paid to the fact that five of the only six states won by Goldwater were in the Deep South, the first time a Republican presidential candidate had carried any of them since Reconstruction. This proved an important step toward realignment of the political parties with regard to race: Northern Democrats were acting decisively against the wishes of their own Southern party members, whereas Goldwater's conservative opposition to federal activism showed its strong appeal to white Southerners (Carmines and Stimson 1989).

There was no let-up in civil rights activity after the election. In 1965 King and the SCLC targeted Selma, Alabama, as the place to force a confrontation on voting restrictions aimed at blacks. Again mass marches and demonstrations met with brutal response from local officials. Scenes of police charging and beating a column of peaceful demonstrators brought cries of outrage from across the political spectrum. The *Washington Post* described the events of March 7, 1965, as follows:

> State troopers and mounted deputies bombarded 600 praying Negroes with tear gas today and then waded into them with clubs, whips and ropes, injuring scores.
>
> The troopers and possemen, under Gov. George C. Wallace's orders to stop the Negroes' "Walk for Freedom" from Selma to Montgomery, chased the screaming, bleeding marchers nearly a mile back to their church, clubbing them as they ran (also see Garrow 1978:80).

Leaders ranging from Michigan Congressman Gerald Ford to Minnesota Senator Walter Mondale denounced the actions and called for federal legislation to protect the rights of blacks to vote. King and other black leaders had succeeded in creating the sense of national emergency needed to obtain the desired federal legislation.

The Johnson administration had wanted to delay additional new legislation until 1966 in order to give the 1964 act some time to be implemented and tested. But King, along with other more militant figures in the civil rights movement, refused to yield, and the sense of urgency grew. In 1965 the administration began to draft voting rights legislation that it hoped would attract bipartisan support in both houses of Congress.

President Johnson signed the Voting Rights Act into law on August 6, 1965, and the Department of Justice made good Johnson's promise of swift implementation. The historian Stephen Lawson reported: "On the first anniversary of the passage of the Voting Rights Act, an average of 46 percent of adult blacks in the five Deep South states to which examiners had been assigned could vote, thereby doubling the percentage from the year before" (1976:330). Mississippi underwent perhaps the most dramatic change. In 1964 only 7 percent of adult blacks in Mississippi were registered to vote; by 1969 that figure had risen to a remarkable 67 percent. As one older black woman put it, "I'm going to vote now. I'm going to vote because I haven't been able to vote in my sixty-seven years" (Lawson 1976:331, 339). The Voting Rights Act has since been heralded as the most effective piece of legislation in American history. The act "succeeded so well because it automatically suspended discriminatory voting qualifications and gave the president the authority to send examiners to register Negroes directly" (Lawson 1976:342).

The 1964 Civil Rights Act and the 1965 Voting Rights Act were, without question, tremendous achievements. But both pieces of legislation, as well as earlier breakthroughs such as the *Brown* decision and the Montgomery bus boycott, had come at a price. The cost in human suffering and lives lost was not small. In June 1963, Medgar Evers, the field secretary of the Mississippi NAACP, was assassinated. Later that year four black children were killed in the bombing of a church in Birmingham. In the summer of 1964 three young men—Michael Schwerner, James Chaney, and Andrew Goodman—who had been working on a black voter registration program in Mississippi were found buried in shallow graves. All three had been severely beaten and then shot. Others also lost their lives in the struggle for black rights, including Jimmy Lee Jackson, the Reverend James Reeb, Jonathan Daniels, and Viola Liuzzo. And these were but the highly publicized instances. The activities of Klansmen and other racists willing to use violence inflicted a higher, though less visible, toll.[12]

There were other blemishes on what from one standpoint was a remarkable record of progress and achievement. The day-to-day lives of ordinary black Americans, especially in terms of educational and economic opportunities, had not been affected by the great gains of the late 1950s and early 1960s. The level of school segregation in the Deep South in 1964, for example, remained virtually identical to what it had been in 1954 (Rodgers 1975). The median family income of blacks fluctuated between 51 percent and 57 percent of that of whites throughout the entire eighteen-year period from 1947 to 1965 (Newman et al. 1978:269). Moreover, the immediate efforts to enforce the Civil Rights Act of 1964, at least in the areas of school desegregation and job discrimination, were weak and ineffectual (Rodgers 1975; Zashin 1978). All too often, it seemed, new principles and laws would be adopted with great ceremony, only to fall short in enforcement and results.

One unusual event during the Kennedy years was a furor over a Department of Labor report called "The Negro Family: The Case for National Action," prepared by Daniel Patrick Moynihan. The "Moynihan Report," as it came to be known, concluded that black urban poverty could be traced in part to a breakdown of black family structure. The conclusion was criticized by many civil rights activists at the time, though more recently has been seen by a number of social commentators as having identified an important social trend, especially in the black population but among whites as well.

Change in the daily lives and experiences of most black Americans remained a remote goal. This fact would be given sudden and dramatic emphasis in places such as Watts, Newark, and Detroit, and in the growing militancy of younger blacks across the nation. With the *Brown* decision fading into the past and landmark legislation on the books, the tortuous and complex task of real implementation and meaningful change had, paradoxically, just begun.

The Unfinished Civil Rights Agenda, 1965–1979

The Urban Riots. On August 11, 1965, less than a week after President Johnson signed the Voting Rights Act into law, the Los Angeles community of Watts exploded with the worst racial disturbance since the Detroit riot of 1943. In more than six days of looting, fires, and violence, approximately 4,000 people were arrested, 34 people (mostly black civilians) were killed, and an estimated $35 million in damage was done (U.S. National Advisory Commission on Civil Disorders 1968:38). The deep alienation, bitterness, and potential for violence seen in Watts would appear again and again across the country. More than 170 cities experienced racial disturbances between 1961 and 1968 (Spilerman 1976). The sense of national emergency became especially acute during the "long, hot summer" of 1967. In the first nine months of that year there were well over 100 civil disorders, 41 of them serious disorders involving fires, looting, violence, and the need for significant numbers of police, National Guardsmen, and even army troops to quell the disturbances (U.S. National Advisory Commission on Civil Disorders 1968). Again in April 1968, following the assassination of Martin Luther King, more than 100 cities experienced violent outbreaks, adding further to the toll of lives lost and the damage to homes and other property.

These events both heralded and spurred a change in the tenor of the campaign for black rights. Most blacks viewed the riots as spontaneous outbursts brought on by years of discrimination and mistreatment (Campbell and Schuman 1968:47–59). They also thought the riots had helped the racial situation by focusing attention on the long-standing economic and social grievances of urban blacks (Sears and McConahay 1973). Some analysts concluded that, in fact, a "riot ideology" had emerged and was attractive to many blacks (Tomlinson 1968; Caplan 1970; Sears and McConahay 1973). For instance, Caplan, after an extensive review of the literature on blacks' riot-related attitudes, concluded, "Militancy in the pursuit of civil rights objectives represents a considerable force within the ghetto. Its support approaches normative proportions and is by no means limited to a deviant and irresponsible minority" (1970:71). In particular, there was mounting evidence that the participants in the riots were not deviants, criminals, or other socially marginal "riffraff." Study after study showed riot participants to have been young black males, born in the North, who felt strong group pride and identity, were more likely than most to be involved in the community, and were deeply distrustful of and dissatisfied with white institutions (Caplan and Paige 1968; Tomlinson 1968; Paige 1970; Sears and McConahay 1973).

White reaction to the riots was divided and ambivalent. Many whites viewed the riots as intolerable lawlessness worthy only of severe punishment. Campbell and Schuman, in a survey of fifteen Northern cities in 1968, found that, of the whites interviewed, "about a third [saw] the riots as largely unjustified but conspiratorial assaults on law and order led by criminal, demagogic, or other undesirable elements, assaults that should be met first of all by firm police action" (1968:50). Another third, however, viewed the riots in much the same way as did blacks: as protests stemming from legitimate grievances. The remaining third held ambivalent views combining both interpretations. A longer-term legacy of the riots was probably an increase in white perceptions of urban ghettos as dangerous places, a consequence still felt in national politics, culture, and attitudes.

The ghetto rebellions and the increasing militancy of black protest prompted a deeper examination of the race problem in America. As the National Advisory Commission on Civil Disorders stated in words that have been quoted many times in subsequent years: "Our nation is moving toward two societies, one black, one white—separate and unequal." As the commission members saw it, the only way to shrink the rift between blacks and whites was through "new attitudes, new understanding, and above all, [a] new will" to address the racial divisions in America (1968:1–2).

Blacks and whites were especially divided in their interpretations of the increasingly popular political slogan "Black Power." In 1967 Joel D. Aberbach and Jack L. Walker asked Detroit residents what the phrase "Black Power" meant to them. The overwhelming majority of whites, 81 percent, interpreted the phrase negatively, usually taking it to mean black rule over whites. Blacks were more wide-ranging in their interpretations of the term: approximately 50 percent offered unfavorable interpretations and 42 percent favorable ones. Despite this split, very few blacks understood Black Power to mean the sort of radical and violent change envisioned by whites. Instead, for them Black Power aroused debates over tactics and strategies in the struggle for equality and integration. In contrast to more extreme advocates of Black Power who favored black separatism, most blacks who were favorably disposed to the slogan took it "as another call for a fair share for blacks or as a rallying cry for black unity" (Aberbach and Walker 1970:373).

The new militant and sometimes separatist thrust of the civil rights struggle split black leaders. The Black Power Movement, fueled by the stormy rhetoric of Stokely Carmichael, Hubert "Rap" Brown, and groups like the Black Panthers, dramatically altered the character and perceptions of the struggle for racial change. Integration, racial harmony, and coalition politics—primary goals of organizations like the NAACP and SCLC—were challenged as accommodationist, weak, and inadequate. Major and increasingly public disputes ensued among black leaders and between black leaders and their white allies.

The nature of these disputes was clearly revealed in two books published in 1967. Martin Luther King's *Where Do We Go from Here: Chaos or Community?* called for a reaffirmation of the values, goals, and strategies of earlier civil rights efforts. King advocated pressing for full implementation of recent court rulings and legislation. Otherwise, he cautioned, black frustration would continue to grow: "The gap between promise and fulfillment is distressingly wide" (1967:40). King characterized the slogan "Black Power," despite a component that emphasized cultural pride and positive change, as mainly a cry of the despairing. He deplored both the increasingly separatist leanings of those calling for Black Power and their willingness to embrace violence as a strategy of protest.

On the other side of the dispute, *Black Power: The Politics of Liberation in America,* by Stokely Carmichael and Charles Hamilton, argued that Black Power meant a positive cultural identity for blacks, a repudiation of "go slow" tactics or of any coalition with whites that curbed or compromised the black demand for freedom, a willingness to respond to violence with violence, and a profound questioning of the goal of integration or assimilation to middle-class values.

The differences between moderate civil rights leaders like King and advocates of Black Power like Carmichael and Hamilton were in some respects matters of emphasis. Both sides agreed that the early victories had mainly established a new framework and new principles, not an entirely new social order in which genuine racial equality reigned. They also agreed that further change would meet more resistance and be even more divisive because it would require upsetting national, not merely Southern, patterns of economic and social inequality between the races. There was consensus over the value of black cultural pride and identity. The great rift between the two camps was over protest strategies and rhetorical emphasis, though there was also some division with regard to the issue of separatism.

The riots and the Black Power Movement had profound effects. They altered black Americans' sense of themselves as a people, and they altered many white perceptions of the struggle for change. More than anything else, however, these developments spoke to the slow pace at which, in the eyes of many blacks, concrete change had been implemented. The Black Power Movement and "the riots crystallized the belief among many blacks that progress was too slight and their status in American society still basically frustrating" (Schuman and Hatchett 1974:125). And in so doing, the riots and black militancy increased the pressure on the nation to address urban economic poverty more generally. Dramatic as the new legislation and court decisions were, racial equality was not much closer for most black Americans.[13]

Some concrete steps on these issues were being taken. In particular, President Johnson's War on Poverty and call to move toward a Great Society had a significant impact on the economic position of blacks (Levitan and Taggart 1976). The Economic Opportunity Act of 1964 created programs such as VISTA, Head Start, and the Job Corps, which provided blacks with greater educational and job-training opportunities. In 1965 the Medicaid and Medicare programs were created to improve health care for the poor and the elderly, and the Elementary and Secondary Education Act, which would greatly increase federal support for poor school districts, was passed. Thus important actions were under way to reduce the effects of economic disadvantage in America. Blacks would benefit greatly from some of these programs, since they were disproportionately represented among the ranks of the ill-housed, the poorly educated, and the recipients of inferior health care, though legislation like Medicare was certainly not focused on blacks in particular.

Johnson's vision of a Great Society began to falter, however. In good part, this occurred as a result of the drain of moral and economic resources caused by the war in Vietnam and by related difficulties with the domestic economy. By mid-1965, public concern over foreign policy (primarily the war in Vietnam) had eclipsed civil rights as "the nation's most important problem" (Smith 1980). The decrease in the number of civil rights demonstrations and racial disturbances after 1968 contributed much to the declining concern with the black struggle.

In part also, the problems of the cities were not as easy to solve as some of the Great Society rhetoric implied. During the presidential campaign of 1968 one of Richard Nixon's key themes was that the Great Society and the black protests had gone too far and needed to be scaled down. Nixon said: "For the past five years we have been deluged by government programs for the unemployed, programs for cities, programs for the poor, and we have reaped from these programs an ugly harvest of frustration, violence and failure across the land" (Levitan and Taggart 1976:3–4). Once elected, Nixon did apply pressure to curb and in some cases to eliminate the social programs started by Johnson, and he deemphasized concern with civil rights.

The Nixon-Ford-Carter Years. From the beginning, Nixon had been viewed with suspicion by many advocates of civil rights. Besides being against welfare, Nixon was perceived as following a "Southern strategy" that promised Southern politicians narrowly construed enforcement of civil rights legislation. His emphasis on law and order also appeared to many as a veiled antiblack appeal.

Nixon's actions in office seemed to lend credence to many of these apprehensions. Early in his first term, his adviser Daniel Patrick Moynihan wrote in a memorandum: "The time may have come when the issue of race could benefit from a period of 'benign neglect.' The subject has been too much talked about" (*Congressional Quarterly* 1970:24). Nixon, moreover, had great difficulty in retaining high-level appointees to civil rights posts (Newman et al. 1978:119–120), and there was mounting criticism of his record on civil rights. He also declared himself opposed to school busing at a time when many courts were turning to busing as the only means to achieve meaningful desegregation of schools (*Congressional Quarterly* 1972). And he initially opposed an extension of the Voting Rights Act, though eventually he endorsed the extension in the face of clear congressional resolve.

During the early 1970s there was a growing belief that the momentum of the civil rights movement had disappeared. *Newsweek* published a special issue in 1973 entitled "Whatever Happened to Black America?" and wrote: "The great surge that carried racial justice briefly to the top of the nation's agenda in the 1960's has been stalemated by war, economics, the flame-out of the old civil rights coalition and the rise to power of a New American Majority. Blacks and their special problems have gone out of fashion in government, politics and civil concern" (*Newsweek* February 19, 1973:29). Not all civil rights issues had vanished, for school busing and affirmative action would receive increasing public attention. Both these issues were the legacies of earlier initiatives, and both concerned the concrete aspects of advancing racial equality. The pressure these policies exerted to close the pervasive gap, however, drew its impetus not from massive social protests but from the courts and the federal civil rights bureaucracy.

Two related factors increased the pressure for school desegregation. First, a series of Supreme Court rulings forcefully mandated compliance with the *Brown* decision and expanded its scope. Second, the Civil Rights Act of 1964 increased desegregation efforts on the part of the Department of Health, Education, and Welfare (HEW) and the Department of Justice. HEW could terminate the flow of federal funds to school systems maintaining segregated schools, and Justice could enter school desegregation cases on the side of the plaintiffs.

The original *Brown* decision had been rendered in two parts: the first ruling, in 1954, *Brown I,* articulated the principle that racially separate schooling was inherently unequal and was an unconstitutional infringement on the rights of blacks. The second ruling, in 1955, *Brown II,* called for the implementation of *Brown I* with all deliberate speed. The phrase "all deliberate speed" was construed very liberally by the affected Southern school systems, especially those in the Deep South, where little noticeable progress toward desegregation was made in the ensuing ten years.

Three crucial Supreme Court rulings attempted to dispel this lethargy. In *Green v. County School Board of New Kent County* (1968) the court ruled that a program that was formally "neutral" with regard to race did not constitute abolition of a dual and segregated system, the remedy called for in *Brown II.* Thus the voluntary desegregation plan that the school board had adopted was held to be insufficient because it achieved no noteworthy progress toward desegregation. The Court took the *Green* ruling a step further in *Swann v. Charlotte-Mecklenburg* (1971). Here the Court held that, where necessary, racial composition quotas might be used as guides to designing desegregation plans and that busing might he used toward implementing such plans. These two decisions, along with threats of funding cutoffs, led to significant increases in the amount of integrated schooling in the South (Rodgers 1975).

These rulings, however, continued the pattern established in *Brown* of applying mainly to Southern states that previously had legally sanctioned segregation. With *Keyes v. School District No. 1, Denver, Colorado* (1973), court-ordered desegregation moved to the North. The Court held that although the Denver school system had not had legally mandated segregation, the school board, as an agent of the state, had intentionally created a segregated school system. The ruling referred to a district court opinion in the case: "Between 1960 and 1969 the

Board's policies with respect to these northeast Denver schools show an undeviating purpose to isolate Negro students in segregated schools 'while preserving the Anglo character of [other] schools'" (pp. 197–198). Such policies, the court held, were a constitutional violation warranting relief.

Busing became an explosive controversy in both North and South. Cities like Pontiac, Michigan, experienced bus burnings and other violence, as district courts ordered desegregation. Boston witnessed large and hostile demonstrations against busing. Several schools required the presence of police to retain order. In Boston, Pontiac, Los Angeles, and many other cities vigorous antibusing protest groups were formed. Many cities facing desegregation orders also experienced significant white flight to unaffected suburban areas (see Farley, Richards, and Wurdock 1980).

School desegregation shared the civil rights limelight during the 1970s with disputes over affirmative action policies. The phrase "affirmative action" had been used originally by President Kennedy. The phrase and later policies were developed further by President Johnson in a speech delivered at Howard University in 1965:

> You do not take a person who for years has been hobbled by chains and liberate him, bring him up to the starting line of a race, and say, "you are free to compete with all the others," and still justly believe that you have been completely fair. Thus it is not enough to open the gates of opportunity. All our citizens must have the ability to walk through those gates. (Johnson 1965)

Guidelines promulgated in 1968 by the Office of Federal Contract Compliance in relation to Title VII of the Civil Rights Act were the serious beginning of the controversy over affirmative action. The guidelines called for employers receiving federal funds of $50,000 or more and firms with 50 or more employees to submit affirmative action compliance plans. In particular, the regulations called for "specific steps to guarantee equal employment opportunity keyed to the problems and needs of members of minority groups, including, when there are deficiencies, the development of specific goals and time tables for the prompt achievement of full and equal employment opportunity" (Glazer 1975:46). Stronger and more specific guidelines were issued in 1970 and again in 1971. The 1971 guidelines called for employer affirmative action programs to analyze the reasons behind "deficient" utilization of minorities and women, and to develop specific plans "to increase materially the utilization of minorities and women" (Glazer 1975:48). Underutilization was said to exist if a particular job category had a lower percentage of minorities or women than would have been expected on the basis of their "availability" in the population. These guidelines in particular have been interpreted by some as requiring "not . . . opportunity, but result[s]" (Glazer 1975:48).[14]

Ironically, in 1969 Nixon's White House agreed to have the Labor Department back the "Philadelphia Plan" for the local construction industry. Thus the first major use of employment targets for blacks was endorsed by a Republican administration. Apparently Nixon saw this affirmative action step partly as a bold way to create some black political support, despite his generally negative civil rights record, and partly as a wedge to split the coalition of civil rights organizations and traditional labor unions that had opposed him in 1968 (Graham 1990).

Although Jimmy Carter was elected president of the United States in 1976 largely as a result of overwhelming black support (92 percent of black ballots), his administration did little to revive government activism in the cause of racial equality. Beyond appointing numerous African Americans to office, including two Cabinet members, thirty federal judges, and twenty-five aides on the White House staff, Carter initiated no new programs and declined to participate in the debate over affirmative action. In addition, the economic specters of inflation and unemployment that bedeviled his term in office hit blacks especially hard. With the jobless rate reaching a ten-year high, Julian Bond, a former Georgia state legislator and black activist, summarized the Carter years by saying, "It is easy to see why many have concluded that we voted for a man who knew the words to our hymns, but not the numbers on our paychecks" (Sitkoff 1993:214–215).

Retrenchment and Reaction, 1980–1997

With the defeat of Carter and the election of Ronald Reagan in 1980, the federal government retreated even further from a commitment to civil rights and affirmative action. Reagan's election, coupled with newly won Republican control of the Senate, was received as distressing news by many blacks and other minorities. Reagan had campaigned against the excesses of "big government," including affirmative action quotas and mandatory busing, as well as the growing Great Society bureaucracy. The apprehensions of civil rights activists seemed confirmed by a number of Reagan initiatives. The Department of Justice now entered school desegregation cases on the side of school districts facing court orders. Virtually all efforts to use busing as a means of achieving desegregation were suspended. There was even an attempt to restore the tax-exempt status of Bob Jones University, a private school that forbade interracial dating. Reagan also was silent on extension of the Voting Rights Act until it became clear that congressional support for it was solid. At that point he agreed to sign the bill. Similarly, he initially opposed a national holiday honoring the birthday of Martin Luther King, Jr., but relented when faced with a united Congress. In the first years of the decade, his administration also cut government aid to historically black colleges and universities, changed the character of financial aid for college students by switching from grants to loans as the primary form of aid, began a policy of rapprochement with the white government of South Africa, restaffed the Civil Rights Commission that had been created in 1957, and launched a major effort to change federal policies on busing and affirmative action (Sitkoff 1993; Franklin and Moss 1994; Marable 1995).

These actions earned Reagan the enmity of many civil rights organizations. One group went so far as to denounce him for unleashing a full-scale assault on the legislative advances of the 1960s. "The Leadership Conference on Civil Rights," reported the *New York Times,* "has charged that under the Reagan Administration 'there [have] been no significant civil rights enforcement activities anywhere in the government'" (June 26, 1984, p. B7). Moreover, polls conducted by several organizations showed blacks, in sharp contrast to whites, to be extremely pessimistic about their future under his administration (*New York Times,* August 24, 1981). Thus began the counterpoint of retrenchment and reaction that has so dominated race relations in this country ever since.

The retreat from civil rights and the exacerbation of racial tensions continued through the presidential election of 1988 and the subsequent term of George Bush. Fear tactics used during the Bush campaign stressed the ubiquity of crime and its concomitant menace in such political advertisements as the "revolving door ad," which pictured dark-complected convicts circling in and out of a prison turnstile (Jamieson 1992). The link with race was made explicit in the infamous Willie Horton political ads, the first of which included a mug shot of the black felon and intoned ominously how he had "murdered a boy in a robbery, stabbing him nineteen times" and then, on a weekend furlough from prison, kidnapped a young couple, "stabbing the man and repeatedly raping his girlfriend." Later ads featured the victims of these criminal acts describing their suffering in inflammatory detail (Jamieson 1992).

Having been elected on the basis of such appeals, Bush did little to counteract their impact during his four years in office. Although he appointed a few more African Americans than Reagan had to the Cabinet and to other highly visible positions in his administration—Colin Powell being the most noteworthy—Bush vetoed important social legislation, including a bill to raise the minimum wage, the so-called motor voter act that would have increased voter registration among African Americans, and most important, the 1990 Civil Rights Act, which he characterized as a "quotas bill." The economic recession that occurred during the final two years of Bush's term brought to an end an administration that had been generally unsympathetic to racial issues.

The tone set by the executive level of government during these years also affected the decisions of the U.S. Supreme Court, now refashioned with Reagan appointees. Approximately ten years after the *Bakke* decision, in a series of four cases decided during 1988 and 1989, the Court narrowed the scope of government policies designed to create greater equality and remedy discrimination. In the first of these cases, the justices declared a contract set-aside program unconstitutional (*City of Richmond v. J. A. Crosson Company,* 1988). Shortly thereafter, they constrained the interpretation of the Civil Rights Act of 1866 (*Patterson v. McLean Credit Union,* 1989), shifted the burden of proof to employees in discrimination lawsuits (*Wards Cove Packing Company v. Antonio,* 1989), and empowered white firefighters in reverse discrimination cases (*Martin v. Wilks,* 1989).

These reversals indicated that the U.S. Supreme Court, which had served as a promoter of civil rights since the 1950s, could no longer be counted on for support in all areas. The appointment of a justice to replace the retiring Thurgood Marshall therefore became a matter of special concern to African Americans. George Bush's nomination of Clarence Thomas, a conservative black Republican with little judicial experience, and Bush's description of him as "the best qualified" among the possible choices, an apparent slip of the tongue (Mayer and Abramson 1994), ignited a controversy over the appointment that has even now scarcely abated among many black and white Americans (see Marable 1995).

Concern about the persistence of poverty, especially among inner-city blacks, also became a growing policy problem during the Reagan and Bush years. Conservative analysts such as Charles Murray and Lawrence Mead painted the social policies of the War on Poverty and Great Society era as having ushered in a dysfunctional pattern of social breakdown and welfare dependency in many poor communities. This debate was crystallized with the publication of William Julius Wilson's important book *The Truly Disadvantaged: The Inner City, the Underclass, and Public Policy* (1987). Wilson made the forceful argument that, following on the heels of generations of racial discrimination, disadvantaged blacks in urban centers were facing sharply rising rates of joblessness as a result of deindustrialization and the deconcentration of industry. The former spoke to a basic shift away from manufacturing toward a more high-technology, service-oriented economy. The latter concerned the movement of much manufacturing work away from inner-city areas to suburban or ex-urban locations. The consequence of these trends was an increasingly sharp mismatch between the skill levels of many inner-city blacks and the available pool of jobs, with the end result of rising black male unemployment (Farley 1996:243–244). The structural problem of joblessness was associated with a series of social changes such as a breakdown of family structure, an increasing number of single-parent, female-headed households, rising welfare dependency, poorly performing schools, and an increase in crime and juvenile delinquency.

Many manifestations of these shifts were readily apparent to most Americans, either through direct observation of communities in decline or, more likely, through news reports and other media outlets. Popular films, even those made by black directors, with titles such as *Boyz N the Hood* and *Menace II Society,* increasingly depicted inner-city ghettos as economically depressed, graffiti-riddled settings. They were portrayed as places for drug trading, seemingly random drive-by shootings that took the lives of innocent people, and incessant gang wars. According to the black urban ethnographer Elijah Anderson, an image of "the black male as predator" was assuming vivid shape in the public mind. "The master status assigned to black males," he wrote, "undermines their ability to be taken for granted as law-abiding and civil participants in public places: young black males, particularly those who don the urban uniform (sneakers, athletic suits, gold chains, 'gangster caps,' sunglasses, and large portable radios or 'boom boxes'), may be taken as the embodiment of the predator" (Anderson 1990:167). This new perception, indeed fear, of the young urban black male affects blacks and whites alike: "In the interest of security and defense, residents adopt the facile but practical perspective that informs the prevailing view of public community relations; whites are law-abiding and trustworthy; anonymous young black males are crime-prone and dangerous. Ironically, this perceived dangerousness has become important to the public self-identity of many local black men" (Anderson 1990:168).

The worsening problem of ghetto unemployment and poverty stands in sharp contrast to the apparent growth, vitality, and success of much of the black middle class. During the 1960s and early 1970s, as the economy grew and as civil rights laws were passed bringing antidiscrimination efforts and pressure for affirmative action, blacks made important relative gains in status. This was true in terms of educational attainment, earnings, and basic placement in the hierarchy of occupations. A major National Academy of Sciences report, entitled *A Common Destiny: Blacks and American Society* (Jaynes and Williams 1989), focused attention on the simultaneous emergence of the new ghetto poor and the expansion of the black middle class. The report declared that "Americans face an unfinished agenda: many black Americans remain separated from the mainstream of national life under conditions of great inequality. The American dilemma has not been resolved" (1989:4). In particular, the report stressed that "since the early 1970s the economic status of blacks relative to whites has, on average, stagnated or deteriorated" (1989:6).

The deterioration in the position of blacks occurred on several key dimensions of social status. First, between 1979 and the mid-1980s there was a sharp decline in the rates of black high school graduates going on to college. This occurred despite evidence of modest relative gains in achievement by African Americans during the same period (Jaynes and Williams 1989; Hauser 1993). Second, the relative employment and earnings of blacks, especially young black men, also stagnated and declined. The growing black-white disparity in employment rates appeared most dramatically among those with only a high school education or less, but the earnings gap between blacks and whites widened most for young, college-educated men (Bound and Freeman

1992). Third, the well-established pattern of racial residential segregation continued to be a problem. Blacks were, and are, far less likely to share residential space with whites than are either Hispanics or Asians (Jaynes and Williams 1989). Sociologists have long held that spatial mobility is a key element in the process of general social mobility. Although there has been some very modest decline in the average level of black residential isolation from whites (Farley and Frey 1994), especially in rapidly growing cities in the West, many black communities remain "hypersegregated," prompting the demographers Douglas Massey and Nancy Denton to characterize the placement of blacks in urban space as "American Apartheid" (Massey and Denton 1993).

The 1980s and early 1990s also saw what appeared to be an increase in incidences of racial harassment and violence within even liberal colleges and universities (see Jaynes and Williams 1989:364–365). The reports of hate speech and hate crimes resulted in several different kinds of initiatives. Colleges hastened to write and approve speech and conduct codes that imposed penalties for both the harmful expression of racial prejudice and overt acts of intimidation, though these codes were sometimes declared unconstitutional infringements on freedom of speech. Congress passed a Hate Crimes Statistics Act in 1990 that required the FBI to report on all "crimes that manifest evidence of prejudice based on race, religion, sexual orientation, or ethnicity" for five years beginning in 1990 (Berry 1994). Other reports also suggested that racial and other kinds of harassment were on the rise. Although the Ku Klux Klan staged rallies throughout this period, its notoriety was eclipsed by the violence associated with groups of "skinheads" that were emerging in the United States and Europe.

Three incidents in the late 1980s and early 1990s symbolized the rise in racial hatred. The attacks on African Americans by whites at Howard Beach and later in the Bensonhurst neighborhood of Brooklyn resulted in senseless deaths and reminded the nation that racial hostility was still a powerful motivator of human behavior. In addition, the subject of police abuse and mistreatment of blacks, always smoldering beneath the surface, came to the forefront in 1991 with the beating of Rodney King by officers of the Los Angeles Police Department. The abuse was captured on videotape by a resident of the neighborhood, and was shown repeatedly on national television. In addition, the campaign of the former Ku Klux Klan member David Duke for the governorship of Louisiana in 1990 provided additional evidence that old, pre–civil rights era ideas lingered in the electorate. Although Duke lost the election, he won a majority of the white vote and also received substantial financial contributions from sympathetic whites in the North (Schuman and Krysan 1996).

The election of Bill Clinton to the White House in 1992 offered a respite from these tensions. He fulfilled his campaign pledge to have the people in his administration resemble the population of the United States by appointing four African Americans and two Hispanics to Cabinet-level positions, as well as tapping numerous African Americans and women to fill lesser positions in the government (Franklin and Moss 1994). He also opposed Republican efforts to eliminate virtually all affirmative action programs, though his proposal "to mend, not end" affirmative action remains unclear as of this writing. In other respects Clinton tried to accommodate conservative critics. He abandoned his choice of Lani Guinier, a black woman, for Assistant Attorney General for Civil Rights after her espousal of proportional voting as a method to increase the influence of blacks at the polls became hotly controversial (Dentler 1995). More generally, the first two years of the Clinton presidency seemed to be "the beginning of a nationwide swing away from the Right and toward the center" (Dentler 1995:28).

The U.S. Supreme Court, with the confirmation of a staunchly conservative justice in Clarence Thomas, continued to whittle away at the basic programs designed in the 1960s and early 1970s to promote equality of outcome across racial and ethnic groups. Between 1992 and 1995, the Court issued a series of opinions that began to redefine the limits of racial policy in the United States. In a particularly striking case (*R.A.V. v. St. Paul, Minnesota,* 1992), the Court supported the right of the Ku Klux Klan to burn crosses as an expression of free speech. As a result, efforts to shield blacks and other minorities from racial epithets and threats of violence suffered a setback. A subsequent case in 1993 *(Wisconsin v. Mitchell),* however, did permit extra penalties when racial hatred motivated violent conduct, but irony here lay in the fact that the victim of racial intimidation in this case was white and the perpetrator black. In 1993 as well *(Shaw v. Reno),* the Court declared that race could not be considered in congressional redistricting after the decennial Censuses. The decision signaled that districts drawn to ensure black majorities after the 1990 Census (such as a district in North Carolina that stretched along 160 miles of highway from Durham to Charlotte) might be rejected. Thus a procedure that had produced substantially greater black representation in Congress seemed threatened (Franklin and Moss 1994), though it had also contributed to increasing Republican dominance outside of black majority areas.

In addition, a conservative Republican tide swept Congress in the mid-term elections of 1994, with implications for civil rights policies. In a flurry of legislation during the new Congress's first one hundred days, the Republicans launched major initiatives that sought to alter the economic and social programs that provided a safety net for the poor and to revoke the affirmative action policies that granted preferential treatment to blacks, women, and other minorities. State governments controlled by Republicans followed suit. In the summer of 1995 the Board of Regents of the University of California system followed Governor Pete Wilson's lead and voted to abolish affirmative action programs on its constituent campuses. The governor also proposed that a referendum on the broader issue be held during the 1996 election. Passage of Proposition 209, or the California Civil Rights Initiative, as it came to be called, would prohibit the state from discriminating against, or granting preferential treatment to, "any individual or group on the basis of race, sex, color, ethnicity, or national origin in the operation of public employment, public education, or public contracting."

After the Republican "Revolution of 1994," the Supreme Court took three actions that further constrained government efforts to promote racial equality. In May 1995, the justices refused to review the decision of the U.S. Court of Appeals that declared race-based scholarships at the University of Maryland unconstitutional. Then in June 1995 they applied the "strict scrutiny" criteria to minority set-aside programs *(Adarand Constructors Inc. v. Pena),* indicating that in the future few of these programs would survive the judicial process. The Supreme Court also supported its 1993 decision on congressional reapportionment by requiring Georgia to redraw three of its districts before the 1996 election.

The turn away from affirmative action policies came at a time of mounting evidence of the persistence of racial discrimination and bias. For example, in the housing market careful auditing studies found high rates of discrimination by landlords and realtors against black home-seekers (Yinger 1996). Evidence also increased that lenders discriminated against blacks who had incomes and credit histories comparable to those of whites (Jackson 1995). In the job market, auditing studies showed significant discrimination against blacks, even in the low-wage, low-skill sector of the economy (Turner, Fix, and Struyk 1991). Indeed, blacks found it difficult to make even modest in-roads to one of the few low-skill, high-paying lines of employment—the construction industry—that had undergone some growth in many urban areas during the 1980s (Waldinger and Bailey 1991). Innovative studies based on in-depth interviews with employers pointed to widespread negative stereotypes of blacks, especially of younger blacks (Kirschenman and Neckerman 1991).

There were many signs that a tightening economy, an increasingly hostile policy climate, and a worsening position for many segments of the black community were producing an acute sense of concern among African Americans, particularly among the African American middle class. Qualitative research studies found that the black middle class faced subtle discrimination in public places such as on the streets, in restaurants, and in stores (Schuman et al. 1983; Feagin 1991). Commenting on the wide occurrence of racial discrimination experienced by otherwise successful, middle-class blacks, the black journalist Ellis Cose wrote: "Despite its very evident prosperity, much of America's black middle class is in excruciating pain. And that distress—although most of the country does not see it—illuminates a serious American problem: the problem of the broken covenant, of the pact ensuring that if you work hard, get a good education, and play by the rules, you will be allowed to advance and achieve to the limits of your ability" (Cose 1993:1). This problem of persistent discrimination and black anger over it runs deep, eliciting concern on the part of the white political scientist Jennifer Hochschild that the core national myth of the "American Dream" is "threatened for all Americans in ways that the disaffection of most middle-class blacks and the fury of a few poor blacks most clearly reveal" (Hochschild 1995:3).

Given the steady rightward swing of government policy from 1980 to 1996, and the worsening conditions for many African Americans during that time (Hacker 1995), it seemed inevitable that there would be some kind of reaction from the black community. There had been a few favorable occurrences—the twenty-five-year extension of the Voting Rights Act, the conviction after thirty-one years of Byron de La Beckwith for the 1963 murder of Medgar Evers, the economic success of the black middle class, and the continued string of firsts by black politicians, such as Carol Mosely Braun (the first black woman ever elected to the U.S. Senate) and Douglas Wilder (the first black governor of Virginia). The initial responses to the conservatism of the 1980s came through mainstream political channels, as Jesse Jackson mounted strong campaigns for the Democratic presidential nominations in 1984 and 1988 by emphasizing essentially left-of-center social programs, including affirmative action (Marable 1995). In addition, as a protest against Reagan administration policies in South Africa, two prominent leaders in Jackson's 1984 primary campaign began a series of demonstrations against apartheid before the South African Embassy in Washington, D.C. As the Free South Africa Movement spread beyond the capital, the U.S. Congress responded to public sentiment by overriding a Reagan veto and joining other nations in an effort to weaken South Africa's commitment to apartheid by imposing economic sanctions.

During the 1980s other, far less mainstream reactions took place. The cultural philosophy of Afrocentrism asserted that people from Africa and non-Western countries understood the human condition in quite different terms from people of European descent. This theory, which called for black children to be educated in separate academies, led to the founding of a number of private schools espousing Afrocentric principles. It also effected changes in the curriculum in many public schools with substantial percentages of black students. The most outspoken proponent of this philosophy has been Leonard Jeffries of the City College of New York. In 1991 Jeffries gained national attention with a speech extolling the virtues of blacks and denigrating those of whites and Jews. His subsequent legal battle to remain chairman of the Black Studies Department at City College lasted four years and was not resolved until 1995, when the U.S. Court of Appeals, under pressure from the U.S. Supreme Court, finally ruled in favor of his demotion.

The Nation of Islam under the direction of Louis Farrakhan represented yet another separatist strain. Decidedly confrontational and hostile, Farrakhan preached a philosophy of black self-help and anti-Semitism that appealed to portions of the African American population. In 1993 one of Farrakhan's associates, Khalid Abdul Mohammad, delivered such an inflammatory speech to students at Kean College that the public uproar eventually forced Farrakhan to relieve him of his official responsibilities in the organization.

The importance of separatist movements, particularly the Nation of Islam, increased as the venerable National Association for the Advancement of Colored People declined in relevance and power (Marable 1995). It was not until the early 1990s that the problems of the oldest civil rights organization in this country became fully evident. With the appointment of Benjamin Chavis as executive director, the NAACP hoped to revitalize both its membership and its mission. As Chavis reached out to the generation of young blacks in the hopes of bringing them into the fold, he also attempted to forge ties between the NAACP and Louis Farrakhan. In the process, he paid too little attention to the financial health of the organization. In 1994 the board of directors voted to oust him. The ensuing controversy clearly indicated that many blacks question the NAACP's "purpose in today's world," and that when they consider the NAACP at all, "it is often in the past tense" (*New York Times,* January 9, 1996, p. A6). With the swearing in of Kweisi Mfume, who had been a respected member of Congress, as the new executive director in February 1996, the NAACP began to reform both its structure and its finances in an attempt to regain its former status (*New York Times,* February 19, 1996, p. A7).

The last sixteen years have also seen large-scale participation by African Americans in marches on Washington. Even before Reagan took office, 100,000 people marched in January 1981 to indicate their support for a national holiday honoring Martin Luther King. The 1983 and 1993 marches celebrated the twentieth and thirtieth anniversaries of the 1963 March on Washington, during which King gave his memorable "I have a dream" speech. After the 1993 march, attended by approximately 75,000 to 100,000 people, some African Americans felt that as "one of the largest public political demonstrations led by African-Americans in the twentieth century," it "might mark the beginnings of a reconfiguration of the entire protest map of black America" (Marable 1995). The size of the crowd paled beside that of the Million Man March, however. This gathering, which took place in 1995 in Washington, drew somewhere between 400,000 and a million plus African Americans from across the country, a substantial proportion of them clearly middle class in education and income level. Sponsored by Louis Farrakhan and the Nation of Islam, the Million Man March may well have signaled a shift of power within the black community. At the least, it is clear that the March tapped a powerful sentiment within the African American community—a sense of growing urgency about race relations and about the situation of blacks, especially but not only poor blacks, in this country (West 1996). The peaceful, dignified, and committed nature of such a huge assembly also was impressive to many whites who had previously viewed black communities largely through media accounts of crime and other signs of deterioration.

Not all mass actions during these years were peaceful, however. Evidence of police brutality and abuse led to racial disturbances in Miami on two occasions in the 1980s. In April 1992 the most destructive protest of this century occurred in Los Angeles as news spread of the acquittal of four white police officers charged with the beating of Rodney King. The civil unrest involved a range of ethnic groups in addition to African Americans, and for three days the authorities struggled to restore peace and order. When calm once more prevailed, fifty-two people had died and property damage topped one billion dollars. (Later the two main police officers charged with the beating of Rodney King were retried under federal civil rights statutes, and this time were convicted and sent to prison.)

The chasm that separates white and black views about the fairness of the criminal justice system grew wider as a result of the Los Angeles disturbances. It came into full and startling focus with the acquittal in October 1995 of O. J. Simpson, a black football hero, for the murder of his former wife Nicole and her friend Ronald Goldman. The defense successfully changed the focus of the trial from Simpson's alleged crime to racism and incompetence within the Los Angeles Police Department. Thus many blacks throughout the nation could rejoice that a black man had managed to defeat what they saw as a corrupt and discriminatory system, while many whites felt shock and disbelief about both the verdict and the scenes of blacks celebrating.

An event that seemed more promising for racial unity was the remarkable boom in support for Colin Powell for the Republican nomination for president. According to the *Gallup Poll Monthly* (November 1995:2), just before Powell announced that he would not be a candidate, "most Americans said they would like to see him run for president, expressed highly favorable feelings about him, and—by a 10-point margin—preferred him over Clinton in the 1996 presidential election." That these reactions to Powell may not have been entirely limited to a uniquely charismatic and nonthreatening general-turned-Republican was indicated by the reelection in 1996 of three of the four black Democratic representatives whose districts had been turned by Court orders from majority black to majority white, despite many predictions that the change would end their tenure in Congress.[15]

A longer-term but important trend affecting African Americans during the 1980s and 1990s also deserves comment. The influx of immigrants during these years has produced a volatile mix of ethnicities and races in large cities. As a result, African Americans are beginning to lose their status as the country's predominant minority. These demographic changes have exacerbated economic tensions among ethnic groups. Furthermore, the discord between blacks and Jews has moved beyond rhetoric into action. Events in the Crown Heights area of New York City that led to the death of a black child, and in retaliation that of a young Jewish man, indicate how destructive such discord can be. In addition, other ethnic groups, particularly Korean merchants, have suffered at the hands of blacks and Latinos. In the Los Angeles disturbances of the spring of 1992, for example, both groups seemed especially to target Korean businesses for destruction. How these tensions will be resolved in the multiethnic future of the United States cannot now be predicted.

Recent events could well confuse any dispassionate observer of race relations in America. The 1996 election saw the California referendum against affirmative action pass by a vote of 54 to 46 percent, followed by a movement headed by a black business leader to spread the same action to other parts of the country. Yet the fact that the opposition vote reached 46 percent might be considered a surprising mobilization of sentiment in support of affirmative action, given the lack of support for such steps in attitude surveys that we describe in Chapter 3. For the time being, the federal courts have prevented the implementation of the referendum.

The controversy over the Oakland, California, School Board's decision to recognize Black English as a distinct language has cut across racial boundaries in unexpected and puzzling ways. Is official recognition of Black English, or Ebonics, a way to help inner-city children succeed and increase their self-esteem, or will it serve only to further stigmatize and set them apart from others? Whites and blacks of distinction can be found championing each side. In contrast to this complex issue, the burning of black churches in the rural South seemed a throwback to the days before the civil rights movement and assumed symbolic significance. According to a listing compiled by the Center for Democratic Renewal that extends from 1990 through May 1996, more than seventy black churches have been destroyed, most of them located in nine Southern states. Although it is not clear that all such acts have been motivated by racism or directed solely at black churches, some certainly have and they have been treated as evidence of a recurrence of Jim Crow terrorism.

The recent revelations of misconduct at Texaco and the subsequent actions taken by the chairman of that corporation send even more mixed signals about the state of race relations in America. Taped conversations showed the willingness of high executives to destroy possibly incriminating evidence about discrimination within their company. This action, along with casual banter demeaning black employees and other evidence of blatant acts of bigotry in many parts of the company, strongly suggested that affirmative action is needed to combat active discrimination, and not simply because color-blind employment policies are insufficient to increase job opportunities for African Americans. Despite antidiscrimination policies that had been in place for some time, there was no visible top-level corporate supervision to prevent prejudiced actions on the part of midlevel Texaco managers (*New York Times,* November 10, 1996, section 3).

But also important were the actions of the chairman of Texaco to address what was an immediate legal and public relations disaster, whatever its ultimate economic effects might turn out to be. Within several weeks he initiated what "civil rights experts described as one of the most comprehensive equal opportunity programs ever adopted by an American corporation . . . [Texaco agreed] to increase its hiring and promotion of minorities and women, set new payment policies to reward managers who meet diversity goals, and do more business with companies owned by nonwhites and women" (*New York Times,* December 19, 1996, D1). Jesse Jackson and others called off a boycott of Texaco and responded positively to the company's plan, which also included mechanisms for monitoring its progress. Thus at the same time that the majority of California's voters were repudiating affirmative action as a general policy and the courts were reacting with increasing skepticism to race-conscious solutions to economic and social inequality, a major corporation put into place a wide-ranging plan of affirmative action, one that we suspect will not easily be dislodged by public opinion or by legal attacks.

At the beginning of this chapter we emphasized that the importance of norms is not only that they can be internalized as personally held attitudes, but also that they can serve as external constraints on action and as the impetus for new action. We have no knowledge of the personal attitudes of Texaco's chairman, and his words denouncing racism may or may not reflect his private feelings. But clearly he acted in ways consistent with norms that have been developing over the past half century to condemn racial and ethnic prejudice and discrimination in the United States. Those norms remain powerful. If supported by enough black and white Americans, they provide some continuing hope that positive changes in American race relations still lie ahead.

With a sense of the larger history in mind, we now shift our attention to trends in racial attitudes, as measured by national sample surveys over nearly six decades. The first questions on racial issues for which trend data later became available were asked in 1942. This was about the time when the first effective actions against racial discrimination were also occurring—Randolph's threat of a March on Washington had forced Roosevelt's Executive Order against discrimination in federal hiring in the previous year—but *de jure* segregation and *de facto* discrimination were still largely unchallenged. Several relevant survey questions were also asked in 1946, but then not again until 1956, two years after the Supreme Court overturned the "separate but equal" doctrine. Another gap in the time series occurred between 1956 and the mid-1960s, when a sizable number of questions began to be repeated on a fairly regular basis.

From 1942 on, then, we have occasional snapshots of American public opinion on racial issues. The trend results allow us to trace changes in white attitudes from the low-activity years of the 1940s and early 1950s; through the late 1950s and early 1960s, which saw major court and legislative actions, the rise of remarkable nonviolent protests against segregation, followed by the appearance of more radical black movements and of widespread urban riots; then during the period of decreasing civil rights activities in the 1970s and early 1980s; until finally we reach the 1990s, with a confusing series of events, both within and outside the government.

As we proceed, the reader may find it useful to refer back to the more important dates in the civil rights struggle. Table 1.1 provides such a chronology. Chapter 2 presents necessary background information for making use of the attitudinal record, and in the last half of the chapter we discuss frankly a series of problems that are important to bear in mind when considering trends in racial attitudes, or indeed racial atti-

Table 1.1   Selected chronology of civil rights events

1896 -*Plessy v. Ferguson* "separate but equal" ruling.
1909 -Founding of the National Association for the Advancement of Colored People (NAACP).
1910 -Founding of the National Urban League (NUL).
1941 -A. Philip Randolph threatens a March on Washington. President Roosevelt issues Executive Order banning discrimination in defense industries.
1942 -Founding of the Congress of Racial Equality (CORE).
1943 -Major race riot in Detroit.
1947 -President Truman's Committee on Civil Rights issues its report.
       -Jackie Robinson joins the Brooklyn Dodgers, breaking the color barrier in baseball.
1948 -President Truman introduces civil rights legislation and issues Executive Orders concerning fair treatment in federal employment and desegregation of the military.
1954 -*Brown v. Board of Education* ruling declares "separate but equal" schooling unconstitutional.
1956 -Montgomery, Alabama, bus boycott begun in 1955 ends after 381 days, drawing national and international attention, and propels Dr. Martin Luther King, Jr., to the forefront of the civil rights crusade.
1957 -Founding of the Southern Christian Leadership Conference (SCLC).
       -Clash in Little Rock, Arkansas, over the desegregation of Central High School. President Eisenhower dispatches federal troops to keep order and enforce desegregation.
       -Passage of the first civil rights legislation since Reconstruction (the Civil Rights Act of 1957).
1960 -Lunchcounter sit-ins by black college students in Greensboro, North Carolina.
       -Founding of the Student Nonviolent Coordinating Committee (SNCC).
1961 -Freedom Rides. President Kennedy sends federal marshals to protect demonstrators.
1962 -James Meredith's attempt to enroll at the University of Mississippi meets violent resistance. President Kennedy dispatches army troops to maintain order and allow Meredith to enroll.
1963 -Mass demonstrations in Birmingham, Alabama, protesting segregation of public accommodations and job discrimination.
       -Black students attempt to enroll at the University of Alabama. Governor Wallace engages in symbolic defiance, standing "in the schoolhouse door".
       -March on Washington. More than 250,000 people gather at the steps of the Lincoln Memorial, where King delivers his "I have a dream" speech.
1964 -Murders of James Chaney, Andrew Goodman, and Michael Schwerner.
       -Passage of the Civil Rights Act of 1964.
       -Martin Luther King receives Nobel Peace Prize.
       -President Johnson reelected in landslide over Senator Barry Goldwater.

Table 1.1 (continued)

1965 -Mass demonstrations in Selma, Alabama, protesting voting hindrances
against blacks.
-Passage of the Voting Rights Act of 1965.
-Rioting in Watts, the worst racial outburst since 1943.
-President Johnson issues Executive Order that fosters affirmative action.

1966 -Stokely Carmichael first uses "Black Power" slogan.
-Founding of the Black Panther Party.

1967 -Rioting in Newark, Detroit, Milwaukee, and other major urban areas.
-Carl Stokes elected mayor of Cleveland, first black mayor of a
major city.
-Thurgood Marshall becomes first black Supreme Court Justice.

1968 -Kerner Commission releases its report on riots, identifying deeply
embedded racism as main cause.
-Martin Luther King, Jr., assassinated by James Earl Ray; rioting in
many cities.
-Passage of the Civil Rights Act of 1968, prohibiting discrimination in
the sale or rental of housing.
-Poor People's March on Washington.
-Richard Nixon elected president over Hubert Humphrey.

1970 -Extension of the Voting Rights Act.

1971 -*Swann v. Charlotte-Mecklenburg* ruling allows busing for desegregation.

1972 -President Nixon calls for a moratorium on court-ordered busing.

1973 -*Keyes v. Denver* ruling opens the way for court-ordered busing in the
North.
-Tom Bradley elected mayor of Los Angeles.

1978 -*Bakke* ruling disallows quotas at U.C. Davis Medical School but affirms
potential for preferential treatment.

1980 -Ronald Reagan elected president.

1982 -Twenty-five-year extension of the Voting Rights Act.

1983 -Harold Washington elected first black mayor of Chicago.

1984 -Rev. Jesse Jackson wages the first major campaign by a black candidate
for the Democratic presidential nomination.
-Ronald Reagan reelected president in greatest Republican landslide in
history.

1986 -First official observation of Martin Luther King Day.
-U.S. Congress overrides President Reagan's veto, joining other nations
in economic sanctions against South Africa to end apartheid.

1988 -George Bush elected president, defeating Michael Dukakis.

1989 -Colin Powell nominated by President Bush as chairman of Joint Chiefs
of Staff.
-Douglas Wilder elected governor of Virginia; David Dinkins elected
mayor of New York City.

1990 -President Bush vetoes a civil rights bill that sought to reverse Supreme
Court decisions weakening discrimination laws on hiring and promoting.

Table 1.1 (continued)

1991	-Thurgood Marshall retires from Supreme Court.
	-U.S. Senate approves nomination of Clarence Thomas to Supreme Court.
	-Videotape of beating of Rodney King shown repeatedly on national television.
1992	-All-white jury acquits four policemen on most counts of beating Rodney King, and Los Angeles is swept by rioting and looting, with 52 lives lost.
	-Bill Clinton elected president.
	-Carol Moseley Braun first black woman elected to U.S. Senate.
1993	-Nobel Prize for Literature awarded to Toni Morrison.
	-Supreme Court disallows congressional districts drawn to produce black majorities.
1994	-Republicans capture both houses of Congress, call for revolutionary changes.
	-Byron de La Beckwith, a white supremacist, convicted of 1963 murder of civil rights leader Medgar Evers in Mississippi.
1995	-Year-long murder trial of O. J. Simpson ends with acquittal, with widely different reactions from blacks and whites.
	-Colin Powell shows great strength in polls as a potential presidential candidate.
	-Million Man March in Washington, led by Louis Farrakhan.
1996	-Taped meeting of Texaco executives planning to impede lawsuit on discrimination; followed by steps by Texaco chairman to show good faith in improving opportunities for minorities.
	-Several black congresspersons from previously black majority districts in South win reelection from new white majority districts.
	-Referendum to end affirmative action passes in California: 54% to 46%.
	-Kofi Annan's election as secretary general of the United Nations brings a black African to prominence on the world scene.
	-Controversy over possible addition of "multiracial" category to Census.
	-Controversy over role of Ebonics in teaching black children.
1997	-Civil trial of O. J. Simpson ends with unanimous verdict that preponderance of evidence shows defendant responsible for deaths of N. Brown and R. Goldman. Racial divide remains after verdict, accentuated by radically different racial compositions of the two juries.

tudes more generally. Chapter 3 reports our main trend results over time for the white population, with additional analysis by region and education. Chapter 4 explores the sources of these trends in terms of changing cohorts and changes within cohorts, and it includes also an analysis of the effects of two additional social background factors, income and gender. Chapter 5 presents a more limited but nevertheless important set of trends in black attitudes. We are certainly not the first to attempt to understand racial trend data, and in Chapter 6 we consider critically several theoretical interpretations offered by others. Chapter 7 provides a brief set of conclusions, though it does not attempt to summarize the entire book.

With this record we hope to document and make more understandable the changing attitudes of the American people toward what W. E. B. Du Bois in 1903 termed "the problem of the twentieth century . . . the problem of the color line" (Du Bois 1961:23).

Problems in Studying
Changes in Racial Attitudes

The survey data available for tracing trends in racial attitudes come
from answers to questions asked of cross-section samples of the American population. In the first section of this chapter, we describe the
survey questions that have been posed on a repeated basis to national
samples, noting also some gaps in question content and time intervals.
The second section is about the nature of the samples of Americans to
which these questions have been put. In the final section we address
important problems that arise when attempting to interpret responses
to survey questions, especially responses that are used to chart change.
Although the focus on problems in the last part of the chapter is meant
to raise cautions for readers, the very fact that we are able to identify
such problems so clearly is a strength, not a weakness, of scientific
surveys. By becoming aware of challenges to valid conclusions, we can
attempt to take them into account in our interpretations—something
less easily done with more qualitative research or with the many varie-
ties of media commentary.

The Survey Questions

Our first step in producing an attitudinal record based on surveys
was to try to identify all survey questions dealing with racial attitudes that had been asked of cross-section samples of the white American population at two or more different times. We were primarily
interested in questions for which answers could be conceptualized
along a dimension that had at one extreme (here labeled "positive" or
"liberal") views favorable to integration, to equal treatment, or to
blacks as a group, and at the other extreme (labeled "negative" or

"illiberal") views supporting segregation or discrimination or unfavorable to blacks.

Only questions asked by nationally recognized organizations and for which trend data could be obtained for at least some reanalysis were useful for our purpose. In the 1985 edition of this book, we were limited to data collected and archived by three survey organizations; in this edition we have added trend data from two more organizations. Of our five sources, the two that continue to contribute the largest share of questions are the leading academic survey research organizations in the United States; the remaining three are commercial survey companies. Each of the five is described briefly below.

The National Opinion Research Center (NORC) at the University of Chicago is the source of the largest number of questions available for trend analysis, and also of those with the earliest baseline date (1942). Prior to 1972, NORC data on racial attitudes were collected as part of a variety of different surveys, but since 1972 a standard set of items has been included in NORC's General Social Survey (GSS). Our GSS data extend through the 1996 survey (except in Chapter 4, where the analysis includes data through 1994). James Davis, the originator of the GSS, fortunately set a policy of keeping the wording and coding of questions unchanged, and this has been maintained well over the years. The GSS Codebook is also for the most part a model of clarity. All NORC data are based on face-to-face interviewing.

The Institute for Social Research (ISR) at the University of Michigan is the source of almost as many of our questions as NORC. Since 1964 these questions have been asked on a fairly regular basis. Most of the surveys were done as part of studies of national elections, first through ISR's Survey Research Center (SRC) and from 1970 on through ISR's Center for Political Studies. With minor exceptions, our main ISR data are also based on face-to-face interviewing, and the data extend through the 1996 National Election Study (NES) survey (except in Chapter 4, where the analysis includes data through 1994). NES has sometimes changed question wording and coding unexpectedly, and we have tried to be aware of and to note the difficulties that this can cause trend analysis.

The Gallup organization has repeated fewer racial questions than NORC and ISR have, but they constitute a valuable source of long-term evidence on several important issues. Particularly for the earliest time points, we have not had direct access to data tapes and so relied on specific cross-tabulations requested from the Roper Center for Public Opinion Research. (This was also true for most NORC data prior to 1972.) Gallup employed face-to-face interviewing over most of its history, but shifted to telephone interviewing in the late 1980s, as the tables in Chapters 3 and 5 will indicate. Fortunately, we are able to include early data from a 1997 Gallup poll just completed as our book is going to press.[1] Some variations in Gallup questions occur mainly in the way volunteered responses to closed questions (for example, "don't know") are handled, a problem we will confront in Chapter 3.

In this edition of the book, we add a small number of questions (four in all) from two additional telephone survey organizations that have become prominent in television and newspaper reporting: the ABC/*Washington Post* (ABC/WP) Poll and the CBS/*New York Times* (CBS/NYT) Poll. In both cases, the organizations asked questions about content areas that were not adequately represented with trend data from the other three organizations. Data from both of these newer polls were obtained through the Inter-university Consortium for Political and Social Research (ICPSR) at the University of Michigan.

Finally, we report several recent replications and a number of experimental studies that we ourselves carried out through the Survey Research Center at the University of Michigan. The questions were included in national telephone surveys in order to clarify issues of question wording, context, and mode of administration, as well as to obtain updated time points for important items that had been asked previously but not recently by one of the main survey organizations. We also refer at certain points to data based on more limited populations, in particular to results from the Detroit Area Study and related research.

The Harris organization has carried out a number of racial studies, but changes in question wording and difficulties in locating and documenting data prevented our use of this source in 1985. We have not altered that decision for this new edition.

The Questions

The primary set of attitude questions that we will examine is identified in Table 2.1 by mnemonic label, survey organization, and time period. Full question wordings follow each of the six large tables in Chapter 3, as noted below, with parallel numbering in Chapter 5. Four basic types of questions used in the 1985 edition remain important, though with some change in content (especially for implementation questions): questions concerned with general *principles* of equal treatment and integration (Table 3.1A and B); questions about the *implementation* of these principles (Table 3.2); questions concerning black-white *social distance* (Table 3.3); and a residual miscellaneous set of questions (Table 3.6).

During the decade since the 1985 edition, new areas of interest and types of questions have become important in the study of racial attitudes. The new areas reflect in many ways the changes in the social and political context of race relations, as described in Chapter 1. We have adequate trend data for some of the new types of questions: those about *explanations* for racial inequality, including perceptions of racial discrimination (Table 3.4), and those about *affirmative action*, including both government expenditures on blacks and preferential treatment for blacks (Table 3.5).

It is important to emphasize the distinction between questions classified as dealing with "affirmative action" and the earlier questions concerned with "implementation." Both types of questions call for policies to be put into effect by the government or in some cases by nongovernment organizations. However, we use the term "implementation" for policies intended to promote principles of equal or neutral treatment regardless of race. Affirmative action policies, by contrast, are those meant to promote equality of outcome as a way of making up for the effects of past discrimination against blacks. Admittedly the line between the two is not always completely obvious, as we will note at later points, but most of the relevant survey items can be seen to fall on one or the other side of the distinction.

It is useful to think of a total sample of trend questions about racial attitudes, and for this purpose we have adopted the approximate number of fifty. The number is necessarily somewhat arbitrary. There are actually fifty-six entries in Table 2.1, but, as the table notes indicate, some of the entries can be treated for analytic purposes as essentially identical. There are also a few other items not shown here that will figure in our later analysis for special purposes.

The fifty questions are the end result of a careful search of all sources we could locate that indexed racial questions of any kind. Questions asked at two or more time points were placed in an initial pool. We then eliminated those questions for which the time span was too limited

Table 2.1 The 51 positive/negative racial trend questions[a] (questions, time span, and time points are for white respondents only)

Gallup questions	ISR questions	NORC questions	ABC/WP questions[b]	CBS/NYT question
Black Candidate (3.1)[c] 1958[13]1997	Residential Choice: 2 alts. (3.1)[f] 1964[6]1976	Same Schools (3.1) 1942[15]1995	Discriminated in Housing (3.4) 1981[3]1994	Preference in Hiring and Promotion (3.5) 1985[7]1995
Intermarriage (3.1) 1958[7]1997	General Segregation (3.1) 1964[8]1978	Equal Jobs (3.1) 1944[5]1972	Disc. in Managerial Jobs (3.4) 1981[3]1994	
Few (3.3)[d] 1958[12]1990	Federal Job Intervention (3.2) 1964[8]1996	Segregated Transportation (3.1) 1942[4]1970	Police Treat Fairly (3.4) 1981[4]1994	
Half (3.3)[d] 1958[12]1990	Federal School Intervention (3.2) 1964[12]1994	Same Accommodations (3.1) 1963[3]1970		
Majority (3.3)[d] 1958[12]1990	Busing (3.2)[e] 1972[5]1984	Residential Choice: 1 alt. (3.1)[f] 1963[18]1996		
Next Door (3.3) 1958[8]1997	Accommodations Intervention (3.2)[g] 1964[6]1995	Black Candidate (3.1)[c] 1972[16]1996		
Great Numbers (3.3) 1958[8]1997	Neighborhood Preference (3.3)[h] 1972[3]1976; 1976[3]1995	Laws against Intermarriage (3.1) 1963[22]1996		
Who to Blame (3.4) 1963[6]1995	Blacks Should Try Harder (3.4) 1972[6]1994	Open Housing (3.2) 1973[16]1996		
Good Chance Jobs (3.4) 1963[8]1997	No Special Favors (3.4) 1986[5]1994	Busing (3.2)[e] 1972[17]1996		

Table 2.1 (continued)

Gallup questions	ISR questions	NORC questions	ABC/WP questions[b]	CBS/NYT question
Ku Klux Klan Rating (3.6) 1965[4]1979	Generations of Slavery (3.4) 1972[6]1994	Few (3.3)[d] 1972[16]1996		
Better Break (3.6) 1984[6]1995	Aid to Minorities (3.5)[i] 1970[13]1996	Half (3.3)[d] 1972[16]1996		
	Federal Spending (3.5) 1984[5]1992	Majority (3.3)[d] 1972[16]1996		
	Preference in Admissions (3.5) 1986[4]1992	Same Block (3.3) 1942[8]1972		
	Preference in Hiring (3.5) 1986[6]1996	Black Dinner Guest (3.3) 1963[12]1985		
	Thermometer Rating of Blacks (3.6) 1964[16]1996	Club Change Rules (3.3) 1977[9]1994		
	Civil Rights Push (3.6) 1964[13]1992	Inequality: Discrimination (3.4) 1977[10]1996		
	Riots (3.6) 1972[4]1992	Inequality: Less Ability (3.4) 1977[10]1996		
		Inequality: No Chance Education (3.4) 1977[10]1996		

Table 2.1 (continued)

Gallup questions	ISR questions	NORC questions	ABC/WP questions[b]	CBS/NYT question
		Inequality: No Motivation (3.4) 1977[10]1996		
		Spending on Blacks (3.5) 1973[20]1996		
		Help Blacks (3.5) 1975[12]1996		
		Black Push (3.6) 1963[15]1996		

a. Numbers in parentheses indicate tables in Chapter 3 that give full question wordings and results for national cross-section white samples. Numbers below question labels indicate the earliest and the most recent time points available for that question, plus the total number of time points. For example, 1958[12]1987 indicates that the question was first asked in 1958, most recently asked in 1987, and asked at 12 time points altogether. (A question asked more than once within a single year is counted as only one time point here, and such replications are averaged for our analysis.)

b. The 1994 time points for all ABC/WP questions were replications conducted for the authors by the Survey Research Center at the University of Michigan's Institute for Social Research.

c. Both NORC and Gallup ask a question about white willingness to vote for a qualified black presidential candidate. The wordings of the two questions are not identical, but the meanings seem so close that we have considered the two as one unit.

d. Few, Half, and Majority refer to three questions concerning degrees of school integration, asked by both Gallup and NORC. The wording of the questions across organizations is almost exactly the same, and we therefore treat these as three rather than six questions, although there are differences in survey dates and in sample definitions that will be noted in Chapter 3.

e. The two Busing questions differ sufficiently to be counted twice.

f. The ISR and NORC Residential Choice questions differ sufficiently to be counted twice. "Alts." stands for "alternatives," i.e., the number of sides of the issue offered to respondents.

g. In 1995, this item was replicated by the Survey Research Center at the University of Michigan's Institute for Social Research. The data are from a telephone survey for that year, while all other time points are from the National Elections Studies and are therefore face-to-face data.

h. Neighborhood Preference refers to two different ISR question versions, one asked in face-to-face surveys and one in telephone surveys. They are counted and shown as a single question here, but are presented separately in Table 3.3 because of wording and mode-of-administration differences.

(for example, if the available time points were very close rather than spread over several years), or where there were other serious problems with the questions. The proliferation of both survey organizations and survey questions over the past ten years led us to be somewhat more selective for this revised edition. Our rule of thumb was to include only those questions that were asked three times or more and that covered at least a ten-year time span. This last requirement was overridden slightly in a few cases, particularly for items concerning topics that have become important in more recent years (for example, affirmative action). Furthermore, wherever the same survey question was asked by more than one survey organization, we usually included data for only the organization that provided trends across the longest time period, though we retain some cases where the same or very similar questions allow a comparison of trends. A more detailed account of our search procedure appears in Appendix A.

Coverage over Time and Issues

Our primary goals in this book are to trace and interpret change over time as fully and adequately as we can. Cross-section attitude surveys began in the United States in the mid-1930s, as indicated by the title of Hadley Cantril's huge compendium, *Public Opinion: 1935–1946* (1951). But as Paul Sheatsley (1966) has noted, the major fact about the study of racial attitudes in the 1930s was the absence of any real interest in that subject on the part of leading polling organizations. Gallup asked three questions about a "lynching bill" that was before Congress in 1937, though race was not mentioned, and in 1939 a question was asked about Eleanor Roosevelt's resignation from the Daughters of the American Revolution to protest their refusal to allow a "well-known Negro singer to give a concert in a DAR hall" (two-thirds of the public approved of the resignation). But no other questions about racial issues seem to have been posed in those first years of polling, and none at all were asked that became part of a long-term trend series until 1942—the earliest point at which our analysis can begin.[2]

The reason for the late start is not hard to find. "The polls, for obvious reasons, tend to ask questions about the issues that are hot, and it is clear that, during the decade preceding World War II, race relations did not qualify on this basis" (Sheatsley 1966:217). Indeed, our good fortune in having several questions from the early 1940s seems to be due largely to the federal government's concern at the beginning of World War II about the effect of racial tension on the war effort. Gallup did not begin a regular series of questions until 1954, when race was becoming a focal issue in the United States, first because of Supreme Court decisions, then later because of the confrontation over school integration in Little Rock, the Montgomery bus boycott, and other events connected to the civil rights movement. Furthermore, nobody carried out a substantial national survey of the racial attitudes of blacks until 1963 (Brink and Harris 1964), but in this case there was the additional complication of the need for special sampling, since black respondents were too few in a typical cross-section national survey to allow for detailed analysis.

An equally serious problem is the different and uneven periods available for different questions. At the extreme, for one question (whether black and white children should go to the same or different schools), we have systematic face-to-face data from both 1942 and 1985, as well as from numerous points in between. For another (whether there should be laws against marriage between blacks and whites), we have data from both 1963 and 1996, as well as twenty additional time points in between. For most other items, the record is truncated at one or both ends. This not only makes for general noncomparability across questions, but also can be seriously misleading: a question asked over one time period (say, 1942 to 1962) may show much more dramatic change than another question asked over a different time period (1964 to 1996), yet it may be impossible to tell whether this difference is due to question content or to variations in the pace of change in different periods. In other words, question content and time period are often confounded, sometimes because questions fit only a particular period (for example, preferential treatment in hiring and promotion as an issue did not appear in surveys until the late 1970s, and our trend data date only from the mid-1980s), but sometimes for reasons that seem more accidental or arbitrary (for example, an important question on the implementation of nondiscrimination in public accommodations was unfortunately dropped by ISR after 1974, despite not having approached a ceiling of 100 percent support).

Regardless of when a question was first and last asked, there is an additional problem whenever the distance between available time points is substantial. For example, because the question about equal

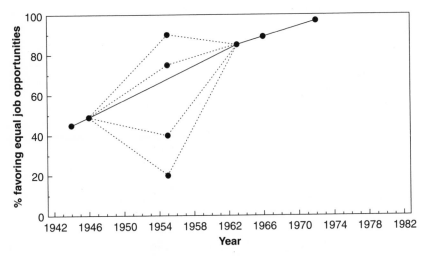

Figure 2.1. Attitudes toward equal job opportunities for blacks and whites: various possible trends for years in which the question was not asked. Equal Jobs question: "Do you think Negroes should have as good a chance to get any kind of job, or do you think white people should have the first chance at any kind of job?"

access to jobs was not asked between 1946 and 1963, a graph of responses to the question (Figure 2.1) encourages us to think of change in attitudes toward this issue between the two dates as constant (as indicated by the solid line in the figure). But this is by no means certain. As the dotted lines suggest, other trajectories were possible; some are perhaps as plausible as the solid straight line. In the absence of other information, we generally connect time points by straight lines, but the larger the time gap, the more uncertain this becomes, and only the points themselves can be thought of as at all firmly established. Figure 2.1 also points up another problem: a ceiling effect as responses approach 100 percent within a single category. Not only does the item cease to register much change, but ordinary percentage differences may not adequately reflect the significance—both statistically and substantively—of what change is occurring when the distribution is so skewed.

It is also important to recognize that our analysis throughout is necessarily limited to what the polls inquired into. In this sense, the polls influence our account of recent history in much the same way that newspapers play an important role in defining news and available

Table 2.2 Trend questions by issue content

Issue content	Year first asked	Question name
Residential integration	1942	Same Block (3.3)
	1958	Next Door (3.3)
	1958	Great Numbers (3.3)
	1963	Residential Choice (1 alternative) (3.1)
	1964	Residential Choice (2 alternatives) (3.1)
	1972	Neighborhood Preference (3.3)
	1973	Open Housing (3.2)
School integration	1942	Same Schools (3.1)
	1958	Few (Gallup, NORC) (3.3)
	1958	Half (Gallup, NORC) (3.3)
	1958	Majority (Gallup, NORC) (3.3)
	1964	Federal School Intervention (3.2)
	1972	Busing (NORC) (3.2)
	1972	Busing (ISR) (3.2)
	1986	Preference in Admissions (3.5)
Job treatment	1944	Equal Jobs (3.1)
	1964	Federal Job Intervention (3.2)
	1985	Preference in Hiring/Promotion (CBS/NYT) (3.5)
	1986	Preference in Hiring/Promotion (NES) (3.5)
Public facilities	1942	Segregated Transportation (3.1)
	1963	Same Accommodations (3.1)
	1964	Accommodation Intervention (3.2)
Political arena	1958	Black Candidate (Gallup, NORC) (3.1)
Economic aid	1970	Aid to Minorities/Blacks (3.5)
	1973	Spending on Blacks (3.5)
	1975	Help Blacks (3.5)
	1984	Federal Spending (3.5)
Personal relations	1958	Intermarriage (3.1)
	1963	Laws against Intermarriage (3.1)
	1963	Black Dinner Guest (3.3)
	1977	Club Change Rules (3.3)
Explanations for racial inequality	1963	Good Chance Jobs (3.4)
	1963	Who to Blame (3.4)
	1972	Blacks Should Try Harder (3.4)
	1972	Generations of Slavery/Discrimination (3.4)
	1977	Discrimination (3.4)

Table 2.2 (continued)

Issue content	Year first asked	Question name
	1977	Less Ability (3.4)
	1977	No Chance for Education (3.4)
	1977	No Motivation (3.4)
	1981	Discriminated in Housing (3.4)
	1981	Discriminated in Managerial Jobs (3.4)
	1981	Police Treat Fairly (3.4)
	1986	No Special Favors (3.4)
Miscellaneous	1963	Black Push (3.6)
	1964	General Segregation (3.1)
	1964	Thermometer Rating of Blacks/Whites (3.6)
	1964	Civil Rights Push (3.6)
	1965	Ku Klux Klan Rating (3.6)
	1972	Riots (3.6)
	1984	Better Break (3.6)

Note: Numbers in parentheses refer to tables in Chapter 3 that give question wording and national trend results for whites.

documents shape knowledge of earlier eras. Just as virtually no racial questions were asked before 1942, so there are important issues for which no trend data at all seem to exist. For example, we could find no questions on voting rights asked on more than one occasion. And although we are able in the present edition to include questions about preferential treatment for the first time, they constitute a fairly narrow interpretation of affirmative action. For example, questions about open listing of employment opportunities and positive efforts at recruiting of minorities seem not to have been asked repeatedly on major surveys of the general public.

Even for topics on which questions were asked, the relative coverage is uneven. Table 2.2 provides one topical way of organizing our pool of questions. As can be seen, there is fairly good coverage of residential issues over the past fifty years, but coverage of employment issues for earlier time points is weaker and only expanded somewhat in the mid-1980s. Also, coverage of interpersonal relations is disproportionately weighted by questions on intermarriage, as against, for example, questions on friendship (see Pettigrew [1997] on the special significance of intergroup friendship).

The Primary Variables

Researchers working within a single set of survey data can readily investigate many relations among variables. We are working, however, with a different data set for every year for every organization. Thus a decision to look at one single type of relation, for example, trends separately for Northerners and Southerners on all items, entailed more than one hundred cross-tabulations. If one additional variable is added (say, education), the number of relationships doubles again. Moreover, even a small change in the definition of the original items (for example, repercentaging without "don't know" responses) again doubles the total number of relationships. For this reason, the number of demographic or background variables that we could examine is much more limited than in reports based on a single cross-section survey, except in Chapter 4 and a few other places where we move to a multivariate statistical approach using regression.

In addition to race and the various attitude questions themselves, our most important variable is "time": most of our tables and figures present attitude responses across years. We also routinely employ "region" because of its historic importance for racial attitudes and behavior in the United States, and a number of graphs in this book separate trends according to a South/non-South distinction. (For convenience, we usually refer to the non-South as "North.") In addition, we frequently use "education" because of its importance as both a social and a psychological indicator, though we point out later in this chapter some uncertainties about exactly what education is really measuring. We have added to this edition an analysis of the effects of education and income, with each controlled for the other and for cohort, region, and gender; this analysis appears in Chapter 4, which includes also a detailed consideration of cohort effects and a briefer discussion of the influence of gender. Finally, in a few cases, attitude questions are cross-tabulated with one another, though that is usually not our main purpose and we are, of course, limited by what questions were asked within the same survey.

Brief definitions of our major analytic variables, along with the typical distribution of cases across categories, are as follows:

Race. Our most basic variable is race, which we treat as a social rather than a biological category. Except where specifically indicated, all results in this chapter and in Chapters 3 and 4 are for the "white population" only, which is ordinarily defined as those classified as white by the survey organization, whether by observation or by self-identification. Chapter 5 deals with the black population, and in all instances we have accepted "Negro," "black," or "African American," again as defined and classified by the survey organization. (We carried out some comparisons of results for race by observation and for race by self-identification, and the differences are trivial.)

Persons classified by one or another survey organization as neither white nor black are omitted from all analysis to the extent that survey codes allowed their identification. This means that our analyses systematically exclude American Indians, Asian Americans, and Pacific Islanders.

The issue is more complicated with regard to respondents of Hispanic background, a group that has become increasingly recognized as having a distinct ethnicity, and whose representation in the population of the United States has grown substantially. Above and beyond the substantive question of whether or not Hispanics should be included or excluded from our analysis of "white" respondents in Chapters 3 and 4, there is the practical issue of whether or not such an identification is possible across all time points and all survey organizations. In a word, ethnic classification in surveys has been quite inconsistent, as reflected, for example, in the changes over time in ISR's National Election Studies. In 1966 these surveys shifted from a trichotomy (white, black, and other) to a more complex coding scheme that specified Mexican (later Mexican American and Chicano), Puerto Rican, American Indian, and Oriental, as well as white and black; at the end of the 1970s another category, "other Hispanic," was added. During this time period, each of these classifications was based on interviewer observation or informal (nonstandardized) inquiry by the interviewer. It was only in 1988 that classification of respondents according to Hispanic identity was standardized in the form of explicit questions directed at the respondent. These shifts make it impossible to systematically include or exclude Hispanics from our analyses of "white" racial attitudes. Furthermore, we do not have adequate numbers of Hispanics to be able to say anything about the racial attitudes of this group taken by itself.[3]

Thus when we speak of our "white" respondents, we are including most, but not all, Hispanics. Specifically, though the vast majority of

Hispanics are classified as "white" (from 1980–1994, between 88 and 95 percent), some are classified as "other" or "black." We therefore cannot say that our white sample includes *all* Hispanics. It should be stressed, however, that the proportion of respondents affected in this way is quite small, especially relative to our large total sample sizes.[4] For recent ISR data we calculated results for twelve questions with and without Hispanics included and found that most time points were changed by less than 1 percent and none greater than 2 percent. The exercise was repeated for the ABC/WP poll and produced the same results.[5]

Region of Current Residence. For NORC, ISR, and Gallup we use the U.S. Census definition of the South: Alabama, Arkansas, Delaware, Florida, Georgia, Kentucky, Louisiana, Maryland, Mississippi, North Carolina, Oklahoma, South Carolina, Tennessee, Texas, Virginia, West Virginia, and the District of Columbia. All other states are defined as North, except for Alaska and Hawaii, which are usually not included in national sample surveys. The division of the white population by region remained fairly constant over the 1942–1972 time span: Southerners constituted about a quarter of the total sample over most of that period. Between the 1970s and the early 1990s, however, the proportion of the white sample residing in the South has increased to around 30 percent. Although fluctuating more because of small sample sizes, black respondents are about evenly split between the North and the South from 1972 to 1996.

Education. We usually separate education into "less than twelve years," "twelve years," and "more than twelve years." (However, 1942 NORC data permit separation only into "less than twelve" and "twelve or more," and in 1944 and 1946 the only separation possible is "twelve or less" and "thirteen or more.") More differentiation of educational categories (for example, separating Some College from College Graduates) does not alter broad trends and becomes impractical with cross-tabulations; however, in Chapter 4, where multiple regression is used, such a finer categorization is employed.

There has been a substantial change over time in the proportion of the white population in the three main educational categories we use in cross-tabulations. The percentage of adults with less than a high school education has declined precipitously in both the North and the

South, while at the same time the percentages graduating from high school and attending college have risen. Survey samples reflect these changes. For example, between the NORC surveys in the early 1940s and the 1996 General Social Survey, the percentage of Southern respondents twenty-one years of age or older with less than a high school education dropped from approximately 60 percent to 21 percent. The percentage of high school graduates increased from a little less than 20 percent to 28 percent. Those with at least one year of college rose from a little more than 20 percent to 50 percent. In addition, most national surveys tend to underrepresent lower educational levels somewhat, as determined by Census data, and this was especially true for samples from the 1940s.

Age. Survey organizations typically sampled only those ages twenty-one and older until the change in the voting age in the early 1970s, at which point surveys began to include those ages eighteen to twenty in their nationally representative samples. In order to address this non-comparability in sample definitions across the total time period covered by our data, we have restricted our analyses to those twenty-one and older.[6] This restriction is noted for conceptual clarity, but the practical effect is minimal because those ages eighteen to twenty constitute only a very small proportion of any given sample. Comparisons of our tabulations with and without this age group typically show no difference at all, or at most a difference of a single percentage point.

The Survey Samples

Sample Sizes and Significant Differences

The total sample sizes of the surveys on which we draw are usually between 1,000 and 2,000, though there are exceptions at both extremes. Specifically, the three NORC surveys from the 1940s were 2,500 and up, and several of ISR's National Election Studies exceeded 2,000. (The 1970 National Election Study, as well as several recent NORC studies, used a split-ballot sample design so that some of the racial attitude questions were asked of only one-half or sometimes only one-third of the respondents, thereby reducing the available sample size to fewer than 1,000.) Unless otherwise specified, figures presented in the tables in Chapter 3 are based on samples of at least 1,000 cases;

wherever there are fewer cases than this, the approximate Ns are presented in footnotes to the table. When we turn to data on black attitudes in Chapter 5, the sample sizes become much smaller, as we will discuss at the beginning of that chapter.[7]

In most survey analysis, statistical significance provides a helpful criterion for distinguishing "real differences" in the population from those differences that may be due to sampling error.[8] Since the samples we work with are almost all clustered, we usually adopted the relatively stringent criterion of a .01 probability level before regarding a difference at the national level as "real." Even so, with samples as large as most of those we work with in Chapter 3, almost any difference in responses between two years that looks real to the eye turns out to be statistically significant. For example, if two simple random samples of 1,000 differ from each other by 6 percent on a response to a dichotomous question, where one is 47 percent and the other is 53 percent, the probability that a difference this large would occur through sampling variation alone is less than 1 in 100 (.01).

Thus for comparing national white responses across years, and for responses of subsamples of Northerners as well, there is rarely any uncertainty as to statistical significance. When only Southern samples are involved, and especially when we divide samples by both region and education (or age), statistical significance cannot so readily be taken for granted. Although we do not usually give explicit significance levels in the text, we have used formal tests (or equivalent rules of thumb) in reporting trends or other differences as "real" and in describing the shape of a trend. At the same time, as examples later in this chapter indicate, statistical significance can only be a starting point in most of our analysis, since there are a number of important factors that can create large response differences but do *not* signify true changes in attitudes for the population.

Sample Coverage

The definitions of the populations to which samples refer have been generally similar across the survey organizations. Only civilian adults living in households in the coterminous United States are sampled. As noted earlier, however, the age specifications for adults have shifted over time, usually from twenty-one and over before the early 1970s to eighteen and over thereafter, coinciding with the change in voting age.

The General Social Survey has added the further requirement that its samples refer only to the English-speaking population of the United States, whereas the ISR National Election Studies sample only citizens of voting age. We have assumed that these minor differences do not create important differences in results by organization, but they probably do cause some minor variations.

A potentially more important difference is caused by the shift to telephone by the commercial survey organizations, though NORC and almost all of the ISR samples we use remain face-to-face. By definition, these telephone samples include only adults living in households with a telephone, and because of this restriction, such samples are likely to underrepresent those with very low income and the related characteristic of low education. Table 2.3 shows a comparison of five demographic characteristics of several 1994 and 1995 samples separately by survey organization and mode of administration. The one systematic difference between the personal interview and telephone interview samples is in educational attainment. As one might anticipate, the telephone samples are more highly educated than the personal interview samples.

Sampling Methods

Regardless of whether the data are collected by personal interview or by telephone, since the early 1950s the organizations that provide most of our data have used full or modified probability sampling methods.[9] However, the three earliest surveys from which we have data were conducted by NORC in the 1940s using quota control sampling—a very different kind of design. "Control factors" upon which the sample distributions were to match the population distributions were defined by NORC: geography (including both region and level of urbanization), sex, race, and "standard-of-living level." Thus, as NORC's Basic Instructions explained to interviewers, "if 7.5 percent of the people in the United States live in the New England states, then 7.5 percent of our sample is drawn from the New England states in a national survey" (NORC 1946). Working in areas that were chosen for their representativeness along several dimensions, interviewers were assigned quotas that indicated how many persons were to be interviewed for each control factor. Then the interviewer was to select respondents "at random—in the home, on the street, in the office, in a store, etc." Although samples drawn in this way are generally believed to be rep-

Table 2.3 Selected demographic characteristics of personal versus telephone survey samples, 1994–1995, selected survey organizations

	Personal interviews			Telephone surveys		
	1994 GSS	1994 NES Panel	1994 NES Cross-Section	1994 Gallup[a]	1994/1995 SRC	1995 CBS/NYT[b]
Education						
< 12 Yrs	17.9	15.4	16.4	11.7	7.7	8.6
12 Yrs	31.4	30.4	35.0	38.5	32.0	34.6
13 Plus	50.7	54.2	48.6	49.7	60.3	56.6
(*n*)	(2800)	(681)	(948)	(468)	(519)	(2055)
Gender						
Male	42.8	47.1	45.6	48.1	47.8	43.7
Female	57.2	52.9	54.4	51.9	52.2	56.3
(*n*)	(2800)	(703)	(961)	(468)	(519)	(2055)
Region						
South	36.8	36.6	36.2	31.4	35.8	33.4
Non-south	63.2	63.4	63.8	68.6	64.2	66.6
(*n*)	(2800)	(703)	(961)	(468)	(519)	(2055)
Race						
White	86.6	86.9	89.2	88.6	88.8	90.4
Black	13.4	13.1	10.8	11.4	11.2	9.6
(*n*)	(2800)	(703)	(961)	(468)	(519)	(2055)
Age						
Mean	46.9	46.7	47.6	47.3	46.3	47.2
Std. dev.	16.8	17.0	17.6	16.9	16.4	16.2
(*n*)	(2800)	(703)	(961)	(468)	(519)	(2055)

a. Results are weighted using Gallup's weighting procedure because that is how we use them in Chapters 3 and 5. Unweighted results are within two percentage points of the weighted results, with the exception of region. For region, the unweighted distribution is 34% south and 66% non-south.

b. Although CBS/NYT provides a weight for their data, these results are unweighted because that is how we use them in Chapters 3 and 5. Weighted results are within two percentage points of the unweighted results, with the exception of education and gender. Weighted, the distribution is as follows for education: 11.8, 48.4, and 39.8, respectively. For gender, the weighted distribution is 47% male and 53% female.

resentative with respect to the control factors, they may be seriously unrepresentative on characteristics not subject to controls (for example, education) and on combinations of control variables (male Southerners, for example) that were not specified in the quotas (Glenn 1975). Moreover, substantial bias could be introduced as the interviewers were given the responsibility of selecting respondents "at random" within quotas. Usually this meant that interviewers chose people who were accessible, and these may have differed systematically in their attitudes from those harder to contact.[10] For these reasons we must be especially careful in drawing on these earliest surveys.

Another potentially important source of variation among organizations, and also between time points for the same organization, is the nonresponse rate: the proportion of people who refuse or are unavailable to take part in a survey. With quota or modified probability sampling, no clear nonresponse rate can be calculated. But whether calculated or not, trends and fluctuations in nonresponse may affect inferences about the percentages and changes in percentages of answers in the target population, for example, the percentage supporting a particular principle or policy. Evidence provided by NORC shows an average (median) nonresponse rate between 1975 and 1996 of 23.5 percent, with no clear trend over that time period (Davis and Smith 1996, table A-3). By far the largest source of nonresponse consists of refusals, which for the NORC data average 17.3 percent of the target sample and do not show a clear change over time. NORC probably does as well as or better than any of the other survey organizations in keeping nonresponse to a minimum, which means that somewhere around 20 percent of target samples (and often well over 20 percent in telephone surveys) decline to be interviewed. (The remaining several additional percentage points of nonresponse are due to not-at-home, ill, or otherwise missed respondents.)[11]

Except where such rates change substantially over time, however, they are unlikely to affect trends greatly, since part of the omitted portion of the sample can be considered random, due to variations in individuals' moods and preoccupations when an interviewer contacts them, and the rest (for example, people who dislike surveys and never agree to be respondents) should be relatively constant over time. There is more danger from variations in nonresponse rates when we compare trends from different organizations, but even in these cases there is not much evidence of a serious problem, as will be seen in later comparisons. The greater risk of misinterpretation comes when we or others report absolute levels of answers (for example, the percentage giving a particular response), since in that case the missing part of the population may well be different from the larger part that is included. Distrust of such absolute levels of answers is a caution we will have good reason to emphasize again when we turn to issues involving the question-answer process itself, though neither we nor any other survey investigator can completely forswear giving some attention to such absolute percentages.[12]

In summary, differences in sample coverage and sampling methods over time and among organizations can lead to some variations in results. This is the first of a number of factors that point to the need for caution in interpreting minor fluctuations in trend data across time or across organizations, *regardless* of their statistical significance. It is important to concentrate on major trends, on the broad picture, and to avoid attempting to interpret every squiggle that catches one's eye.[13]

Interpreting Trend Data

Suppose that in 1942 only 32 percent of a sample of white Americans favored the integration of public schools, but by 1995 the figure had risen to 96 percent, as shown in a later table. Before taking this dramatic evidence of change at face value, we must consider the nature of the sample and the sampling method used at each time point, as discussed in the previous pages. In addition to sampling considerations, however, there are a number of other features of surveys that must be taken into account if one is to avoid serious misinterpretation. These involve the exact questions asked, the larger questionnaires in which the questions were embedded, the survey organizations that directed the work, the characteristics of the interviewers who posed the questions, and the method by which they asked the questions—that is, the mode of administration.

Consistency of Question Wording

There is no more important point in survey research than the need to keep the wording of questions constant for all comparisons. Even variations in wording that seem minor can produce important differences in response and sometimes in relationships as well. For example, both NORC and ISR ask a question on residential integration. At first reading, the one question might be thought of as a shorter version of the other:

Residential Choice, 1 alternative plus scale (NORC): "Here are some opinions other people have expressed in connection with black-white relations. Which statement on the card comes closest to how you feel? White people have a right to keep blacks out of their neighborhoods if they want to, and blacks should respect that right." [Respondents are presented with a card and asked to choose one of four responses: strongly agree, slightly agree, slightly disagree, strongly disagree.]

Residential Choice, 2 alternatives (ISR): "Which of these choices would you agree with more: (1) White people have a right to keep blacks out of their neighborhoods if they want to. (2) Black people have a right to live wherever they can afford to, just like anybody else."

Part of the wording of these two questions is identical: "White people have a right to keep blacks out of their neighborhoods if they want to," and the differences between the two questions might at first seem unimportant, since they do not change the basic issue of whether white people have a right to prevent blacks from moving into their (white) neighborhoods.

However, the NORC question is almost certainly easier for respondents to "agree to," which means approving of racial discrimination, because it does not present the other side of the picture, namely, black rights to residential choice. In addition, this version places the burden on blacks to "respect" white rights. From past research (Schuman and Presser 1981, chapter 8) we would expect the NORC version of the question to elicit less positive responses (that is, a lower degree of support for open residential choice by blacks) than the ISR version, which pits two arguments against each other and requires the respondent to choose between them. If we dichotomize the NORC four-point scale in what seems the most natural way (strongly agree + agree vs. disagree + strongly disagree) in order to create greater comparability, this is indeed the case for white respondents, as shown in Figure 2.2. Wherever the same years are involved, on the average about 25 percent more respondents give a response favoring black rights on the ISR version than on the NORC version. This is an example of why one cannot shift in midstream from one question wording to another. It also indicates why the absolute percentages for any particular wording should not be given much weight: a different wording might have yielded different percentages.[14]

Even when two somewhat different questions on the same issue yield different absolute percentage levels, they may nevertheless show much

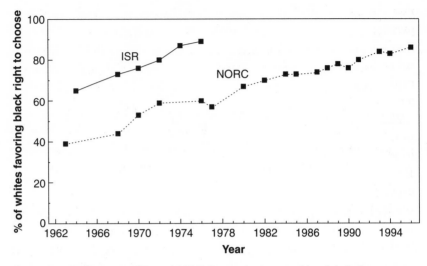

Figure 2.2. Response to ISR and NORC questions on residential choice.

the same trend over time. Indeed, there is evidence that in most cases this is likely to occur, but it cannot be taken for granted. Figure 2.2 provides mixed indications on this point for the two Residential Choice questions. Both versions clearly reveal increased support by whites for free residential choice by blacks. However, whereas the change is quite steady for the ISR version, the NORC version seems to level or even dip slightly during the 1970s, after which it continues a steady upward climb into the mid 1990s.[15] We have not been able to determine why this different pattern occurs, but it warns us that we must look carefully at the trend for every item that is available for study on a given issue, and not take any single trend as definitive. Of course, we could average all trends over all items (for example, by creating a single summary index of all items in Table 2.1), which would produce an overall mild positive record of change—but, as will become evident, this would obscure much more than it would clarify.

Missing Data

As with the example just discussed, all the questions available for our analysis are "closed" in the sense that respondents are offered two or more explicit alternatives to choose from. Sometimes, however, respondents reject such choices and insist on giving another response, most often (or at least most often recorded as) "don't know" (DK). For racial questions, such nonsubstantive responses are not very common, seldom more than 5 percent of all responses to a given question. However, they can complicate the analysis and presentation of data: for example, by transforming a simple dichotomous question into a three-alternative item.

We initially included "don't know" and similar nonsubstantive responses in tables in order to determine whether they affected conclusions about substantive trends. In most cases they had virtually no effect at all; that is, percentaging data with and without nonsubstantive responses did not appreciably alter trend lines or other results and conclusions. In Figure 2.3, we repeat the results for the ISR and NORC Residential Choice questions used in Figure 2.2. This time, however, we show two trend lines for each question. One line includes the "DK" responses when calculating substantive percentages; the other, identical to Figure 2.2, excludes the "DK" responses. As can be seen, although the trend lines are at slightly different levels, particularly for the ISR version, conclusions about substantive trends do not differ appreciably depending upon whether "DK" responses are included or excluded. There are a few cases where spontaneous "don't know" or other "missing data" responses throw some light on a trend, usually because

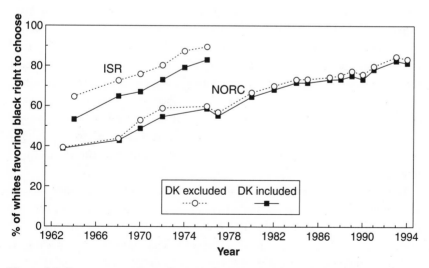

Figure 2.3. Response to ISR and NORC questions on residential choice excluding and including "don't know" responses.

a change in the "don't know" level reflects a change more in one than in another substantive response, and we will note these cases when they seem to be of importance. Our general practice, however, is to exclude spontaneous "don't know" and similar responses, with two exceptions, as noted in the Chapter 3 tables—where the percentage of "don't know" and "other" responses were consistently high and substantively meaningful.

Our procedure is different when a nonsubstantive or similar response such as "no interest" or "in between" is offered to respondents as an explicit alternative to a question. The proportions of respondents who choose these alternatives are often substantial, and of course the alternatives are intrinsic parts of the questions as asked. Therefore they are included in our main tables, though often omitted from figures in order to simplify the presentation. Again, such simplification seldom changes conclusions to any appreciable extent.

Effects of Context

Even where careful attention is paid to maintaining identical question wording, there is an added problem for time series analyses: the "context" of a question—what questions were asked prior to the question of interest—can change from year to year if the exact same questionnaire is not used. There is increasing awareness among survey investigators of the effects of question order or context on responses.[16] Such effects do not appear to be frequent, but when they occur they can be fairly large (Schuman and Presser 1981: chapter 2). This means that the same question in different surveys may yield different results not because of true change but because its placement within the surveys differs. Even in the NORC General Social Survey, where there is considerable emphasis on keeping items constant from year to year, there have been substantial variations in context because of the rotation of items into and out of the questionnaire.

We carried out two important context experiments as part of our efforts to understand unexpected trends for certain questions. One of the experiments, which dealt with a general question on attitudes toward segregation (Table 3.1, the General Segregation item), produced dramatic results that help to explain a curvilinear trend radically out of line with findings on closely related items. These results are discussed in detail in Chapter 3, since they bear heavily on substantive conclu-

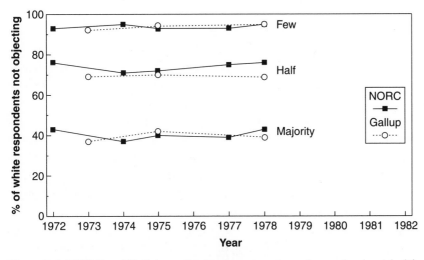

Figure 2.4. NORC and Gallup results for three questions about schools with different proportions of blacks.

sions in that chapter. The other experiment concerned the Few, Half, and Majority school-integration items (shown in Figure 2.4). In this case, which is also discussed in Chapter 3, the experiment did not confirm a suspected context effect and therefore supported a more substantive interpretation of the trend in question. In both of these instances, the experimental results contribute significantly to our understanding, and we wish it had been possible to carry out similar experiments with all of the items that figure importantly in this book, though none of the others seemed so obviously open to contextual influence.[17]

The lesson to be learned from these context experiments is about the importance of looking for evidence of systematic change, or lack of change, over as many time points as possible. A single outlier, even if significantly different from other points, does not deserve too much effort at substantive interpretation in terms of change, since it may result from questionnaire context rather than from events in the external social or political environment.

Organizational Differences

We have discussed how our analysis of time trends must pay attention to issues of question wording, response options, and question context.

One might think that we should add still another concern: the use of data collected by different organizations. For example, the comparison of Residential Choice questions in Figure 2.2 involves a difference between two organizations, ISR and NORC, as well as a difference in question wording. It might seem as though this could present a serious problem, but comparisons of such "house differences" among high-quality organizations indicate that they are seldom an important source of variation in survey results (Smith 1984). There is some difference in the way "don't know" and other unsolicited responses are handled by interviewers trained by different organizations, but once substantive alternatives to a question are repercentaged to exclude such responses, even small differences across organizations tend to disappear.

We do not have any trend question asked by different organizations to exactly the same type of sample at exactly the same time points, but a valuable approximation is available for three questions about sending white children to schools attended by varying proportions (a few, half, more than half) of black children. (These are the questions listed as Few, Half, and Majority in Tables 2.1 and 2.2, with detailed wording shown in Table 3.3.) Gallup asked the three questions to parents with children in school over the period 1958 to 1990. NORC asked exactly the same questions to cross-section samples from 1972 to 1996. Unfortunately, the NORC questionnaire does not provide information that would allow reduction of the sample to fit the Gallup sample specifications, but there is no theoretical reason to expect the differences in the samples to have large effects, though of course there could be some difference. Figure 2.4 shows both sets of data for the time points that are most comparable (excluding 1990 because in that year the Gallup shifted to a telephone survey, whereas the NORC data continued to be based on face-to-face interviews).

The comparisons in Figure 2.4 are instructive in several respects. First, there do not appear to be important differences by organization either in absolute levels or in trends. Wherever year and mode of administration are identical, the largest absolute difference attributable to the organizations is 7 percent; another is 4 percent; there is no difference at all for one time point; and for the remaining points the difference is only 2 percent. Because of the large sample sizes, the 7 percent difference for Half in 1978 is significant at the .01 level, and even the 4 percent difference for Majority in 1978 is near the .05 level. But these differences at specific time points are so small and unsystematic that we believe it best to treat them as lacking substantive significance. (It is difficult even to attribute them to variations in the way the two samples were defined, since they are too inconsistent for such an explanation.) Furthermore, differences in trends by organization are even less evident for the time period 1972–1978, and a summary statement for both organizations would stress the lack of visible change in either a positive or a negative direction on any of the three questions.

Second, it is useful to note that in comparison with the nonexistent or trivial variation by organization, the variation by question *content* is quite large over this same time period (1972–1978), averaging 94 percent acceptance of integration for the question about a few blacks in a school, 72 percent for the question about a school that is half black, and only 40 percent for the question about a school with more than half the students black. It obviously makes a great deal of difference which description of integration is used, and it is clear that the distinction is one of substance. The huge difference of 54 percent between the Few and Majority questions indicates that a large proportion of the respondents take the exact meaning of the question seriously, rather than answering carelessly or simply in terms of some general "set" such as a desire to appear unprejudiced, although such sets may also occur.

Third, the data presented in Figure 2.4 are confined to the period 1972–1978, but we have data for Gallup going back to 1958, and as Figure 2.5 shows for the Half question, the stability from 1972 to 1978 was reached only after a steep climb during the previous decade. Moreover, as one might expect, the climb occurred almost entirely in the South and during the years after the 1954 *Brown* decision. (The Few question shows much the same trend, and the Majority question also shows a similar picture except that the slope for the South is not quite as steep.) This is clearly a case in which a straight line would not represent well the course of change over the total period 1958–1980.

In sum, the Few, Half, and Majority questions illustrate quite nicely that question wording, time, and region are all important in understanding trends in racial attitudes, whereas survey organization as such has little or no role in producing variation.[18]

In another and quite different way, however, organizational differences have been important in past findings and interpretations of trends in racial attitudes. Prior to the 1985 edition of this book, and to a considerable extent still today, most published analyses have been con-

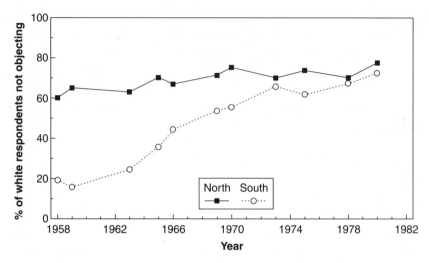

Figure 2.5. Attitudes toward half-black, half-white school, by region and year (Gallup data).

fined to data collected by a single organization. One early series of articles in *Scientific American* (discussed in Chapter 6) used only NORC data, and the same has been true of many later articles; other publications have relied only on ISR data; and of course Gallup compilations have printed only Gallup results. This has tended to limit the view of any single analyst, a narrowing accentuated by the fact that the *types* of questions asked tend to differ from one organization to another. Questions about broad principles of racial integration, for example, have been prominent especially in NORC surveys. This means that analysts of NORC data are more affected by such content and analysts of ISR data less affected insofar as question content produces distinctive trends over time. Questions about the implementation of principles present just the reverse picture—dominance in ISR surveys and few such items in NORC surveys.

As in the story of the blind men and the elephant, the analyst working with data from only one organization perceives only a part of the creature. A primary aim of this book is to draw on several different sources of racial trend data and therefore to obtain a fuller view of the complexity of change. At the same time, we must acknowledge that our own views are largely limited to the questions we consider, and we almost certainly miss or misinterpret some trends that have not been measured well or not measured at all. This is merely to acknowledge that a full understanding of social change even in a single area is a goal to move toward, not one likely to be attained completely.

Race of Interviewer

There is considerable evidence that responses to many questions concerning racial issues are influenced appreciably by whether interviewers and respondents perceive themselves to be of the same or different races. For black respondents, this was first clearly demonstrated more than four decades ago by Hyman (1954), and it has subsequently been replicated many times by many different investigators (Williams 1964; Schuman and Hatchett 1974; Finkel et al. 1991; and others noted below), often using experimental randomization of the race-of-interviewer variable.[19] The main result is that blacks tend to give fewer responses that might be interpreted as antiwhite when the interviewer is white than when the interviewer is black. A parallel phenomenon occurs with white respondents; for example, in one experimental study positive answers toward intermarriage rose by 46 percent when the interviewer was black rather than white (Hatchett and Schuman 1975–76; see also Schaeffer 1980). In both cases the most straightforward explanation is one of avoidance of offense. As one of the early studies put it: "To accept a guest into your house and then proceed to explain that you neither trust nor feel friendly toward people of her race probably takes more *chutzpah* than the average respondent possesses" (Schuman and Converse 1971:58).

None of the major face-to-face surveys handles this problem well, despite the fact that each one has devoted considerable resources to asking questions about racial issues to both white and black respondents. It is understandable that practical constraints prevent national surveys from following an ideal design, which would involve random assignment by race of interviewer. Somewhat less understandable is the failure—despite the obvious administrative difficulties and expenses—to match race of interviewer and race of respondent on a regular basis, on the assumption that this will usually lead to more candor and in any case will at least provide constancy over time.[20] Least understandable is the fact that none of the three major face-to-face survey organizations has routinely included race of interviewer as a variable that can be used or controlled in analysis. As of the present date, no such variable seems to be available in NORC's General So-

Table 2.4 Effect of race of interviewer on thermometer ratings[a]

	Rating	No. of cases	No. of interviewers
A. Black respondents rate whites:			
When interviewer is white	76.9	168	57
When interviewer is black	55.8	26	4
B. White respondents rate blacks:			
When interviewer is black	77.9	13	5
When interviewer is white	60.5	1417	134

a. Respondents are shown a picture of a thermometer and asked to rate a number of groups in terms of how warm or cold they feel toward each group, where maximum warmth is represented by 100, minimum warmth by 0. Data are from 1994.

cial Survey, nor was there one in Gallup data prior to 1997. Such a variable has been included in ISR National Election Study files only since 1986 and is still not available in the cumulative file for these surveys, which is of course of particular relevance for studying attitude change.

What little we know about the composition and effects of race of interviewer in NORC and ISR surveys comes from individual scholars who have themselves developed the necessary information for analysis. Schaeffer (1980) analyzed the 1972 to 1977 NORC General Social Surveys, and Anderson et al. (1988a, 1988b) analyzed the 1964 to 1986 ISR National Election Studies. Both show important effects on both black and white respondents, effects that are consistent with earlier experimental studies that randomized race of interviewer. Both also note that these effects make for special difficulties in research on attitude change because the racial composition and assignment of interviewing staffs may have shown undocumented shifts over time. Quite apart from the interpretation of results at any particular time point, apparent changes in attitude might result simply from changes in the proportions of black and white interviewers.

A simple example of the importance of race of interviewer for our data is presented in Table 2.4, using the 1994 ISR survey where a race-of-interviewer variable is available. The table reports ratings on ISR's "feeling thermometer" scale, which asks the respondent to express warmth or coldness of feelings toward a variety of groups. This variable has often been used as a relatively pure measure of attitude in the sense of affect by respondents toward blacks or toward whites (see

Sears 1988). The ratings in Table 2.4 are tabulated separately by race of respondent and race of interviewer. Black respondents rate whites twenty-one scale points higher when the interviewer is white than when the interviewer is black. White respondents rate blacks seventeen points higher when the interviewer is black than when the interviewer is white. These differences are quite substantial in size and highly significant statistically, despite small numbers of cases for two of the averages.[21]

The problem presented by race-of-interviewer effects is a serious one in face-to-face surveys, but probably much less so for white respondents than for black respondents. As Table 2.4 suggests, most interviewers are white and most white respondents are interviewed by white interviewers. There is some general documentation of this for both early NORC and more recent ISR surveys: the proportion of whites interviewed by blacks has been minimal, no more than 6 percent and usually less (Schaeffer 1980; Anderson et al. 1988b).

Schaeffer's NORC data cover only the 1970s, however, and she further notes that "when year effects are . . . small, even slight changes in the size of the race-of-interviewer effect or the racial composition of the interviewing staff could distort conclusions about attitude change" (1980:415).

The problem is much more severe for black respondents, since as Table 2.4 indicates, they may actually be interviewed in ISR surveys more often by whites than by blacks, and there is also probably considerable variability over time and across organizations. Between 1964 and 1986, the proportion of black respondents in ISR's National Election Studies who were interviewed by black interviewers ranged from a high in 1964 of 43 percent to a low in 1984 of 13 percent (Anderson et al. 1988b). Although the General Social Survey seems to have had a higher degree of race-matching (ranging from 36 percent to 78 percent) in the past, the proportion fluctuated considerably from year to year (Schaeffer 1980). So far as we have been able to discover, no systematic information is available at all for the past two decades (as reported by Tom Smith in personal communications, 1995 and 1996).

In sum, the high and possibly varying proportions of black Americans interviewed by whites makes our later chapter on black attitude change much more subject to doubt on the basis of interviewer effects than the chapters on white attitude change. Our only safeguard is to keep in mind the likely direction of such bias (in particular, to make blacks appear more favorable toward whites than they would be if interviewed entirely by blacks). Furthermore, for both whites and blacks, but again especially for blacks, we must recognize that conclusions about attitude change over time may also be confounded with changes in the racial composition of interviewing staffs.

We should add that racial attitudes, as stressed earlier, are often ambivalent, and that it is too simple to assume that validity always lies in the direction of matching interviewer and respondent by race (Schuman and Converse 1971). Pressure to conform to the expectations of the interviewer can work in either or even in both directions. It depends on the commitment that respondents have to expressing their own preferences regardless of social constraints, and on the assumptions they make about the expectations of their interviewer, whether black or white. Thus some black respondents may feel more pressure to express antiwhite sentiments to a black interviewer because she is believed—whether correctly or not—to want to hear them. Furthermore, Anderson et al. (1988a) provide some evidence that reports by blacks of having voted may be more valid when the interviewers are white. Nevertheless, having stated these qualifications, we believe it is safest for our present research to assume that in most cases there is likely to be greater candor in discussing the "other" race when not talking directly to a person of that race. Even if the attitudes do vary by racial context, unless we can have both contexts, as is possible in experiments, it is probably more useful to know how attitudes are expressed in same-race situations.

The Move to Telephone Surveys

In the 1985 edition of this book we were in a position to exclude data not based on face-to-face interviews, because at that point telephone surveys were still the exception. Although this remains true for the major national surveys by ISR and NORC, during the last decade Gallup has moved more and more to telephone interviewing, and our two new sources of data—ABC/*Washington Post* and CBS/*New York Times*—are based entirely on telephone surveys. If we were to continue to exclude this mode of administration, we would be unable to analyze adequately some questions on important new racial issues, such as attitudes toward affirmative action and perceptions of the prevalence of discrimination against blacks. In drawing on telephone data, however, we must be cautious because of differences between telephone and personal interviews. As already noted, sample coverage is one such problem, and there are other differences as well (Groves et al. 1988). It is thus better, wherever possible, to avoid combining face-to-face and telephone data from different periods to construct a single trend.

It might seem as though race of interviewer would present less of a problem with telephone than with face-to-face surveys, but apparently voice and perhaps other cues make it still a potent variable for white respondents (Cotter et al. 1982; Finkel et al. 1991), and for black respondents as well (Sanders 1995). Moreover, there is more chance assignment—though seldom carefully randomized assignment—by race of interviewer in telephone surveys than in face-to-face surveys, since the interviewing is usually centralized in one location (for example, New York City), rather than delegated to interviewers in terms of their own neighborhoods. The CBS/NYT telephone polls have provided information on race of interviewer since late in 1991, and our analysis of a selection of these studies indicates that a significantly higher proportion of white respondents are interviewed by black interviewers, as compared with the evidence we have from face-to-face surveys. Over a two-month period in 1995, for example, 74 percent of white respondents were interviewed by white interviewers, 20 percent by black interviewers, and the remaining 5 percent by Hispanic interviewers. By contrast, 75 percent of black respondents were interviewed by white interviewers in the CBS/NYT polls.

These variations in the rate of race-matching in telephone versus face-to-face interviews are particularly important for questions that are especially susceptible to race-of-interviewer effects. For the most part they are questions that indicate rejection or hostility toward the other race, though occasionally even political items that at first sight seem nonracial in content have been found to be affected (Schuman and Hatchett 1974; Finkel et al. 1991).

Furthermore, there may be differences between face-to-face and telephone modes of administration that derive from characteristics of interviewers more subtle than race. Consider the following striking example. A question to whites that we employ about preferences for different degrees of racial mixture in a neighborhood was also included by Groves and Kahn (1979) in a larger, experimentally controlled comparison of telephone and face-to-face surveys. We reanalyzed their data separately for white Southern and white Northern respondents,

hypothesizing that the regional variation would be particularly important in this case. Face-to-face interviewers normally come from the
same local area—and therefore have the same local accents—as their
respondents, whereas the telephone interviewing was done centrally
from Ann Arbor and most of the interviewers were Northerners. For
those living in the South, responses on preferred racial composition of
neighborhood were significantly more favorable toward residential integration from those who were interviewed by telephone than from
those who were interviewed face-to-face (see Table 2.5). A plausible
interpretation is that Southern whites are more likely to express preferences for residential segregation when talking face-to-face in their
living rooms with Southern white interviewers than when responding
by telephone to voices in Ann Arbor that they perceive as Northern
(and conceivably as black).[22] This is still another indication that we
should avoid so far as possible treating face-to-face and telephone data
as equivalent when studying trends in racial attitudes. Where we cannot
avoid linking the two modes in tracing a particular trend, extra caution
is needed in drawing conclusions.

The Issue of Privacy: Mail versus Face-to-Face Surveys

At the heart of the interviewer problem is the more general issue of
candor in responding to survey questions about racial issues. In today's
social and racial climate, it is possible that even with race-matching
there may be pressures on white Americans to give more racially liberal
responses, because the long-term normative change in this country has
been in that direction. Moreover, if these pressures have increased over
time, conclusions based on survey data about the increasingly liberal
racial attitudes of whites may be overstated. In addition, if the pressures
are experienced more intensely by some parts of the white population
(in particular, the more highly educated, who are apt to be more aware
of broad cultural norms) than by other parts (the less educated), our
conclusions about the correlates of change may also require some
qualification.

One of the present authors (Krysan 1995) recently investigated this
fundamental issue by carrying out an experimental study that varied
modes of survey administration in terms of the sense of privacy likely
to be felt by white respondents. She compared responses to three modes
of survey administration:

Table 2.5 Responses to Neighborhood Preference question, by mode of administration and region, 1976

Mode of administration	North					South				
	All white	Mostly white	Mixed[a]	Total	N	All white	Mostly white	Mixed[a]	Total	N
Telephone	22%	31	46	100	(927)	38%	29	33	100	(370)
Face-to-face[b]	23%	36	42	100	(874)	51%	27	22	100	(368)
Difference	−1	−5	+4			−13	+2	+11		

Question (ISR): "Would you personally prefer to live in a neighborhood with mostly whites, mostly blacks, or a neighborhood that is mixed half and half?"

[IF MOSTLY WHITE] "Would you prefer a *mostly* white neighborhood or an all-white neighborhood?"

a. "No difference" was accepted if offered spontaneously, but is combined here with mixed half and half. DK responses are omitted; they were almost identical for both modes in both regions. Only two persons gave the response "mostly blacks" and these are included here under "mixed."

b. Restricted to households owning telephones.

Mode 1. A standard face-to-face interview condition where interviewers asked all the questions;

Mode 2. A modified face-to-face interview condition where respondents answered a subset of racial questions in a self-administered form while the interviewer waited;

Mode 3. A noninterview condition where questionnaires were mailed to respondents and returned through the mail.

The study was conducted on a cross-section of the white population of the Metropolitan Detroit area. A sample of the results from this extensive experiment is presented in Table 2.6, focusing on questions that are either similar in content to, or exact replications of, the questions used in the national trend analyses we report in later chapters.[23]

Two important conclusions can be drawn from Table 2.6. First, in comparing modes 1 and 2, it does not appear that being able to record privately one's answers in the context of a face-to-face interview makes any difference in responses: none of the items shows a significant difference between these two kinds of face-to-face interviews (column 1 vs. column 2), even though mode 2 affords more temporary privacy than mode 1. Apparently one does not obtain greater candor by interrupting an interview for a few minutes of self-administered questions.[24]

Second, it appears that administering the survey entirely by mail does result in differences in responses. Indeed, seven of the eleven items available for comparison in Table 2.6 show statistically significant differences between the mail and the combined face-to-face conditions. Five of the differences are in the direction the researcher anticipated on the assumption that the mail mode of administration afforded a great deal more privacy than either of the face-to-face modes, and would therefore allow expression of more counternormative attitudes. Respondents in the mail condition expressed less willingness to vote for a black presidential candidate, were less likely to attribute black disadvantages to racial discrimination, and were less supportive of various kinds of policies and programs to assist blacks. Furthermore, additional analysis (not shown here) indicates that it is those with a college degree who are most affected in this way by being able to report their answers in private in the mail survey. A persuasive interpretation is that it is better-educated white Americans who are most aware of the social norm to appear racially tolerant, and who thus feel more strongly the pressure to respond in that direction when an interviewer is present, even an interviewer of their own race.

Surprisingly, two agree-disagree items—one attributing racial inequality to in-born ability and another attributing inequality to a lack of motivation—showed significant differences in the opposite direction. That is, in the *less* private personal interview, respondents gave *more negative* answers: they agreed more often with characterizations of blacks as having less in-born ability and as lacking motivation and will power. Additional analysis showed that this unexpected finding is concentrated among *less*-educated respondents, and is best interpreted as evidence of what has been called acquiescence bias—the tendency, particularly among the less well educated, to agree to sweeping statements read by survey interviewers (Campbell et al 1960; Lenski and Leggett 1960). This tendency is apparently reduced both in a mail survey and in the self-administered portion of a face-to-face interview, since in neither is there pressure to agree or disagree quickly to a statement read aloud by an interviewer.

What implications do these new findings have for our interpretation of trend data, which are based on face-to-face and telephone interviews, not on mail surveys? The results provide an empirically documented warning that at least some white respondents feel pressure in an interview situation to appear more racially liberal than they would indicate under conditions of greater privacy, and that this tendency is probably accentuated for more-educated respondents. As we noted in Chapter 1, such behavior shows the power of norms, but at the same time it indicates that we should interpret differences by education as carrying an extra weight of normative influence. How that difference by education would affect actions outside the survey setting presumably would depend on the degree to which the new situation is subject to similar normative influence. In addition, the study reinforces our inclination to be wary of questions that use an agree-disagree format, since they may produce acquiescence bias, especially by the less educated.

Unfortunately, we do not have experimental mail survey data from earlier time points, and so it is not possible to investigate directly whether the effects identified by Krysan (1995) have changed over time. Nor do any of the data we analyze in later chapters come from mail surveys. As we interpret both trends over time and educational differences in racial attitudes, however, this recent study of mode of administration alerts us to the social pressures inherent in the process of collecting survey data, especially data on racial attitudes.

*　　*　　*

Table 2.6 Racial attitude items by mode of administration, 1994 Detroit Area Study and Tri-County Study (white respondents only; weighted by education and gender)

Question	(1) Standard FTF (%)	(2) Self-admin. FTF (%)	(3) Mail survey (%)	(4) Standard FTF vs. SA FTF (sign.)	(5) Combined FTF vs. mail survey (sign.)
Principles					
Black Candidate					
Yes, would vote	89.5	86.2	78.4		
No, would not vote	10.5	13.8	21.6	n.s.	**
(*n*)	(190)	(187)	(486)		
Intermarriage					
No, would not object	47.3	n/a	50.6		
Yes, would object	52.7		49.4	n/a	n.s.
(*n*)	(203)		(522)		
Implementation					
Open Housing					
Homeowner cannot refuse	52.2	54.0	51.2		
Homeowner can decide	47.8	46.0	48.8	n.s.	n.s.
(*n*)	(201)	(191)	(522)		
Social distance					
Same Block					
Not mind at all	72.3	70.1	72.9		
Mind a little	21.8	26.5	21.3		
Mind a lot	5.9	3.4	5.7	n.s.	n.s.
(*n*)	(202)	(193)	(522)		
Explanations for inequality					
Discrimination					
Strongly agree	9.9	8.2	7.3		
Somewhat agree	43.8	44.5	37.0		
Somewhat disagree	30.5	33.8	27.6		
Strongly disagree	15.8	13.5	28.1	n.s.	**
(*n*)	(203)	(193)	(520)		
Less Ability					
Strongly disagree	55.0	55.6	66.2		
Somewhat disagree	24.3	29.5	21.1		
Somewhat agree	16.8	11.8	10.9		
Strongly agree	4.0	3.0	1.8	n.s.	**
(*n*)	(202)	(194)	(519)		

Table 2.6 (continued)

Question	(1) Standard FTF (%)	(2) Self-admin. FTF (%)	(3) Mail survey (%)	(4) Standard FTF vs. SA FTF (sign.)	(5) Combine FTF vs. m: survey (sig:
No Motivation					
Strongly disagree	18.2	22.7	25.8		
Somewhat disagree	21.2	17.9	20.0		
Somewhat agree	41.4	42.1	37.3		
Strongly agree	19.2	17.3	16.9	n.s.	†
(n)	(203)	(193)	(515)		
No Special Favors					
Strongly disagree	0.5	0.9	0.4		
Disagree	9.4	6.8	9.1		
Neither agree/disagree	14.3	21.8	14.4		
Agree	46.8	43.3	40.0		
Strongly agree	29.1	27.3	36.1	n.s.	†
(n)	(203)	(193)	(275)		
Perceptions of discrimination					
Discriminated in Managerial Jobs					
A lot	7.6	8.2	7.4		
Some	57.4	61.9	58.0		
Not at all	35.0	29.8	34.5	n.s.	n.s
(n)	(197)	(187)	(487)		
Affirmative action					
Education and Training					
Strongly favor	6.9	6.5	5.9		
Favor	23.3	22.4	15.9		
Neither favor/oppose	31.2	33.8	31.8		
Oppose	24.3	22.0	28.6		
Strongly oppose	14.4	15.2	17.9	n.s.	**
(n)	(202)	(190)	(517)		
Preferences in Hiring and Promotion					
Strongly favor	0.0		0.9	n/a	*
Favor	5.9		3.4		
Neither favor/oppose	22.2		18.4		
Oppose	41.9		39.6		
Strongly oppose	30.0	n/a	37.6		
(n)	(203)		(516)		

Note: FTF = face-to-face; SA = self-administered. Columns 4 and 5 give the approximate level of statistical significance according to a two-tailed t-test of the tau-b statistic, where n.s. is not significant at $p < .10$ or higher; † $p < .10$; * $p < .05$; ** $p < .01$.

As each of the preceding examples indicate, analyzing trend data on racial attitudes (and on most other attitudes as well) is more than a matter of simply stringing together results from whatever surveys are at hand. Great care must be exercised to make certain the data sets are as comparable as possible and to take account of noncomparability when it occurs. Despite all feasible precautions, however, it is evident that not every variation, nor even every statistically significant variation, necessarily represents real change over time in the attitudes of the population. We cannot avoid all problems inherent in our data, but we should also remind readers again that an important *advantage* of scientific surveys—as reflected in the research described in this chapter—is to make us aware of possible problems and to provide ways of discovering how and where they occur. Throughout the analysis that follows we have tried to exercise both caution and judgment in inferring change in the underlying racial attitudes of the American population over the past half century.

3

Trends in
White Racial Attitudes

The question of how white racial attitudes have changed over the past half century has no simple answer. Even a cursory glance at the evidence shows that trends differ greatly depending on the kind of question asked. For this reason, we organize the available trend questions by their substantive content, and take account also of question form, wording, and context in our interpretations.

Six types of questions have sufficient data for trend analysis:

1. *Principles of equal treatment.* These are questions that ask respondents whether they endorse broad principles of equal treatment regardless of race in important areas of life. It is no accident that such questions are the earliest we have in terms of start date, with several having begun as far back as the 1940s. The earlier principles of discrimination and forced segregation that had crystallized at the end of the nineteenth century were the first walls to be breached when racial issues moved to the fore in the middle of the twentieth century.

Most of the "principle questions" available for trend analysis come from NORC surveys, but fortunately there are some from Gallup and ISR as well, so that the content of this category does not overlap entirely with that of survey organization. The partial overlap of conceptual content and survey organization here and for other categories of questions is a factor we noted in Chapter 2 and will discuss further in Chapter 6.

2. *Implementation of equal treatment.* These questions deal with steps that the government (usually but not always the federal government) might take to put principles of equal treatment into effect by ending discrimination and enforced segregation. The first implementation questions were asked in an ISR survey in 1964, following the major

Civil Rights Act of that year. The legislation concerned, among other things, the areas of employment, public accommodations, and school integration, and for each of these issues the ISR survey included a question that was then repeated over a number of subsequent years. A little later NORC added questions on open housing laws and busing that we also put under the heading of implementation, though one could argue that busing is closer to the affirmative action questions described below.

There are fortunately some close parallels between principle and implementation questions. These will be particularly important for interpretation, since a central issue in the study of racial attitudes is the degree to which support for principle leads to support for implementation of the same principle (see Prothro and Grigg 1960; Jackman 1978; Pettigrew 1979).

3. *Social distance*. These questions ask how the respondent would react in particular situations that involve some degree of integration at a personal level. Thus the questions also deal with a form of implementation of principle, but they do so in terms of the individual's own behavior or feelings about being *personally* involved in racial change. The questions can be considered abstract in another sense, however, for they ask people to predict how they would act in hypothetical situations, and there is no direct evidence on actual behavior. The term "social distance" comes from the name of a classic attitude scale developed long ago by Bogardus (1928), though none of the original items was carried over in an exact way into these national surveys.

4. *Beliefs about inequality*. These questions attempt to determine how cross-sections of white Americans interpret continuing black-white differences in socioeconomic levels. Occupational, income, and educational differences between blacks and whites were obvious at the beginning of the civil rights movement, but at that point only two types of explanations for these differences were considered seriously by most writers. On the one hand, traditional racist explanations were seen as focusing on the supposed innate superiority of the white race and therefore the lack of any real possibility for racial equality. On the other hand, those involved in or sympathetic to the civil rights movement emphasized the hundreds of years of racial oppression, with blacks always denied opportunities for advancement, as well as the psychological effects of being treated as second-class citizens in one's own country. By the early 1970s, surveys began to include questions

that attempted to determine how white Americans explain continuing black-white differences in education, occupation, and income. Such items have increasingly been an object of analysis by social scientists, and there are now sufficient data over time to provide important evidence for our consideration. In addition, beginning in the 1980s direct questions about white beliefs concerning current levels of discrimination began to be repeated across time, and these more specific trend data are also considered here.

5. *Affirmative action.* These questions concern positive actions that government or other organizations might take to improve the economic and social status of African Americans. The riots in major American cities in the middle and late 1960s made it evident that not all black Americans felt they were benefiting from what had seemed to many white Americans to be substantial racial change. The continuing racial differences in economic and social status became a new focus, and steps were proposed to promote greater equality on these scores, rather than simply ending legal segregation or preventing open discrimination.

The first affirmative action steps had been attempts to eliminate what came to be called "institutional racism," as exemplified by traditional forms of hiring that preclude or discourage black applicants, such as advertising jobs via individuals or media having ties only to a white community.[1] A second, more active type of affirmative step was to devote government funds to improving the lives of black Americans, for example, providing additional money to inner cities caught up in the consequences of poverty. Finally, a third and still more dramatic step was to give preference to blacks in employment and educational situations, as a way of both making up for past discrimination and accelerating the move toward equality of outcomes. In this book we use the term "affirmative action" to cover all of the approaches that use race-conscious methods to promote racial equality, rather than equating the term with any single method (for example, preferential treatment).

As typically happens, survey questions followed after the issues became salient in the public arena. Thus questions on the second of these steps—government expenditures to improve the status of blacks—began to be asked at the end of the 1960s, especially in ISR's National Election Study, probably because of its general concern with government policies. A decade later, several survey organizations began to include questions about specific types of preferential treatment in educational and employment settings. (The simplest form of affirmative action that calls for efforts to ensure racially neutral recruitment never became a focus in surveys, probably because it was not a very controversial policy change.)

Questions about affirmative action deal with policies, just as do questions about the implementation of equal treatment, but as we noted in Chapter 2 (p. 61), the two types of policies have different goals. Implementation questions, as originally developed in the early 1960s, focused on policies that attempt to prevent unequal treatment by race in particular situations (public accommodations, employment, and so on). The emphasis was on the creation and practice of color blindness. Most affirmative action questions concern policies intended to lead to greater equality of outcome (for example, more black students graduating from medical schools), even where immediate white discrimination is not at issue, though they also guard against such discrimination toward blacks. Necessarily, such questions emphasize color consciousness, not color blindness. In practice, the two types of questions are not always clearly demarcated. One complication that we discuss at later points is the possible change over time in the perception of the meaning of what was originally thought of as an implementation question (for example, Federal Job Intervention in Table 3.2) into a question about preferential treatment.[2]

6. *Miscellaneous racial questions.* This category includes a few trend questions of interest that do not fit well into any of the above categories, nor occur in sufficient number to justify creation of a further new category. For example, we include here a measure of "warmth of feelings" toward specific racial groups, which has been asked regularly in ISR surveys since 1964 and has been used in a number of analyses as a more or less pure indicator of general white attitude or affect toward blacks.

Each of the six sets of questions just outlined will be presented and discussed in turn. For each set, an initial table shows trends for the white adult population as a whole and includes the exact wording of all questions.[3] Graphs are used to highlight particular trends and comparisons among trends. We also discuss differences between Northern and Southern respondents and by broad levels of education. Chapter 4 then looks systematically at the degree to which shifts in racial attitudes can be attributed to changes within individuals, as against the replacement of older cohorts by younger cohorts. In addition, education as a causal factor is considered again, this time with cohort, income, gender, and region controlled (see pp. 231–234). The effects of both income and gender are likewise analyzed with other variables held constant.

Our organizing scheme is certainly not the only one possible. But since all of the questions and overall trends are presented in the main summary tables of this chapter (Tables 3.1 to 3.6), readers are free to consider other ways of thinking about the evidence, as indeed we ourselves do at some points. Whatever organizing scheme is adopted, we should keep in mind that although our focus is necessarily on questions, our ultimate concern is with the people who answered the questions and even more with the changing (or unchanging) attitudes of these people as we infer them from the trend data.

Principles of Equal Treatment

Table 3.1 presents questions concerned with broad principles of non-discrimination and integration.[4] Results are given for all available time points for samples intended to represent the total white adult population.[5] The questions deal with most of the major racial issues that became focal in the middle of the twentieth century: integration of public accommodations, school integration, residential integration, and job discrimination. In addition, two more symbolic issues, racial intermarriage and willingness to vote for a black presidential candidate, are represented, and there is one quite general item about segregation as an overall principle. The table is divided into two parts, A and B, to accommodate different sets of dates.

Schools

1. *Overall trends.* The trends that occur for most of the principle items are quite similar and can be illustrated in Figure 3.1, using attitudes toward school integration as an example. The figure shows that there has been a massive and continuing movement of the American public from overwhelming acceptance of the *principle* of segregated schooling in the early 1940s toward acceptance of the *principle* of integrated schooling. In 1942 almost seven out of ten white Americans chose the pro-segregation schooling response; by 1985, more than nine out of

Table 3.1A Questions concerning principles, 1942–1995 (white respondents)[a]

Question	42	43	44	45	46	48	50	56	58	60	61	62	63
Same Schools (NORC)													
% Same	32	—	—	—	—	—	—	50	—	—	—	—	65
Separate	68	—	—	—	—	—	—	50	—	—	—	—	35
Equal Jobs (NORC)													
% As good a chance	—	—	45	—	49	—	—	—	—	—	—	—	85
White people first	—	—	55	—	51	—	—	—	—	—	—	—	15
Segregated Transportation (NORC)													
% No	46	—	—	—	—	—	—	62	—	—	—	—	79
Yes	54	—	—	—	—	—	—	38	—	—	—	—	21
Same Accommodations (NORC)													
% Yes	—	—	—	—	—	—	—	—	—	—	—	—	73
No	—	—	—	—	—	—	—	—	—	—	—	—	27

Question wordings and variants

Same Schools (NORC): "Do you think white students and (Negro/black) students should go to the same schools or to separate schools?" Sample size was fewer than 1,000 cases in 1985 (*n* = 638). Data for 1995 are from a telephone survey conducted by the Princeton Survey Research Associates, as reported in the Roper Center's *Public Perspective*, vol. 7 (2), 1996, p. 40. Because of this, respondents aged 18–20 are not excluded in 1995.

    1. Same
    2. Separate
(**Variant:** in 1964 added "but equal" after "separate.")

Equal Jobs (NORC): "Do you think Negroes should have as good a chance as white people to get any kind of job, or do you think white people should have the first chance at any kind of job?"

    1. As good a chance
    2. White people first

ten chose the pro-integration response. At that point, NORC concluded that there was too little variation in answers to make the question useful for further analysis and dropped it from their annual General Social Survey.[6] (Results still closer to the 100 percent ceiling appeared in an independent telephone replication of the question in 1995; they are shown in Table 3.1A, but not in Figure 3.1.) With other questions about principles, we will see that the type of change reflected in the school integration item has continued well into the 1990s.

It is striking that the trend in Figure 3.1 follows closely the path of a straight line upward.[7] Also shown in the figure are a few of the important events that might have increased, disturbed, or even reversed its trajectory. Some of the events were government actions that sup-

								Year of survey									
4	65	66	68	70	72	74	76	77	78	79	80	81	82	83	84	85	95
3	70	—	73	75	86	—	85	86	—	—	88	—	90	—	92	93	96ᵗ
7	30	—	27	25	14	—	16	14	—	—	12	—	10	—	8	8	4ᵗ
—	—	89	—	—	97	—	—	—	—	—	—	—	—	—	—	—	—
—	—	11	—	—	3	—	—	—	—	—	—	—	—	—	—	—	—
—	—	—	—	88	—	—	—	—	—	—	—	—	—	—	—	—	—
—	—	—	—	12	—	—	—	—	—	—	—	—	—	—	—	—	—
—	77	—	—	88	—	—	—	—	—	—	—	—	—	—	—	—	—
—	23	—	—	12	—	—	—	—	—	—	—	—	—	—	—	—	—

Question wordings and variants

Segregated Transportation (NORC): "Generally speaking, do you think there should be separate sections for Negroes in streetcars and buses?"
  1. Yes
  2. No

Same Accommodations (NORC): "Do you think Negroes should have the right to use the same parks, restaurants, and hotels as white people?"
  1. Yes
  2. No

a. Here and throughout the book, percentages may not sum to 100 due to rounding.
t. Data collected through telephone survey rather than personal interview.

ported civil rights; some were nonviolent protest activities by blacks; some involved widespread and frightening urban violence that challenged the sense of American progress in civil rights; and some seemed at the time to represent conservative political reaction hostile to further civil rights progress. What is most remarkable about Figure 3.1 is that the trend upward in support of the principle of school integration appears entirely unaffected by these external events. For example, although at one time or another there was much talk of a white "backlash," there is virtually no sign of such a reaction in the figure.[8]

In Chapter 4 we will see that the kind of trend reflected in Figure 3.1 can be attributed both to the replacement of older generations or cohorts by younger ones and to individual attitude change within

Table 3.1B Questions concerning principles, 1958–1997 (white respondents)

Question	Year of survey													
	58	59	61	63	64	65	67	68	69	70	71	72	73	74
Residential Choice 1 alt. (NORC)														
% Disagree strongly	—	—	—	19	—	—	—	19	—	34	—	34	—	—
Disagree slightly	—	—	—	20	—	—	—	25	—	19	—	25	—	—
Agree slightly	—	—	—	21	—	—	—	25	—	18	—	18	—	—
Agree strongly	—	—	—	39	—	—	—	31	—	29	—	23	—	—
Residential Choice 2 alt. (ISR)														
% Blacks rights	—	—	—	—	65	—	—	73	—	76	—	80	—	8
Keep blacks out	—	—	—	—	35	—	—	27	—	24	—	20	—	1
Black Candidate (Gallup)														
% Yes	37	46	50	45	—	58	52	—	71	—	71	—	—	—
No	63	54	50	55	—	42	48	—	29	—	29	—	—	—
Black Candidate (NORC)														
% Yes	—	—	—	—	—	—	—	—	—	—	—	73	—	8
No	—	—	—	—	—	—	—	—	—	—	—	27	—	1
Laws against Intermarriage (NORC)														
% No	—	—	—	38	40	—	—	44	—	50	—	60	61	6
Yes	—	—	—	62	60	—	—	56	—	50	—	40	39	3
Intermarriage (Gallup)														
% Approve	4	—	—	—	—	—	—	—	—	—	—	27	—	—
Disapprove	96	—	—	—	—	—	—	—	—	—	—	73	—	—
General Segregation (ISR)														
% Desegregation	—	—	—	—	27	—	—	33	—	37	—	38	—	36
Something btwn.	—	—	—	—	48	—	—	50	—	46	—	48	—	53
Strict segregation	—	—	—	—	25	—	—	17	—	18	—	15	—	1

Question wordings and variants

Residential Choice, 1 alternative (NORC): "Here are some opinions other people have expressed in connection with (Negro/black)–white relations. Which statement on the card comes closest to how you, yourself, feel? White people have a right to keep (Negroes/blacks/African Americans) out of their neighborhoods if they want to, and (Negroes/blacks/African Americans) should respect that right." Sample sizes fewer than 1,000 cases occurred in 1988–1993 and 1996, and ranged from 724 to 875.

1. Agree strongly
2. Agree slightly
3. Disagree slightly
4. Disagree strongly

									Year of survey									
'5	76	77	78	80	82	83	84	85	86	87	88	89	90	91	93	94	96	97
—	34	28	—	38	39	—	46	43	—	46	49	53	48	55	62	56	65	—
—	26	29	—	29	31	—	27	30	—	28	27	25	28	25	22	27	21	—
—	18	21	—	17	15	—	16	16	—	16	16	15	15	12	11	11	7	—
—	22	23	—	17	15	—	11	11	—	10	9	8	9	8	4	6	6	—
—	90	—	—	—	—	—	—	—	—	—	—	—	—	—	—	—	—	—
—	11	—	—	—	—	—	—	—	—	—	—	—	—	—	—	—	—	—
—	—	—	78	—	—	81	81	—	—	84	—	—	—	—	—	—	—	95ʳ
—	—	—	22	—	—	19	20	—	—	16	—	—	—	—	—	—	—	5ʳ
81	—	78	83	—	86	85	—	83	86	—	79	82	86	88	87	90	92	—
9	—	22	17	—	14	16	—	17	14	—	21	19	14	12	13	11	8	—
60	66	71	—	68	66	—	72	71	—	73	74	77	79	80	81	84	87	—
40	34	29	—	32	34	—	28	29	—	27	26	23	21	20	19	16	13	—
—	—	—	34	—	—	39	—	—	—	—	—	—	—	51ʳ	—	51ʳ	—	67ʳ
—	—	—	66	—	—	61	—	—	—	—	—	—	—	49ʳ	—	49ʳ	—	33ʳ
—	36	—	34	—	—	—	—	—	—	—	—	—	—	—	—	—	—	—
—	53	—	60	—	—	—	—	—	—	—	—	—	—	—	—	—	—	—
—	11	—	6	—	—	—	—	—	—	—	—	—	—	—	—	—	—	—

Question wordings and variants

Residential Choice, 2 alternatives (ISR): "Which of these statements would you agree with: White people have a right to keep (Negroes/black people) out of their neighborhoods if they want to, or, (Negroes/black people) have a right to live wherever they can afford to, just like anybody else?"

1. Keep blacks out
2. Blacks have rights

(Variant: in 1964 replaced "anybody else" with "white people.")

Black Candidate (Gallup): From 1958 to 1978, question wording was as follows: "There's always been much discussion about the qualifications of presidential candidates—their education, age, race, religion, and the like. If your party nominated a generally well qualified man for president and he happened to be a Negro, would you vote for him?" See notes below for question variants in other years. In 1987 and 1997, the results include

Table 3.1B (continued)

Question wordings and variants

---

respondents aged 18–20, and the 1987 data are based on published data reported in the Gallup Monthly Report, June 1987.

    1. Yes
    2. No

(**Variants:** Introductions to this item frequently refer to an upcoming election year or convention. This is the case in 1958 [reference to the 1960 election], 1959 [reference to the 1960 election], 1961 [reference to the 1964 election], and 1978 [reference to the 1980 convention]. In 1983, the question did not refer to either an election or a convention, but instead was asked as follows: "If your party nominated a generally well qualified man for president and he happened to be black, would you vote for him?" In 1984, the question wording was: "This year there has been much discussion about the qualifications of presidential candidates—their education, age, religion, race, and the like. If your party nominated a generally well qualified man for president, would you vote for him if he happened to be black?" In 1987, the 1983 question wording was used, but with reference to the 1988 conventions. Other groups [most notably Jews, Catholics, and women] have also been offered to respondents as potential presidential candidates. Blacks were the first group mentioned in 1958, 1959, 1961, 1971, 1978, and 1984; the last group mentioned in 1963 and 1965; and the third of several groups mentioned in 1967 and 1969. In 1983 and 1997, only a question about a black presidential candidate was asked. In 1987, four groups were asked about, in the following order: Jews, atheists, blacks, and women. In 1997, the question wording was changed from "man" to "person.")

Black Candidate (NORC): "If your party nominated a (Negro/black/African American) for president, would you vote for him if he were qualified for the job?" Sample sizes fewer than 1,000 cases occurred in 1988–1993 and 1996, and ranged from 716 to 836.

    1. Yes
    2. No

Laws against Intermarriage (NORC): "Do you think there should be laws against marriages between (Negroes/blacks/African Americans) and whites?" Sample sizes fewer than 1,000 cases occurred in 1988–1993, and ranged from 728 to 844.

    1. Yes
    2. No

Intermarriage (Gallup): (1994: In general) "Do you approve or disapprove of marriage between whites and nonwhites (1983–1997: between blacks and whites)?" For 1997, the results include respondents aged 18–20.

    1. Approve
    2. Disapprove

General Segregation (ISR): "Are you in favor of desegregation, strict segregation, or something in between?" Sample size fewer than 1,000 cases occurred in 1970, when $n = 630$.

    1. Desegregation
    2. Strict segregation
    3. Something in between

    t. Data collected through telephone survey, rather than personal interview.

generations. For now it is sufficient to note that most questions that we will discuss about broad principles of equal treatment and integration show much the same almost inexorable upward movement. A revolution in what the white American population took for granted about the relation of blacks and whites occurred between the 1940s and today.

    2. Regional trends. In Figure 3.2 the sample is divided by education

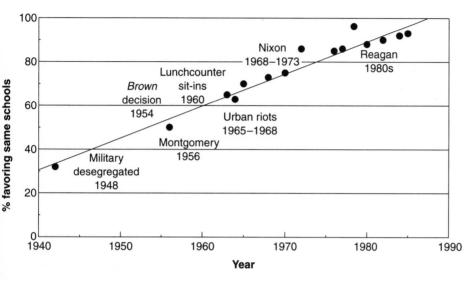

Note: Dark circles represent data points.

Figure 3.1. Attitudes toward integrated schools over time.

and region in order to give some sense of the variation across important parts of the population. (See Chapter 2 for further discussion of the meaning of these social background characteristics.) We employ the starting date of 1956 in this figure because full information about respondents' education is not available before that time. The findings can be summarized as follows:[9] From the beginning, there has been a sizable gap between attitudes in the South and the North, though both regions have shown essentially the same type of change over time. Gradually, the two regions appeared to converge, although this may be due largely to the fact that acceptance of the principle of integrated schooling in the North is approaching 100 percent, thus creating a ceiling constraint. At the earliest point in 1942 (not shown in Figure 3.2), the Same Schools response was chosen by only 2 percent of Southern respondents and only 42 percent of Northern respondents; by 1985 the two figures were 86 percent and 96 percent, respectively. The regional differences and their decrease over time are clearly related to the events surrounding school desegregation in the South, as discussed in Chapter 1.

3. *Trends by education.* Responses indicating acceptance of integrated schooling are positively and clearly associated with respondents' education at each point throughout the entire time period. Since the

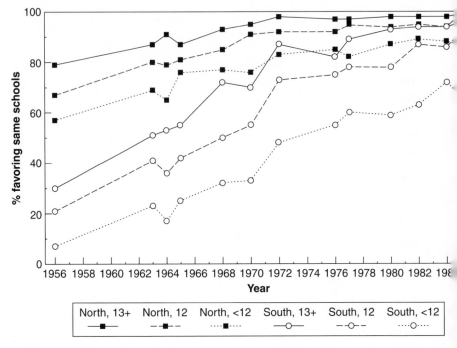

Figure 3.2. Attitudes toward integrated schools over time, by region and education.

trend over time is much the same for each educational category, there is no substantial shift in the association between education and acceptance. However, the least-educated Southerners remain distinctly lower in acceptance of the principle of integrated schooling than the other five groups, whereas the most-educated Southerners have moved to the level of the most-educated Northerners. Indeed, in 1985 the proportion of respondents with thirteen or more years of education who claimed to support "same schools for blacks and whites" reaches 99 percent in both regions! As we discussed in Chapter 2 and will return to again at later points, this response is best treated as a new social norm for well-educated white Americans. We will need to determine its practical effects more clearly on the basis of later questions that distinguish among different methods and degrees of integration.[10]

Jobs, Public Accommodations, Transportation

The trends shown in Figures 3.1 and 3.2 for attitudes toward the principle of school integration apply almost identically for attitudes

toward principles of equal treatment in employment, in public accommodations, and in seating on public transportation. This is true not
only in terms of overall change, as shown in Table 3.1A, but in terms
of trends by region and education as well. There are, to be sure,
some small variations in results due to differences in issue content. For
example, there was greater divergence between Northern and Southern
respondents in the 1940s for the Segregated Transportation and Same
Schools questions than for the Equal Jobs question; this was almost
certainly due to the existence of legal segregation of schools and transportation in the South at that time. But such variations are small
compared with the great similarity in overall trends for all three questions.

The most rapid and largest change of all was on the Equal Jobs
question, which focuses openly and squarely on discrimination, rather
than on supposedly "separate but equal" segregation. By 1972, when
the Equal Jobs question was dropped from NORC surveys, 97 percent
of the white population rejected the principle of explicit discrimination
against blacks in the area of employment. There was still considerable
verbal opposition to some forms of *integration* at that point, but only
a tiny minority of white respondents could bring themselves to defend
the blatant discrimination against black Americans that was so explicit in the Equal Jobs question—a form of discrimination that had
been freely accepted by the majority of white Americans (55 percent)
only a generation earlier in 1944. Two other questions were also
dropped in the early 1970s: Same Accommodations and Segregated
Transportation. Neither had reached the kind of ceiling shown by the
jobs question and, a little later, the school question, but both dealt
with what by then seemed settled issues of public policy in support
of desegregation. Thus survey measures were clearly headed toward
100 percent acceptance of the principle of desegregation in these public spheres where interracial contact is typically transient and impersonal.[11]

Residential Integration

A fifth important area dealt with at the level of principle is residential
integration. In this case, Table 3.1B reports two questions labeled
Residential Choice, one from NORC beginning in 1963 and one from
ISR beginning in 1964.[12] Both Residential Choice questions offer in
their wording specific rationales for the principle stated. The NORC

version is clearly more one-sided, however, since it refers only to the rights of whites to keep blacks out of neighborhoods. The ISR version, by contrast, pits white rights against the rights of blacks to live wherever they can afford to. This difference in question wording undoubtedly accounts for much of the difference between the two versions in levels of support for residential integration, and may have affected the difference in trends (slopes) as well, as discussed earlier in Chapter 2.

The ISR Residential Choice question, which forces respondents to choose between white rights to keep blacks out of their neighborhoods and black rights to live wherever they can afford to, produces overall trends and regional and educational results much like those for attitudes toward equal treatment in public accommodations, schools, employment, and transportation. The percentage choosing black rights by 1976, when the question was unfortunately dropped, is not quite as high as attained by some of these other issues, but it reaches 90 percent and might well have exceeded that level had the question been asked beyond the mid-1970s. (The other distinctive result for this item is that a volunteered "it depends" response was appreciable in the early years—one out of every seven responses given—but decreased regularly over time to one out of fourteen in 1976. But this has little effect on the substantive trends, and its inclusion in percentaging for the trend analysis would not alter the results importantly, except to show that in earlier years respondents found the forced choice more difficult than in later years.)

The more one-sided NORC Residential Choice question that asks respondents only to agree or disagree to white rights to keep blacks out presents a similar picture, with a continued rise in disagreement through the early 1990s. The slope is less sharp than the ISR question, however, and even in 1996 the most liberal response (disagree strongly) is chosen by only 65 percent of white Americans, though the opposite extreme of a strong defense of white rights to segregation (agree strongly) had declined to just 6 percent.[13] In addition to its one-sided argument, the NORC question offers a scale of four alternatives, thus allowing a substantial proportion of the population—approximately a third during the 1990s—to indicate ambivalence on the issue of residential segregation by choosing "slightly" agree or disagree. The ambivalence manifested by those in the middle categories can help explain why actual segregation of residential areas has shown only modest

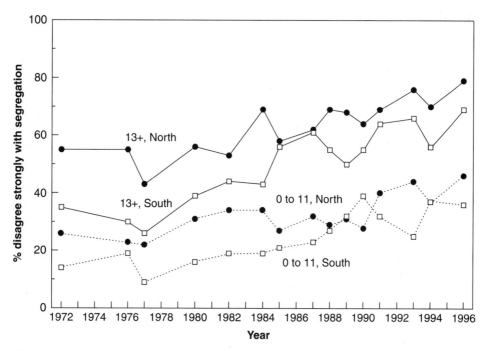

Figure 3.3. Attitudes toward residential integration (NORC).

changes over the period we are considering (Massey and Denton 1993; Farley and Frey 1994).[14]

Figure 3.3 presents the NORC Residential Choice results by region and by high and low educational categories, omitting the middle (twelve years) category because there would be too much overlap for the figure to be read easily. The results show considerable variability from year to year, especially for the less educated, where the number of cases becomes very small, but the basic trends are similar to Figure 3.2 (Same Schools): more Northerners than Southerners and more highly educated than less educated respondents reject the claim that whites have the right to keep blacks out of a neighborhood. However, education is an even stronger variable here than it was for the Same Schools question, overriding the effect of region wherever the two compete. This may be due partly to the fact that residential segregation does not have quite the same historical roots in the South as does school segregation (Massey and Denton 1993). In addition, it is less-educated whites who are likely to feel most threatened by neighborhood desegregation because it is their neighborhoods that are usually closer to densely populated black areas and more similar to them in terms of housing costs.

Black Presidential Candidate

There are also two different versions of a question about willingness to vote for a black presidential candidate of one's own party, but in this case (as Table 3.1 shows) the questions are quite close to each other in wording. Both questions ask how respondents would vote in a hypothetical situation, and in this sense they are similar to the social distance questions to be discussed below. But because voting does not call for personal involvement in an integrated living situation, we view voting intention as a way of measuring attitudes toward nondiscriminatory political choices generally. The voting questions are therefore best classified as dealing with basic principles of equal treatment, though that might change if in the coming years one of the major parties does nominate a black candidate. It should be noted that both the Gallup and the NORC questions speak of a black candidate *nominated* by one's party, and thus cannot be directly compared with actual white voting for a black candidate such as Jesse Jackson who attempts to win a party nomination. A more appropriate comparison appeared in a Gallup Poll of a national sample in November 1995 where Colin Powell had the support of 52 percent over Bill Clinton's 42 percent, with 6 percent having no opinion (*Gallup Poll Monthly*, November 1995), but of course other factors such as partisan attachment also influenced these preferences.

Between 1972 and 1996 NORC measured more abstract attitudes toward support for a qualified black presidential candidate and reached 92 percent support at the latest time point (see Table 3.1B). The overall trend in both regions is clearly positive, with the North always more positive than the South. The three educational categories are also separated much as in Figure 3.2, and each shows an overall movement upward. The Gallup version of the Black Candidate question provides a longer time series, extending from 1958 through 1997 (though with the most recent time point shifted to a telephone survey). Recent percentages are similar to those for NORC, but we can see that in the late 1950s only a little more than a third of white Americans said they would support "a generally well qualified" black candidate for president.

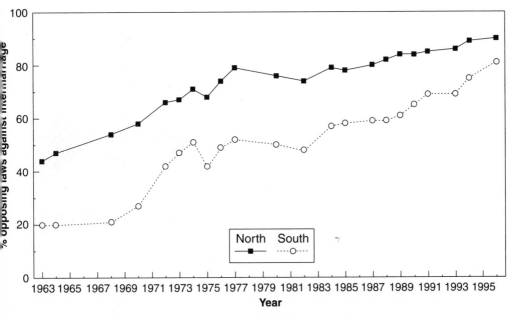

Figure 3.4. Attitudes toward laws against intermarriage.

Intermarriage

We turn to two items that concern a very different issue, but that still are phrased in a way that can be considered to deal with basic principles of integration and nondiscrimination. Both NORC and Gallup have asked questions on racial intermarriage, although the questions were formulated in quite different ways. The NORC question, the one most clearly embodying an abstract principle, asks whether there should be laws against intermarriage. In a sense this also involves an inquiry about implementation, but here the issue is whether government should *stop* intervening to prevent a form of integration, rather than whether it should intervene to bring about integration. The overall trend for this question, as shown in Figure 3.4, is positive in both regions, with a noticeable plateau effect between 1977 and 1982.

In the previous edition of this book, the most recent time point available was 1982, and we speculated that the trend upward might have halted. We also noted the lack of convergence of responses in the North and South, and a similar lack of convergence for the three main educational categories. Thus we wrote that the issue of intermarriage—

with such a long history of emotional weight for white Americans—
appeared to present a trajectory different from more public issues such
as jobs and schools.

Our speculation in 1985 turns out to have been incorrect, however,
pointing up the importance of continued data collection over time
rather than too quick a projection based on a limited set of time points.
As Figure 3.4 makes clear, the plateau of the late 1970s and early 1980s
proved only a temporary one, and the subsequent years show essentially the same upward movement as was true for other principle
questions. Moreover, there is evidence of convergence between North
and South in the figure, a convergence quite likely to increase as the
North approaches the ceiling of 100 percent.

Likewise, there are signs of convergence for this question by educational levels (not shown), slight at present but almost certain to increase: the high-education groups are moving toward the 100 percent
ceiling, while those with lower education continue to move upwards
also. (In 1996, of respondents in the North with at least some college
education, 96 percent opposed laws against intermarriage, and in the
South the parallel figure reached 92 percent.) Moreover, as with the
Same Schools question (Figure 3.2), highly educated Southerners have
moved from a position lower than all Northern educational groups to
a position second only to college-educated Northerners—a dramatic
indicator of change in what was once considered the most sensitive of
all interracial spheres, especially for Southern whites.

Thus our additional ten years of data suggest that the Laws against
Intermarriage question is likely to have the same fate as the principle
questions on schools, accommodations, and transportation. That is,
these latter questions are no longer included in national surveys because
of the virtual unanimity in support of the equal treatment principle. It
is important to recall that the Laws against Intermarriage question
yielded only 38 percent liberal answers in 1963, when it was first asked.
This level is not so very different from the 32 percent liberal answers
to the Same Schools question when it was first asked two decades
earlier in 1942. Figure 3.5 compares the trends for the Same Schools
and Laws against Intermarriage questions with their start dates fixed
at the same position on the left; the actual dates of each are shown
below the horizontal axis, for example, 1942 for the start of the Same
Schools question, and 1963 for the start of the Laws against Intermarriage question. Looked at in this way, despite some difficult-to-interpret

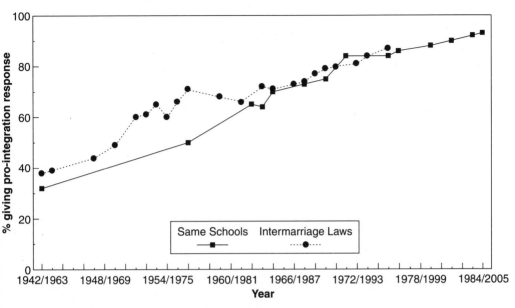

Figure 3.5. Comparison of trends for Same Schools and Laws against Intermarriage.

differences in the two trends, the questions show similar long-term change, and indeed at their most recent equivalent point (1975/1996), they reveal very similar proportions of liberal answers. Data for the Same Schools question are available for nearly four and a half decades—from 1942 until 1985, when the question was dropped from the General Social Survey. Because it was first asked some twenty years later (in 1963), the Laws against Intermarriage question will need to be repeated until the year 2005 to cover an equally long period. By, or perhaps even before that point, we can expect the Laws against Intermarriage question to be dropped, just as the Same Schools question was, as a result of near unanimity of responses in the liberal direction. In other words, a question we believed in 1985 to be somehow different from the other principle questions is really not different at all in its trajectory.

Gallup's question on intermarriage asks not about laws against intermarriage but about approval of intermarriage. This seems a more pertinent inquiry at present, but it is also somewhat less a matter of general principle and more a matter of personal preference. As might be expected, a much lower proportion of the population approves of

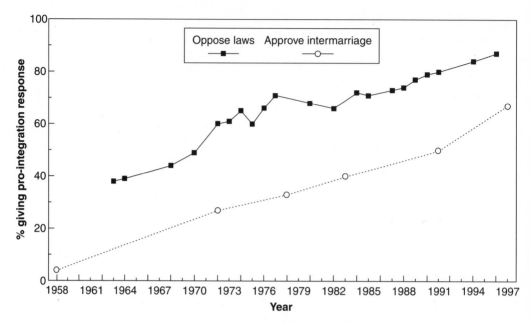

Figure 3.6. Comparison of Laws against Intermarriage and Approval of Intermarriage.

intermarriage than opposes laws banning intermarriage (see Figure 3.6). Yet the Gallup data suggest a pattern much like that for the NORC Laws against Intermarriage question: the slopes are similar for the two questions, but because the starting point is so much lower for the Gallup Intermarriage question, hypothetical extrapolation toward 100 percent can be expected to occur over a longer time than has been true for the Laws against Intermarriage and other principle questions already discussed. Apart from this difference, the two items behave similarly in terms of their relations to region and education, with education the more powerful predictor. It is useful to note here that actual new black-white intermarriage figures, though much lower, also show a sharp increase over time (see Figure 7.1 in our concluding chapter).[15]

General Segregation/Integration

The final question in Table 3.1B, labeled General Segregation, appears to embody the principle of desegregation at the most general level, and thus might be expected to show even more clearly the main trends we have found for all other principle items: continuous positive change over the entire time period, a regional difference but with convergence toward a ceiling, and a clear positive association with educational level.

In fact, however, the results ran counter to these expectations in important ways during the fifteen years that the question was asked. True enough: few people even in the early 1960s claimed to favor segregation in general, and their number decreased regularly between 1964 and 1978; there was also a clear but decreasing North-South difference in this attitude; and at each time point general segregationist sentiments declined as education increased. But the opposite findings do not hold with regard to the *desegregation* response. Beginning about 1970 this response showed a tradeoff with the vague middle response "something in between," producing a curvilinear effect for this alternative. Moreover, this effect occurred almost entirely in the North and was especially pronounced among the college-educated. Figure 3.7 presents the three responses separately for college-educated Northern respondents, and the trade-off and curvilinearity are striking. (No point in this figure is based on fewer than 120 cases, and most are based on more than 350 cases.)

One possible interpretation of these trends, so different from all others in Table 3.1, is that the provision of an ambiguous middle

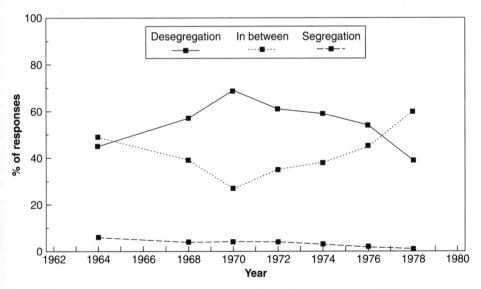

Figure 3.7. Attitudes toward segregation as a principle, among Northern, college-educated whites.

response ("something in between") allows whites an acceptable way of expressing their anxieties and reservations about integration, and that these anxieties and reservations suddenly took on new life around 1970 and increasingly thereafter. If so, responses to the General Segregation question could be seen as a harbinger of things to come, conceivably continuing through the present day. The fact that it is college-educated Northerners who showed the reversal most clearly would be all the more meaningful, since they are both the best-informed and normally the most liberal part of the population on questions dealing with principles of integration.

If this interpretation were correct, the General Segregation question would be of major importance. However, we found no other evidence of such a curvilinear trend for principle questions, or indeed for any question for which trend data are available. Although no other principle question provides a middle alternative quite like the one in the General Segregation item, other questions do code ambivalent volunteered responses (such as "depends") or provide middle responses (as in the NORC Residential Choice question), yet none shows a pattern of change quite like that in Figure 3.7. (But see also note 18 in this chapter.) The crucial issue here is *not* whether provision of a middle alternative allows more expression of ambivalence than a dichotomous forced-choice question, for that is certainly the case, but rather whether this changes the basic shape of the time trend.

For the moment we leave open the issue of whether the General Segregation question points to an important feature of change not captured by other items, or whether it indicates a trend of much less significance. In the following section we will present experimental data involving context effects created by another question that points to a narrower interpretation of the curvilinear trend, though one that is still of importance. The delay is required because the related question deals not with principles but with the implementation of principles—the issue we turn to after summarizing our results thus far.

Conclusions about Principles of Equal Treatment

Almost all of the principle questions show substantial positive trends over time. If only this set of questions were available to trace white racial attitudes over the past five decades, it would be reasonable to conclude that there has been a remarkably large, wide-ranging, and generally consistent movement toward white acceptance of the principles of equal treatment and integration in most important areas of American life. Moreover, clear-cut educational differences support the assertion that more-educated respondents are more liberal in their responses, and consistent regional differences indicate a historic North-South difference that disappears only when a ceiling of 100 percent is approached.

The one disturbing note is a peculiar reversal on a single item that asks about general attitudes toward integration, but in the absence of corroboration from other questions, this singular result remains a puzzle—and one that we will shortly show is best considered an accident of context rather than a sign of broader reversals to come. Of more general importance for the principle area, a question on intermarriage that had seemed at the time of the first edition of this book to have reached a plateau resumed movement in a liberal direction over the past decade. Thus, for the major public areas of life, overall trends on these principle questions over the half century since the early 1940s appear to justify the optimistic belief of Hyman and Sheatsley (1964) that "in the minds and hearts of the majority of Americans the principle of integration seems already to have won" (p. 23). But when we turn to questions on *other* kinds of racial issues, the picture changes markedly. Our primary challenge in the end will be to make sense of results that seem on the surface to contradict one another.

Implementation of Equal Treatment

Questions about implementation deal with support or opposition to actions that the government—usually the federal but in one case local government—should take to end discrimination and coerced segregation. The questions are important because one of the two main ways that such institutional change has occurred in the United States is through government enforcement, the other being collective action by African Americans themselves, as in the lunchcounter sit-ins of the early 1960s and similar actions before and after (McAdam 1982; Morris 1984). Thus white willingness to support government enforcement of equal treatment has often been regarded as the touchstone in gauging genuine support for civil rights, as distinct from merely verbal approval of high-sounding principles.

We should emphasize that the pure form of implementation question has to do *only* with requiring equal treatment regardless of race, not with any kind of preference toward blacks (as considered in a later section under affirmative action), though certain items we have classified here (for example, Federal Job Intervention) may be interpreted otherwise by some respondents. Some writers would also argue that busing is a form of affirmative action, and as we note later, the wording of the question about school implementation is somewhat ambiguous. Thus the term "implementation" in the strict sense of government enforcement of color-blind behavior encompasses only two of the six questions in this section—Accommodations Intervention and Open Housing—and even those have special characteristics that limit generalization somewhat.[16]

It is also important to bear in mind that even though questions about implementation focus on actions and are sometimes referred to as if they point directly to "behavior," this is only an analogy. Implementation responses in surveys are no less verbal than responses about general principles—symbolic answers to symbolic questions, as LaPiere (1934) would have put it. These considerations cut both ways in terms of the validity of the responses. On the one hand, answers to implementation questions certainly do not involve the kind of commitment necessary for behavior outside the interview setting. On the other hand, in an interview it would be relatively easy for respondents to try to *appear* consistent in all their answers by giving liberal responses to questions on *both* principles and implementation. If in fact they do not do this, but appear inconsistent—showing themselves to be liberal on principle questions but illiberal on implementation questions—we might well see this not as hypocrisy but as a distinction that is meaningful in their own minds.

The questions we classify as dealing with implementation of equal treatment are shown in Table 3.2, with results for the white population as a whole. For comparison purposes, it would be useful if there were a number of parallel principle and implementation questions in terms of both content and dates. This is not always the case, but it does occur enough to provide insight into the level of white support for concrete steps that might be taken to put principles of equal treatment into practice.

School Desegregation

We saw earlier that in 1985, when NORC stopped asking the Same Schools question on the principle of school integration, 93 percent of

Table 3.2 Implementation questions (white respondents)

Question	Year of survey													
	62	64	66	68	69	70	71	72	73	74	75	76	77	78
Federal School Intervention (ISR)														
% Govt. see to it	—	42	48	36	—	47	—	35	—	31	—	21	—	27
Govt. stay out	—	47	42	53	—	41	—	54	—	52	—	49	—	54
No interest	—	11	11	11	—	12	—	12	—	17	—	30	—	20
Busing (ISR)														
% Bus (1–3)	—	—	—	—	—	—	—	5	—	5	—	5	—	—
Neutral (4)	—	—	—	—	—	—	—	4	—	4	—	5	—	—
In n'hood (5–7)	—	—	—	—	—	—	—	85	—	83	—	81	—	—
Not thought	—	—	—	—	—	—	—	6	—	8	—	9	—	—
Busing (NORC)														
% Favor	—	—	—	—	—	—	—	13	—	15	14	12	12	17
Oppose	—	—	—	—	—	—	—	87	—	85	87	88	88	83
Accommodations Intervention (ISR)														
% Govt. see to it	—	44	—	51	—	60	—	60	—	65	—	—	—	—
Govt. stay out	—	45	—	38	—	28	—	29	—	21	—	—	—	—
No interest	—	11	—	11	—	12	—	11	—	14	—	—	—	—
Open Housing (NORC)														
% Owner cannot refuse	—	—	—	—	—	—	—	—	—	34	—	34	35	—	37
Owner can decide	—	—	—	—	—	—	—	—	—	67	—	66	65	—	63
Federal Job Intervention (ISR)														
% Govt. see to it	—	38	—	37	—	—	—	40	—	36	—	—	—	—
Govt. stay out	—	50	—	51	—	—	—	42	—	40	—	—	—	—
No interest	—	13	—	12	—	—	—	18	—	24	—	—	—	—

Question wordings and variants

Federal School Intervention (ISR): "Some people say that the government in Washington should see to it that white and black (1972: Negro) children (1964–1978: are allowed to go) go to the same schools. Others claim that this is not the government's business. Have you been concerned (1986, 1990: interested) enough about (in) this question to favor one side over the other? [If yes] Do you think the government in Washington should see to it that white and black children go to the same schools, or stay out of this area, as it is not its business?" Sample sizes fewer than 1,000 occurred in 1970, 1986, and 1990, and ranged from 570 to 807. Data for 1974 are from an ISR Omnibus Survey; all other years are from the NES.

    1. Government should see to it
    2. Government should stay out
    3. No interest

Note: Important variations in the way the Federal School Intervention question was asked between 1964 and the present are reported on p. 128. (Also, an earlier version of the question was used in 1962, but wording changes were too great for inclusion in trend analysis. The question read: "The government in Washington should see to it that white and colored children are allowed to go to the same schools. Do you have an opinion on this or not? [If yes] Do you agree that the government *should* do this or do you think the government

Table 3.2 (continued)

								Year of survey									
79	80	81	82	83	84	85	86	87	88	89	90	91	92	93	94	95	96
—	—	—	—	—	—	—	26	—	—	—	28	—	29	—	25	—	—
—	—	—	—	—	—	—	42	—	—	—	35	—	39	—	41	—	—
—	—	—	—	—	—	—	32	—	—	—	37	—	32	—	34	—	—
—	5	—	—	—	6	—	—	—	—	—	—	—	—	—	—	—	—
—	5	—	—	—	7	—	—	—	—	—	—	—	—	—	—	—	—
—	86	—	—	—	82	—	—	—	—	—	—	—	—	—	—	—	—
—	5	—	—	—	6	—	—	—	—	—	—	—	—	—	—	—	—
—	—	—	15	21	—	18	25	—	28	25	30	32	—	26	28	—	33
—	—	—	85	79	—	82	75	—	72	75	70	68	—	74	72	—	67
—	—	—	—	—	—	—	—	—	—	—	—	—	—	—	—	56[r]	—
—	—	—	—	—	—	—	—	—	—	—	—	—	—	—	—	21[r]	—
—	—	—	—	—	—	—	—	—	—	—	—	—	—	—	—	23[r]	—
—	40	—	—	46	50	—	48	50	54	57	54	60	—	65	62	—	67
—	60	—	—	54	50	—	52	50	46	43	47	40	—	35	38	—	33
—	—	—	—	—	—	—	33	—	30	—	—	—	34	—	—	—	28
—	—	—	—	—	—	—	34	—	30	—	—	—	34	—	—	—	36
—	—	—	—	—	—	—	33	—	40	—	—	—	32	—	—	—	36

Question wordings and variants

should not do it?" Of the white respondents, 49 percent supported government action, 30 percent opposed it, and 15 percent said they had no opinion. Versions involving even more substantial changes in wording were asked in 1956, 1958, and 1960.)

Busing (ISR): "There is much discussion about the best way to deal with racial problems. Some people think achieving racial integration of schools is so important that it justifies busing children to schools out of their own neighborhoods. Others think letting children go to their neighborhood schools is so important that they oppose busing. Where would you place yourself on this scale, or haven't you thought much about this?" Sample size fewer than 1,000 cases occurred in 1984 (*n* = 796). (Show card with 7-point scale)

1. Bus to achieve integration
2.
3.
4.
5.
6.
7. Keep children in neighborhood schools
0. Not thought about this

Table 3.2 (continued)

Question wordings and variants

Busing (NORC): "In general, do you favor or oppose the busing of (Negro/black/African American) and white school children from one school district to another?" Sample sizes fewer than 1,000 cases occurred in 1988, 1989, 1991, 1993, and 1996, and ranged from 727 to 810.
  1. Favor
  2. Oppose

Accommodations Intervention (ISR): "As you may know, Congress passed a bill that says that black people should have the right to go to any hotel or restaurant they can afford, just like anybody else. Some people feel that this is something the government in Washington should support. Others feel that the government should stay out of this matter. Have you been interested enough in this to favor one side over another? [If yes] Should the government support the right of black people to go to any hotel or restaurant they can afford, or should it stay out of this matter?" Sample sizes fewer than 1,000 cases occurred in 1970 ($n = 615$) and 1995 ($n = 412$). For 1964–1972, data are from the NES; 1974 data are from an ISR Omnibus Survey. In 1995, the data come from an add-on to the October and November Survey of Consumer Attitudes conducted by the Survey Research Center at ISR.
  1. Government should see to it
  2. Government should stay out
  3. No interest
  (**Variant:** in 1964 replaced "anybody else" with "white people.")

Open Housing (NORC): "Suppose there is a community-wide vote on the general housing issue. There are two possible laws to vote on. One law says that a homeowner can decide for himself who to sell his house to, even if he prefers not to sell to (Negroes/blacks/African Americans). The second law says that a homeowner cannot refuse to sell to someone because of their race or color. Which law would you vote for?" Sample sizes fewer than 1,000 cases occurred in 1988, 1989, 1991, 1993, and 1996, and ranged from 755 to 819.
  1. Homeowner can decide
  2. Homeowner cannot refuse to sell

Federal Job Intervention (ISR): "Some people feel that if black people are not getting fair treatment in jobs, the government in Washington ought to see to it that they do. Others feel that this is not the federal government's business. Have you had enough interest in this question to favor one side over the other? [If yes] How do you feel? Should the government in Washington see to it that black people get fair treatment in jobs or (1964, 1968, 1972: should the government in Washington leave these matters to the states and local communities) is this not the federal government's business?" Sample sizes fewer than 1,000 cases occurred in 1986 ($n = 842$). Data from 1974 are from an ISR Omnibus Survey; all other years are from the NES.
  1. Government should see to it
  2. Government should stay out
  3. No interest

t. Data collected through telephone survey rather than personal interview.

white Americans claimed to believe that "white students and black students should go to the same schools . . . [not] to separate schools." Since 1964, ISR's National Election Study has included an implementation question asking whether "the government in Washington should see to it that white and black children are allowed to go to the same schools" or whether "this is not the government's business" (see Table 3.2 for the wording, plus important variations in wording that we will

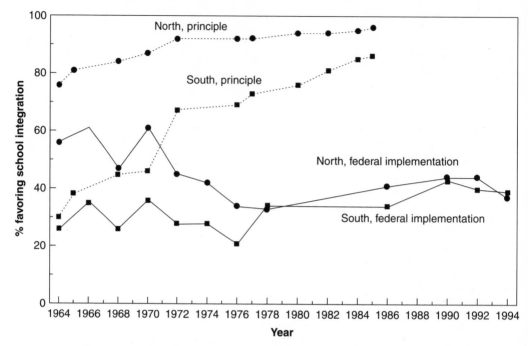

Figure 3.8. Attitudes toward principle of school integration and toward federal implementation of school integration.

note shortly). Thus the content of the two questions is close, although the ISR implementation question offers an explicit alternative whereby the respondent can avoid a substantive choice by indicating that he or she has "no interest" in the issue. Furthermore, both questions were being posed fairly regularly to the American public over two decades between 1964 and 1985–1986, and therefore we compare trends for this period for the two questions in Figure 3.8, separately by region.

The contrast in results for the principle and implementation school questions in Figure 3.8 is both striking and complex.[17] During the time period shown, attitudes favoring the principle of school integration rose by 30 percent (1963–1986), whereas support for federal implementation of school integration *dropped* by 9 percent (1964–1986), with virtually the whole decline occurring in the North.[18]

It is sometimes argued that lack of support for implementation is due to philosophic objections to actions by the federal government, not to specific race-related issues (see Kuklinski and Parent 1981; Margolis and Haque 1981). This is an argument that we will explore more directly at later points, and in the present instance of school integration it could conceivably explain the overall gap between principle and implementation responses in the late 1960s. But the sharp drop in Northern support for federal intervention after 1970 seems much more likely to have been due to particular events that occurred at that point in time than to a more general attitude like antipathy toward the federal government. Moreover, in 1964 support for federal school intervention was greater among the more educated, but differences by education tended to disappear after 1970. By 1994 there is a trend for the more educated to be *less* supportive of federal implementation in this area, as shown below:

	1964			1994		
	0 to 11	12	13 and up	0 to 11	12	13 and up
Government see to it	40%	51%	55%	50%	32%	38%
Government stay out	60	49	46%	50	68%	62%
Total	100	100	100	100	100%	100
N	(437)	(378)	(286)	(113)	(276)	(495)

This reversal in the results for education also suggests something more specific than a generalized antigovernment or antifederal attitude.[19]

The pattern of results in Figure 3.8 seems to fit the following interpretation. Support for federal desegregation efforts was high in the early 1960s, especially among more educated Northern whites, because attention was focused on ending *de jure* segregation in the South. The media presented the federal effort as essential in the face of crude and often violent attempts by Southern whites to circumvent decisions of the Supreme Court that required an end to enforced segregation of schooling (see Chapter 1 for an overview of these events). But Northern support began to erode at the beginning of the 1970s, when attention shifted to altering *de facto* segregation in the North, especially but not only through court-ordered busing.[20] Figure 3.8 shows a precipitous drop at about that point in the North, with only a slight recovery in support in more recent years.[21] In the South, by contrast, the modest but stable or even slightly rising support for federal intervention probably indicates limited acceptance, however reluctant, of the federal role in ending legalized school segregation. Paradoxically, the two regions

began to converge by the end of the 1970s, but they did so in the form
of a low level of support for the implementation of school desegregation, far from the kind of convergence due to ceiling effects that occurs
for the Same Schools principle question.[22]

Unfortunately, a careful examination of the wording of the Federal
School Intervention question reveals peculiarities that leave this comparison less certain than we would like. The phrase white and black
children "are allowed to" go to the same schools is consistent with a
color-blind enforcement of the 1954 Supreme Court decision. However,
once respondents said that they did have an opinion on the issue, the
follow-up probe to obtain that opinion omitted "are allowed to," thus
transforming the question into something closer to affirmative action
(the government should see to it that white and black children go to
the same schools). It is impossible to know how much respondents
remembered the complete phrasing. Moreover, for no obvious reason
"are allowed to" was dropped entirely from both parts of the item from
1986 on, thus definitely changing it into a question about affirmative
action.[23] In sum, we believe that our previous conclusions are correct
about the downturn in Figure 3.8 of the Federal School Intervention
item, but problems of question wording with this ISR item leave some
uncertainty.

Busing

As just noted, the loss of support for federal intervention occurred at
about the same time that busing became a salient issue. Attitudes
toward busing are shown in Table 3.2 for both an NORC question and
an ISR question. What is most evident is the overwhelming opposition
to busing by white respondents during the 1970s and early 1980s. The
ISR question, which poses the hotly debated issues more sharply, shows
even less support than the slightly more ambiguous NORC question.
Only the NORC question has been asked in recent years, and it indicates a definite increase in support for busing over the past decade or
so, though still a great deal of opposition.[24] The increase is consistent
with the leveling off or slightly positive direction of change with regard
to school implementation in recent years.

We are not certain of the explanation for the recent increase in
support for busing, but our analysis of cohort differences in Chapter
4 indicates that the youngest cohort is noticeably less negative about

busing than the rest of the sample. The same is true with regard to federal implementation of school integration generally, though to a lesser degree. It is possible that this cohort difference results simply from the decreased salience of the busing issue itself in recent years. But it is also possible that there is a genuine increase on the part of the youngest cohort in acceptance of this method of implementing school integration. At the same time, it is important to keep in mind that a clear majority of whites oppose busing in all years, so that the increase in support leaves it still a quite unpopular method of promoting integration.[25]

Effects of School Implementation on the
General Segregation Item

The nearly unanimous opposition of whites to busing during the 1970s may well have had an impact that extended beyond questions on the implementation of school integration. Recall the puzzling reversal in responses to the very general question dealing with the broad principle of desegregation, segregation, or "something in between" (Figure 3.7). That reversal occurred in 1970, exactly when the decline in support for federal implementation of school desegregation started, as shown in Figure 3.8. This suggests that the two trends may be linked in some way. Furthermore, there is evidence from other studies that very general items such as the General Segregation question are especially subject to context effects, presumably because their meaning is vague and therefore tends to be interpreted in terms of the more specific questions that precede them (Schuman and Presser 1981). And, in fact, in all of the ISR surveys in which the General Segregation question appeared, it was asked soon after the School Intervention item. Thus we hypothesize that the downturn after 1970 in apparent support for the general principle of desegregation was at least partly due to the change in attitudes toward the specific issue of federal intervention to promote school integration, which in turn occurred as the busing issue became prominent.

This hypothesis cannot be tested directly, but it is possible to determine whether responses to the General Segregation question can be affected by its placement after the Federal School Intervention question. We carried out such a split-sample experiment in January 1983: half of a national telephone sample was asked the General Segregation question after the Federal School Intervention item; the other half was asked the General Segregation question after the Equal Jobs principle item, which was chosen because it elicits almost 100 percent agreement for the pro-integration response (see Table 3.1). The findings from this experiment lend clear support to our hypothesis:

Response to General Segregation item	When preceded by Equal Jobs item	When preceded by School Intervention item
Desegregation	61.4%	38.9%
Something in between	36.1	57.1
Segregation	2.5	4.0
Total	100	100
N	(158)	(149)

There is a 23 percent difference in the choice of the "desegregation" response between the two contexts, with most of the shift involving the "something in between" response ($x^2 = 15.6$, d.f. = 2, $p < .001$). This finding suggests that the pattern presented in Figure 3.7 was at least partly an artifact resulting from a combination of the vagueness of the General Segregation question, its regular placement after the Federal School Intervention question in the ISR surveys, and the fact that the Federal School Intervention item itself showed an important decline during the same period. In sum, what appeared to be a decrease in support for the broad principle of desegregation—a decrease inconsistent with trends on other principle items—was probably in good part a reflection of a more specific decrease in support for the implementation of school desegregation through busing or other federal action. It would have been useful if the General Segregation question had been asked in recent years in order to study its movement further, but otherwise such general questions have limited value precisely because of this problem: they lend themselves to varied and changing meanings.[26]

Public Accommodations

When the civil rights movement rose to prominence in the 1950s, one of the first issues that captured national attention was that of equal access to restaurants, hotels, and similar public settings. As described in Chapter 1, in the years following black protests such as the lunch-counter sit-ins, Congress passed important legislation in support of equal treatment in public accommodations. Indeed, this is probably the one sphere in addition to voting rights where very substantial movement toward ending discrimination has taken place in American life, even though there continue to be instances, subtle and not so subtle, in which unequal treatment still occurs.

By 1970, as shown previously in Table 3.1, 88 percent of the white American public responded that in principle blacks "should have the right to use the same parks, restaurants, and hotels as white people." During approximately the same period, ISR's National Election Study posed a very similar public accommodations issue in terms of federal implementation:

> As you may know, Congress passed a bill that says that black people should have the right to go to any hotel or restaurant they can afford, just like anybody else. Some people feel that this is something the government in Washington should support. Others feel that the government should stay out of the matter. Have you been interested enough in this to favor one side over another? [If Yes] Should the government support the right of black people to go to any hotel or restaurant they can afford, or should it stay out of the matter?

Thus the two questions focus on essentially the same issue, with the main difference being that the principle question is about "rights" only and the implementation question is about the role of the federal government in supporting these same rights.

The overall trends for the two questions, one phrased in terms of pure principle and one in terms of federal implementation of that principle, are presented in Tables 3.1 and 3.2, and are compared directly by region in Figure 3.9. Three conclusions can be drawn from the comparison. First, support for the principle of equal treatment was appreciably greater throughout this period than was support for its implementation by the federal government. The overall difference was about 24 percent at the beginning of the period and 21 percent in 1970, the last good point for comparison. In the absence of other evidence, this gap can be interpreted as the reflection of a negative attitude toward federal intervention generally, though it can also be argued that refusal to endorse the enforcement of principle reveals shallow support for the principle itself (see Jackman 1978). Whichever interpretation is

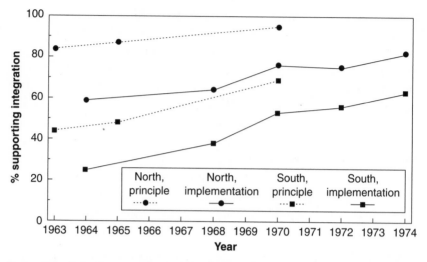

Figure 3.9. Attitudes toward principle of integration of public accommodations and toward implementation of the principle.

preferred, it is useful to note that the gap here is similar in size to differences *among* principle items that deal with different issues. For example, in Table 3.1 consider the 20 percent difference between the Equal Jobs question and the Same Schools question in 1963. Thus there may not be anything more fundamental or more insurmountable about the gap in Figure 3.9, even though in the present case it is based on a distinction between principles and implementation instead of a distinction between two different principles.

Second, both Accommodation items show much the same trend upward over time. Thus there was reason to believe that the implementation question would have continued to move toward 100 percent during the later years of the 1970s and perhaps early 1980s, though unfortunately this was not tested because the item was dropped from ISR's National Election Study after 1974. More generally, the 21 percent increase over the ten-year period in support for federal intervention to guarantee blacks access to public accommodations (Table 3.2) was of the same order of magnitude as the increase for comparable lengths of time in support shown for particular principles (Table 3.1). Again, the data do not support the uniqueness of implementation with regard to this question. From the vantage point of the mid-1970s it may well have seemed that acceptance of government implementation in this area of public life was moving toward the 100 percent ceiling.

Indeed, this may have been the reason the question was dropped after 1974, though we have no direct information on the decision and it was clearly a mistake.

Third, attitudes toward implementation in the sphere of public accommodations show clear regional and educational differences: support for implementation is more positive in the North and more positive as education increases. The relation to education does not vary systematically over the limited ten-year period when the question was asked by ISR, but the gap in implementation by region decreases reliably over the five surveys (from a 34 percent difference in 1964 to an 18 percent difference in 1974). Moreover, support for the implementation of the principle is actually higher in the North during the 1960s than is support for just the principle in the South, as can be seen in Figure 3.9.

In sum, although the change in questioning from an emphasis on principle to an emphasis on government implementation of the principle undoubtedly lowers support at any one point in time, it did not seem to lead to a radically new or different picture in other respects. Opposition to federal intervention *per se* does not, as some have argued, provide a wholly adequate explanation for opposition to implementation of the principles of nondiscrimination.[27]

To the preceding conclusions, however, we must add very recent findings from a set of questions that we included in an ISR telephone survey carried out in October-November of 1995. A replication of the Accommodations Intervention question actually produced somewhat *lower* support for government action (56 percent) than did the last regular face-to-face survey administration of the question in 1974 (65 percent). The main change over the twenty-one-year period is an increase in "no interest" responses, reminiscent of a similar pattern on the Federal School item (see note 18 above). If this response is excluded, the distribution of support and opposition is identical in the 1974 and 1995 surveys. Both the increase in "no interest" responses and the leveling off of support are disturbing findings that are in definite need of further research, especially since there is little evidence that behavior (that is, integration of public accommodations) has reversed directions.

This result must be viewed with caution because the mode of survey administration changed from face-to-face to telephone, though there is no obvious reason why this would have lowered support for accommodations intervention. Furthermore, the twenty-one year gap between

1974, when ISR last administered the question, and our replication in 1995 presents exactly the problem illustrated in Chapter 2 (Figure 2.1) about the difficulty of knowing how to connect two time points when they are separated by a long span of years. It is possible that the height of support for government intervention in the area of public accommodations was reached in the mid-1970s and never exceeded that level thereafter. It is equally possible that support continued to rise after 1974 but then dropped again as civil rights faded from the national agenda and opposition to federal intervention more generally increased in the 1980s. In any case, support for government implementation of equal treatment in public accommodations is today still far below 100 percent, though its level of support is considerably greater than the question on implementation of school integration discussed previously.

Open Housing Laws

The implementation question on open housing is distinctive because it refers not to enforcement by the federal government but rather to a personal vote on a local referendum about whether the respondent's community should have a law requiring nondiscrimination in the sale of housing. As Table 3.2 shows, support for such a law has climbed steadily since 1973, when the question was first asked, and has now reached 67 percent—the highest level of support for any implementation item.

Furthermore, differences by region and educational levels are crystal clear throughout the entire time span: Northerners and more educated persons support open housing laws more than do Southerners and the less educated, with the education relation essentially monotonic in all years. The picture is much like that for the principle of school integration in Figure 3.1, except that without ceiling constraints there are not yet signs of convergence by region or education.

It is also useful to compare the Open Housing implementation question with the earlier Residential Choice questions that dealt only with the principle of residential nondiscrimination. Recall that Residential Choice questions appeared in both ISR and NORC surveys, with the ISR question offering an argument on each side of the issue and the NORC question more one-sided in the sense of offering a justification only for the discriminatory side of the issue. Furthermore, the NORC

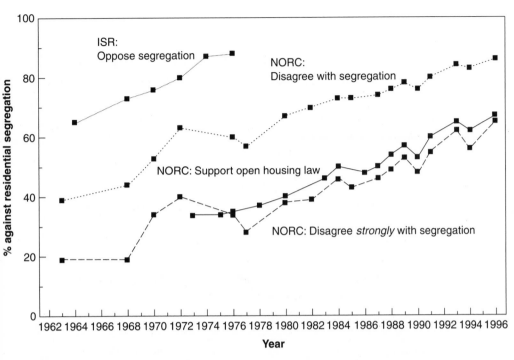

Figure 3.10. Residential segregation: comparison of ISR principle question, two scorings of NORC principle question, and NORC Open Housing implementation question.

version of the question provided a four-point scale that allowed respondents to distinguish a strong position from a not-so-strong position. All of these possibilities are brought together in Figure 3.10, in order to compare further the principle-implementation distinction with the distinction in terms of degree of support for the principle per se.

This rather complex but quite informative figure shows attitudes toward residential integration from four standpoints:

1. Opposition to residential segregation on the dichotomous ISR principle question (from Table 3.1);

2. Combined strong and not strong opposition to residential segregation on the scale offered by the NORC principle question (from Table 3.1);

3. *Strong* opposition to residential segregation considered separately on the scale offered by the NORC principle question (from Table 3.1);

> 4. Support for government implementation of an open housing law (from Table 3.2).

Two important conclusions can be drawn from the comparisons possible in Figure 3.10. First, no matter how the questions were asked, a trend toward acceptance of residential integration is clear in terms of support for *both* principle and implementation. Second, if we assume that support for open housing laws is a touchstone of conviction on this issue, then the implication of Figure 3.10 is also clear: the level and trend in support for open housing laws over time is essentially the same as the level and trend shown for those people who *strongly* reject the NORC statement of principle that seems to justify continued residential segregation. This reinforces the idea raised earlier that the distinction between principle and implementation can be seen as reflecting points along a larger continuum, one that *also* reflects intensity of commitment to integration, rather than as defining a unique and insurmountable qualitative difference between two different types of questions (principle vs. implementation). This is a notable conclusion, and if it is supported in future research, the debate over "principle" versus "implementation of principle" will be clarified considerably.

Jobs

The implementation question available for the area of employment is unfortunately so general in wording that its meaning may never have been entirely what was intended and, more important, could easily have changed since the question was first asked in 1964:

> Some people feel that if black people are not getting fair treatment in jobs, the government in Washington ought to see that they do. Others feel that this is not the federal government's business. Have you had enough interest in this question to favor one side over the other? [If yes] How do you feel? Should the government in Washington see to it that black people get fair treatment in jobs or leave these matters to the states and local communities?

If "fair treatment" is taken to mean *equal treatment* without regard to race, then the question provides a close parallel to the principle question we labeled Equal Jobs. But especially in recent years, "fair treatment" might be interpreted by some to mean a degree of preferential employment of blacks. Indeed, the variation in responses to this item in different experimental orders that was reported earlier (Chapter 2, note 17) may well be due to the generality of the phrase "fair treatment in jobs" and its susceptibility to different interpretations in different contexts.

Therefore, we will not attempt a detailed comparison of the Equal Jobs principle question and the parallel question on Federal Job Intervention, but simply note that the gap between them was quite large even in the 1960s, when their meanings were more likely to be the same. Likewise, the Equal Jobs principle question showed a sharp rise over time in support for equal treatment, whereas the implementation question shows only a small increase of 7 percent over twenty-eight years, and even that increase depends on repercentaging to omit the "no interest" alternative. However, any attempt to interpret these differences is compromised by the vague wording of the implementation question, a defect that makes the item of less value today.[28]

Conclusions about Implementation of Equal Treatment

The questions about government implementation of principles of equal treatment and integration produce results more complex than those produced by the questions about the principles themselves. First, fewer people endorse the implementation of a principle than endorse the principle itself in every area we were able to investigate. Since there are always possible objections, whether sincere or not, to a particular type of government implementation, it is not surprising that levels of support go down whenever concrete action is proposed. This probably happens not just with racial policies but in almost every instance where general principles must be translated into specific actions. (See also Burstein's [1985:56–60] discussion of the principle-implementation gap with regard specifically to equal employment opportunity.)

More important for the study of attitude change is whether implementation items move in a more liberal direction, as was true for almost all items about principles. Here the evidence is mixed: for the two questions—Public Accommodations and Open Housing—that seem the purest measures of color-blind implementation, support follows much the same upward trajectory that we found for questions on principles, except that there is unexpected evidence of retrenchment on the Accommodations question in 1995. For a question about school

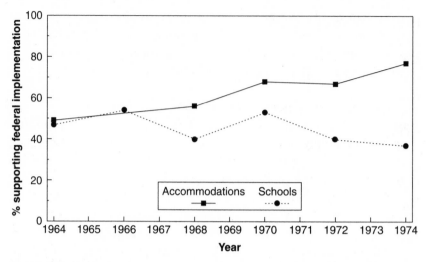

Figure 3.11. Federal implementation of school desegregation versus federal implementation of accommodations intervention.

integration, the long-term trend is actually down, and we think this reflected a genuine decrease in support for school integration as national attention shifted from South to North. For a question on employment the results are ambiguous, though this may be because the question is worded in so general a way as to have changed in meaning over time.

The contrast in trends on implementation items is brought out well in Figure 3.11, where we compare implementation of accommodations and implementation of school integration (with "no interest" responses omitted) over essentially the same time span. For the period in which both questions were asked, the two start with the same level of support for federal action, but then support continues to rise for public accommodations while it drops for school integration. This sharp divergence provides persuasive evidence that federal implementation in and of itself cannot be the sole deciding factor. Other differences between the two questions and the two areas of life must be crucial.

We have also shown that though questions about implementation are more difficult for white respondents to answer in a liberal direction than are questions about general principles, so are questions about the *principle* of racial intermarriage more difficult than questions about the *principle* of equal treatment in hotels and restaurants. We seem then to be dealing with a broad continuum of "difficulty" rather than with an absolute and categorical distinction between two entirely different realms of response. It is useful to recognize the importance of the distinction between principle and implementation, but it should not be reified into the single overarching source of division in racial attitudes. The strength with which an attitude is held may be the most important factor to consider.

We have been impressed by the continued increase through 1996 of support for an open housing law—clearly a strong form of implementation. We also noted that these responses show the same relations to region and education as do most questions dealing with principles of equal treatment. There are suggestive qualitative data that the statement of principle ("cannot refuse to sell to someone because of their race or color") makes the antidiscrimination alternative very appealing, and that what was intended as an excuse for discrimination ("a homeowner can decide for himself") is interpreted as "prejudice" and therefore unacceptable to many white respondents (Krysan 1995). Thus the Open Housing question combines the equal treatment (color-blind) principle with a proposed policy in a way that gives the principle maximum leverage. Furthermore, the same research by Krysan (1995), which is summarized in Chapter 2 (see Table 2.6), showed responses on the Open Housing question to be essentially the same in an interview setting as in a private, self-administered setting. This provides some evidence that the choices respondents make on the question are not easily swayed.

Social Distance

A third set of trend questions asks white Americans how they themselves would feel or act in particular situations that involve racial integration. Thus the questions, shown in Table 3.3, inquire about a kind of personal implementation of principles, as distinct from implementation that involves government policies. For most respondents, of course, the situations are hypothetical, and we are not here directly concerned with whether the predictions would turn out to be valid if we could test them by observing actual behavior—useful as that would be. Instead we take the predictions as informative in their own right, as respondents attempt to state in a survey interview what they would

Table 3.3 Social distance questions (white respondents)

Question	58	59	63	64	65	66	67	68	69	70	72	73	74	75	7⟨
Few (Gallup)															
% No objection	75	81	77	—	84	90	—	—	89	92	—	92	—	94	—
Objection	25	19	23	—	16	10	—	—	11	8	—	8	—	6	—
Half (Gallup)															
% No Objection	50	55	52	—	60	60	—	—	67	70	—	69	—	70	—
Objection	50	45	49	—	40	40	—	—	33	30	—	31	—	30	—
Majority (Gallup)															
% No objection	33	31	29	—	35	35	—	—	39	39	—	37	—	42	—
Objection	67	69	72	—	65	65	—	—	61	61	—	63	—	58	—
Few (NORC)															
% No objection	—	—	—	—	—	—	—	—	—	—	93	—	95	93	—
Objection	—	—	—	—	—	—	—	—	—	—	7	—	5	7	—
Half (NORC)															
% No objection	—	—	—	—	—	—	—	—	—	—	76	—	71	72	—
Objection	—	—	—	—	—	—	—	—	—	—	24	—	29	29	—
Majority (NORC)															
% No objection	—	—	—	—	—	—	—	—	—	—	43	—	37	40	—
Objection	—	—	—	—	—	—	—	—	—	—	57	—	63	61	—
Next Door (Gallup)															
% No	56	—	55	—	63	66	63	—	—	—	—	—	—	—	—
Yes, might	23	—	24	—	23	21	24	—	—	—	—	—	—	—	—
Yes, definitely	22	—	21	—	15	13	12	—	—	—	—	—	—	—	—
Great Numbers (Gallup)															
% No	21	—	23	—	28	30	28	—	—	—	—	—	—	—	—
Yes, might	29	—	28	—	30	31	32	—	—	—	—	—	—	—	—
Yes, definitely	50	—	49	—	42	38	41	—	—	—	—	—	—	—	—
Same Block (NORC)[b]															
% No	—	—	65	66	69	71	—	78	—	—	86	—	—	—	—
Yes	—	—	35	34	31	29	—	22	—	—	14	—	—	—	—
Neighborhood Preference A (ISR-Personal)															
% Mixed/makes no difference	—	—	—	—	—	—	—	—	—	—	31	—	27	—	2
Mostly white	—	—	—	—	—	—	—	—	—	—	23	—	34	—	3
All white	—	—	—	—	—	—	—	—	—	—	46	—	39	—	4
Neighborhood Preference B (ISR-Telephone)															
% Mixed/makes no difference	—	—	—	—	—	—	—	—	—	—	—	—	—	—	4
Mostly white	—	—	—	—	—	—	—	—	—	—	—	—	—	—	3
All white	—	—	—	—	—	—	—	—	—	—	—	—	—	—	2

							Year of survey											
7	78	80	81	82	83	84	85	86	87	88	89	90	91	93	94	95	96	97
—	95	95	—	—	—	—	—	—	—	—	—	99[t]	—	—	—	—	—	—
—	5	5	—	—	—	—	—	—	—	—	—	1[t]	—	—	—	—	—	—
—	69	76	—	—	—	—	—	—	—	—	—	90[t]	—	—	—	—	—	—
—	31	24	—	—	—	—	—	—	—	—	—	10[t]	—	—	—	—	—	—
—	39	42	—	—	—	—	—	—	—	—	—	66[t]	—	—	—	—	—	—
—	61	58	—	—	—	—	—	—	—	—	—	34[t]	—	—	—	—	—	—
3	95	—	—	94	95	—	96	95	—	96	97	97	97	96	97	—	98	—
7	5	—	—	6	5	—	4	5	—	4	4	3	3	4	4	—	2	—
5	76	—	—	76	75	—	77	75	—	79	77	79	80	80	83	—	81	—
5	24	—	—	24	25	—	23	25	—	21	23	21	20	20	17	—	19	—
9	43	—	—	43	37	—	41	37	—	43	41	41	47	45	48	—	51	—
1	57	—	—	58	63	—	60	63	—	57	59	60	53	55	52	—	49	—
—	86	—	—	—	—	—	—	—	—	—	—	95[t]	—	—	—	—	—	98[t]
—	10	—	—	—	—	—	—	—	—	—	—	4[t]	—	—	—	—	—	1[ta]
—	4	—	—	—	—	—	—	—	—	—	—	1[t]	—	—	—	—	—	1[ta]
—	46	—	—	—	—	—	—	—	—	—	—	75[t]	—	—	—	—	—	75[t]
—	33	—	—	—	—	—	—	—	—	—	—	7[t]	—	—	—	—	—	7[ta]
—	21	—	—	—	—	—	—	—	—	—	—	18[t]	—	—	—	—	—	18[ta]
—	—	—	—	—	—	—	—	—	—	—	—	—	—	—	—	—	—	—
—	—	—	—	—	—	—	—	—	—	—	—	—	—	—	—	—	—	—
—	—	—	—	—	—	—	—	—	—	—	—	—	—	—	—	—	—	—
—	—	—	—	—	—	—	—	—	—	—	—	—	—	—	—	—	—	—
—	—	—	—	—	—	—	—	—	—	—	—	—	—	—	—	—	—	—
—	—	—	42	—	—	—	—	—	—	—	—	—	—	—	—	57	—	—
—	—	—	34	—	—	—	—	—	—	—	—	—	—	—	—	30	—	—
—	—	—	24	—	—	—	—	—	—	—	—	—	—	—	—	13	—	—

Table 3.3 (continued)

	Year of survey														
Question	58	59	63	64	65	66	67	68	69	70	72	73	74	75	7€
Black Dinner Guest (NORC)															
% Not at all	—	—	52	—	—	55	—	—	—	65	71	69	73	—	72
Mildly	—	—	17	—	—	21	—	—	—	17	16	15	16	—	1§
Strongly	—	—	30	—	—	24	—	—	—	18	14	16	11	—	1₹
Club Change Rules (NORC)															
% Yes would	—	—	—	—	—	—	—	—	—	—	—	—	—	—	—
No would not	—	—	—	—	—	—	—	—	—	—	—	—	—	—	—

Question wordings and variants

Few (Gallup): "Would you, yourself, have any objection to sending your children to a school where a few of the children are black? Sample sizes fewer than 1,000 cases occurred in 1958, 1959, 1973–1980, when they ranged from 619 to 871, and 1990 ($n = 409$). Gallup asked this and the following two questions only of white respondents with children in school.
    1. Yes
    2. No

Half (Gallup): [If No to FEW] "Where half of the children are black?" Sample sizes for all years were the same as Few (Gallup). Note that percentage "Yes" includes those who objected to Few.
    1. Yes
    2. No

Majority (Gallup): [If No to HALF] "Where more than half of the children are black?" Sample sizes for all years were the same as Few (Gallup). Note that percentage "Yes" includes those who objected to Few and Half
    1. Yes
    2. No

Few (NORC): "Would you, yourself, have any objection to sending your children to a school where a few of the children are (Negroes/blacks/African Americans)?" Samples sizes were fewer than 1,000 cases in 1988, 1989, 1991, 1993, and 1996, and ranged from 769 to 881.
    1. Yes
    2. No

Half (NORC): [If No or DK to FEW] "Where half of the children are (Negroes/blacks/African Americans)?" Sample sizes were same as for Few (NORC). Note that percentage "Yes" includes those who objected to Few.
    1. Yes
    2. No

Majority (NORC): [If No or DK to HALF] "Where more than half of the children are (Negroes/blacks/African Americans)?" Sample sizes were same as for Few (NORC). Note that percentage "Yes" includes those who objected to Few and Half.
    1. Yes
    2. No

Next Door (Gallup): "If black people (1958–1967: colored people; 1978: blacks) came to live next door, would you move?" For 1997, the results include respondents aged 18–20.
    1. Yes, definitely
    2. Yes, might
    3. No

							Year of survey											
7	78	80	81	82	83	84	85	86	87	88	89	90	91	93	94	95	96	97
1	—	74	—	78	—	81	77	—	—	—	—	—	—	—	—	—	—	—
7	—	15	—	12	—	12	12	—	—	—	—	—	—	—	—	—	—	—
2	—	11	—	10	—	7	11	—	—	—	—	—	—	—	—	—	—	—
2	—	—	—	—	—	—	52	63	—	59	61	61	66	67	67	—	—	—
9	—	—	—	—	—	—	48	37	—	41	39	39	34	33	33	—	—	—

Question wordings and variants

Great Numbers (Gallup): "Would you move if black people (1958–1967: colored people; 1978: blacks) came
o live in great numbers in your neighborhood?" For 1997, the results include respondents aged 18–20.

1. Yes, definitely
2. Yes, might
3. No

Same Block (NORC): "If a Negro with the same income and education as you have moved into your block,
ould it make any difference to you?"

1. Yes
2. No

Neighborhood Preference A (ISR-Personal): "Would you personally prefer to live in a neighborhood with all
hite people, mostly white people, mostly blacks, or a neighborhood that's mixed half and half?" The 1974
ata come from an ISR Omnibus Survey; data for all other years are from the NES.

1. All white
2. Mostly white
3. Mostly blacks
4. Mixed
5. No difference (volunteered)

(**Variant:** in 1976, the question read, "Would you personally prefer to live in a neighborhood that is all
hite, mostly white, about half white and half black, or mostly black?")

Neighborhood Preference B (ISR-Telephone): "Would you personally prefer to live in a neighborhood with
ostly whites, mostly blacks, or a neighborhood that is mixed half and half? [If Mostly whites] Would you
efer a mostly white neighborhood or an all-white neighborhood? [If Mostly blacks] Would you prefer a
ostly black neighborhood or an all-black neighborhood?" Sample sizes were fewer than 1,000 cases in 1981
= 539) and 1995 (n = 438). Data for 1995 are from add-ons to the Survey of Consumer Attitudes
nducted in December 1994 and January 1995 by the Survey Research Center at ISR.

1. All whites
2. Mostly whites
3. Mostly blacks
4. Mixed
5. All black
6. No difference (volunteered)

Table 3.3 (continued)

Question wordings and variants

Black Dinner Guest (NORC): "How strongly would you object if a member of your family wanted to bring a (Negro/black) friend home to dinner? Would you object strongly, mildly, or not at all?" Sample size was fewer than 1,000 cases in 1985 ($n = 643$).

    1. Strongly
    2. Mildly
    3. Not at all
    (**Variant:** in 1966 used "Negro" instead of "Negro friend".)

Club Change Rules (NORC): "If you and your friends belonged to a social club that would not let (Negroes/blacks) join, would you try to change the rules so that (Negroes/blacks/African Americans) could join?" Sample sizes were fewer than 1,000 cases from 1988 to 1994, and ranged from 372 to 818.

    1. Yes (including volunteered response "wouldn't belong to club")
    2. No

a. From 1958 to 1990, the options "Yes, might" and "Yes, definitely" were both accepted by interviewers (and were options in the interview schedule, though not explicitly provided to the respondent). However, in 1997, these qualified "Yes" options were apparently not accepted by interviewers. For 1997, the "Yes, might" category consists of respondents who said "don't know" or who refused to answer the question.

b. The trend for this question also has time points in 1942 and 1956. The percentage of white respondents indicating "No" in 1942 was 36, and in 1956 it was 53 percent.

t. Data collected through telephone survey as opposed to personal interview.

do in the situations interviewers describe. Three important areas of integration are dealt with: schools, neighborhoods, and informal social activities.

School Composition

Three school composition questions, which we have labeled Few, Half, and Majority, ask whether white respondents would object to sending their own children to a school with different proportions of black children: "a few," "half," and "more than half." The same questions were administered by both Gallup and NORC, with most of the Gallup data from earlier years and the NORC data starting in 1972 and continuing through 1996. In order to present the maximum time series, we have combined the Gallup and NORC results in constructing Figure 3.12. (Although the Gallup sample was restricted to parents of children in school as compared with the full adult sample used by NORC, the two organizations show essentially the same overall levels of support for comparable years from 1970 through 1978, as can be seen in Table 3.3. For the purposes of depicting long-term trends, the overall differences by organization are minor.)[29]

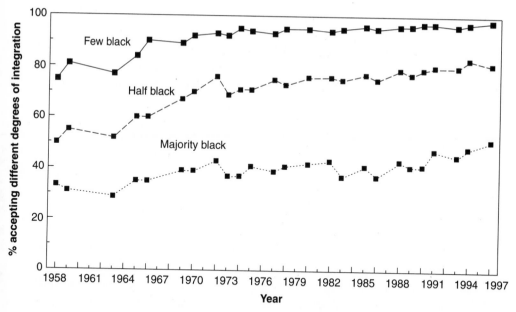

Figure 3.12. Attitudes toward white children's attending schools with different proportions of blacks.

The first available time point of 1958 occurred four years after the Supreme Court's unanimous decision on *Brown vs. Board of Education* altered fundamentally the legal status of school segregation, and a year after President Eisenhower ordered federal troops to enforce court-ordered desegregation in Little Rock, Arkansas, as described in Chapter 1. Quite likely if we had data from time points prior to the 1954 decision, considerable change would be recorded for the 1950s. In any case, already by 1958 three-quarters of the white population claimed to have no objection to integration involving "a few" black children, and by the 1990s the figure reached a ceiling of close to 100 percent. At the other extreme reflected in this sequence of three questions, there is a relatively small increase (18 percent) in acceptance of a school in which the majority of children are black. In between, the increase where "half the children are black" is substantial: from 50 percent in 1958 to 81 percent in 1996.

North-South differences were quite large on all these questions when they were first asked in the late 1950s (see, for example, Figure 2.5), but the regional differences are now much smaller and seem likely to disappear in the not too distant future, at least for the questions about a few or half of the children being black, since these two trends appear to be moving toward a ceiling. Our three standard educational categories varied slightly but consistently in acceptance of school integration in earlier years (for example, acceptance of a few black children in 1982 is 88 percent for less than high school, 95 percent for high school graduates, and 98 percent for those with at least some college). But by 1996 the difference on the Few question between the two higher educational levels disappears almost entirely (98 and 99 percent, respectively) and only the least educated remain somewhat distinctive (91 percent). For a school that is fifty-fifty in racial composition, education is positively related to lack of objection (71, 76, and 85 percent for the three educational categories). For a school described as having the majority of children black, educational differences cease to have an effect below the college level, but show 9 percent more acceptance by the college category.

A useful feature of all the findings from these three school integration questions is the sharp difference in answers that the words "few," "half," and "more than half" evoke. Those who claim that most white respondents do not reveal anti-integration sentiments in survey interviews should take note of the willingness of a considerable number of respondents to give different responses to questions that vary only in the degree of integration posed. For example, in 1996 hardly any white respondents object to a school with a few black children, but almost half (49 percent) say they would object to a school in which black children were in the majority. This kind of variation in response does not mean that respondents always express their true attitudes to interviewers—our earlier discussion in Chapter 2 indicates otherwise—but it is apparent that a major determinant of responses to these racial questions is the substance of the question itself. Many white respondents are quite open in distinguishing between degrees of integration that they find acceptable and unacceptable.

At the same time, even the Majority question produces surprisingly high acceptance of school integration—51 percent of the white NORC sample in 1996 claim to have no objection to such a school. Since the three questions were always asked in the same sequence by both Gallup and NORC, we wondered about the possibility of an effect due to question order. Specifically, some white respondents who genuinely feel and report "no objection" to having their children in a school with a *few* black children might feel constrained to answer "no objection" to the next question about a fifty-fifty situation, and even to the third question about a majority black school. In order to test this possibility we carried out an experiment that varied the order of the Few and Half questions. To our surprise, there was no evidence at all that responses to the Half question are inflated by a question-order effect. If anything, acceptance of a school with half the children black is lowered when that question follows one about a few black children.[30]

Residential Integration

We do not have a set of questions on residential integration that vary like the three school-composition items. But there are two Gallup items that come close to paralleling the extremes of "few black" and "more than half black" children, since one asks about a single black family moving into the neighborhood and the other about "great numbers" of blacks moving in. There is also a differently worded NORC item that provides further data about integration by a single black family. In addition, an ISR question approaches the issue of residential integration more broadly by asking respondents for their personal preferences with regard to different proportions of whites and blacks in a neighborhood.

The wordings and detailed percentages for the four questions are presented in Table 3.3, and overall results for the NORC and Gallup questions are depicted in Figure 3.13. All four questions show an upward trajectory similar to that for school integration, and they also show appreciable differences in levels of acceptance of integration as a function of the proportion of blacks said to be involved. Note, however, that the NORC question asks whether integration "would make any difference to you," the two Gallup questions ask "would you move," and the ISR question asks about what you would "personally prefer"— three different types of reaction to residential integration that are not comparable in a literal way.

The question by NORC clearly involves a single black person or family, specifies that income and education are the same as the respondent's, and speaks of the "same block" rather than "next door"—all of which might encourage more white acceptance. The question was unfortunately discontinued after 1972, but during the period when both it and the Gallup "next door" item were asked, they show quite similar upward trends, with the NORC question registering a few

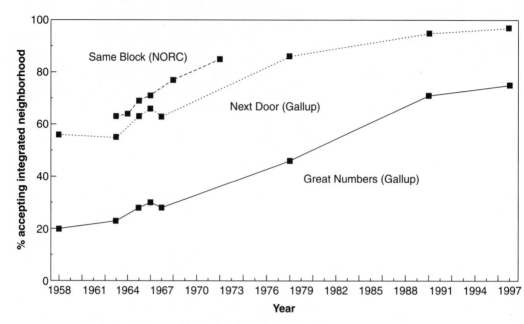

Figure 3.13. Personal preferences about living in integrated neighborhoods.

points higher in acceptance of integration, as might have been expected because of its more focused wording. (In Chapter 7, pp. 321–322, we report an experiment that compared variants of the NORC item with and without the phrase "same income and education as you" in order to determine how much effect it has on responses.)

The first of the two Gallup questions asks white respondents whether they would move "if black people came to live next door," which we assume is interpreted by most respondents to refer to a single black family, with no other changes in the neighborhood. A second Gallup question then asks about moving "if black people came to live in great numbers in your neighborhood." The two questions were always asked together in that sequence, and both show a clear upward trend between 1958 and the 1990s in acceptance of integration. At the same time, there is much greater willingness on the part of whites to say they would move if "great numbers" of blacks are referred to than when a single black family is described, as is evident in Figure 3.13.[31]

The fourth question available to measure attitudes toward residential integration takes a quite different tack. It asks about the kind of neighborhood the respondent "personally prefers": all-white, mostly white, or mixed.[32] In addition, volunteered responses of "it makes no difference" were recorded and were fairly frequent. This neighborhood preference question was asked by ISR three times in face-to-face interviews during the 1970s and, in a slightly different question format, three times at more recent points by telephone. (The third telephone point was obtained at our initiative over the two-month period of December 1994 and January 1995, and we refer to it as 1995 data.) We do not think it wise to combine the different face-to-face and telephone formats and modes of administration into a single time series, for reasons explained in Chapter 2. This complication, plus the complex set of alternatives offered by the question, makes it impractical to include the neighborhood preference trends in Figure 3.13, though all the percentages by year are shown in Table 3.3. However, a simple summary of the results can be conveyed if we focus on the racially conservative response of "white only" and restrict ourselves to the more recent series of three telephone surveys. From Table 3.3, the decline over time in the choice "all white" is clear-cut:

28% in 1976
24% in 1981
13% in 1994

However, the proportion choosing "mostly white" neighborhoods hardly changes. What is happening is the decreased willingness of respondents to insist on complete racial segregation, the stability of the "mostly white" preference in aggregate terms, and the increase in those choosing "mixed" or saying "no difference."[33]

As noted earlier, residential segregation in the South lacks the same heritage of legal segregation as does school segregation, but there is little difference between the residential questions and the school questions in terms of regional variation. All four questions about neighborhood integration show Southern whites more reluctant than Northern whites to accept neighborhood integration, as happened also with the school questions. Furthermore, education is positively related to acceptance of a limited number of black neighbors, regardless of how the question is phrased. But in the case of the question about "great numbers" of blacks moving into the neighborhood, educational differences tend to disappear. The phrasing of the "great numbers" question may be taken to imply imminent turnover of the neighborhood from white to all black, and thus integration in the usual sense may no longer be seen as at issue. When the inquiry allows more distinction among proportions of blacks and whites, as does the ISR question about preferences, education is more clearly related to rejection of all-white neighborhoods and preference for a "mixed" neighborhood. We should also note, however, that other evidence makes it clear that for most whites "mixed" means a substantial white majority and a small number of blacks (Farley et al. 1978; Farley et al. 1994).

Social Interaction

School integration and neighborhood integration are two classic areas in which not only personal preferences but fundamental policy issues are at stake. Hence we have considered each issue under the headings of both government implementation and social distance. We now turn to two items that deal with what continue to be regarded as more informal and voluntary types of personal contact between whites and blacks, and thus where behavior is not constrained by laws or administrative orders. One question asks about willingness to have "a member of your family . . . bring a black friend home to dinner," the other about willingness to object to blacks' being excluded from one's social club (see Table 3.3 for complete wording and detailed results). The question about approval or disapproval of intermarriage—shown earlier in Table 3.1 and Figure 3.6—might well have been included here also: we treated it then as dealing with "principles" because of its general phrasing, but the line between attitudes toward principle and personal preferences is not always clear, as the Intermarriage question illustrates.

Each question shows steady growth over the past two to three decades, though neither is very close to a ceiling. There is clearly more willingness to entertain a black dinner guest than there is to call for integration of one's social club, but how much this is due to the distinction between a single dinner and continuing social membership, and how much to the difference between the passive and active tones of the two questions, is impossible to determine. Degree of intimacy also plays a role in this sphere, as traditionally found to be the case in race relations (Myrdal 1944:60–61). Thus we note that the percentage approving intermarriage is considerably lower than the percentages registered for either having a black dinner guest or seeking to integrate a social club. For both the Dinner Guest and the Club Change Rules questions, as well as for the Intermarriage item, region and education present patterns that will be familiar by now: Northerners are more accepting of reduced social distance than are Southerners, and the higher educated are more accepting than the less educated.

It is interesting to note that the choice of the middle alternative "mildly" to the Dinner Guest item is always low (around 15 percent) and shows little sign of changing over the period tracked (see Table 3.3). The visible shift in answers over time is mainly from one extreme ("object strongly") to the other ("not at all"). Thus there is no sign here of the phenomenon observed for the question on general attitudes toward segregation, where a middle alternative seemed to offer respondents a way to backtrack in recent years from an earlier acceptance of desegregation (pp. 118–120 above).

There is some indication that responses to the Dinner Guest item had leveled off before the question was dropped in 1984 and that the Club Change Rules question has also leveled off in the 1990s. We are hesitant to draw this conclusion, however, because previous interruptions of upward trends have been only temporary (for example, the Laws against Intermarriage question in Table 3.1). The same will probably be true for these more personal types of interaction—provided that nothing happens on the national scene to reverse the post–World War II norm of equal treatment regardless of race.

Conclusions about Social Distance

Despite some puzzles, the social distance questions produce a generally meaningful pattern of results both internally and in relation to the principle and implementation questions. It is important to note that Northern white acceptance of, or rather lack of objection to, "a few" black children in a school has been quite high almost from the earliest date the question was asked by Gallup—1958—and Southern responses to the question arrived at nearly the same level by the mid-1980s. Acceptance of a single black family's moving into one's immediate neighborhood started at a noticeably lower level in 1958, but then showed a sharp climb over the time period for which data are available. By the 1990s the national figure had reached almost the same level as the school question on a few black children.

The difference between the two types of questions probably reflects the fact that a school defines a neighborhood setting that is a

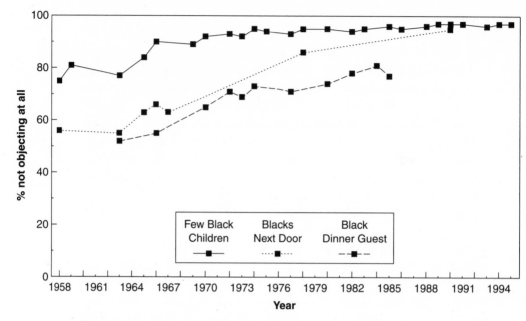

Figure 3.14. Comparison of three degrees of social distance.

good deal wider and less personal than a person's own block—and indeed throughout the North some small amount of integration of schools has long been more common than integration within blocks. The upward slope for the residential questions thus represents the increasing verbal acceptance in the past four decades of small-scale neighborhood integration, bringing it to the same level as small-scale school integration. The question about a black dinner guest shows a similar but less steep upward trend, though the more clearly personal and voluntary nature of the situation probably accounts for its slower climb toward the ceiling of 100 percent acceptance than some other items. The trends are compared graphically in Figure 3.14 for all three of these questions dealing with desegregation in the limited sense of white acceptance of single or small numbers of blacks.

Acceptance of larger numbers of blacks into previously white schools or neighborhoods is clearly much more limited, though it registers as surprisingly high. We thought at first that questionnaire order might play a role here, but experimental evidence indicates that the sequence of questions is not a source of consistency of response. The upward trend does not seem to match reality if compared with the exodus of white families that often occurs when large numbers of black families move into a previously white neighborhood. We can add that the 1997 time point for the Great Numbers question comes from a Gallup study in which race-of-interviewer effects were measured, and white respondents expressed 9 percent more support when the interviewer was black than when the interviewer was white. This indicates that some of the support is situational rather than firm even at the verbal level.

Most of these questions reveal a relation to education that is similar to that for questions dealing with abstract principle: the more education, the more positive the view of one or a few blacks in a school, on a block, or as invited guests. The relation to education is strongest for the most voluntary and individualized action, namely, inviting a black dinner guest, and for the Neighborhood Preference item that deals with wishing to live in a somewhat integrated neighborhood. The relation is weaker, tending to disappear, where the proportion of blacks becomes large—where indeed whites might no longer constitute a clear majority.

Southern respondents generally show less acceptance of personal involvement in desegregated situations, but the regional difference has tended to decrease in recent years. This decrease occurs most strikingly for acceptance of token school integration; a large North-South difference in earlier decades—no doubt due to the heritage of legal segregation of schools in the South—virtually disappeared by the 1980s.

Beliefs about Inequality

The Causes of Black Disadvantage

In a survey carried out for the National Advisory Commission on Civil Disorders three decades ago, Campbell and Schuman (1968) asked white respondents an open-ended question about why blacks have "worse jobs, education, and housing than white people." Only a small proportion of the respondents (6 percent) offered an explanation in terms of differences in innate ability, but at the same time only a minority (19 percent) gave racial discrimination as a primary cause. Instead of either the classic racist response in terms of ability or the classic egalitarian emphasis on discrimination, the largest proportion of answers attributed black disadvantage to lack of motivation (for example, "not trying"). This was offered by respondents as a self-sufficient explanation, one that in effect assumes "free will" as the main source of success in America (Schuman 1969). Later more systematic explorations of these and other white explanations were provided by Apostle et al. (1983) and Kluegel and Smith (1986), and this has now become an important focus for research on racial attitudes and beliefs.

Trend data on white explanations for black disadvantage have been gathered by NORC, ISR, and Gallup using closed questions, and the results are presented in Table 3.4A. The NORC questions open by stating that blacks on the average "have worse jobs, income, and housing than white people," and then present four possible explanations, each in the form of a separate agree-disagree item.[34] Three of the items offer the explanations of in-born ability, discrimination, and motivation ("will power") discussed above, and a fourth adds the alternative of lack of opportunity for education.[35] The total set of questions—the first four rows in Table 3.4A—is self-contradictory in that each explanation is presented as though it should be treated as primary (for example, "*most* blacks have less in-born ability to learn" and "*mainly* due to discrimination" are two of the phrasings [italics added here]). Yet each question is asked regardless of answers to a previous question, and thus the series allows a person to respond by saying "yes" to all four explanations of inequality. And in fact 30 percent of those who attribute "most" black disadvantage to "less in-born ability" also claim that the differences are "mainly due to discrimination!"

The tolerance for inconsistency that is built into the structure of the questions is both a weakness and a strength. On the one hand, failure to require respondents to confront their own contradictions makes it impossible to know what would happen if they were forced to choose between incompatible answers, or at least to provide weights among them (for example, "mostly discrimination but also in some part due to lack of ability"). On the other hand, the inconsistencies indicate clearly the ambivalence that white Americans manifest when they are asked to account for black disadvantage, though it is hard to know how much the ambivalence is genuinely internal and how much a matter of self-presentation to others. The inconsistencies also provide once again a warning against taking any particular set of percentages too literally.[36] What we can do is look at trends over time for each explanation and for the differences among them.

Trends for the four explanations are presented in Figure 3.15 (p. 161), with all percentages shown for the agreeing responses in order to facilitate comparisons among them. Two of the explanations exhibit highly significant trends in opposite directions. In-born ability as an explanation was not heavily chosen (26 percent) even in 1977 when the set of questions was first asked, and by 1996 it was agreed to by only 10 percent of the white population.[37] Taken alone, this decrease might well suggest that explanations in terms of "discrimination" have found increasing support within the white population. On the contrary, discrimination is also mentioned decreasingly, and significantly so, over time. The change between 1977 and 1996 in beliefs about discrimination is not great, only 7 percent, but it is definitely downward.

No other explanation for inequality clearly replaces the declining percentages for ability and discrimination as an explanation for black disadvantage. Low motivation remains the most popular explanation among whites, though with some decrease over time. Lack of opportunity for education, the second most widely affirmed explanation, shows a small rise and then a recent drop. Overall, an explanation that stresses lack of will power continues to compete with lack of education to attract the largest proportion of the white population.

The four NORC explanations of black disadvantage can be ordered in terms of who is responsible for the problem: ability, motivation, education, and discrimination. At one extreme, the low-ability explanation attributes the problem entirely to blacks, with no hint of the possibility of change. At the other extreme, the discrimination explanation attributes the problem entirely to white behavior, behavior that evidently could be changed, whether by whites as individuals or through the enforcement of laws. The two intermediate explanations, which are the more common ones, are ambiguous as to where ultimate responsibility lies, but both allow for improvement in the conditions of blacks. Lack of motivation places responsibility for black disadvantage on blacks, does not deal with causes beyond individual free will, and implies the possibility of change if blacks will just decide to try harder. Lack of education focuses on external constraints, clearly allows for the possibility of change, but is vague as to what caused the problem in the first place. If we adapt the terminology used by Kluegel (1990) and earlier by Kluegel and Smith (1986), the discrimination and education explanations are "structural" in emphasis, whereas the motivation and ability explanations concern limitations in individuals.[38]

The two explanations that focus on the responsibility of blacks for their own disadvantage (ability, motivation) are positively correlated,

Table 3.4A Explanations for inequality (white respondents)

Question	Year of survey									
	63	68	72	77	78	80	81	82	83	84
Inequality due to:										
Discrimination (NORC)										
% Yes	—	—	—	41	—	—	—	—	—	—
No	—	—	—	59	—	—	—	—	—	—
Less Ability (NORC)										
% No	—	—	—	74	—	—	—	—	—	—
Yes	—	—	—	27	—	—	—	—	—	—
No Chance for Education (NORC)										
% Yes	—	—	—	50	—	—	—	—	—	—
No	—	—	—	50	—	—	—	—	—	—
No Motivation (NORC)										
% No	—	—	—	34	—	—	—	—	—	—
Yes	—	—	—	66	—	—	—	—	—	—
Blacks Should Try Harder (ISR)[a]										
% Disagree strongly	—	—	na/10	—	—	—	—	—	—	—
Disagree somewhat	—	—	na/21	—	—	—	—	—	—	—
Neither agree/disagree	—	—	na/na	—	—	—	—	—	—	—
Agree somewhat	—	—	na/39	—	—	—	—	—	—	—
Agree strongly	—	—	na/30	—	—	—	—	—	—	—
No Special Favors (ISR)										
% Disagree strongly	—	—	—	—	—	—	—	—	—	—
Disagree somewhat	—	—	—	—	—	—	—	—	—	—
Neither agree/disagree	—	—	—	—	—	—	—	—	—	—
Agree somewhat	—	—	—	—	—	—	—	—	—	—
Agree strongly	—	—	—	—	—	—	—	—	—	—
Generations of Slavery/Discrimination (ISR)[a]										
% Agree strongly	—	—	na/29	—	—	—	—	—	—	—
Agree somewhat	—	—	na/43	—	—	—	—	—	—	—
Neither agree/disagree	—	—	na/na	—	—	—	—	—	—	—
Disagree somewhat	—	—	na/16	—	—	—	—	—	—	—
Disagree strongly	—	—	na/12	—	—	—	—	—	—	—
Who to Blame (Gallup)[b]										
% White people	70/43	30/23	—	—	—	—	—	—	—	—
Blacks themselves	30/19	70/58	—	—	—	—	—	—	—	—
Both (vol.)	na/29	na/na	—	—	—	—	—	—	—	—
Neither (vol.)	na/na	na/na	—	—	—	—	—	—	—	—
No opinion (vol.)	na/10	na/20	—	—	—	—	—	—	—	—

					Year of survey						
85	86	87	88	89	90	91	92	93	94	95	96
41	40	—	39	38	36	35	—	37	36	—	34
59	60	—	62	63	64	66	—	63	64	—	66
78	79	—	80	81	81	85	—	88	86	—	90
22	21	—	20	19	19	16	—	12	14	—	10
52	52	—	52	53	52	52	—	54	49	—	45
48	48	—	48	47	48	48	—	47	51	—	55
39	36	—	38	38	35	39	—	46	45	—	48
61	64	—	62	62	65	61	—	54	55	—	52
—	9/10	—	6/7	—	8/10	—	6/6	—	5/5	—	—
—	20/23	—	19/22	—	19/23	—	19/21	—	17/19	—	—
—	13/na	—	14/na	—	16/na	—	12/na	—	13/na	—	—
—	36/42	—	37/43	—	34/40	—	41/46	—	38/44	—	—
—	22/26	—	24/28	—	23/27	—	23/26	—	27/31	—	—
—	5	—	2	—	4	—	4	—	2[c]	—	[c]
—	17	—	13	—	14	—	11	—	11	—	[c]
—	12	—	9	—	12	—	8	—	11	—	[c]
—	34	—	33	—	40	—	35	—	40	—	[c]
—	33	—	42	—	30	—	42	—	37	—	[c]
—	17/19	—	12/13	—	15/18	—	15/17	—	11/13	—	—
—	42/46	—	35/39	—	36/41	—	36/40	—	33/38	—	—
—	10/na	—	12/na	—	12/na	—	11/na	—	11/na	—	—
—	19/21	—	27/30	—	24/27	—	24/27	—	25/28	—	—
—	13/14	—	15/17	—	13/15	—	15/16	—	19/22	—	—
—	—	—	—	20/17[t]	—	20/10[t]	20/17[t]	—	—	20/14[t]	—
—	—	—	—	80/58[t]	—	80/54[t]	80/54[t]	—	—	80/56[t]	—
—	—	—	—	na/17[t]	—	na/21[t]	na/18[t]	—	—	na/23[t]	—
—	—	—	—	na/4[t]	—	na/5[t]	na/5[t]	—	—	na/3[t]	—
—	—	—	—	na/4[t]	—	na/11[t]	na/6[t]	—	—	na/4[t]	—

Table 3.4B Perceptions of discrimination (white respondents)

Question	Year of survey						
	63	70	78	80	81	83	84
Good Chance Jobs (Gallup)							
% Not as good a chance	49	—	18	—	—	—	—
As good/same chance	51	—	82	—	—	—	—
Discriminated in Housing (ABC/WP and ISR/1994)							
% Yes	—	—	—	—	17ᵗ	—	—
No	—	—	—	—	83ᵗ	—	—
Discriminated in Managerial Jobs (ABC/WP and ISR/1994)							
% Yes	—	—	—	—	26ᵗ	—	—
No	—	—	—	—	74ᵗ	—	—
Police Treat Fairly (ABC/WP and ISR/1994)							
% Disagree	—	—	—	—	39ᵗ	—	—
Agree	—	—	—	—	62ᵗ	—	—

Question wordings and variants

Inequality due to Discrimination (NORC): "On the average, (Negroes/blacks/African Americans) have worse jobs, income, and housing than white people. Do you think these differences are . . . mainly due to discrimination?" For this item, and the next three, the sample sizes were fewer than 1,000 cases in 1988, 1989, 1991, and 1993, when they ranged from 759 to 840.
  1. Yes
  2. No

Inequality due to Less Ability (NORC): "Do you think these differences are . . . because most (Negroes/blacks/African Americans) have less in-born ability to learn?"
  1. Yes
  2. No

Inequality due to No Chance for Education (NORC): "Do you think these differences are . . . because most (Negroes/blacks/African Americans) don't have the chance for education that it takes to rise out of poverty?"
  1. Yes
  2. No

Inequality due to No Motivation (NORC): "Do you think these differences are . . . because most (Negroes/blacks/African Americans) just don't have the motivation or will power to pull themselves up out of poverty?"
  1. Yes
  2. No

Blacks Should Try Harder (ISR): (1986, 1990: "In past studies we have asked people why they think white people seem to get more of the good things in life in America—such as better jobs and more money—than black people do. These are some of the reasons given by both blacks and whites. Please tell me whether you agree or disagree with each reason as to why white people seem to get more of the good things in life.) (1988, 1992: Now looking, at the respondent booklet for your choices, here are several more statements.) It's really a matter of some people not trying hard enough; if blacks would only try harder they could be just as well off as whites." Sample sizes were fewer than 1,000 cases in 1986 (*n* = 856) and 1990 (*n* = 782). (Show card)
  1. Agree strongly
  2. Agree somewhat
  3. Neither agree nor disagree
  4. Disagree somewhat
  5. Disagree strongly

					Year of survey					
85	87	88	89	90	91	92	93	94	95	97
—	—	—	26[t]	21[t]	26[t]	—	28[t]	—	29[t]	19[t]
—	—	—	74[t]	79[t]	74[t]	—	72[t]	—	71[t]	81[t]
—	—	—	21[t]	—	—	—	—	18[t]	—	—
—	—	—	79[t]	—	—	—	—	82[t]	—	—
—	—	—	24[t]	—	—	—	—	20[t]	—	—
—	—	—	76[t]	—	—	—	—	80[t]	—	—
—	—	—	52[t]	—	—	47[t]	—	47[t]	—	—
—	—	—	48[t]	—	—	53[t]	—	53[t]	—	—

Question wordings and variants

No Special Favors (ISR): (Same introductions as Blacks Should Try Harder) "Irish, Italians, Jewish and many other minorities overcame prejudice and worked their way up. Blacks should do the same without any special favors." Sample sizes fewer than 1,000 cases occurred in 1986 (*n* = 858) and 1990 (*n* = 785). (Show card)

1. Agree strongly
2. Agree somewhat
3. Neither agree nor disagree
4. Disagree somewhat
5. Disagree strongly

Generations of Slavery/Discrimination (ISR): (Same introductions as Blacks Should Try Harder) "Generations of slavery and discrimination have created conditions that make it difficult for blacks to work their way out of the lower class." Sample sizes fewer than 1,000 cases occurred in 1972, 1986, and 1990, when they ranged from 780 to 892. (Show card)

1. Agree strongly
2. Agree somewhat
3. Neither agree nor disagree
4. Disagree somewhat
5. Disagree strongly

Who to Blame (Gallup): "Who do you think is more to blame for the present conditions in which blacks (1968: Negroes) find themselves—white people or blacks (1968: Negroes) themselves?" In 1995, the results include respondents aged 18–20, and are based on published data reported by the Gallup organization.

1. White people
2. Blacks themselves
3. Both (volunteered)
4. Neither (volunteered)
5. No opinion (volunteered)

(**1963 Variant:** "Who do you think is more to blame for the present position of the Negro race in American life—Negroes or white people?")

Good Chance Jobs (Gallup): (1989–1991: "For the next few questions I'd like you to think about your own community. 1995: I have a few questions about race relations in this country. First, . . .) In general, do you think blacks (1963 and 1978: Negroes) have as good a chance as white people in your community to get any

Table 3.4A & B (continued)

Question wordings and variants

---

kind of job for which they are qualified, or don't you think they have as good a chance?" Sample sizes were fewer than 1,000 cases in 1993 ($n = 830$) and 1995 ($n = 983$). In 1997, the results include respondents aged 18–20.

    1. As good a chance
    2. Not as good a chance
    3. Volunteered: same ("same" coded separately only in 1963.)

Discriminated in Housing (ABC/WP and ISR/1994): "In your area, would you say blacks generally are discriminated against or not in getting decent housing?" Sample size was fewer than 1,000 cases in 1994 ($n = 238$). Data for 1994 are from an add-on to the Survey of Consumer Attitudes conducted in August 1994 by the Survey Research Center at ISR.

    1. Yes, discriminated against
    2. No, not discriminated against

Discriminated in Managerial Jobs (ABC/WP and ISR/1994): "In your area, would you say blacks generally are discriminated against or not in getting managerial jobs?" Sample size was fewer than 1,000 cases in 1994 ($n = 228$). Data for 1994 are from an add-on to the Survey of Consumer Attitudes conducted in August 1994 by the Survey Research Center at ISR.

    1. Yes, discriminated against
    2. No, not discriminated against

Police Treat Fairly (ABC/WP and ISR/1994): "I am going to read you a few statements, and for each I'd like you to tell me whether you tend to agree or disagree with it, or if, perhaps, you have no opinion about the statement. These days police in most cities treat blacks as fairly as they treat whites." The 1992 survey was conducted following the riots that occurred after the Rodney King verdict was announced in Los Angeles. Sample sizes were fewer than 1,000 in 1992 ($n = 388$) and 1994 ($n = 240$). Data for 1994 are from an add-on to the Survey of Consumer Attitudes conducted in August 1994 by the Survey Research Center at ISR.

    1. Agree
    2. Disagree
    3. No Opinion

    a. In 1972, this question was asked without the "neither agree nor disagree" option presented to the respondent. Thus the response options for 1972 are not comparable to the response options for the 1986–1994 data. For comparison purposes, we have presented the 1986–1994 data in two ways. First, we present the data with the middle alternative included. Second, we present the numbers excluding those respondents who indicated "neither agree nor disagree." For trend purposes, the second numbers presented for 1986–1994 may be compared with the 1972 results, if one is willing to make the assumption that if the respondents who selected the middle alternative in 1986–1994 were not given this option, they would have been distributed proportionately across the remaining response options.

    b. Across time, Gallup has been inconsistent in its coding of various "volunteered" responses to this question, which in some years have been substantial. Sometimes specific volunteered responses (e.g., "both" or "neither") are coded separately from "don't know," and in other years they are indistinguishable from each other. It should be noted, however, that in all years, these options were strictly volunteered by the respondents; they were not offered as explicit choices to them. Because of these inconsistencies in coding, the data are presented in two ways. The first set of figures provides all response options that were coded for a given year; thus, it includes the various "volunteered" responses. The second set of figures excludes the volunteered responses, showing results only for the two explicitly offered options.

    c. The No Special Favors question was included in the NORC General Social Survey in 1994, with the following percentages: 3 (Disagree strongly), 9, 10, 30, 48 (Agree strongly). It was repeated in 1996, with these percentages: 4, 8, 11, 29, 48.

    t. Data were collected by telephone survey as opposed to personal interview.

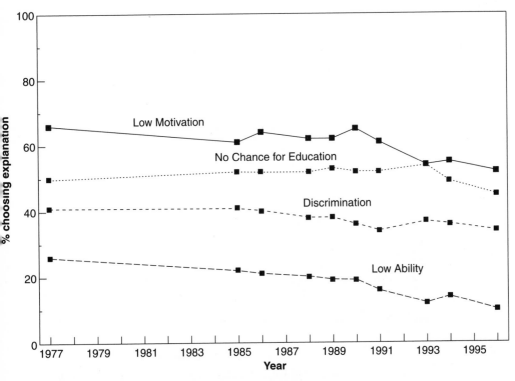

Figure 3.15. White explanations for racial inequality (NORC).

as are the two more structural explanations (education, discrimination). In both cases the associations are asymmetrical. Thus 90 percent of those who cite low ability also cite low motivation, but only 29 percent of those who cite low motivation cite low ability. This indicates that for some whites the two explanations are essentially identical and imply permanent black defects, whereas other whites shy away from such traditional racist expression and frame the issue of black motivation entirely as a matter of individual free will. For the two structural explanations, 72 percent of those who agree that discrimination is the problem also agree that low education is a barrier, and probably see the two as directly connected. However, only 53 percent of those who agree with the low-education reason also agree that discrimination is a cause. This suggests that the remainder do not blame the educational deficiency on white discrimination. In sum, the two extreme positions on the scale, low ability and discrimination, are relatively simple categories in terms of meaning—traditional racism vs. traditional emphasis

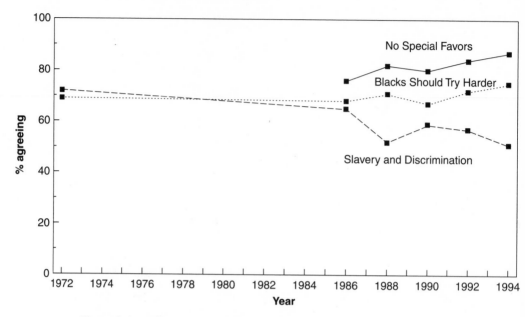

Figure 3.16. White explanations for racial inequality (ISR).

on discrimination—whereas the middle positions of motivation and education are more ambiguous in interpretation and avoid attributing black disadvantage to either limitations in black ability or discrimination by whites.

ISR has also asked agree-disagree questions in order to obtain white explanations for black disadvantage. The questions concern only motivation and discrimination. The percentages agreeing over time are shown graphically in Figure 3.16, and the results are presented in full in Table 3.4A.[39] Essentially the same level of agreement (about 70 percent) was produced by the two statements first asked in 1972, one of which attributed black disadvantage to "not trying hard enough" and the other to "generations of slavery and discrimination." In later years, however, the "not trying hard enough" question increased in its level of agreement, whereas the attribution to "slavery and discrimination" lost support. Moreover, beginning in 1986, when a new question was added that touts the achievements of other ethnic groups ("Irish, Italians, Jewish and many other minorities") in overcoming obstacles, agreement that blacks should be able to do the same is even higher than for the "not trying hard enough" question, as Figure 3.16 shows.[40] Although we cannot take the tabled percentages literally, there can be little doubt that white Americans find very appealing those explanations of black disadvantage that focus on blacks as responsible in motivational terms for their own success or failure.

The ISR question about past discrimination as a cause of black disadvantage may seem similar to the NORC item about discrimination as a cause of black disadvantage, but as Kluegel and Bobo (1993) note, it is actually rather different because the wording about "slavery and discrimination" focuses on past events (especially slavery) rather than on current discrimination for which whites today bear responsibility. This is probably the reason that the percentage of total agreement is higher for the ISR wording (51 percent in 1994) than for the NORC wording (36 percent in 1994), though even with the emphasis on the past, agreement shows signs of declining in recent years and the trends for both questions are basically similar.

At the same time, the ISR question about blacks' needing to "try harder" also registers more agreement (75 percent in 1994) than the NORC question about motivation (55 percent in 1994). The explanation for this difference is not obvious, but the positive ISR wording ("if blacks would only try harder they could be just as well off as whites") may be somewhat more inviting than the NORC wording. It is less easy to account for the fact that the percentage of whites agreeing to the NORC motivation explanation seems to have gone down in recent years (see Figure 3.15), whereas the percentages giving the ISR motivation explanation appear to have increased over roughly the same period. Because of this unexplained inconsistency in direction over the past several years, we think it best to regard the changes in direction as inconclusive for now and to focus on differences in overall levels of agreement between the items.[41]

Beginning in 1963, Gallup asked a more general question about the source of black disadvantage: "Who do you think is more to blame for the present conditions in which (Negroes/blacks) find themselves—white people or blacks themselves?"[42] The question was repeated in 1968 after the urban riots of the previous year, though unfortunately with different coding of volunteered responses, and then not again until 1989 and two subsequent years, providing five time points in all.[43] Consistent with results already discussed, from 1968 onward, most white respondents attribute "the present condition" of blacks to blacks themselves rather than to whites, but in 1963 whites were seen as the main source of the problem. The change between 1963 and 1968 is extraordinarily large, and we would feel more secure if there were some supporting data from another organization.

It is true, however, that 1963 must have been at or near the high point in white sympathy for blacks, because the focus then was on the violent suppression in the South of the nonviolent civil rights movement, whereas by 1968 the focus had shifted to urban rioting by blacks in Northern cities like Newark and Detroit (see the account in Chapter 1, together with the chronology in Table 1.1). Taken at face value, the results are of great importance, for they indicate that at the peak of the civil rights movement, whites rather than blacks were seen as mostly responsible for black disadvantage—a conclusion very different from that drawn from the attributional research subsequent to 1968 (for example, Kluegel and Smith 1986).[44]

We should also note the relatively high proportion of people who *volunteered* "both blacks and whites," even though it was not mentioned explicitly, suggesting that many more would have chosen such an alternative if it had been included in the question. This indicates that there is greater willingness by whites to accept a role in having produced racial inequality if the responsibility is phrased as shared rather than placed entirely on whites themselves. In this sense, arguments over discrimination versus motivation may be counterproductive in reaching the white population, for if whites are forced to choose, the burden will more often be placed solely on blacks themselves.

Differences due to region and education are clear on almost all of these questions concerning explanations for racial inequality. For the four NORC items, the least educated are much more likely than the most educated to agree with the explanation of lower black ability, and the same relation holds a little less strongly for the motivation explanation. The explanation that speaks of black educational disadvantage is agreed to disproportionately by more educated respondents, and the discrimination explanation shows very little relation to education, though there is a slight tendency for it to be endorsed more by the college educated. Approximately the same findings occur when region is substituted for education, with Northerners behaving like the higher educated and Southerners like the lower educated, though the discrimination explanation shows a sharper relation to region than it does to education.

Similar relations for region and education occur for the three ISR questions: the two statements suggesting that blacks can succeed if only

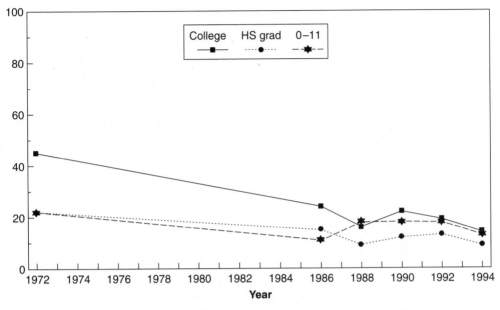

Figure 3.17. Generations of slavery and discrimination as a cause of black disadvantage, by education.

they try harder are agreed to disproportionately by the less educated and by Southerners, whereas the statement that black disadvantage can be traced to "generations of slavery and discrimination" is agreed to most by Northerners and the more educated. In the latter case the difference is entirely between the college educated and all others, and it tends to disappear in recent years. The Gallup question also shows region and education relations in the same directions, and stronger in earlier than in more recent years.

Most of the associations just described do not change appreciably over time—with one important exception shown in Figure 3.17. The relation of education to strong agreement with the ISR item attributing black disadvantage to "generations of slavery and discrimination" decreases noticeably and reliably between its first asking in 1972 and later time points. What was a fairly substantial relationship in 1972 had become virtually nonexistent by the 1990s. College-educated whites show the greatest change over time, moving from 45 percent in 1972 agreeing strongly that slavery and discrimination have been an important cause of black disadvantage to only 14 percent indicating this in 1994. The NORC question about the importance of discrimination as an explanation also shows a small drop in its relation to education over time: the relation was slight but significant in 1977, is no longer significant in 1992, and reverses slightly in 1996. Thus an emphasis on past oppression of blacks as a basic source of racial inequality has lost support over the past two decades, particularly among more educated white Americans. This probably reflects the fading of reports of obvious racial oppression from the media, and their replacement by stories about forms of affirmative action intended to benefit blacks.

Perceptions of Amount of Discrimination

There are also trend data on the extent to which whites believe that specific types of discrimination against blacks currently exist, regardless of whether discrimination is treated as a basic cause of larger inequalities. Table 3.4B (pp. 158–159) presents four questions that concern important spheres of daily life. One is a general question about employment first asked by Gallup in 1963 and not repeated again until 1978 and subsequent years. The other three questions concern housing, movement into managerial positions, and treatment by police, and were initiated by the ABC/WP poll in 1981. In order to extend these data beyond the three time points available from the archives, we replicated the three ABC/WP questions in an SRC monthly survey in 1994 and include the results in Table 3.4B as well, though caution is needed with such an extension in a different survey.[45]

The longest trend in this set is for the Gallup Good Chance question on whether "blacks have as good a chance as white people in your community to get any kind of job for which they are qualified." The fifteen-year span from 1963 to 1978 showed a substantial *decrease* in beliefs in the existence of discrimination or other barriers to employment equality, with little change over later years through a very recent time point in 1997. Northerners tend to perceive more discrimination than do Southerners, and the higher educated more than the less educated.

Perceptions of discrimination in housing, managerial positions, and treatment by police for the three ABC/WP questions are shown graphically in Figure 3.18. It is useful to note first that the percentage of whites who perceive inequality of managerial employment opportunity on this question (20 percent in 1994) is similar to the percentage that perceived unequal treatment in employment more generally on the

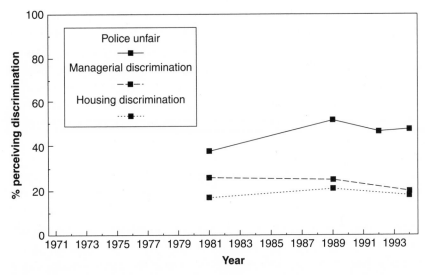

Figure 3.18. White perceptions of discrimination in housing, managerial jobs, and police treatment.

Gallup question during the same period (average of 24 percent in 1995–1997). Thus, from the late 1970s onward, about three-quarters of the white population *reject* the proposition that blacks as a group face important barriers in the area of jobs, either generally or at higher managerial levels.

The greatest amount of discriminatory treatment that whites perceive has to do with the police, with nearly half the sample *dis*agreeing that "these days in most cities police treat blacks as fairly as they treat whites." Quite likely this relatively high perception of discrimination occurs because of the publicity given to particular incidents of police mistreatment of blacks, though it is difficult to pinpoint the source of the increase in perceptions of unfairness between 1981 and 1989. The apparent decline in such perceptions between 1989 and 1992 is not statistically significant, but it is somewhat puzzling because the widely publicized beating of Rodney King by Los Angeles police occurred in 1991 and should have increased white perceptions. What is evident, however, is that white perceptions of unfair practices are more widely held with regard to the police than with regard to the more general areas of housing and employment.

At the same time, there is a somewhat lower perception of discrimination in the area of housing than in the other two areas asked about, despite—or because of—the high degree of residential segregation that exists in the United States (Massey and Denton 1993; Farley and Frey 1994). Whites may be shielded from direct knowledge of residential discrimination, since such gate-keeping tends to be lodged in institutional practices like real estate steering that do not require actions by most whites as individuals (Jackman 1994). Moreover, even the presence of a single black family in a neighborhood—a type of integration that has become more common in recent years—may create the sense among many whites that racial discrimination in the sale or rental of property is absent or unimportant (Sigelman et al. 1996). Both of these explanations can be interpreted to fit employment as well, and to some extent, even police-citizen relations.

A further complication with respect to the housing question is the belief by many whites that blacks *prefer* to live in all or mostly black neighborhoods. In the 1995 survey in which we asked whites about their preferences for living in segregated vs. integrated neighborhoods (as discussed earlier, pp. 148–149), we followed with an inquiry about how these same white respondents thought most blacks would answer a parallel question about their own preferences. We hypothesized that whites who themselves prefer a particular degree of segregation or integration will believe that blacks prefer the same degree of segregation or integration, as has been shown in a number of other areas of life (Fields and Schuman 1976; Ross, Greene, and House 1977). The table below provides striking evidence in support of this hypothesis:

Beliefs about black preferences by actual white preferences

White beliefs about black preferences	White preferences		
	All white	Mostly white	Mixed, no difference
All black	52%	11%	10%
Mostly black	17	60	28
Mixed, no difference	31	30	63
Total	100	100	100
N	(52)	(132)	(217)

Thus,

- of those whites who prefer all-white neighborhoods, 52 percent state that blacks prefer all-black neighborhoods;

- of those whites who prefer mostly white neighborhoods, 60 percent state that blacks prefer mostly black neighborhoods;
- of those whites who prefer mixed neighborhoods, 63 percent state that blacks prefer mixed neighborhoods.

In sum, white respondents tend to see their own desires for segregation or integration mirrored by black respondents. Although this might be interpreted as a kind of rationalization on the part of whites, the same type of "looking-glass" perception occurs in many other areas of life where rationalization would not be expected. The more plausible interpretation is that the beliefs result from a straightforward projection of a person's own ethnocentric preferences onto others—a propensity to assume that one's own nature reflects "human nature."[46]

Our data on associations of these three questions with education and region are less adequate than for earlier analyses, because some of the samples are small and not every data set includes education and region variables. The one clear relation is for respondent education to be positively associated with perceptions of police unfairness, probably because accounts of particular incidents appear in newspapers and other media attended to most by those with more education. There are small trends of a similar sort for employment and housing, but they are not statistically reliable within individual years and can be considered trivial at best. Region also shows only small, nonsignificant tendencies for Northerners to perceive discrimination more than do Southerners.

Conclusions about Beliefs concerning Inequality

White respondents have some difficulty when asked to account for black disadvantage. The type of explanation that has greatest appeal is one that focuses on a lack of motivation by blacks to improve their own status in America. If blacks really wanted to, and were willing to work hard, so the explanation goes, their problems could be solved. At the same time, there is not much recognition of past or present discrimination as a factor impeding black achievement, and there is evidence that even limited recognition of discrimination as a source of black disadvantage has decreased over time.

A fundamental premise of the civil rights movement and of a number of past court and legislative actions is that blacks have suffered and continue to suffer unfair treatment in many areas of life. Evidently such a belief was widely held among whites during the height of the civil rights movement in the late 1950s and early 1960s, but in more recent years the majority of whites in America do not appear to have shared this premise. Moreover, unlike most other areas we have dealt with, there is not a great difference by region or by education in the failure of whites to believe in the existence of serious discrimination against blacks.[47]

To the extent that whites are willing to take responsibility for inequality of outcomes, this occurs mainly by emphasizing traditional obstacles to equal education faced by blacks, though exactly why these obstacles arose in the first place is not explored by the available survey questions. White acceptance of *any* role in having created black disadvantage occurs most clearly when responsibility is treated as shared by both groups, rather than as focused entirely on whites themselves. Finally, innate differences between blacks and whites are seldom chosen as important when offered in surveys; the publicity given to Hernstein and Murray's (1994) *Bell Curve* may have some effect in the future and needs to be studied, but we doubt that its impact will be very great, at least with respect to answers to survey questions by the general population. Since most whites are almost certainly aware of the traditional stereotype regarding black-white ability differences (Devine and Elliot 1995), most either reject it or treat expressing such a stereotype as counternormative.

Affirmative Action

Earlier we considered questions about the implementation of broad principles of equal treatment and integration. What is called "affirmative action" might also be viewed as a form of implementation, where the goal is to bring blacks on the average closer to whites in such spheres as education, occupation, and income. Initially affirmative action was developed as a way of preventing the omission of blacks, whether intentional or unintentional, from candidate pools that lead to employment positions or college admissions. When the policies were begun in the early 1960s, the basic idea was that those making admission and hiring decisions should be required to demonstrate that African Americans were included in lists of candidates and given full consideration. Apparently Colin Powell was first added to a list of names to be reviewed for promotion to general in order to meet affirmative action requirements in this sense of being given full and fair consideration (Powell 1995). No trend questions have been asked about this basic meaning of affirmative action, however, which is indeed rather subtle to present in ordinary survey questioning.

Instead, affirmative action has come to be identified in many quarters with giving preference to blacks when final decisions are made about admission or employment, particularly if they would otherwise be greatly underrepresented among the people finally selected. This practice could be justified on at least two grounds that are different from the ideas behind the questions about principles that we considered at the beginning of this chapter. First, most blacks were seen as hampered by the effects of hundreds of years of racial oppression, and therefore prevented from obtaining the capital and skills needed to compete on equal terms in contemporary American society. Second, it seemed clear that in many areas of life (for example, the health professions and the police), the country would be better off if minorities were represented in approximately the same proportion that they are in the population, and that, more generally, greater equality of outcomes could reduce the kind of tensions that had erupted in urban violence in the late 1960s. Of course, preferential treatment can also be justified as a remedy where specific acts of discrimination can be shown to have occurred. (We continue to use the term "liberal" to refer to support for preferential treatment, as well as for other forms of affirmative action.)

The kinds of affirmative action questions that have been asked over time in surveys deal mainly with preferential treatment to compensate blacks on the assumption that they continue to face unique barriers to advancement. We have seen, however, that the majority of whites deny the importance of discrimination and place most of the burden for black disadvantage on blacks themselves, putting primary emphasis on inadequate black motivation. Given these findings, we have little reason to expect that affirmative action steps—especially in a form that can be characterized as giving any hint of preference to blacks—will have much support in the white population. The actual findings are not quite as simple as this reasoning suggests, and here as in other areas a good deal depends upon the kind of affirmative action being proposed and the alternatives offered to respondents.

Our data on affirmative action are of two different types, as presented in Table 3.5. Part A concerns broad issues of economic help to black communities, which best fits under the generic heading of affir-

Table 3.5A Affirmative action questions—government expenditures (white respondents)

Question	Year of survey									
	70	72	73	74	75	76	77	78	80	8
A. Government expenditures										
Spending on Blacks (NORC)										
% Too little	—	—	27	26	21	23	20	18	20	—
About right	—	—	46	48	49	46	49	50	51	—
Too much	—	—	27	26	30	30	31	32	29	
Help Blacks (NORC)										
% Gov't help (1–2)	—	—	—	—	20	—	—	—	—	—
Agree with both (3)	—	—	—	—	22	—	—	—	—	—
No special treatment (4–5)	—	—	—	—	58	—	—	—	—	—
Federal Spending (ISR)										
% Increased	—	—	—	—	—	—	—	—	—	—
Same	—	—	—	—	—	—	—	—	—	—
Decreased/vol: cut out	—	—	—	—	—	—	—	—	—	—
Aid to Minorities (ISR)										
% Gov't help (1–3)	22	26	—	22	—	24	—	21	a	—
Mid-point (4)	25	23	—	23	—	19	—	24	a	—
Help themselves (5–7)	45	42	—	44	—	42	—	47	a	—
Not thought	9	9	—	11	—	15	—	9	a	
Aid to Blacks (ISR)										
% Gov't help (1–3)	—	—	—	—	—	—	—	—	—	—
Mid-point (4)	—	—	—	—	—	—	—	—	—	—
Help themselves (5–7)	—	—	—	—	—	—	—	—	—	—
Not thought	—	—	—	—	—	—	—	—	—	—

mative action, even though it is not always thought of in that way. Part B of the table deals with the focus of most recent debate: explicit recognition of race as a factor in decisions about hiring and promotion in employment and about admission to colleges and universities.[48]

Government Expenditure

We begin with four general questions (one of which is in two versions) about government expenditure to assist blacks. Two questions were asked by NORC and two by ISR, with some of the results stretching over twenty-five years. Each organization asked one question that was substantively balanced in the sense that an argument is presented on each side, for and against special expenditures for blacks. Each organi-

							Year of survey							
82	83	84	85	86	87	88	89	90	91	92	93	94	95	96
22	27	32	28	29	31	31	30	34	29	—	32	25	—	26
53	51	49	47	50	51	48	51	48	52	—	49	49	—	48
25	23	19	24	20	18	21	19	19	19	—	19	26	—	26
—	13	14	—	13	15	12	14	15	15	—	12	10	—	12
—	26	31	—	28	30	29	28	34	31	—	32	29	—	28
—	61	55	—	59	55	59	58	51	54	—	56	61	—	60
—	—	14	—	17	—	16	—	20	—	18	—	—	—	—
—	—	62	—	62	—	57	—	61	—	54	—	—	—	—
—	—	24	—	20	—	27	—	19	—	28	—	—	—	—
9	—	24	—	23	—	22	—	—	—	—	—	—	—	—
7	—	28	—	29	—	22	—	—	—	—	—	—	—	—
2	—	36	—	40	—	46	—	—	—	—	—	—	—	—
2	—	12	—	8	—	10	—	—	—	—	—	—	—	—
—	—	—	—	14	—	16	—	20	—	17	—	17	—	16
—	—	—	—	30	—	23	—	25	—	26	—	25	—	27
—	—	—	—	49	—	52	—	47	—	49	—	53	—	49
—	—	—	—	7	—	10	—	8	—	9	—	6	—	8

zation also asked a second question that is more one-sided, with expenditures on blacks raised as one item in a list of possible uses for government funds. Question wordings and detailed results are presented in Table 3.5A.[49]

A summary of the percentages showing positive support for expenditures for blacks is presented in Figure 3.19, as against both opposition and middle positions (that is, "agree with both").[50] The main conclusion to be drawn from the figure is the lack of either much support or much change in level of support over the twenty-five-year period. One question, Spending on Blacks (NORC), does show noticeably higher support than the other three questions, but it is unbalanced in form and the wording indicates that blacks do need such help. The other NORC question on helping blacks offers reasons on both sides

Table 3.5B Affirmative action questions—preferential treatment (white respondents)

	Year of Survey									
Question	70	72	73	74	75	76	77	78	80	81
B. Preferential treatment										
Preference in Admissions (ISR)										
% Favor strongly	—	—	—	—	—	—	—	—	—	—
Favor not strongly	—	—	—	—	—	—	—	—	—	—
Oppose not strongly	—	—	—	—	—	—	—	—	—	—
Oppose strongly	—	—	—	—	—	—	—	—	—	—
Pref. Hiring/Promotion (ISR)										
% Favor strongly	—	—	—	—	—	—	—	—	—	—
Favor not strongly	—	—	—	—	—	—	—	—	—	—
Oppose not strongly	—	—	—	—	—	—	—	—	—	—
Oppose strongly	—	—	—	—	—	—	—	—	—	—
Pref. Hiring/Promotion (CBS/NYT)										
% Yes	—	—	—	—	—	—	—	—	—	—
No	—	—	—	—	—	—	—	—	—	—
Depends/DK (vol.)	—	—	—	—	—	—	—	—	—	—

Question wordings and variants

Spending on Blacks (NORC): "We are faced with many problems in this country, none of which can be solved easily or inexpensively. I'm going to name some of these problems, and for each one I'd like you to tell me whether you think we're spending too much money on it, too little money on it, or about the right amount . . . . Improving the conditions of blacks. Are we spending too much, too little, or about the right amount on improving the conditions of blacks?" Improving the conditions of blacks is eighth in a list of 15 problems, following such things as improving and protecting the environment, halting the rising crime rate, and improving the nation's education system. Sample sizes were fewer than 1,000 cases in 1984–1993, when they ranged from 360 to 606.

    1. Too Much
    2. Too Little
    3. About the right amount

Help Blacks (NORC): "Some people think that (Negroes/blacks/African Americans) have been discriminated against for so long that the government has a special obligation to help improve their living standards. Others believe that the government should not be giving special treatment to (Negroes/blacks/African Americans). Where would you place yourself on this scale, or haven't you made up your mind on this?" Sample sizes were fewer than 1,000 cases in 1988, 1989, 1991, and 1993, when they ranged from 786 to 837. (Show card)

    1. I strongly agree the government is obligated to help blacks
    2.
    3. I agree with both answers
    4.
    5. I strongly agree that government shouldn't give special treatment
    8. Don't know

Federal Spending (ISR): "If you had a say in making up the federal budget this year, for which (1986–1992: of the following) programs would you like to see spending increased and for which would you like to see spending decreased? . . . Should federal spending on programs that assist blacks be increased, decreased, or kept about the same?" In 1988 and 1992, volunteered "cut out entirely" answers were accepted by interviewers and coded separately. In Table 3.5A, this small group of respondents are included in the "Decreased" category.

							Year of Survey								
2	83	84	85	86	87	88	89	90	91	92	93	94	95	96
—	—	—	—	11	—	12	—	13	—	11	—	—	—	—
—	—	—	—	18	—	16	—	17	—	15	—	—	—	—
—	—	—	—	22	—	20	—	24	—	24	—	—	—	—
—	—	—	—	49	—	52	—	46	—	51	—	—	—	—
—	—	—	—	5	—	6	—	8	—	6	—	4	—	6
—	—	—	—	10	—	7	—	9	—	8	—	6	—	6
—	—	—	—	22	—	17	—	21	—	18	—	21	—	17
—	—	—	—	63	—	70	—	63	—	68	—	69	—	71
—	—	—	33[t]	—	35[t]	—	—	23[t]	12[t]	34[t]	25[t]	—	23[t]	—
—	—	—	53[t]	—	59[t]	—	—	62[t]	69[t]	53[t]	61[t]	—	66[t]	—
—	—	—	14[t]	—	6[t]	—	—	16[t]	19[t]	13[t]	14[t]	—	11[t]	—

Question wordings and variants

1. Increased
2. Decreased
3. Same
4. Volunteered "cut out entirely" (1988 and 1992)

(Variant: In 1984, the question was asked as follows: "If you had a say in making up the federal budget this year, which programs would you like to see increased and which reduced . . . Should federal spending on assistance to blacks be increased, decreased, or kept about the same?")

Aid to Minorities (ISR): "Some people feel that the government in Washington should make every possible effort to improve the social and economic position of blacks (1970: Negroes) and other minority groups. Others feel that the government should not make any special effort to (1972–1988: help minorities because they should help themselves) (1970: but they should be expected to help themselves). Where would you place yourself on this scale, or haven't you thought much about this?" Sample sizes were fewer than 1,000 cases in 1986 (n = 859) and 1988 (n = 811). (Show card with 7-point scale)

1. Government should help minority groups (1988: minorities)
2.
3.
4.
5.
6.
7. Minority groups (1988: minorities) should help themselves
0. Haven't thought much about this

Aid to Blacks (ISR): "Some people feel that the government in Washington should make every possible effort to improve the social and economic position of blacks. Others feel that the government should not make any special effort to help blacks because they should help themselves. Where would you place yourself on this scale, or haven't you thought much about this?" Sample sizes were fewer than 1,000 cases in 1986 (n = 836) and 1988 (n = 785). (Show card with 7-point scale)

1. Government should help blacks
2.

Table 3.5A & B (continued)

Question wordings and variants

3.
4.
5.
6.
7. Blacks should help themselves
0. Haven't thought much about this

(**Note:** In 1986 and 1988, a split-ballot design was used to phase out the use of the "Aid to Minorities" version of this question, and to phase in the use of the "Aid to Blacks" version of the question. Thus both versions were used in 1986 and 1988. Beginning in 1990, however, only the "Aid to Blacks" form of the question was asked.)

Preference in Admissions (ISR): "Some people say that because of past discrimination it is sometimes necessary for colleges and universities to reserve openings for black students. Others oppose such quotas because they say quotas give blacks advantages they haven't earned. What about your opinion—are you for or against quotas to admit black students? (If for) Do you favor quotas *strongly* or *not strongly?* (If against) Do you oppose quotas *strongly* or *not strongly?*" Sample sizes were fewer than 1,000 cases in 1986 (*n* = 815) and 1990 (*n* = 744).

1. Favor Strongly
2. Favor not strongly
3. Oppose not strongly
4. Oppose strongly

Preference in Hiring/Promotion (ISR): "Some people say that because of past discrimination, blacks should be given preference in hiring and promotion. Others say that such preference in hiring and promotion of blacks is wrong because it gives blacks advantages they haven't earned. What about your opinion—are you *for* or *against* preferential hiring and promotion of blacks? (If for) Do you favor preference in hiring and promotion *strongly* or *not strongly?* (If against) Do you oppose preference in hiring and promotion *strongly* or *not strongly?*" Sample sizes were fewer than 1,000 cases in 1986 (*n* = 826); 1990 (*n* = 753).

1. Favor strongly
2. Favor not strongly
3. Oppose not strongly
4. Oppose strongly

Preference in Hiring/Promotion (CBS/NYT): "Do you believe that where there has been job discrimination against blacks in the past, preference in hiring or promotion should be given to blacks today?" In 1987, volunteered "depends" responses were not reported separately from DK. In all other years, "depends" was coded as a separate category. Sample size was fewer than 1,000 cases in 1990 (*n* = 885).

1. Yes
2. No
3. Depends/don't know (volunteered)

(**1991 Variant:** "Do you believe that where there has been job discrimination against blacks in the past, preference in hiring should be given to blacks today?")

a. In 1980 the phrase "even if it means giving them preferential treatment in jobs" was added to the first sentence. It is quite probable that this change in wording altered the meaning of this question for respondents and therefore we do not include the 1980 data in our trend analysis. For interested readers, however, 15 percent supported government aid to minorities, 73 percent thought minorities should help themselves, and 12 percent said they hadn't thought much about the issue.

t. Data were collected through telephone survey rather than personal interview.

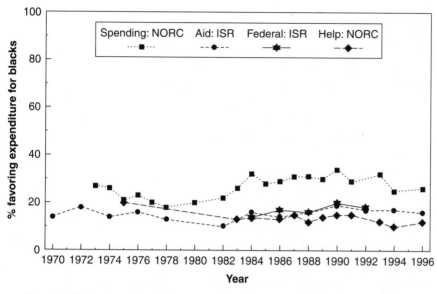

Figure 3.19. Support for government expenditures on blacks.

of the issue, and the level of support in this case is less than half as great in recent years as the support for NORC's Spending on Blacks question. ISR also asked one question with substantive arguments on each side (Aid to Minorities/Blacks) and one that implies the need for support without a counterargument (Federal Spending), and neither garners much white support for government expenditures on blacks.[51] Overall, in recent years only a small part of the white population has been favorable to increased efforts by the government to improve the economic and social position of black Americans. However, it is also important to note that a large proportion of whites will opt for a vague middle position (for example, spending should be "kept about the same") when that is offered. Indeed, for the two questions that offer just three alternatives, Spending on Blacks and Federal Spending, the middle alternatives ("about right" and "same") attract more responses than either of the extremes. Although there is not strong support for increased expenditure for blacks, there is also not a lot of opposition either, and this suggests that political leaders may have a fair amount of leeway on the issue.[52]

For most of the issues discussed in earlier sections of the chapter, our findings on region and education indicated that Northerners and more educated respondents express more liberal sentiments on racial issues than do Southerners and the less educated, though there were some exceptions where little association was found. When we come to government expenditures for improving black conditions, the results are surprising in two regards. First, the relation of education to the four government expenditure items tends to be somewhat curvilinear in most cases, with most support for expenditures expressed by the most educated, the next most by the least educated, and the least support by the middle educational ranks. When we introduce a control for income differences in Chapter 4, however, the relation of support for government expenditures to education does become monotonic, though it is still weaker than in most other areas that we have considered.[53] The results suggest that to the more liberal social expression of those who complete college, we may need to add the capacity of less educated whites to feel somewhat more solidarity with blacks said to be in economic need than might have been expected—a point to which we return in the next section on preferential treatment, where the result is much stronger.

Second, what may seem surprising about the results for region is, paradoxically, that the North-South difference we have found for most earlier questions continues to hold and strongly so, even though we are no longer dealing with an area of life that has anything to do with the legacy of legal segregation, nor with upholding social separation. The government expenditure questions are entirely concerned with efforts to improve the economic well-being of blacks, rather than with relations between blacks and whites. It would be worth exploring this further to determine how much the regional difference represents traditional white economic domination of blacks and how much it reflects the rise of a new Republican conservatism in the South, perhaps partly based on recent white migrants.[54]

Preferential Treatment

We now turn to affirmative action in its most controversial form: preferential treatment in employment and education. Table 3.5B presents overall trends for three questions we have available for detailed analysis. Two of the questions have been asked by ISR since 1986 and deal, respectively, with college admissions and with hiring and promotion, but are otherwise similar in wording. Both are balanced substantively in the sense that the questions include an argument for each side

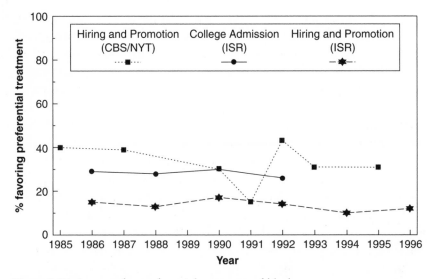

Figure 3.20. Support for preferential treatment of blacks.

of the issue: preferential treatment is justified on the basis of "past discrimination," and it is challenged because "it gives blacks advantages they haven't earned." Each question also offers gradations in support or opposition ("strongly" versus "not strongly"). The third question, asked in CBS/NYT surveys since 1985, is substantively unbalanced, focusing more clearly on remedying actual instances of job discrimination: the question asks in yes/no format about preference in cases "where there has been job discrimination against blacks in the past." Based on past research on balanced and unbalanced questions, we expect the unbalanced question to show greater support for preferential treatment, especially since it seems to focus directly on situations where past discrimination has occurred, whereas the ISR questions speak of preferential treatment as a more general compensatory policy.

These several variations in wording produce quite different levels of support, ranging from only about 6 percent voicing "strong support" on the ISR question about hiring and promotion to around a third indicating support (with no gradations offered) on the CBS/NYT question. The ISR question on college admission yields an intermediate figure with some 12 percent giving strong support.

In Figure 3.20 we have collapsed the ISR responses of "agree strongly" and "agree not strongly" into a single "favor" category in order both to simplify the graph and to allow a more appropriate comparison with the "yes" response to the dichotomous CBS/NYT question. Focusing first on the two ISR questions, which are close to each other in wording, it is evident that preferential treatment has a good deal more support for college admission than for hiring and promotion. We suspect that this is because preferential treatment in education can be seen as an attempt to "level the playing field," whereas employment is seen as the final game itself. Moreover, we found earlier that a substantial part of the white population views lack of education as a major cause of black disadvantage, and thus preference in college admission may be regarded as helping blacks overcome this obstacle.

The CBS/NYT results are less stable over time than the ISR trends. However, at most points they yield greater support for preferential treatment, in keeping with the wording differences noted above. Nearly a third of the white population expresses backing for preferential treatment in hiring and promotion when, according to the wording of the CBS/NYT question, it is applied to situations in which there has been past discrimination. This should be regarded as the high water mark, however, for once preferential treatment in employment is presented as a general policy by the ISR questions, with a reason included for opposing it, the total for support (strong plus not strong) never reaches a fifth of the white population. None of the three items shows a consistent trend over time that is up or down in direction.

The relation of education to support for preferential treatment presents the most unexpected results in all of our analysis: opposition to preferential treatment of blacks is lowest among the least-educated members of the white population. This is shown in Figure 3.21 for the six surveys in which the question was asked. The four-point scale has been reversed in the figure in order to make a high score represent support for preferential treatment. Although no educational group is highly in favor of preferential treatment for blacks, those with the lowest education (zero to eleven years) are more supportive in each of the six years. There is little difference between the other two educational levels.

Similar findings occur for preferential treatment in admission to college in the same ISR surveys, and also for preferential hiring and promotion in the CBS/NYT surveys. The latter is especially important as a cross validation because it involves an entirely different set of surveys by a different organization using a different item format with a

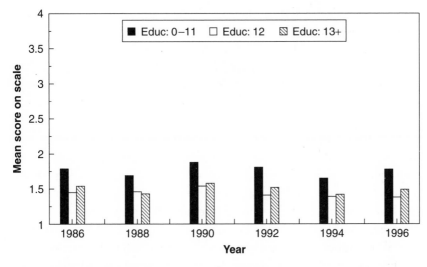

Figure 3.21. Support for preferential treatment of blacks in hiring and promotion, by education (ISR).

different mode of administration (telephone rather than face-to-face). Furthermore, the education relation just described continues to hold up well when we subject the preferential treatment items to additional controls in Chapter 4.

Such consistency over time and across surveys makes it difficult to question the findings showing greater support for preferential treatment among the least educated. But since the results go against almost all previous associations between education and racial attitudes, we felt it essential to test the findings further. One additional step has been to explore the relation between support for preferential treatment and other available questions in the ISR surveys. Both overall *and within* the less educated group, those who support preferential treatment tend to give more liberal responses to other types of racial questions, for example, whether the government should take actions to support the integration of schools. Thus, although the least educated are most likely to oppose school integration, those who *do* favor integration are especially likely also to support preferential treatment.

In sum, there is good reason to believe the surprising results about education reported here. We conclude that the least-educated whites are able to feel greater sympathy toward black disadvantage than the more educated, leading to disproportionate support for giving blacks a preference in jobs and college admission, even though the least educated are *not* the most supportive of integration, nor most in favor of pro-black policies on other items we have considered in previous sections of this chapter. Still, we remain uncertain about this conclusion and consider the findings in great need of additional research that can illuminate them further.

With regard to region, there is little difference between Northerners and Southerners on any of the questions, though Northerners are slightly more supportive of preferential treatment than are Southerners. This is somewhat different from the results with a number of other questions, where the regional difference was sharp and consistent. Moreover, unlike some results for earlier questions, the lack of a regional difference here cannot be attributed to ceiling effects, since the level of support for preferential treatment is quite low for the sample as a whole.

Conclusions about Affirmative Action

White support for affirmative action in the sense of compensatory preferential treatment for blacks has never been close to being the majority position during the relatively brief period since 1985, when these trend questions were first asked. Depending on phrasing, support has ranged from at most a third of the white public down to just a few percentage points, and with little evidence of change over time. The least support occurs when preferential treatment is generalized beyond particular settings in which discrimination is said to have taken place in the past.

Positive support for increased economic assistance to black communities is likewise not very great, nor does it change much over the nearly twenty-five years for which trends are available. However, here there is more evidence for acceptance of whatever is said to be the "present" level of support, the nature of which is, of course, not spelled out in these simple attitude questions.

Regional and educational sources of support and opposition for both types of questions were unexpected and not easily interpreted. Northerners show more support than Southerners for economic assistance to blacks, but the regional difference tends to disappear for preferential treatment. The least educated also show somewhat greater sympathy for government expenditures on blacks than do those who have completed high school, though the greatest support comes from those with at least some college education and the overall association becomes monotonic when further controls are introduced (see Chapter 4).

What is most striking of all our results is the finding that the least-educated whites in these samples show disproportionately greater willingness to accept preferential treatment for blacks. This quite unexpected finding has held up under considerable scrutiny. The finding is so different from those on all other questions we have considered, but also so important both theoretically and practically if valid, that further replication and exploration should be a high priority. This is a case where open-ended follow-up "why" inquiries might be extremely useful in order to clarify what respondents, especially the less educated, have in mind when they answer questions about preferential treatment.

Miscellaneous Racial Questions

Included here are six questions that do not fit easily under concepts already discussed. Each has some value but also some limitations. For example, there are considerable trend data for white "thermometer ratings" of blacks, but there are problems in interpreting the results, especially their bearing on change over time. In other cases the questions are of obvious interest (for example, on the Ku Klux Klan), but there are no recent time points and the topic is one for which information about the recent past is crucial. All six questions are shown in Table 3.6.

Attitudes toward Blacks

In the standard ISR thermometer series, respondents are asked to indicate on a scale of zero to one hundred how warm or cold (favorable or unfavorable) they feel toward various groups, with blacks always one of the groups named. If the warm-cold dimension is taken at face value, one might treat the item as measuring affect toward blacks on the part of whites, thus reflecting a continuing underlying emotional orientation much like that described in the literature on symbolic racism (see Sears 1988). In support of this interpretation, the thermometer scores are related to *all* other racial questions available in the same ISR surveys: the more positive the thermometer rating, the more

Table 3.6 Miscellaneous questions (white respondents)

Question	Year of survey											
	42	44	46	56	63	64	65	66	68	70	72	73
Thermometer Rating of Blacks (ISR)												
Mean of 100-pt scale	—	—	—	—	—	60	—	60	61	58	61	—
Thermometer Rating of Whites (ISR)												
Mean of 100-pt scale	—	—	—	—	—	85	—	84	81	77	79	—
Ku Klux Klan Rating (Gallup)												
% Highly unfavorable (−4, −5)	—	—	—	—	—	—	84	—	—	79	—	75
Unfavorable (−1, −2, −3)	—	—	—	—	—	—	9	—	—	13	—	16
Favorable (1,2,3)	—	—	—	—	—	—	5	—	—	5	—	5
Highly fav. (4,5)	—	—	—	—	—	—	1	—	—	3	—	5
Civil Rights Push (ISR)												
% Too slowly	—	—	—	—	—	4	—	3	5	6	5	—
About right	—	—	—	—	—	22	—	17	24	32	41	—
Too fast	—	—	—	—	—	74	—	80	71	61	54	—
Black Push (NORC)												
% Disagree strongly	—	—	—	—	9	—	—	7	8	8	11	11
Disagree slightly	—	—	—	—	13	—	—	16	13	8	13	15
Agree slightly	—	—	—	—	27	—	—	26	31	24	31	30
Agree strongly	—	—	—	—	51	—	—	51	48	59	45	45
Riots (ISR)												
% Solve (1–3)	—	—	—	—	—	—	—	—	a	a	51	—
Mid-point (4)	—	—	—	—	—	—	—	—	a	a	16	—
Use force (5–7)	—	—	—	—	—	—	—	—	a	a	24	—
Not thought	—	—	—	—	—	—	—	—	a	a	9	—
Better Break (Gallup)												
% Keep down	—	—	—	—	—	—	—	—	—	—	—	—
Whites don't care	—	—	—	—	—	—	—	—	—	—	—	—
Blacks get break	—	—	—	—	—	—	—	—	—	—	—	—

Question wordings and variants

Thermometer Rating of Blacks (ISR):[b] "There are many groups in America that try to get the government or the American people to see things more their way. We would like to get your feelings toward some of these groups. Blacks. Where would you put them on the thermometer?"

Response: Mean of a 100-point scale

Thermometer Rating of Whites (ISR):[b] "There are many groups in America that try to get the government or the American people to see things more their way. We would like to get your feelings toward some of these groups. Whites. Where would you put them on the thermometer?"

Response: Mean of a 100-point scale

Ku Klux Klan Rating (Gallup): "How far up the scale or how far down the scale would you rate the following organizations: Ku Klux Klan?"

1. Highly favorable (4,5)
2. Favorable (1,2,3)

Year of survey																		
'4	75	76	77	79	80	81	82	84	85	86	88	89	90	91	92	94	95	96
3	—	58	—	—	60	—	61	62	—	62	58	—	66	—	61	61	—	63
9	—	74	—	—	76	—	71	74	—	—	72	—	—	—	70	71	—	70
—	—	—	—	71	—	—	—	—	—	—	—	—	—	—	—	—	—	—
—	—	—	—	17	—	—	—	—	—	—	—	—	—	—	—	—	—	—
—	—	—	—	8	—	—	—	—	—	—	—	—	—	—	—	—	—	—
—	—	—	—	3	—	—	—	—	—	—	—	—	—	—	—	—	—	—
5	—	5	—	—	9	—	—	8	—	9	11	—	9	—	13	—	—	—
6	—	49	—	—	52	—	—	57	—	62	60	—	58	—	58	—	—	—
8	—	47	—	—	40	—	—	36	—	29	29	—	33	—	28	—	—	—
—	10	12	9	—	12	—	16	19	16	—	—	—	—	—	—	29	—	31
—	15	16	18	—	20	—	23	22	23	—	—	—	—	—	—	27	—	28
—	28	29	29	—	32	—	32	31	35	—	—	—	—	—	—	29	—	25
—	47	43	45	—	36	—	29	28	27	—	—	—	—	—	—	16	—	17
6	—	41	—	—	—	—	—	—	—	—	—	—	—	—	42	—	—	—
9	—	18	—	—	—	—	—	—	—	—	—	—	—	—	22	—	—	—
1	—	21	—	—	—	—	—	—	—	—	—	—	—	—	23	—	—	—
4	—	20	—	—	—	—	—	—	—	—	—	—	—	—	13	—	—	—
—	—	—	—	—	—	—	—	18	—	—	5[t]	21[t]	—	10[t]	8[t]	—	11[t]	—
—	—	—	—	—	—	—	—	33	—	—	35[t]	36[t]	—	28[t]	31[t]	—	37[t]	—
—	—	—	—	—	—	—	—	48	—	—	60[t]	43[t]	—	61[t]	61[t]	—	53[t]	—

Question wordings and variants

3. Unfavorable (-1,-2,-3)

4. Highly Unfavorable (-4,-5)

(Note: The Ku Klux Klan was the first organization to be rated in 1970 and 1979, the fourth in 1965, and the third in 1973. The YMCA, CORE, and the FBI were first, second, and third, respectively, in 1965; CORE and the FBI were first and second, respectively, in 1973.)

Civil Rights Push (ISR): "Some say that the civil rights people have been trying to push too fast. Others feel they haven't pushed fast enough. How about you: Do you think that civil rights leaders are trying to push *too fast*, are going *too slowly*, or are they moving at *about* the *right* speed?" Sample sizes were fewer than 1,000 cases in 1966, 1970, 1984, 1986, and 1990, when they ranged from 607 to 995.

1. Too fast

2. Too slowly

3. About the right speed

Table 3.6 (continued)

Question wordings and variants

Black Push (NORC): "Here are some opinions other people have expressed in connection with (Negro/black)–white relations. Which statement on the card comes closest to how you, yourself, feel? (Negroes/blacks/African Americans) shouldn't push themselves where they're not wanted." Sample size was fewer than 1,000 cases in 1985 (*n* = 632).

1. Agree strongly
2. Agree slightly
3. Disagree slightly
4. Disagree strongly

Riots (ISR): "There is much discussion about the best way to deal with the problem of urban unrest and rioting. Some say it is more important to use all available force to maintain law and order—no matter what the results. Others say it is more important to correct the problems of poverty and unemployment that give rise to the disturbances. (1992: And, of course, other people have opinions in between.) Where would you place yourself on this scale, or haven't you thought much about this?" (Show card with seven-point scale)

1. Solve problems of poverty and unemployment
2.
3.
4.
5.
6.
7. Use all available force
0. Not thought much about this

Better Break (Gallup): "On the whole, do you think most white people want to see blacks get a better break, or do they want to keep blacks down, or don't you think they care either way?" In 1991, the results include those aged 18–20, and are based on published figures reported in the Gallup Monthly Report, June 1992. Data for 1995 are from a telephone survey conducted for the *New York Times*, and reported in the Roper Center's *Public Perspective*, vol. 7 (2), 1996, p. 22. Because of this, respondents aged 18–20 are included in 1995 results.

1. Better break
2. Keep blacks down
3. Don't care either way

a. In 1968 and 1970 the Riots question was asked *without* the interest filter, and for that reason we have not included those time points in our trend analysis. For interested readers, however, 37 percent of the white respondents in 1968 and 1970 said that we should solve poverty and unemployment (1–3), and 32 percent and 34 percent, respectively, in 1968 and 1970 supported the use of all available force to maintain law and order (5–7).

b. The wording of the introduction is as shown here for 1964, 1966, and 1968. A small change occurred in 1970: the second sentence was replaced with "Please use the thermometer again—this time to indicate your feelings toward these groups or persons." More changes too cumbersome to report in detail (and unlikely to affect results) were made in the introduction to the thermometer rating at the remaining time points (1972–1996). Generally, respondents were asked to express their feelings toward a number of groups (an average of roughly 22 different groups or organizations across the 16 surveys involved), with blacks falling about 13th on average. The relative order of the ratings of blacks and whites was highly inconsistent across time: about 1/2 the time points, whites were rated before blacks, and the reverse was true in the other 1/2 of the time points. In two years, whites were not asked about at all, and in only one year were whites and blacks asked about contiguously. Other groups asked about most regularly were liberals, conservatives, Democrats, Republicans, big business, labor unions, and poor people. "Don't know" responses were automatically coded as 50 in 1964, 1966, 1968, and 1970, but were coded separately in later years; for all analyses we have rescored "don't know" to 50.

t. Data were collected through telephone survey as opposed to personal interview.

favorable the respondent is likely to be toward integration, government implementation, and so forth. When all available items are intercorrelated, the associations involving the thermometer scale are at about the same level as the correlations among the other items.[55]

A striking feature of white thermometer scores about blacks, however, is that they have hardly varied at all over the past three decades.[56] The rating in 1964, when whites were first asked to rate blacks, was sixty, and in 1994 it was sixty-one, as shown in Table 3.6. Yet during that long span of years when black scores were unchanged, other questions associated with the thermometer scores changed considerably—in particular, the question about federal implementation of school integration, which was losing support, and the question about public accommodations, which was gaining support (both shown earlier in Figure 3.11). Thus, on the one hand, it might be argued that thermometer ratings are important because they provide evidence of an underlying constancy in basic white attitudes toward blacks, despite apparent shifts registered by more specific questions. On the other hand, this constancy makes thermometer ratings less useful if our goal is to portray or understand trends in policy-related attitudes, since the lack of change for the thermometer despite its association with more volatile issues suggests that affect toward blacks is not important as either a cause or an effect of *changes* in other attitudes.

One other feature of the thermometer ratings makes it difficult to know exactly what they measure. It seems reasonable to compare white ratings of blacks with white ratings of whites (that is, of themselves), and then use the *difference* between them as the more sensitive measure of racial attitudes, rather than the absolute level of either. For this reason, Table 3.6 also reports ratings of whites for the years when they were obtained, and the comparison of the two trends turns out to present a considerable puzzle. It is reasonable that the ratings of whites are noticeably higher than the ratings of blacks, but it is surprising to find that the ratings of whites declined substantially between 1964 and 1996, the total change being nearly fifteen points. This also means that the white-black difference shrinks over the twenty-year period, which taken at face value could imply that white attitudes toward blacks have become much more favorable—but only because whites have become less favorable toward themselves!

This is not a very plausible scenario, and indeed it casts some doubt on the interpretation of thermometer ratings as measuring some underlying affect not subject to the same vicissitudes as policy-related attitudes. A quite different and opposite interpretation of the variations in white ratings of whites is that they are easily influenced by questionnaire context. For example, if the ratings of whites were obtained in interviews after the ratings of blacks, then an increase in the norm of "even-handedness" might lower ratings of whites over time (Schuman and Ludwig 1983). Other possible contextual effects can also readily be imagined. However, the position of the various objects of thermometer ratings has shifted from one year to the next quite a bit in ISR surveys, and we are unable to find any pattern that provides a clear interpretation in terms of context.[57] What we did show earlier in Chapter 2 is that thermometer ratings are greatly affected by the race of the interviewer.

There are other puzzles as well. In 1992 when Jews were also asked about, blacks were rated only slightly lower (a score of sixty-two, as against a score for Jews of sixty-four), suggesting that negative attitudes toward blacks are only a bit stronger than negative attitudes toward Jews, which seems unlikely on the basis of other data comparing attitudes toward the two groups. Scores for blacks are also higher (more favorable) than scores for "wealthy" people (fifty-six in 1994), Democrats (fifty-two in 1994), and a number of other groups. In sum, although it is tempting to treat thermometer scores as measuring a profound affective orientation by whites toward blacks, an orientation that remains constant over the long stretch of time that has seen more "superficial" measures vary, it is far from clear exactly what is captured by these scores and how meaningful they are. Since our main concern in this study is with change over time, we have not pursued the thermometer scores further for whites, but discuss them again in Chapter 5 on black attitudes.[58]

Attitudes toward the Ku Klux Klan

A second rating question, used by Gallup, provides a quite different object of affect. Respondents are asked to rate on a scale of -5 to $+5$ (with zero omitted) a number of groups, including the Ku Klux Klan. Data are available at four time points from 1965 to 1979. Most respondents—at least 75 percent—place the Klan on the unfavorable side of the scale (-5 to -1) at all four times, but there was a significant lessening of *un*favorability in the North at the two more recent time points. This shows up most clearly if we contrast extreme negative scores (−4 and −5 combined) with all others, as shown in Table 3.6. Moreover, the sharper decrease in extreme disapproval of the Klan occurred in the North, lessening somewhat a large gap between the two regions in 1979, the most recent year for which we have data. The change seemed to involve all educational levels, though the most visible shift was among high school graduates in the North. Unfortunately, the question has not been repeated since 1979, despite the rise of other manifestations of antiblack activity such as the several candidacies of David Duke and the increased salience of white supremacy groups.

Civil Rights Push and Black Push

These two questions benefit from substantial trend data but are of somewhat limited value because of their ambiguity. On whether "civil rights people" are pushing too fast, too slow, or at the right speed, the long-term trend is fairly clear: whites have increasingly seen the movement as about right in speed, whatever that may mean. Only a tiny proportion of whites have ever rated the push as too slow, though there has been some increase in this proportion. Trends in the North and South are similar, with Southerners more likely at all time points to say too fast. People with less education are also more likely to state that civil rights leaders are moving too fast.

One interpretation of these trends is that whites have increasingly accepted civil rights as a legitimate pursuit and thus have increasingly seen the current level, whatever it may be, as the right speed. But another and different interpretation is that civil rights leaders have gone more slowly in the last decade, and that the reduced pace is approved by the majority of whites. One point seems evident: there was no increase in rejection of civil rights activism in recent years, a time when we noted there was an increase in opposition to federal intervention to ensure integration of schools (see Table 3.2).

The question we have labeled Black Push is also somewhat uncertain in meaning, but NORC resumed asking it in 1994 after a hiatus of nearly a decade. The question can be taken as a negative way of asking about the principle of integration: disagreement with the statement that blacks are "pushing themselves where they're not wanted" can indicate acceptance of blacks into presumably all-white spheres of life. On the other hand, the question has a ring of implementation in the word "push," though the implementation is not through government action. In either interpretation, the question is more loaded than most, for a respondent might feel that no one, of any race, should push in where not wanted; that is, the cliché might be accepted without much thought.

The overall trend for the item is one of decreasing choice of the "strongly agree" response, but its replacement differs somewhat by region. In the South the main replacement is "slightly agree," so that what occurs is some moderation of response but not a change in direction. In the North the change involves some movement into the "disagree" categories, that is, more positive views of blacks pushing into new areas, though what these areas are is not defined by the question.

Riots and Better Break

In the previous edition of this book we included as an implementation item a question on how "urban unrest and rioting" should be responded to, and the question might also be seen as tapping support for a kind of affirmative economic action. In either case, there is not much evidence of change over the four time points at which the question has been asked: a plurality of respondents favor force more than economic efforts to prevent urban unrest and rioting, but support for economic steps is also fairly strong. The question is probably most meaningful in the wake of a riot, and its replication in 1992 occurred after the Los Angeles riot earlier that year, precipitated by the failure of a jury to convict police accused in the beating of Rodney King. However, there is little sign of change except for a decrease in the "not thought about it" alternative.

The Better Break question is more relevant to black perceptions than to white, but we include the trend data here for later comparison by race. There is little change over time, and, not surprisingly, relatively few whites believe that "most white people want to . . . keep blacks down," though a quarter to a third say that most whites simply don't care (about blacks) one way or the other. In Chapter 5 we will see that it is that belief that accords with what blacks themselves increasingly see to be true.

Conclusions about Miscellaneous Questions

The most interesting and frequently repeated question in this set of miscellaneous items is the thermometer scale used to measure white affect toward blacks as a group. These self-reported affect ratings cannot be dismissed as unimportant, since at any given time point they are associated in a meaningful way with attitude questions dealing with particular issues. But the interpretation of the scale values presents a number of problems, which make them of uncertain value in terms of our interest here in changes in racial attitudes.

Conclusions about Changes in White Attitudes

We have covered a wide range of trends in this chapter: some questions show a large increase over time in racially liberal attitudes, some show no change at all, and a small number show an actual decline. In addition, differences by both region and education vary greatly in size and in some cases even in direction. Although a reader starting from a particular theoretical perspective might wish to regard some of the results as more valid than others, we think it is useful to begin by treating each set of findings as meaningful in its own way. We can then attempt to determine whether the different results taken together provide a plausible picture of changes in white attitudes.

1. *Principles of equal treatment.* On questions concerning principles of equal treatment of blacks and whites in the major public spheres of life (jobs, schools, residential choice, public accommodations, transportation), there has been a strong and generally steady movement of white attitudes from denial to affirmation of equality—so much so that some questions have been dropped by survey organizations because answers were approaching 100 percent affirmation. Even questions that reveal lower levels of support for integration, for example, a question on intermarriage that had seemed to reach a plateau a decade ago, have continued their upward movement during the past several years. Thus a graph showing all these questions (or all but one that we think is probably an aberration due to context effects) would reveal a set of approximately parallel linear trends upwards, differing in levels (intercepts) primarily due to the degree of intimacy that equal treatment would bring about.

Furthermore, in all these cases, the trend over time is accompanied by more support in the North than in the South and by more support at higher than at lower educational levels—at least until distributions are compressed as a ceiling of 100 percent is approached. Thus wherever questions show change over time, they also tend to show substantial differences by region and education.

2. *Implementation of equal treatment.* Results for questions on gov-

ernment action to implement the principles just mentioned differ in two respects from results for the questions on the principles themselves. First, there is noticeably less support for the implementation of principles than for principles as such. Differences in question wording make it impossible to offer a precise estimate of the size of these gaps, but they are fairly large across all the comparisons of principle and implementation that we are able to make. However, we also showed in the case of support for an open housing law that the gap disappears when we are able to focus on those who hold the principle with great strength. This suggests that the underlying dimension may be degree of commitment to the principle rather than an ineluctable distinction between principle and implementation.

A second important difference is that unlike principle questions, implementation questions do not all show a clear positive trend over time, or indeed any single direction of change. A question on federal intervention in support of school integration revealed a dramatic drop in support beginning around 1970, with the loss especially affecting well-educated Northerners, the opposite of results for questions on principles. But the question on support for an open housing law has shown a clear upward trend, along with regional and educational differences similar to those for most principle questions. To complicate matters further, a question on the seemingly settled issue of government support for equal treatment in use of public accommodations showed a clear upward trend until 1974, when it was unfortunately discontinued, then evidence of a drop in support when we included the same question in a 1995 survey of our own. Thus it is not possible to generalize in a simple way about the direction of trends regarding government implementation.

From the standpoint of attitude measurement, two forces are probably needed for an implementation question to show positive change over time. First, the question must emphasize equal treatment regardless of race, so that the principle itself is one that has gained the greatest acceptance. This probably accounts for why the Open Housing question has shown such clear upward movement over time, though the question is certainly also focused on the difficulties that blacks face in buying homes. Second, the substantive issue must not have been turned into a debate about other widely held values, as occurred in connection with school integration and busing. Once issues like "neighborhood schools" and their emotional correlates are invoked (for example, the safety of children), the principle that must underlie support for implementation tends to lose its force.

It is also important to recognize that just as the color-blind norm of equal treatment changed during the 1960s and 1970s into a more color-conscious norm of affirmative action, so at least one of the questions we originally selected to measure government implementation of equal treatment may have metamorphosed into a measure of affirmative action for some respondents. The Federal Job Intervention question is so vaguely phrased that its meaning may have changed even though the wording remains the same. Furthermore, questions about busing that we originally included under government implementation might be considered to lie midway between implementation and affirmative action.

In the previous edition of this book we gave great emphasis to the principle vs. implementation distinction, as have some other writers before and since, including several reviewers of our earlier edition who were attracted by one side or the other of the divide. We still believe it to be important, but the distinction now seems to us somewhat less fundamental for the reasons discussed here.

3. *Social distance.* A third type of question that we examined concerns white willingness to participate personally in integrated situations, insofar as this can be measured by asking about intentions and feelings. The clearest result for these items is that white responses vary according to the proportions of blacks and whites in the hypothetical situations described. Very few whites object to school or residential integration involving a small number of blacks; such questions show upward trends and other associations much like questions about abstract principles of equal treatment. However, objections are much more frequent when substantial numbers of blacks are involved and whites are at risk of becoming the minority, though even here verbal support is greater than one might expect given actual patterns of neighborhood and school integration.

4. *Beliefs about inequality.* When white Americans are asked to account for black disadvantage, the most popular explanation is that blacks lack motivation or will power to get ahead. Lack of opportunity for education is also frequently selected as a reason. Least likely to be cited are differences in ability by race, and there is also not much emphasis on racial discrimination as a causal factor. It is important to keep in mind, however, that many white Americans hold more than

one explanation for black disadvantage, even where the explanations are phrased so as to be logically inconsistent with one another. In addition, there is evidence that between the height of the nonviolent civil rights efforts in the South (around 1963, which saw Martin Luther King's "I have a dream" speech during the March on Washington) and the height of the urban riots in the North in the late 1960s, white beliefs about who is to blame for black disadvantage shifted sharply from whites to blacks. There is also evidence that more whites will accept some white responsibility for black disadvantage when it is combined with an emphasis on black responsibility as well.

Much civil rights activity, including support for affirmative action, is based on the assumption that discrimination against blacks continues to be an important obstacle in many areas of American life. However, the majority of whites do not share this assumption, and even the minority that holds it has become smaller in recent years. There are only small differences by region and education in the belief that discrimination is a continuing problem.

5. *Affirmative action.* Affirmative action in the form of preferential treatment has very little support among white Americans, with not much indication of change over the decade in which such questions have been asked. There is somewhat more support for government expenditure to improve the conditions of blacks generally, though the support shows up mostly in acceptance of the status quo when it is offered vaguely as an alternative to either "more" or "less" spending for this purpose. It is interesting to note that Southern whites are clearly more resistant than Northerners to government expenditures for blacks, and this calls for additional interpretation: it may represent simply the legacy of the Southern past or it may also reflect a new Southern Republican conservatism.

Our results for associations between education and attitudes toward affirmative action are quite surprising and difficult to interpret: the least-educated respondents (less than high school graduation) are more positive about preferential treatment for blacks than are both high school graduates and those with college experience. This relation, which is the opposite of most findings about the association of education and pro-black attitudes, appears to be quite robust, and it sets a challenge for future analysis and interpretation.

Unfortunately, there are no trend questions about affirmative action in the sense of enlarging candidate pools, providing extra training or remedial forms of education, or even setting nonmandatory goals with regard to integration in employment or in other areas of life. (In Chapter 6 we will present one relevant experimental comparison of two different types of affirmative action.) But if the basis for stronger forms of affirmative action is the assumption that blacks are faced with *external* barriers to achievement, then such an assumption is not found widely at present in white thinking. We have too little data to trace confidently white perceptions of the problems that blacks confronted in the early 1960s, when white support for civil rights activity was probably greatest, but in recent years the explanation of black disadvantage that appeals most to white Americans is that black Americans lack adequate motivation to get ahead.

6. *Two final qualifications.* Most of our conclusions thus far are based on analyzing questions exactly as they were asked by major survey organizations. Sometimes the questions are dichotomous in form, sometimes they include a middle alternative such as "no interest," sometimes they involve longer scales of four or more points. Evidence has turned up at several junctures that these and other variations in format can make an important difference in the conclusions drawn about trends over time. When additional problems such as effects due to questionnaire context, race of interviewer, and social desirability are also called to mind, one realizes that our knowledge of white racial attitudes is far from complete even for the substantive areas most adequately covered by the major surveys. Sweeping summary statements by ourselves or others must be qualified by the need to understand more adequately the relation between substantive issues and the way the questions are asked in surveys.

There is also a need to understand more adequately the meaning of the effects of education reported in this chapter, including its frequent positive relation to liberal racial attitudes, the absence of clear relations in certain instances, and even a reversal of relation in two different but important cases (pp. 126–127 and pp. 180–182). For the purpose of such further understanding, it is essential to control for variables like income that are related to education, which we do in Chapter 4, pp. 231–235; to take account of the relation of greater schooling to awareness and acceptance of changing social norms, as considered in Chapter 2, pp. 92–97; and to enrich interpretation by use of additional open-ended questioning (Krysan 1995).

Sources of Change
in White Racial Attitudes

This chapter considers several social background factors that can help us understand how changes in racial attitudes take place and where the changes are located in the white population. The first part of the chapter deals with the difference between changes that occur *within* individuals, as when a person responds to events by altering his or her own attitudes, and changes that occur in the total population as older people die and are replaced by younger people with different attitudes.

The second part of the chapter picks up our earlier interest in the effects of education on attitudes, contrasting them with the effects of income on attitudes. Income and education are themselves positively related, but they do not always have the same relation to particular attitudes. The different effects of these two social class variables prove informative. In addition, we consider the association of gender with various racial attitudes, and find it to be generally consistent and meaningful.

Throughout the chapter we hold constant all variables except the one that is of direct interest. For example, unlike Chapter 3, we examine here the relation of education to a particular attitude while controlling for income, cohort, gender, and region. This requires use of a somewhat more technical form of analysis than that employed in other chapters, but we have tried to keep the statistical machinery in the background and thus make the chapter accessible to readers less interested in the technical aspects.

The Question of Cohort Effects

The three most frequently cited sources of change in the attitudes of a population—for example, the white American population—are public events or *period* influences that may affect individuals irrespective of age or cohort, a process that Davis (1992) calls "conversion"; generational or *cohort* differences among groups of people born at different times; and the developmental stages in the life-course associated with *aging*.

Thus, as described in Chapter 1, the use of violence by segregationist white police in Birmingham in 1963 shocked the general white public and, as a result, created more sympathy for the goals of the civil rights movement among individuals of all ages and cohorts than would have occurred otherwise. This is change at the individual level that we call "attitude conversion" or a "period effect." Cohort (generational) effects can also lead to change because older persons holding one set of attitudes die and younger persons holding different attitudes replace them in the adult population. Thus Southern children experiencing integration in restaurants and other public accommodations may grow up with racial attitudes quite different from those of their parents, who experienced only segregation when they were growing up. Even if no single individual changes his or her own opinion, this demographic process of cohort replacement can shift the overall attitudes of the population. Finally, changes due to aging presumably reflect biological and psychological developments that are thought to be more or less independent of specific times and places. The supposed tendency of people to become more conservative as they grow older would be an instance of change occasioned by this kind of life-course factor. It is possible for all these types of change to occur simultaneously as well as in various combinations. If any two take opposite directions, they may even cancel each other out in terms of net effects.[1]

Most previous research on changes in racial attitudes has focused primarily on two of these explanations: conversion of individual attitudes and cohort replacement. In the 1985 edition of this book, we found that both processes had contributed positively to the development of racial tolerance in the last half of the twentieth century, and our assessment built on, and has subsequently been corroborated by, the work of others (Davis 1975, 1992; Smith 1981, 1985; Firebaugh and Davis 1988; Mayer 1992). We continue to treat the two processes of conversion and cohort replacement as the basic causes of changes in racial attitudes. There is reason to focus especially on cohort replacement because certain political events over the past half century, such as the rise and decline of the national civil rights movement in the 1950s and 1960s and a possible retreat from a commitment to integration during the 1980s and 1990s, have created quite disparate milieus for various generations of young adults.

Before we examine in detail how these two processes have operated over the last fifty years, however, we must decide whether or not aging, the third explanation, has had a substantial impact. When life-course developments, as well as cohort and period effects, contribute importantly to major changes in racial attitudes, the three influences become confounded in a way that makes them impossible to separate (Glenn 1976, 1989; Fienberg and Mason 1985; Rodgers 1990). Thus the question of how much aging helps to explain changes in racial attitudes must be resolved.

Two hypotheses link the process of aging with increasing social and political conservatism. The more widely accepted explanation states that as individuals reach late middle age they become more conservative owing to a number of physiological, psychological, and social factors (Sears 1983). Davis (1975, 1992) has confronted this hypothesis directly and to date has found no evidence to support it. In addition, Danigelis and Cutler have studied attitude trends for cohorts born before 1939 and concluded that aging is not accompanied by "either increasingly rigid or increasingly conservative attitudes with respect to race relations" (1989:19; also see Danigelis and Cutler 1991). More general research on attitude change at the individual level using panel data and covering a multitude of social and political topics finds members of the oldest age groups (fifty-eight to sixty-five and sixty-six to eighty-three) no more nor less likely to change their attitudes than any other age group over thirty-three (Krosnick and Alwin 1989). The main conclusion of yet another study using both cross-section and panel data is that "older people are as capable of attitude change as younger people" when they are exposed to "change-inducing experiences" (Tyler and Schuller 1991).

The second hypothesis about aging also makes a connection between growing older and conservatism, but much earlier in the life-course. The supposed idealism of youth gives way by early middle age under the pressures of marriage, parenthood, and work—as when, for example, the radical yippie becomes a stockbroker. If this aging effect indeed exists, we would expect trends on social and political attitudes within cohorts to show noticeable declines in liberalism between young adulthood and early middle age. However, previous research on racial attitudes indicates that cohorts, regardless of birth date, became more, not less, integrationist over the period from 1972 to 1990 (Schuman et al. 1985; Davis 1992; Steeh and Schuman 1992).

In the absence of evidence that either of these life-course effects operates as hypothesized, we are willing to assume explicitly, as Davis (1992) does, that the aging process has very little or no impact on changes in racial attitudes and, therefore, that trends are the result of a combination of period effects and cohort replacement. In our own previous work (Steeh and Schuman 1992), we took the precaution of eliminating the oldest cohorts, those coming of age prior to the 1960s, in order to guard against the possibility that they may be more susceptible to influences associated with aging than are younger cohorts. We have now decided that this was an overly cautious approach and that there are advantages to be gained from extending our analyses to the entire adult population represented in national samples, including those people who grew up before the civil rights movement became salient.[2]

Perspectives on Cohort Effects

To explore properly the process of cohort replacement, we need to understand why there might be differences in attitudes among groups of people born and raised in different eras. Firebaugh and Chen (1995) posit two possibilities: the relative sizes of cohorts and history. For some scholars, size has been all important (Easterlin 1980), but our interest, like Firebaugh and Chen's, centers on the historical sources of cohort differences. We expand their interpretation, however, by subdividing these historical influences into two types:

The Continuous Socialization Model. This model is assumed to result from a process of change that is ongoing and cumulative. Younger generations, for example, those who have grown up in less racially hostile environments, are presumed to be more tolerant than older generations (Stouffer 1955; Hyman and Sheatsley 1956). This produces a monotonic ordering of cohorts with the oldest being the least tolerant and the youngest being the most tolerant. Thus an ever-improving spiral develops that would not "soon, if ever, reverse itself" (Hyman and Sheatsley 1956:39). This model does not pinpoint specific ages as particularly formative for racial attitudes but implies a learning period that stretches from childhood through at least early adulthood. Over the years this type of cohort effect has assumed a prominent place in the literature on racial attitude change since it seems to fit well the gradually liberalizing trends revealed by national survey data of the 1950s, 1960s, and 1970s (Hyman and Sheatsley 1964; Greeley and Sheatsley 1971; Taylor, Sheatsley, and Greeley 1978; Hyman and Wright 1979).

The Unique Events Model. This model defines cohort effects in a different and more specific way. Starting from the suggestions of Mannheim ([1928] 1952), much work of the last few years has stressed the impact of particular historical events on the character of generations. Public events experienced at a "critical period" in the life-course, usually defined as the years of adolescence and early adulthood, produce a distinctive set of attitudes in an entire cohort that persists throughout its lifetime (Roberts and Lang 1985; Schuman and Scott 1989; Firebaugh and Chen 1995). Sharing of great events supposedly creates a distinct generational consciousness. Thus we speak and read about the Great Depression generation (Elder 1974), the sixties generation (Gitlin 1987; Whalen and Flacks 1989), the generation of young Nazis in prewar Germany (Weil 1987; Braungart and Braungart 1990), and even Generation X, a title that has been used to refer to adults born roughly from the mid-1960s to the mid-1970s (Holtz 1995). If the continuous socialization model produces gradual change, the occurrence of important historical events may result in abrupt and discontinuous shifts in attitudes that allow for considerable variation in the ordering of cohorts. Rather than always being more tolerant, younger generations may instead be swayed by historical events to become less tolerant than previous cohorts (Weil 1985). Under conditions such as these, intercohort differences in liberalism are not very likely to be monotonic. Furthermore, intracohort trends could stall or reverse direction, creating a downward rather than an upward spiral. In addition, rates of change within cohorts might diverge considerably, creating differences in the directions of trend lines that produce statistical interactions. It is also possible that one cohort, particularly affected by historical circumstances, would stand out as being distinctively more or less liberal than all the others.

Much in this second conception of cohort differences seems at first sight to be appropriate for studying changes in racial attitudes. The national population can readily be thought of as consisting of cohorts that differ in the racial events they experienced during their adolescence and early adulthood. Some cohorts went through this potentially critical life period in the heyday of Jim Crow. Others grew into adulthood at the height of the civil rights movement, when segregation was successfully challenged. Still others came of age during the years of the urban riots, the busing controversy, and the Nixon period of benign neglect. The youngest adults now available for interview in surveys matured in the 1980s and 1990s, when rising hostility to affirmative action and a focus on inner-city crime and deterioration may have counteracted the effects of being raised by ever more liberal parents.

Although we acknowledge the difficulties in establishing the impact of events occurring during a person's adolescence on their later attitudes (Schuman and Rieger 1992; Firebaugh and Chen 1995), we nevertheless hold that any differences among cohorts defined in terms of their historical backgrounds cannot be explained as parsimoniously in any other way. Thus we apply both the continuous socialization and the unique event explanations of cohort differences to our data and attempt to assess in a rough way the relative strength of each. At the same time we want to take into account overall period influences so that we can determine whether or not a combination of period and cohort effects would best fit the data.

The Analytic Strategy

To study attitude change within a population along the lines we have indicated, we first place respondents into one of four cohorts. In doing this we assume that the four groups are basically distinct from one another, even though such an assumption clearly violates reality and risks underestimating cohort effects. Undoubtedly the boundaries between these large cohort groups, rather than being clearly demarcated, as our conception implies, blend gradually one into the other. Thus some of the change that we will attribute to period effects may, in fact, be due to differences among smaller cohorts that exist within the larger category (Firebaugh and Davis 1988). We are willing to take this risk for two reasons. First, we are interested in determining if the differences in attitude between successive cohorts are approximately equal or not. This is important for gauging the impact of unique generation effects. By treating cohort as a series of dummy variables rather than as a continuous variable, we are able to circumvent a linearity assumption in our analyses and thus to allow for the possibility of unequal differences. Second, we choose to limit the number of groups to four because the historical events we discussed in Chapter 1 seem to fall naturally into four eras and because a smaller number of clearly meaningful groups makes the results easier to interpret. The four cohorts are defined by the following criteria:[3]

1. *Pre–civil rights movement cohort.* This oldest cohort contains the people who grew up and were socialized into American life before the civil rights movement. The youngest members of this cohort would have reached the age of eighteen in 1953, one year before the U.S. Supreme Court declared racial segregation of the nation's public schools unconstitutional. In ISR's 1970 survey, the earliest one for which we have usable data for at least three cohorts, this group constituted 70 percent of the white population. By the 1994 ISR study, its proportion had declined to 29 percent.

2. *Civil rights movement cohort.* This cohort consists of those individuals who reached adulthood during the early, successful struggle of the civil rights movement from 1954 to 1965. In 1970 members of this cohort made up 25 percent of the white adult population, but only 16 percent by 1994.

3. *Post–civil rights movement cohort.* Adults in this cohort came of age during the mid to late 1960s and the 1970s (1966–1980), the years of the urban riots, the Vietnam war, and the Nixon-Ford-Carter administrations. This group ranged in size from a mere 4 percent of whites in 1970 to 36 percent by 1994.[4]

4. *Reagan-Bush cohort.* Our youngest group, roughly the same as Generation X, entered adulthood from 1981, when Ronald Reagan was inaugurated as president, to the mid-1990s. Besides having matured in what many consider the most conservative political climate in many years, the most recent cohort is also distinguished by its innocence of the historic struggle waged by African Americans for equality. Since members of this generation have no firsthand knowledge of the events that occurred in the 1950s and early 1960s, they can hardly feel the outrage and sense of urgency that swept through the nation at that time. The Reagan-Bush cohort first appeared in the 1984 ISR study representing 1 percent

of the white population. By 1994 this percentage had increased to 19. Because this cohort is so small during its first years, we exclude any time point with a sample size of fewer than fifty. Practically, this means that the cohort first appears in 1988 for analyses that involve NORC questions and in 1986 for analyses of ISR items.[5]

Using repeated samples of the population from many different time points, we track each cohort over an extended period. Even though the same individuals are not interviewed in the surveys we analyze, the random samples are intended to represent the same cohort at each time point and can be compared to determine whether and how much attitudes have changed (*intra*cohort change). This difference across time constitutes a measure of the net amount of conversion in individual attitudes that has occurred within a cohort during a designated period.[6] Since period effects are usually experienced by members of all cohorts simultaneously, it seems logical to hypothesize initially that these will be approximately the same across cohort groups. Thus conversion of individual attitudes can occur independent of cohort membership.[7] For example, everyone, young or old, could have watched on television as the Birmingham, Alabama, police released attack dogs and turned fire hoses on innocent civil rights marchers during the nonviolent protests of 1963. The resulting outrage undoubtedly crossed generational boundaries. In our analyses, however, we also want to be open to other possibilities—for example, that younger cohorts change somewhat more quickly and older cohorts somewhat more slowly than others. When rates of change diverge considerably across cohorts, we have evidence that attitude conversion and cohort membership are not independent but related, and we speak of an interaction effect, for example, convergence or divergence of intracohort trends over time.

Evidence of change due to cohort replacement (*inter*cohort change) is reflected by the differences *among* the four cohorts at specific points in time. With data from many different years, we can assess whether or not each new cohort entering the population is more liberal on racial issues than the ones that preceded it, and whether or not these differences are relatively equal and constant over time, as the continuous socialization model implies. We are especially interested in gauging the impact of two historical eras with quite opposite dynamics that seem potentially important for differentiating cohorts in relation to racial issues. In the one case, the years of the civil rights movement may have left an indelibly liberal mark on the generation growing up at that time. In the other, the racial climate following Reagan's election to the presidency may have led to a conservative backlash among the young men and women reaching adulthood over the succeeding decade. Thus, if Mannheim's ideas hold, we should see something unique about the cohorts that came of age during one or both of these periods.

In sum, we are proposing that specific historical events work in two ways. They fashion a distinct generational consciousness in particular cohorts, on the one hand, and, on the other, they provide the impetus for change in individual attitudes that may affect the entire adult population.

In addition to the measures of net change among individuals and of cohort differences, our analyses also include the basic background factors of education, region of residence, gender, and family income. We create a slightly more refined measure of education than the one employed in Chapter 3 by dividing those with more than a high school education into those who attended college but never graduated and those who received a college degree. The region variable is identical to the North-South division we used in Chapter 3, and gender is a natural dichotomy. (For technical reasons, these three factors, plus cohort, are treated as dummy variables in our analysis, with the omitted groups being, respectively, people in the pre–civil rights movement cohort, those with less than a high school education, Southerners, and males.) In order to maintain comparability over time, income is conceived in relative terms as quartiles (the 25 percent at the bottom of the income distribution, the low middle 25 percent, the high middle 25 percent, and finally the top 25 percent) except for ISR surveys, where income can only be divided into three equal categories (the lowest third, the middle third, and the top third).[8]

Taking these background factors into account may modify our estimates of the cohort and period effects in which we are most interested. Thus our strategy differs from models that concentrate exclusively on period and cohort (Firebaugh and Davis 1988; Davis 1992; but see Firebaugh and Chen 1995). To explain our decision, we look briefly at a few of the resulting benefits. Controlling the level of formal education turns the cohort variable into a purer measure of the other socializing experiences that may differentiate cohorts, such as directly experiencing the events of the civil rights movement. By the same token, a specific region variable takes into account the influences that different subcultures exert upon attitude formation, since there is a good deal of evidence that Southerners are socialized to be less liberal on racial issues than Northerners (Chapter 3; Taylor et al. 1978; Wilson 1986).[9] Furthermore, scattered research suggests that women as a group are more supportive than men of policies that aid the poor, the unemployed, the sick, and people in need (Baxter and Lansing 1983; Shapiro and Mahajan 1986). Including family income allows us to eliminate yet another influence that might otherwise affect our interpretations, especially our assessments of the effects of education. These controls do mean, however, that we underestimate the *total* effect of intercohort differences insofar as they may be due to education or other of the control variables we include (Firebaugh and Davis 1988; Mayer 1992).

Intracohort trends and intercohort differences in this chapter will be based on multiple regression models and will be presented in a way that can be understood by readers not interested in the technical details.[10] These models will be calculated for questions from each of the issue areas we explored in Chapter 3. In order to ensure that our results are reliable, we limit our analyses to those items for which we have at least three years of data at the individual level. It should also be emphasized that the change analyzed here is only a subset of the change we discussed in Chapter 3. Individual-level data from early NORC surveys were not available to us, and so our focus in this chapter centers on NORC data collected in the General Social Survey, which began in 1972. On the whole, we were able to obtain complete data for ISR surveys.[11]

Presentation of Results

We present the results of our analyses in graphs just as we did throughout Chapter 3. Now, however, we display cohort and period effects after removing differences among the four cohorts in education, income, gender, and region. We can estimate these "pure" effects using regression, and in the graphs that follow we show them for a specific subset of our sample population: white Northern males with a high school education and an income in the second quartile of the income distribution (basically lower middle class).[12] Our choice of this group has no substantive meaning, and we could as easily have decided to graph the effects for female Southerners with a college degree and a higher (or lower) level of income. We only need to specify a subset in order to equalize the four cohort groups on the background factors that have been included in the analysis. Had we used Southern females instead of Northern males, the lines would slope in exactly the same direction and the distances between the trends would remain the same. However, all the lines would be moved upward or downward on the scale to fit the average attitude values for that particular group.[13]

Because we have chosen a specific subset of people, any variation in cohort and period effects that occurs cannot be attributed to differences among the cohorts on the characteristics that define the subset. In this way we are able to approximate an experiment by holding other things equal—the other things in this case being education, income, region of residence, and gender. Because we are plotting values estimated from regressions, all the lines in the graphs of this chapter will be straight and will communicate simply and clearly the impact of cohort and period influences after controlling for background factors.[14]

Thus the graphs that follow will contain four trends, one for each cohort. Figure 4.1 is an example. The trends across time indicate *intra*cohort changes, that is, the amount of net conversion in individual attitudes (period effects). *Inter*cohort differences (cohort effects) are represented by the vertical distances between trend lines. We begin with the hypothesis that the continuous socialization model will fit the results for most of our questions. Thus each successively younger cohort should become more liberal than its immediate predecessor, and the distances between cohorts should be approximately equal and remain constant over time.

Although we hypothesize the operation of this continuous model, we want to be alert to evidence that indicates the unique impact of historical events on attitudes and suggests that the continuous model may need modification. It seems reasonable to assume that the civil rights movement powerfully affected the attitudes of adults coming of age at that time, but, to date, its influence has been difficult to detect. Perhaps there are signs of its importance that researchers have overlooked, such as a sizable difference between the oldest, pre–civil rights movement cohort and all subsequent cohorts, or a conversion effect that is substantially more positive for the civil rights movement cohort than for other cohorts. Furthermore, in order to infer the impact of the conservative Reagan era, we do not need to find that the young adults of the 1980s and 1990s are the most conservative of all the cohorts. We must

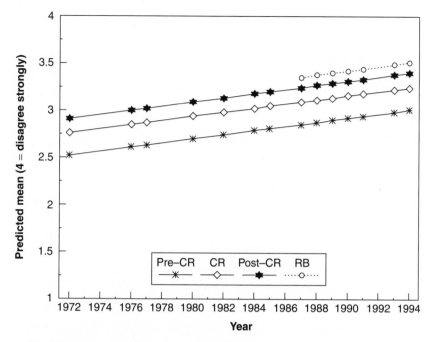

Figure 4.1. Residential Choice, by cohort, NORC, 1972–1994

Pre–CR = Pre–civil rights movement cohort
CR = Civil rights movement cohort
Post–CR = Post–civil rights movement cohort
RB = Reagan-Bush cohort

demonstrate only that they are either at the same level as their immediate predecessor (the post–civil rights cohort) or just slightly more liberal, provided that there are no ceiling effects.

The graphs in this chapter will plot two different types of numbers, depending on whether an attitude question has dichotomous response options or can be regarded instead as a scale with three or more points. Wherever the response options for a dependent variable consist of three or more ordered categories, the values in the graph are those that are predicted by an ordinary least squares regression equation for each cohort and year, rather than the actual percentages in favor of a principle or policy as in Chapter 3. Thus in Figure 4.1 the four alternatives to the NORC Residential Choice question are scored from one (agree strongly with white rights) to four (disagree strongly with white rights, the racially liberal response), and each point represents the predicted

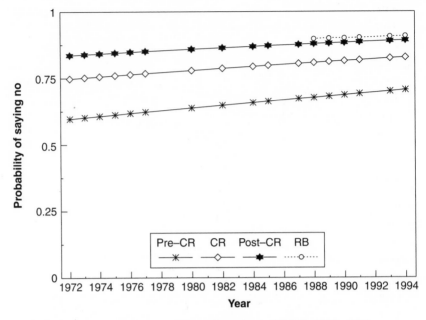

Figure 4.2. Laws against Intermarriage, by cohort, NORC, 1972–1994

Pre–CR = Pre–civil rights movement cohort
CR = Civil rights movement cohort
Post–CR = Post–civil rights movement cohort
RB = Reagan-Bush cohort

score for a particular cohort at a particular time, after controlling for the background factors specified earlier. Whenever the dependent variable is dichotomous, however, logistic regression is the preferred statistical method, especially where an item is extremely skewed. In this case, the number plotted in a graph, such as Figure 4.2, is the probability that a group has given a liberal rather than a conservative response.

Despite the different metrics in Figures 4.1 and 4.2, the plotted values in each case are the cohort and period effects after removing the influences of education, income, gender, and region. Nontechnical readers do not need to be concerned about the difference between probabilities and predicted values since in practice they can be interpreted in essentially the same way. At any rate, high scores usually represent attitudes that favor equal rights, integration, or are pro-black in other ways. (Each figure shows clearly the definition of a high score for the particular question being graphed.)

Generally we will follow the main topical areas developed in Chapter 3. Usually one question will serve as a prototype and others will be mentioned in relation to it. If a question deviates from the prototype sufficiently, we will discuss the deviations in more detail. Throughout these analyses, as in Chapter 3, the population will be defined as white adults age twenty-one and over. All response scales, except those for the questions we have categorized as explanations of inequality, have been ordered from conservative to liberal.

Principles

Four of the eleven questions about principles of equal treatment and integration have sufficient data for analyzing sources of attitude change. Figure 4.1 displays the pattern of intracohort trends and intercohort differences for the NORC question Residential Choice, which will serve as our prototype. For this question as well as for the other three items, Laws against Intermarriage, Black Candidate, and Same Schools, the data generally cover the period from 1972 through 1994.[15]

From these results, we draw several conclusions about the processes of change as they are reflected in white attitudes toward the principles of equal treatment and integration. First, the intracohort trends (slopes) seem approximately alike as they move upward across all cohorts. The absence of significant interaction effects indicates that all cohorts have changed in a liberal direction over time at about the same rate. Thus there is evidence of a broad period effect over the entire population.

Second, the differences between the cohorts are also clearly evident, since each succeeding group proves to be more liberal than the one immediately before it.[16] Thus the prototype for the principle questions conforms roughly to the continuous socialization model. However, the distances between adjacent cohorts shrink as we move from older to younger groups. The oldest, pre–civil rights cohort is clearly the most conservative in its attitude toward the principle of blacks' having the right to live wherever they can afford to, with the distance fairly large between its line and that of the civil rights cohort. At the same time, although the position of the Reagan-Bush adults on residential choice is the most liberal, it is only a little more liberal than that of the post–civil rights movement cohort. Thus there is also evidence in Figure 4.1 for the unique events model, since the conservatism of the pre–civil rights cohort might be traced to its socialization prior to the salience of the civil rights movement that began in the mid-1950s, and the lack of substantial liberalism of the Reagan-Bush cohort could be explained by its socialization after the civil rights movement had for all practical purposes ended.

Figure 4.2 indicates that the conclusions we would draw had we chosen one of the other three principle questions would be similar (though for these dichotomous items we use logistic regression and graph probabilities rather than predicted values). In the case of the question about laws against intermarriage, the gap between the oldest and the next oldest cohort is somewhat larger than in Figure 4.1, whereas the difference in degree of liberalism between the two younger cohorts almost disappears.

Thus the basic ordering of the four cohorts remains the same for the several items dealing with principles, but the magnitudes of the differences do vary somewhat depending on the nature and distribution of the item. Two other questions about principles were plotted and studied, though the graphs are not shown here. Although school integration is supported strongly by all cohort groups, the intercohort differences remain stable and are consistently positive and monotonic. The levels of approval for the Black Candidate question, like those for the Same Schools question, approach a ceiling for all but the pre–civil rights movement cohort. By the late 1980s the trends for the three youngest cohorts begin to intertwine, as a result of slight period and cohort interactions, and the monotonic pattern disappears. Only the oldest cohort remains distinctly less liberal throughout the period from 1972 to 1994.

Summary. From our discussion of these four questions tapping approval of principles of equal treatment and integration, we are able to fashion a common portrait. It appears that change due to the net conversion (period effect) of individual attitudes has proceeded slowly over the last two and a half decades, partly because of the high level of support most of these issues already enjoyed by 1972. In addition, distinct and sometimes sizable cohort differences have existed, especially between the oldest pre–civil rights cohort and the others. Equally notable is the fact that the difference between the two youngest cohorts tends to be small, so that the Reagan-Bush cohort is only slightly, if at all, more liberal about issues of principle than the post–civil rights movement cohort that immediately precedes it. Thus much of the remaining intercohort variation involves the oldest pre–civil rights cohort.

Elements of both sources of attitude change—cohort and period—appear in the years from 1972 through 1994 for principle questions. Each successive cohort is usually more liberal than the one immediately preceding it, and period change occurs gradually. However, conformity to the continuous model of cohort differences is not complete: the youngest cohort is less liberal than we might expect, while the conservatism of the oldest cohort can be interpreted to fit either model. Furthermore, if the youngest cohorts continue to become more alike in the future, replacement will ultimately cease to provide an explanation of attitude change, though there will continue to be some overall liberalization within the total population until the oldest, most conservative cohort becomes too small to matter. (The gradual disappearance of the oldest cohort helps account for the striking picture of change shown for principle questions in Chapter 3, for example, Figure 3.1.) But as we examine other attitude areas, we will see that this summary does not always hold, and that the attitudes of the Reagan-Bush cohort vary more across types of racial questions than we or most other observers expected.

Implementation

As we showed in Chapter 3, questions about the implementation of principles of equal treatment enjoy less support among whites than questions about the principles themselves. The existence of this principle-implementation gap has led some scholars to treat approval for government efforts to promote integration as the more valid measure of genuine commitment to racial justice. Therefore, we might also expect to find very different cohort and period effects for the two categories of questions. Our analysis in Chapter 3, however, suggested that generally the overall trends and relationships for the implementation questions did not lead to a radically new perspective, but fell instead on the same continuum as the principle questions. Thus a difference between a principle and an implementation item might be no greater than a difference between two questions about principles. In this chapter we subject this finding to a more difficult test by determining how closely the cohort effects for the four implementation items we consider in this section (Open Housing, Federal School Inter-

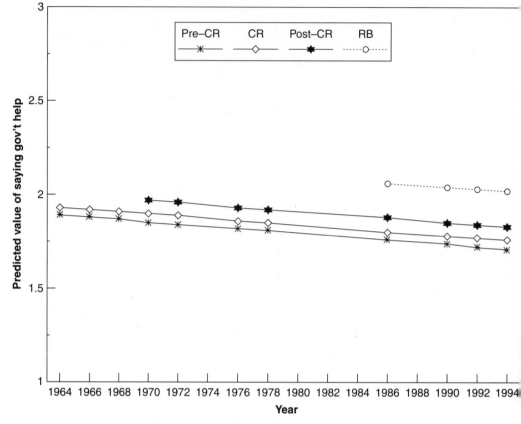

Figure 4.3. Federal School Intervention, by cohort, ISR, 1964–1994

Pre–CR = Pre–civil rights movement cohort
CR = Civil rights movement cohort
Post–CR = Post–civil rights movement cohort
RB = Reagan-Bush cohort

vention, Federal Job Intervention, and NORC's Busing question) parallel those for the principle items.

Just as we might expect on the basis of our conclusions in Chapter 3, the implementation questions display a more complex variety of cohort and period effects than the principle questions.[17] The intracohort trends (period effects) generally reflect the direction of overall change we found in Chapter 3. Support for the federal government's efforts to ensure school integration generally declines (Federal School Intervention in Figure 4.3), whereas support for Open Housing laws

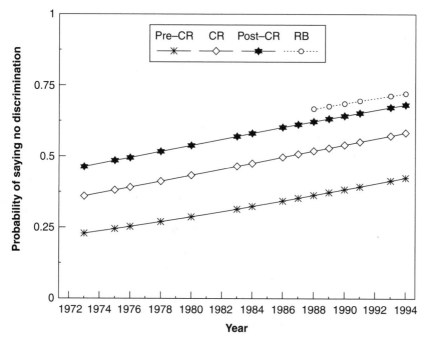

Figure 4.4. Open Housing, by cohort, NORC, 1972–1994

Pre–CR = Pre–civil rights movement cohort
CR = Civil rights movement cohort
Post–CR = Post–civil rights movement cohort
RB = Reagan-Bush cohort

increases (Figure 4.4). On a third item, Federal Job Intervention, the four intracohort trends scarcely change over the thirty years the question has been asked (the trends are not shown, but note the overall coefficient of .000 for year in Appendix B).[18] Finally, the NORC Busing item in Figure 4.5 seems to show the three oldest cohorts becoming more favorable to busing and the Reagan-Bush cohort declining slightly from its relatively high level of support. However, the statistical evidence for the decline is mixed (the interaction with year is significant but the coefficient for the slope within the Reagan-Bush cohort itself is not), and we are somewhat skeptical about its reliability. There is some corroboration of the decline for that cohort on a few other NORC questions, but not at all on ISR or Gallup questions. Thus we are uncertain about how seriously to take the unusual Reagan-Bush slope for the Busing item.[19] We do feel confident, though, that the Reagan-

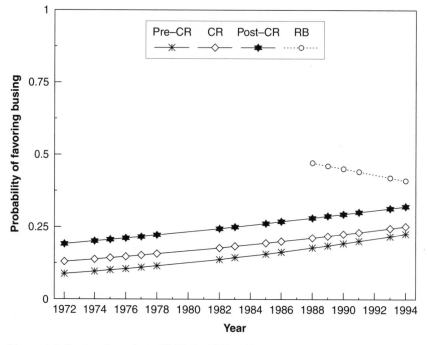

Figure 4.5. Busing, by cohort, NORC, 1972–1994

Pre–CR = Pre–civil rights movement cohort
CR = Civil rights movement cohort
Post–CR = Post–civil rights movement cohort
RB = Reagan-Bush cohort

Bush cohort is on the average much more liberal on this issue than the other cohorts, and it is this difference in levels of liberalism that we stress here.

The negative or stable period effects that exist for the two federal intervention questions (Schools and Jobs) would seem to suggest a pattern of attitude change that is quite different from the pattern common to the principle questions. We proposed in Chapter 3 that these effects are largely due to changes in the meaning of questions (Federal Job Intervention) or to the sudden prominence of the controversy over busing or other innovative methods to achieve racial integration (Federal School Intervention). The item about nondiscrimination through Open Housing is relatively free from these kinds of influences, and conversion occurs in a liberal direction just as it did for the principle questions.

Intracohort trends, however, tell only a part of the story. The differences among cohorts are equally revealing. Although the cohorts for Open Housing (Figure 4.4) and Federal Job Intervention (not shown) maintain the liberal monotonic order from oldest to youngest that is characteristic of the principle questions, they also repeat another striking characteristic—the small difference between the two youngest groups. The cohorts for the remaining two items—Federal School Intervention (Figure 4.3) and Busing (Figure 4.5)—possess the same monotonicity, but here the youngest cohort proves to be much more liberal than any other group. This unexpected liberalism of the youngest cohort explains the apparent recovery of some support for Federal School Intervention shown earlier in Chapter 3 (Figure 3.8): the recovery must be due to the entry into the population of the Reagan-Bush cohort in the mid-1980s since the three older cohorts continue in Figure 4.3 to show a decline through 1994. For the Busing question, there is a similar contribution by the Reagan-Bush cohort, but conversion in a liberal direction also helps create the recent rise in support shown in Table 3.2.

In trying to understand why the youngest cohort takes such a leading position on both Federal School Intervention and Busing, we turn back to our analysis in Chapter 3. Both questions deal with policies that foster school integration, and we saw how interrelated the two issues became in the minds of survey respondents during the 1970s. It is conceivable that the same influences also produce similar patterns of intercohort differences. Thus the underlying reason for young adults' greater approval of government efforts in this area may stem from the historical conditions that mold the attitudes of young adults. Because busing is no longer a salient pro-integration strategy, adults coming of age in the 1980s have not been exposed to the arguments against it that proliferated in the early 1970s. As a result, there may have been "generational forgetting" that carries over to affect attitudes toward federal intervention to desegregate schools. With no historical memory of the busing controversy, young adults do not have as strong a motive for opposing desegregation policies.[20] However, the small liberalization in attitudes toward busing that has occurred among the oldest groups in recent years does not seem to have had the carryover effect to implementation of school integration that we might have anticipated.

Summary. The intercohort pattern that occurs for the implementation questions shown in Figures 4.3 and 4.5 differs in what are probably two interrelated ways from questions about broad principles. On the one hand, the youngest cohort of adults is exceptionally liberal on the two implementation items, and on the other hand, the oldest cohort is not as conservative as it was on the principle items. We will see that this pattern recurs with some later types of questions. The Open Housing question in Figure 4.4, however, acts more like the principle items—oldest cohort very conservative, youngest only slightly more liberal than its predecessor—as indeed it had in most other respects in our analysis in Chapter 3. This pattern also recurs with some future items. We are not able to interpret fully the difference between these two types of patterning, but the distinction is noteworthy and calls for future explanation. (The Federal Job Intervention question is closer to the Open Housing pattern, but perhaps because of the ambiguity of the question it is less clear-cut.)

Our results suggest that both cohort and period influences will affect the future course of attitudes toward implementation issues, but in different directions. For only two questions (Open Housing and Busing) will period and cohort effects both work together to promote liberal change as they did for the principle items. Federal Job Intervention seems immune to period influences and may become slightly more liberal in the future only as a result of cohort replacement, depending on how the ambiguity of the phrase "fair treatment in jobs" is interpreted. By contrast, Federal School Intervention would show a steady overall decline in approval due to period effects except for the existence of the youngest cohort, whose attitudes are decidedly more liberal on this item than are those of any other group. Here the two sources of change counterbalance each other. Across the implementation questions as a whole, the different processes produce the overall trends we traced in Chapter 3.

Social Distance

In Chapter 3 we discussed three areas of life that bring blacks and whites into personal contact with one another. Posed as hypothetical situations, the items we call social distance asked white respondents how they might react to associating with blacks in schools, in neighborhoods, and in informal social activities. From the thirteen items in Table 3.3 that fall into these categories, we have sufficient data to look at those from two areas: school desegregation and informal social activities. We first examine the NORC questions involving various

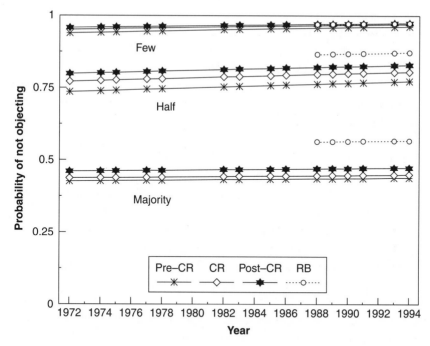

Figure 4.6. Level of school integration, by cohort, NORC, 1972–1994
Pre–CR = Pre–civil rights movement cohort
CR = Civil rights movement cohort
Post–CR = Post–civil rights movement cohort
RB = Reagan-Bush cohort

degrees of racial integration in schools (Few, Half, and Majority black schools).[21] As Figure 4.6 indicates, most white people would be willing to place their children in a school setting with a few blacks. We therefore concentrate on the trends and intercohort differences for Half and Majority black schools, which are also graphed in Figure 4.6.

Besides the great difference in levels of support for Half versus Majority black schools, which we noted in the last chapter, the cohort analysis helps us understand the evidence of upward change on these items reported in Chapter 3. The rates of intracohort change for both questions are quite small, vanishingly so for the Majority question. It is the entrance of the Reagan-Bush adults into the sample population that accounts for much of the upward movement that occurs between 1972 and 1990 (see Table 3.3 or Figure 3.12) on both Half and Majority black schools. As with the school-related implementation questions, the youngest cohort appears clearly most liberal here, especially on the Majority question, producing an intercohort pattern quite different from the one we saw for the principle questions. In addition, although the order of cohorts remains monotonic for Half black schools, there is only a small distance between the two oldest cohorts, and those same two cohorts converge completely on the Majority question—again a very different pattern from that shown by the principle questions.

The question about a black friend's coming to dinner (Black Dinner Guest) shows a pattern very much like that of Half black schools— small intercohort differences, a monotonic ordering of cohorts, and small amounts of positive intracohort change (results not shown).[22] Since the Dinner Guest question was dropped by NORC after 1985, we do not have enough time points and cases to establish an intracohort trend for the youngest (Reagan-Bush) group, but its mean on the item shows it to be clearly and significantly the most liberal of the four cohorts.

When the issue becomes changing club rules to allow blacks to join, as Figure 4.7 illustrates, the intracohort rise is similar to that for the principle questions, except that some convergence occurs between 1977, when the question was first asked, and 1994.[23] The intercohort effect is unusual, with both the oldest and the youngest cohorts distinctive. Conceptually the question has elements of principle, of social distance, and of implementation, since it is about actively changing a norm as well as about personal preference. This probably accounts for its similarity to several of the patterns already discussed.

Summary. On most issues involving social distance between the races, white Americans, regardless of generation, seem to share a common outlook. The main deviation from this consensus involves the youngest cohort, whose perspective is clearly more liberal than everyone else's. In addition, although the oldest cohort is usually the most conservative, it does not stand out as being extreme in this respect, as it did on questions about broad principles.

The basic pattern exhibited by the social distance questions suggests that only limited liberal change will occur in the future for most of them and that it will come almost entirely from cohort replacement. In the case of attitudes about changing the rules of social clubs, however, period and cohort effects may act to ensure greater liberalization. Given

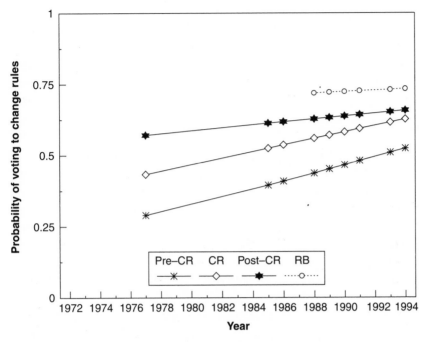

Figure 4.7. Clubs Change Rules, by cohort, NORC, 1977–1994
Pre–CR = Pre–civil rights movement cohort
CR = Civil rights movement cohort
Post–CR = Post–civil rights movement cohort
RB = Reagan-Bush cohort

the high level of approval that whites now espouse for most but not all types of social interaction with blacks—majority black schools being the primary exception—period influences will not lead to much change, unless of course public events occur that divert them to a negative course.

Explanations of Inequality

As we saw in Chapter 3, the questions that explore beliefs about the sources of economic inequality between whites and blacks reveal considerable ambivalence. On the one hand, whites overwhelmingly reject a categorical explanation that relies on in-born ability to account for racial differences. But on the other hand, only a minority of whites attribute black disadvantages to racial discrimination, and instead the most frequent explanation focuses on black motivation. Perhaps because of this pattern, these questions, though relatively recent additions to national surveys, have assumed increasing importance as indicators of current white opinion, displacing to some extent traditional beliefs and attitudes about race (Kluegel 1990; Kluegel and Bobo 1993). Thus it is fortunate that we have a varied set of questions on this topic—seven items with sufficient data for us to analyze at least partially.[24] As we have already discussed in Chapter 3, NORC and ISR have each asked a set of items designed to elicit opinions about different types of explanations. We conceptualized the dimensions represented by these questions along a continuum ranging from explanations that identify in-born characteristics of blacks as the source of their unequal position to explanations that hold white society responsible (Chapter 3, p. 155). This continuum can be described as moving from "individualistic" explanations, which place the blame on individual blacks, to "structural" explanations, which place the blame on discrimination by whites, with intermediate explanations as well (Kluegel and Smith 1986).

We hypothesize that most inequality items will *not* have cohort differences that conform to those in the continuous socialization model as originally stated by Hyman and Sheatsley (1956). Instead, successively younger cohorts will become *less* liberal over time as the goals of the civil rights movement are realized. Thus younger adults may see less discrimination in the world around them than did their predecessors, either because there actually is less *or* because they believe there is less. In either case, any continued inequality can easily be viewed as resulting from the failures of individuals to achieve rather than to racial discrimination by whites. The one qualification to this hypothesis concerns the NORC item about blacks' having less in-born ability than whites, since we know that this element of traditional racism from the nineteenth and early twentieth century has been disappearing from verbal responses in much the same way that defense of principles of discrimination has faded over the past half century.

We might also expect intracohort trends to diverge from those that are specified in the continuous model. Among whites, perceptions of improving conditions for blacks, whether real or assumed, would produce a declining awareness of discrimination regardless of cohort and an increase in the percentages of respondents who accept individualistic explanations.

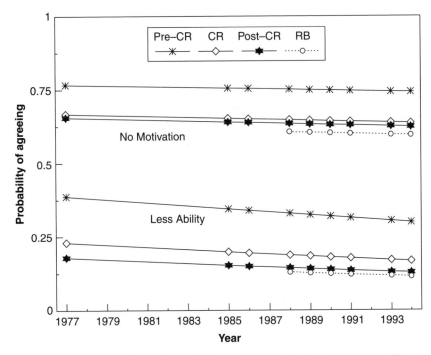

Figure 4.8. Inequality due to Less Ability and No Motivation, NORC, 1977–1994

Pre–CR = Pre–civil rights movement cohort
CR = Civil rights movement cohort
Post–CR = Post–civil rights movement cohort
RB = Reagan-Bush cohort

As expected, NORC's Less Ability question in Figure 4.8 shows a substantial difference in level between the pre–civil rights cohort and the other three, and downward slopes for all four cohorts. Thus both intercohort and intracohort effects contribute to the decline in expression of beliefs in lower black ability. Contrary to our expectation, however, a similar pattern occurs for the NORC No Motivation item in Figure 4.8, with a marked difference between the oldest and the other three cohorts, and some intracohort decline as well. It is possible that an order effect in the NORC series of questions on accounting for black disadvantage has influenced these responses, since the No Motivation question follows one asserting that blacks have not had a chance for a good education, and the No Motivation results differ from two similar questions in ISR surveys (below).

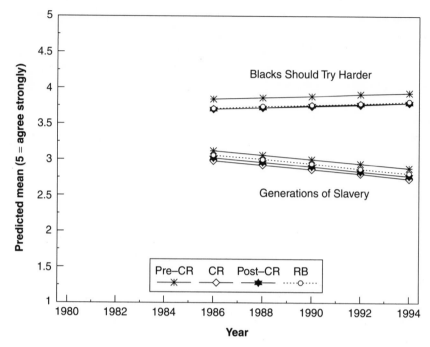

Figure 4.9. Inequality due to Blacks not Trying Hard and Generations of Slavery, ISR, 1986–1994

Pre–CR = Pre–civil rights movement cohort
CR = Civil rights movement cohort
Post–CR = Post–civil rights movement cohort
RB = Reagan-Bush cohort

Once we move away from the NORC questions, we find that our hypothesized pattern emerges. Instead of becoming more liberal, intra-cohort trends tend to slope in conservative directions, and the ordering of cohorts is not predictable. Figure 4.9 graphs Blacks Should Try Harder (ISR) and Generations of Slavery (ISR). If we take Blacks Should Try Harder as the prototype, we see that the oldest cohort is still the most likely to attribute inequality to the fact that blacks do not try hard enough. However, the other three cohorts are indistinguishable—appearing so close together in their views of how hard blacks try that they seem to form a single, larger cohort. Furthermore, the intracohort trends move toward increased agreement on this item, indicating that across all cohorts respondents have by 1994 become slightly more individualistic and conservative in the way they explain inequality.[25]

Whether they measure support for structural or for individualistic explanations, the remaining items show results similar to that for the prototype, Blacks Should Try Harder (ISR). The question comparing blacks' experience with that of other ethnic groups (No Special Favors) repeats the identical cohort pattern, whereas the questions proposing that Generations of Slavery (ISR), No Chance for Education (NORC), or Discrimination (NORC) are responsible for black disadvantage differ only because the distance separating the oldest cohort from all the others is narrower (see Generations of Slavery graphed in Figure 4.9). The trends within cohorts for most of these questions move in a conservative direction, rising when the item refers to an individualist explanation and declining when the explanation is structural (see Figure 4.9). When the explanation involves a lack of education, the overall impression is one of relatively little change over time for any cohort. Across all the items that ask about racial inequality, except for the two NORC questions concerning ability and motivation in Figure 4.8, the intercohort differences and intracohort trends indicate that respondents have less liberal explanations for racial differences now than in the past.

When we ask what is happening with the youngest cohort on these matters, we discover that it almost never stands out as either much higher or much lower than its predecessors. The one exception to this generalization is shown in Figure 4.10, on discrimination as a possible cause of inequality. For this broad question, the Reagan-Bush cohort *enters* adulthood much more willing than any other group to say that inequality between blacks and whites is due to discrimination. After that, the decline is steady and by 1994 the youngest cohort cannot be distinguished from the other three cohorts. Although the decrease is most obvious for the youngest cohort, a similar tendency occurs for the post–civil rights movement cohort as well. The resulting convergence is plainly evident in Figure 4.10.[26]

Summary. For the survey questions that ask people about their understanding of racial inequality, we first located each item along a continuum that ranges from explanations blaming blacks for their problems to those blaming whites and racial discrimination. We then suggested that the prototypical cohort pattern for all of these questions would have the following characteristics: (1) reordering of cohorts so that the oldest cohort is not always the most conservative and the youngest group not always the most liberal; and (2) negative rather than positive intracohort trends. Of the six questions we consider (other than Less

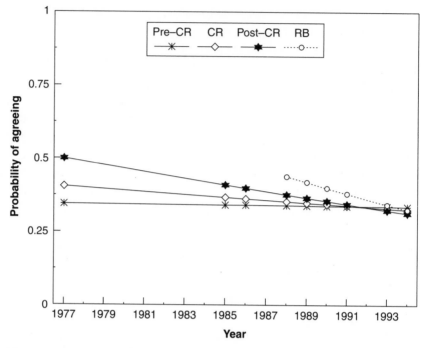

Figure 4.10. Inequality due to Discrimination, NORC, 1977–1994

Pre–CR = Pre–civil rights movement cohort
CR = Civil rights movement cohort
Post–CR = Post–civil rights movement cohort
RB = Reagan-Bush cohort

Ability), all but one (NORC's No Motivation item) manifest these traits. We did not predict the disappearance of meaningful cohort differences, but the evidence for this seems convincing for most of the questions.

It is also possible to speculate about future changes in white attitudes toward the sources of racial inequality. Cohort replacement will be an important factor only for the two NORC explanations involving ability and motivation. Very small cohort differences for the other questions suggest either that any continued liberalization due to cohort replacement may be offset by the increasing conservatism of the youngest adults, or that changes in attitudes toward these issues may not be fueled by cohort replacement at all. As a result, conversion, that is, changes in individual opinions, will assume greater importance for these types of questions than for the other types we have discussed (principle, implementation, and social distance). Whether the declining liberalism that will result from the operation of these processes can ever be reversed will depend on public events that may take place in the future.

Affirmative Action

In Chapter 3 we distinguished between two types of affirmative action questions: those that ask whether the government should act directly to remedy black disadvantage, such as by spending money on programs of economic aid, and those that ask whether blacks should be given preference in hiring, promotion, and admissions to college. In our cohort analysis, we find that there are common traits characteristic of all the questions: only small differences exist among cohorts; the traditional liberal order of cohorts from oldest to youngest is often disrupted; there is little change in attitudes within any cohort; and the youngest cohort is usually the most liberal.[27]

The prototype can be seen in Figure 4.11 for the ISR question, Preference in Hiring and Promotion. The levels of those saying that blacks should be given preferences are narrowly monotonic, with the oldest adults being the least supportive of preferences. The youngest cohort is the most in favor of preferences, though by only a small amount. The question on preferential treatment in college admissions presents similar results, except that the small intracohort decline visible in Figure 4.11 is even smaller and no longer significant in the college case.

The pattern common to four other affirmative action questions, Federal Spending, Help Blacks, Aid to Blacks, and the CBS/NYT version of Preferences in Hiring and Promotion, is similar, differing only in the absence of such clear monotonicity. However, the two remaining items, Spending on Blacks (shown in Figure 4.12) and Aid to Minorities, deviate somewhat from this prototype. Since both questions have a longer time span than most of the affirmative action items, we suspect that they indicate what earlier patterns might have looked like for the questions that do not go back so far in time. During the 1970s the cohorts for both Aid to Minorities and Spending on Blacks were discernibly separate in level and assumed the traditional order from oldest as most conservative to youngest as most liberal. For both items a convergence began in the late 1970s. Rising levels of support among

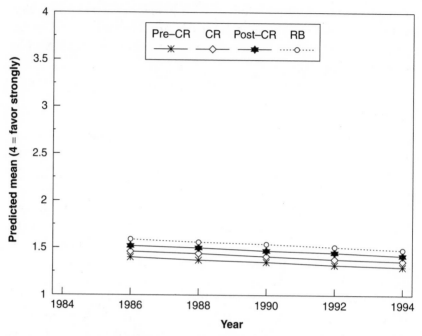

Figure 4.11. Preferences in Hiring and Promotion, by cohort, ISR, 1986–1994

Pre–CR = Pre–civil rights movement cohort
CR = Civil rights movement cohort
Post–CR = Post–civil rights movement cohort
RB = Reagan-Bush cohort

the oldest cohort and possible declining levels of support among the youngest virtually wiped out the intercohort differences.[28] The decline within the youngest cohort for Spending on Blacks, pictured in Figure 4.12, like the decline in attitudes toward Busing (Figure 4.5), should be treated somewhat skeptically. The size of the youngest cohort from 1988 through 1990 is small for this item (approximately fifty cases per year) and there are only six time points, hence there is reason to be cautious in interpretation without further evidence. Thus we stress here the greater liberalism of the youngest cohort compared with the other cohorts, a difference that is quite reliable, and reserve judgment on the reliability of its apparent decline in slope. More generally, by the 1980s and 1990s the cohort effects for these two questions had assumed some of the features common to the other affirmative action items. Apparently we have come full circle from the principle questions, where both cohort and period influences affect changes in attitudes, to the affirmative action questions, where neither works to alter overall distributions of opinion, except slightly as the youngest, more liberal cohort will make up a larger proportion of the adult population in the future.

Summary. We began this chapter by discussing a set of questions concerning principles of equal treatment and integration that had a definite prototype representative of all items in the set. We end this section of the chapter with a similarly consistent set of questions concerning affirmative action, but one where the results differ greatly from the prototype for principles—little change over time for any cohort group, small intercohort differences that are usually not monotonic, and a less prominent role for the oldest cohort than the large differences shown in Figures 4.1 and 4.2. As for future change, we expect very little to

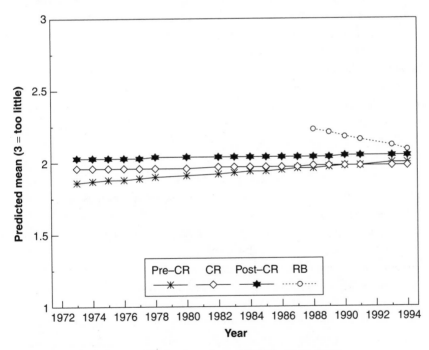

Figure 4.12. Spending on Blacks, by cohort, NORC, 1972–1994

    Pre–CR = Pre–civil rights movement cohort
    CR = Civil rights movement cohort
    Post–CR = Post–civil rights movement cohort
    RB = Reagan-Bush cohort

occur. Support for preferences in jobs and college admissions and for spending on blacks and economic aid is already so low within each cohort (including even the youngest) that it is difficult to see how it can decline much more. The slight liberalization that will result as the youngest adults increasingly replace the older cohorts could conceivably be balanced by a slight decline in support due to the forceful attack on affirmative action that has occurred in the mid-1990s.

Conclusions about Cohort Effects

In a provocative discussion, Davis (1992) suggested that conversion and replacement effects can assume very different patterns depending on the issue being studied, a proposition that our discussion has confirmed. We now know that the extent to which cohort or period or both affect racial attitudes depends on the topic of the question. Thus the conclusions of Firebaugh and Davis (1988), which were mainly derived from principle questions and can be interpreted to fit the continuous socialization model, cannot be generalized to most questions involving implementation issues and affirmative action policies. Further, although we agree that there has been a lessening of the difference between the two youngest cohorts (but no reversal), as Dowden and Robinson maintain (1993), this would be largely true of questions that deal with racial equality as a matter of principle or with explanations about racial inequality.[29] By the same token, our previous work (Steeh and Schuman 1992) offers a misleading generalization by focusing on implementation and affirmative action questions that show the youngest generation to be distinctly more liberal than any of its predecessors. Our contention that these implementation and affirmative action questions provide the most rigorous test of the hypothesis that young white adults have become *less* rather than more liberal in the 1980s and 1990s needs to be abandoned and our conclusions limited to the type of questions we considered.

The analyses of this chapter refine another proposition advanced by Davis (1992). In his view, cohort replacement should continue to have a liberal influence on attitudes for some time into the future, though not indefinitely. This is a position that holds well for racial attitudes about abstract principles, issues of implementation, and social distance. The absence of substantial intercohort differences for most items about affirmative action and most explanations for inequality means that liberalization from cohort replacement in these cases will be very weak. This outcome fits with research that looks at change through a broader lens than ours and finds a conservative swing during the 1980s across an array of social and political attitudes (Smith 1990; Stimson 1991; and with more in the way of qualifications, Davis 1996).

Our examination has also indicated that both the continuous socialization and the unique event models of cohort effects are present to some degree in most of our questions. For the principle items we find evidence of the continuous socialization process in the usually monotonic ordering of cohorts along a liberal dimension from oldest to youngest, but the positions of the oldest and youngest cohorts can be interpreted also to fit the unique events model. For other questions the unique event concept of generation formation applies primarily to the youngest cohort, but the divergent directions of change for these adults coming of age in the 1980s and 1990s—some in a liberal direction (Majority Black Schools) and some in a conservative direction (Inequality due to Discrimination)—present a conundrum that we are not able to unravel here. This is the cohort for which we have the fewest time points and usually the smallest number of cases, and it is possible that future surveys will have more success in resolving the issue.

The mixture of cohort effects that we find for many of our questions casts doubt on the universal validity of the continuous socialization model. When Stouffer (1955) and Hyman and Sheatsley (1956) first proposed this model, it did seem to fit the data then available from national surveys. The questions on racial attitudes asked mostly about abstract principles, and each succeeding generation appeared to be more liberal than the last. Survey data from the 1970s, 1980s, and 1990s show that the process of change cannot be conceptualized so simply. It appears that unique public events have the potential to cause the gears of change to shift in new directions, as Mannheim predicted.[30]

The Influence of Income, Education, and Gender

We now wish to analyze the effects of two variables that are not often considered in connection with racial attitudes—family income and gender—and also to reconsider the effects of education when income, gender, region, and cohort are held constant.

First, does family income, in accordance with rational choice theory, decrease support for policies that involve expenditures of public money for blacks? And if so, what of attitudes that are unrelated to spending money in any direct sense, such as questions about principles of equal treatment? Furthermore, since income and education are positively related, what happens to the association of each with various racial attitudes when the other is held constant? More generally, our inclusion of education as a variable in Chapter 3 did not control other background variables (except region). Here we will look at the effects over time of both education and income, with the other held constant, while also controlling for cohort, region, and gender.

Second, we examine the effects of gender, following leads obtained in an earlier analysis (Steeh and Schuman 1992). Again we control for the same background variables (education, income, region, cohort) in order to look more closely over time at whether men and women differ in their racial attitudes.[31]

Income and Education Considered Simultaneously

Income. We find that of the twelve questions in the affirmative action and implementation categories, eleven show large negative effects of income.[32] Only the implementation question about open housing laws fails to show differences of opinion by income level. Yet income just as consistently has a positive effect on attitudes about abstract principles, a fact that is not surprising given that questions dealing with the principles of equal treatment and questions dealing with policy issues such as affirmative action and implementation share few characteristics. These opposing relationships are illustrated in Figure 4.13, using one question from each group (Preference in Admissions and Black Candidate).[33] Higher income is positively related to willingness to vote for a black candidate, but it is negatively related to support for special programs to advance the economic position of blacks.

For two of the items dealing with explanations of inequality (Discrimination and Generations of Slavery), the relationship is strongly negative (greater income leads to disagreement that discrimination is the source of racial inequality). For most of the other inequality items, greater income also leads to individualistic explanations of racial differences, though the effects tend to be weak and nonsignificant. Only when the inequality is said to result from in-born differences in ability does increasing family income promote liberal racial attitudes.

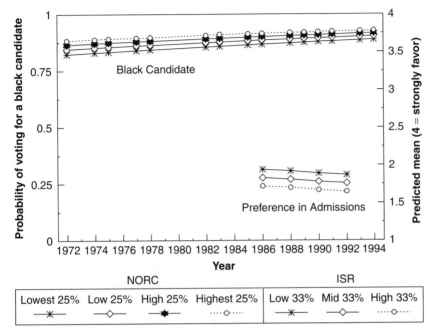

Figure 4.13. Black Candidate (NORC) and Preference in Admissions (ISR), by family income, 1972–1994

It is almost impossible to locate a single relationship that will characterize most of the social distance questions. Higher income seems to promote approval of contact with African Americans in both private and public settings where the number of blacks is small, such as a school with a few black students or a family member's bringing a black friend home to dinner. Whenever the number of black students in a school reaches 50 percent or more, however, higher income substantially reduces support for integrated settings. Thus the one element that seems to explain the varying relationships is the number of blacks mentioned in the hypothesized contact. We offer this interpretation tentatively because the questions available for analysis are limited in the types and degrees of intergroup contact they specify.

Education. In Chapter 3 we generally found a positive, monotonic relationship between education and attitudes: those who did not graduate from high school were the least liberal, and those who had at least some college were the most liberal on racial issues. The major exception to that positive relationship occurred with affirmative action questions. Education showed some evidence of a U-shaped curvilinear relationship to questions about government expenditures and economic aid to blacks, with the least support coming from those with middling education (high school graduates). Even stronger and more striking were the questions about preferential treatment: Figure 3.21 showed the least-educated respondents (zero to eleven years of schooling) taking the most liberal position (support for preferential treatment), with both the college educated (thirteen years or more) and the high school graduates relatively far behind. Within other categories of questions in Chapter 3, the exceptions to the pattern of monotonic, positive effects for education are confined to one or two items and indicate the lessening rather than a reversal of a relationship to education.

We now ask what happens to these relationships when we control income (along with gender, region, and cohort) in our analysis. Fortunately, we can be very specific about the direction of the changes we expect to find, since we start with the knowledge that income and education are positively correlated. If the impact of income on an attitude is negative, the influence of education should be strengthened once we eliminate the effects of income. Thus we may discover education effects that we did not find in Chapter 3. Because the relationship of income to attitude is the most consistently negative for questions involving policies of economic aid and affirmative action, we hypothesize that holding constant the income variable will have the greatest potential to increase the magnitude of the education-attitude relationship for questions that mention or imply spending public money. When the impact of income is positive, however, the education effect should be weakened, and the effects that we found previously may no longer appear. (Furthermore, in these multivariate analyses we divide the highest education level used in Chapter 3 into those who attended college but did not earn a degree and those who obtained at least one college degree. In this way we are able to extend our previous findings by determining the effects on racial attitudes of a little versus a lot of postsecondary education.)

The results of our multivariate analysis reveal that a monotonic positive pattern of education effects appears when we control for income in fifteen of the twenty-nine questions discussed in this chapter. All principle items, all but one of the social distance questions (Majority), and all but two of the explanations for inequality questions show a positive and significant impact of schooling on racial attitudes. For the other fourteen items, the monotonic ordering is sometimes disrupted, primarily for the implementation and affirmative action questions and most often at lower educational levels.

When we look at the education relationships for the questions that make up the implementation category, we find solid evidence of the liberalizing influence of having graduated from college. The education relationships for this group are positive and highly significant for all questions except Busing.[34] In addition, the multivariate analyses containing income confirm our earlier analysis that willingness to send a child to a majority black school is associated with education beyond the high school level.

Finally, when we look for the U-shaped effects on affirmative action that we discovered in Chapter 3, we find that one remains robust, whereas another that was weaker disappears. The questions involving preferential treatment for blacks are still characterized by an order that begins with the least educated (those with less than a high school education) taking the most liberal position, followed by the most highly educated (college graduates), and then by the other two educational categories (high school graduates and some college). However, the U-shape that seemed to occur for questions asking about economic aid and government spending has been replaced by a pattern that is basically positive, ranging from the two less educated groups that are relatively conservative to approximately the same degree, through those with some college, and finally to those with at least a college degree who express the most liberal attitudes.

These patterns are displayed in the following table of *differences* among regression coefficients for the four educational categories.[35] In a monotonic ordering, all differences would be positive, which is true for the first item, Spending on Blacks. Across the next four questions, which are all concerned with economic aid and government spending, the negative differences indicate that people with a high school education are slightly less liberal than those who do not have a high school diploma, and thus there is a faint sign of the curvilinearity reported in Chapter 3. After that the differences assume a positive direction, with each more highly educated group becoming more liberal. Thus for the five questions involving spending and economic aid, entering income into the analyses has altered the effect of education by moving the relationship in a monotonic direction, though this is partly because we have split the college category between those who have and those who have not earned a college degree.

Affirmative action item	1. High school grad *minus* less schooling	2. Some college *minus* high school grad	3. College grad *minus* some college
Spending on Blacks	+.030	+.068	+.159
Aid to Minorities	−.029	+.198	+.407
Aid to Blacks	−.077	+.232	+.426
Federal Spending	−.055	+.028	+.128
Help Blacks	−.093	+.112	+.349
Hiring (ISR)	−.302	−.039	+.211
Hiring (CBS/NYT)	−.454	−.324	+.149
Admissions	−.290	−.036	+.238

For the three preferential treatment questions, however, the difference between educational levels is positive only among those with a college degree. The positive movement, however, is not great enough to make the college graduates as supportive of preferential treatment as the least educated. Therefore, the striking curvilinear relation reported in Chapter 3 is maintained even after we control for income and other background variables: it is the least-educated white respondents who express the most support for preferential treatment of blacks.

In sum, it appears that taking account of income does affect the relationship of education to racial attitudes in many of the ways we predicted. However, the effects are seldom large enough to change most of the major substantive conclusions we drew in Chapter 3. When the income-attitude relationship is positive, as with the principle items, we might expect the effect of education to be somewhat weaker. Yet we find that its impact is still strong and highly significant. If anything, including income has only served to confirm the importance of education in promoting the expression of liberal racial attitudes on most of the issues we have dealt with in this book.

Gender

We find that for most types of questions the effect of being female has a liberalizing influence on racial attitudes. This is especially true for questions that fall under the headings of explanations of inequality and affirmative action. Without exception, women are significantly more likely than men to agree with the structural explanations of racial inequality and to feel that preferences for African Americans are acceptable government policy.[36] Although most items in both the implementation and the social distance categories also show positive relationships, there are a few questions that do not conform, primarily Federal Job Intervention and Half black schools, which show no difference between women and men, and Majority black schools, which displays a highly significant negative association. Women, it seems, are less willing than men to send their children to a school that is made up mostly of black students.

The relation of gender to attitudes regarding principles of equal treatment is different for each question, however. Only the question asking about the acceptability of a qualified black presidential candidate matches the strong positive relationship typical of the other categories of questions. Three items (Laws against Intermarriage, Residential Choice, and Same Schools) show very little difference between men and women in their support of principles, probably because general agreement with the pro-integration response for two of the items has reached very high levels. The Gallup item gauging approval of intermarriage itself indicates, however, that women are more likely than men to disapprove. The strong objections women have both to intermarriage and to schools that have a mostly black student body suggest that in these more intimate areas of racial contact, being female hinders rather than promotes racial integration. Figure 4.14 graphs the attitudes of women and men toward an affirmative action issue (Aid to Blacks) about which women tend to be more liberal and a principle item (Intermarriage) about which they tend to be more conservative than men.[37]

Conclusions about Income, Education, and Gender

In this section we have explored the effects of additional social background variables on racial attitudes. Both gender and income are im-

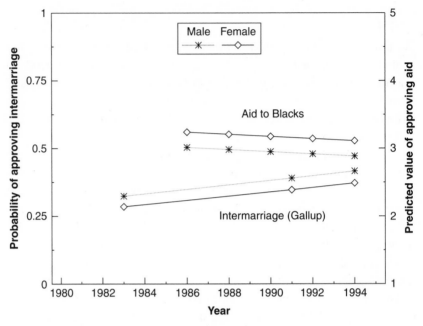

Figure 4.14. Intermarriage (Gallup) and Aid to Blacks (NES), by gender, 1983–1994

portant sources of differences in opinion. Gender is almost uniformly positive and highly significant, indicating that women are more liberal in their racial attitudes than men. The most consistent exceptions appear when items imply a very intimate contact between the races (intermarriage or having children attend predominantly black schools). In these cases, women are significantly more conservative than men.

The impact of income level on racial attitudes varies according to the topic of the question. Items asking about abstract principles of racial equality have positive and highly significant income effects, whereas items asking about affirmative action and implementation policies show negative effects that are just as significant. The other categories of questions have relationships that tend not to be significant. Thus a negative relationship of income and attitude is not broadly characteristic of racial issues, but tends to hold for those specific questions that deal with policies where government expenditures seem likely and thus opposition can be seen as a matter of self-interest.

Overall, it appears that controlling for income only serves to strengthen the liberalizing effect of education on the expression of most racial attitudes, consistent with our reporting in Chapter 3. Attitudes on a few questions that had seemed unrelated to education now appear more clearly connected to schooling in systematic ways. At the same time, the unexpected and challenging finding that it is the least educated who show the most support for preferential treatment for blacks receives further confirmation in the analysis of this chapter.

5

Trends in
Black Racial Attitudes

Recent events have dramatized the gulf between black and white Americans' perceptions of both specific occurrences and the general state of race relations.[1] In this chapter we will draw on black responses to the same trend questions that we employed in Chapter 3 on white attitudes. Our main concern will be the comparison over time of black and white responses to the same basic issues.

Trend data are sparser and sample sizes much smaller for black racial attitudes than for white, though more questions and more time points are available for recent years than was the case in the previous edition of this book. In addition, as discussed in Chapter 2, the problems presented by race-of-interviewer effects on black respondents are much more serious than they are for white respondents because of the high proportion of face-to-face interviews with blacks that have been conducted by white interviewers. We have no entirely adequate way to control for these effects, and can only assume that many of the differences we discover between the attitudes of black and white Americans would be even larger if each racial group had been interviewed entirely by persons of its own race.[2]

Our data on black Americans are also limited in scope because they are based almost entirely on questions developed originally for whites and then at some later point asked of blacks also. This occurred because during the 1940s and 1950s, survey investigators interested in racial issues saw the problem as almost entirely one of white acceptance of equal treatment across racial lines. After all, laws and administrative rules constructed by white Americans had created and enforced racial segregation, and large parts of the white population still supported segregation as a general principle. As Paul Sheatsley, one of the major initiators of research in this area, commented: "It never occurred to us when we wrote questions in the Forties and Fifties to ask them of blacks because Myrdal's dilemma was a white dilemma and it was white attitudes that demanded study" (personal communication, 1984).[3] Added to this was the fact that some of the main issues inquired into, such as whether "whites should have the first chance at jobs," might have seemed both nonsensical and demeaning if asked of blacks.

With the rise of new and diverse forms of political ideology, action, and organization among blacks in the 1960s, survey investigators (almost all of whom were white at that point) realized that blacks were not merely passive players in the rapidly changing racial scene and that black attitudes should not be assumed to be either self-evident or fixed. A series of special survey studies of blacks was carried out during the 1960s: Brink and Harris (1964), Marx (1967), Murphy and Watson (1967), Campbell and Schuman (1968), Caplan and Paige (1968), Aberbach and Walker (1970), Sears and McConahay (1973). However, the very fact that issues important to blacks appeared to be changing so rapidly made for considerable discontinuity from one study to the next. Within a short period of time in the mid-1960s, for example, the term "militancy" changed from indicating nonviolent action against white-imposed segregation to suggesting support for violent rebellion and separatism. Furthermore, the samples used in these special surveys were seldom national and often quite different from one another. As a result of these various factors, it is virtually impossible to draw on these studies for trend data, despite the importance they may still have for other purposes.

In the 1960s and 1970s, the major survey organizations began to ask a few questions on racial issues of blacks as well as whites. For example, the NORC Same Schools principle question (Tables 3.1A and 5.1A) was first asked of whites in 1942, but was not asked of blacks until 1972. The ISR election surveys generally asked questions of both blacks and whites beginning in the mid-1960s. Even for those surveys that did ask questions of blacks, however, another problem becomes that of small numbers of cases. A typical national sample of 1,500 to 2,000 Americans yields only 150 to 200 or so black respondents, and the effectiveness of such small numbers is further diminished by design effects in large-scale survey samples.[4] The smaller sample sizes for the black data make it even more important here than in the discussion of white attitudes to avoid emphasis on a single point in a time series.

Table 5.1A Questions concerning principles, 1942–1995 (black respondents)[a]

Question	Year of survey													
	42	43	44	45	46	48	50	56	58	60	61	62	63	6
Same Schools (NORC)[b]														
% Same	—	—	—	—	—	—	—	—	—	—	—	—	—	—
Separate	—	—	—	—	—	—	—	—	—	—	—	—	—	—

Question wordings and variants

Same Schools (NORC): "Do you think white students and (Negro/black) students should go to the same schools or to separate schools?" Data for 1995 are from a telephone survey conducted by the Princeton Survey Research Associates, as reported in the Roper Center's *Public Perspective*, vol. 7 (2), 1996, p. 40. Because of this, respondents aged 18–20 are included in the results for 1995.
    1. Same
    2. Separate

a. NORC data for 1982 and 1987, and NES data for 1964, 1968, and 1970, had oversamples of black respondents. The figures presented throughout Chapter 5 *include* those oversamples. In cases where such an

Some recent studies have focused specifically on black attitudes, but we do not attempt to discuss the results of such studies in this book.[5] Thus our treatment of black attitudes is less comprehensive than our treatment of white attitudes, and focuses instead on direct comparisons of black and white attitudes on the same issues.[6] It is still of considerable value, despite needing to be qualified in the several ways discussed in this introduction.

Questions about Principles

When discussing the questions about broad principles in Table 5.1, we are prompted to reconsider the distinction between the concept of "equal treatment" and the concept of "integration." For white Americans the distinction is usually unimportant, for it is probably assumed by white respondents that equal treatment is intended to lead to integration. For example, the response to a question on residential choice stating that "black people have a right to live wherever they can afford to" is almost certainly interpreted by whites to mean movement of blacks into residential areas largely or entirely white in composition. For black Americans, however, a basic distinction between equal treatment and integration is important. The principle that "black people have a right to live wherever they can afford to" might well be sup-

									Year of survey								
5	66	68	70	72	74	76	77	78	79	80	81	82	83	84	85	95
—	—	—	—	96	—	98	93	—	—	97	—	97	—	97	(97)	99[t]
—	—	—	—	4	—	3	7	—	—	3	—	3	—	3	(3)	1[t]

Question wordings and variants

clusion leads to results that differ by more than 3 percentage points, a note has been made. For the 1982 NORC data, our including the oversamples represents a departure from the 1985 edition. Only one item in the NES—the Thermometer Ratings of Blacks and Whites (Table 5.6)—does *not* include the cases from the black versample.

b. Here and throughout the chapter, results are presented in parentheses in order to identify those questions nd time points in which the sample sizes ranged from 50 to 100 cases. Instances in which there are fewer than 0 cases are considered inadequate, and so results are not presented.

t. Data collected through telephone survey rather than personal interview.

ported even where respondents have no particular interest in moving into an integrated area, let alone a largely white area. Thus we need to consider carefully the *meanings* to blacks of the questions on principles in Table 5.1, and how they may differ from the meanings the same questions have for whites—meanings that we took largely for granted when we considered them in Chapter 3.[7]

From the standpoint of blacks, the two Residential Choice questions in Table 5.1B are probably viewed as primarily about equal treatment, with no necessary implication about a desire for integration. As such, we would expect something close to unanimity in the answers of black respondents. This does occur for the dichotomous ISR question, with choice of the equal treatment response reaching 99 percent when the question was last asked in 1976, as compared with 90 percent for whites in the same year. There is good reason to think the same unanimity for blacks would occur if the question were repeated today.

The much more one-sided NORC Residential Choice question with its four-point scale was first asked of blacks in 1980. At that time point only 66 percent disagreed strongly with the statement that "white people have a right to keep blacks out of their neighborhoods if they want to, and blacks should respect that right." This lack of unanimity in rejecting overt discrimination should be seen primarily as a reflection of the power of question form and wording to shape answers. Thus something on the order of 33 percent of blacks (99 minus 66) were

Table 5.1B Questions concerning principles, 1958–1997 (black respondents)

Question	58	59	61	63	64	65	67	68	69	70	71	72	73	7
Residential Choice 1 alt. (NORC)														
% Disagree strongly	—	—	—	—	—	—	—	—	—	—	—	—	—	—
Disagree slightly	—	—	—	—	—	—	—	—	—	—	—	—	—	—
Agree slightly	—	—	—	—	—	—	—	—	—	—	—	—	—	—
Agree strongly	—	—	—	—	—	—	—	—	—	—	—	—	—	—
Residential Choice 2 alt. (ISR)														
% Blacks rights	—	—	—	—	99	—	—	98	—	98	—	100	—	9
Keep blacks out	—	—	—	—	2	—	—	2	—	2	—	0	—	
Black Candidate (Gallup)														
% Yes	92	98	97	96	—	98	93	—	100	—	95	—	—	
No	8	2	3	4	—	2	7	—	0	—	5	—	—	
Black Candidate (NORC)														
% Yes	—	—	—	—	—	—	—	—	—	—	—	—	—	9
No	—	—	—	—	—	—	—	—	—	—	—	—	—	
Laws against Intermarriage (NORC)														
% No	—	—	—	—	—	—	—	—	—	—	—	—	—	—
Yes	—	—	—	—	—	—	—	—	—	—	—	—	—	—
Intermarriage (Gallup)														
% Approve	—	—	—	—	—	—	—	—	—	—	—	76	—	—
Disapprove	—	—	—	—	—	—	—	—	—	—	—	24	—	—
General Segregation (ISR)[a]														
% Desegregation	—	—	—	—	78	—	—	79	—	78	—	69	—	6
Something btwn.	—	—	—	—	17	—	—	18	—	19	—	29	—	3
Strict segregation	—	—	—	—	6	—	—	4	—	3	—	2	—	

Question wordings and variants

Residential Choice, 1 alternative (NORC): "Here are some opinions other people have expressed in connection with (Negro/black)–white relations. Which statement on the card comes closest to how you, yourself, feel? White people have a right to keep (Negroes/blacks/African Americans) out of their neighborhoods if they want to, and (Negroes/blacks/African Americans) should respect that right."

    1. Agree strongly
    2. Agree slightly
    3. Disagree slightly
    4. Disagree strongly

Residential Choice, 2 alternatives (ISR): "Which of these statements would you agree with: White people have a right to keep (Negroes/black people) out of their neighborhoods if they want to, or, (Negroes/black people) have a right to live wherever they can afford to, just like anybody else?"

    1. Keep blacks out
    2. Blacks have rights

(**Variant:** in 1964 replaced "anybody else" with "white people.")

Black Candidate (Gallup): From 1958 to 1978, question wording was as follows: "There's always been much discussion about the qualifications of presidential candidates—their education, age, race, religion, and the like.

								Year of survey										
75	76	77	78	80	82	83	84	85	86	87	88	89	90	91	93	94	96	97
—	—	—	—	66	81	—	69	63	—	80	82	(81)	(80)	84	81	79	86	—
—	—	—	—	19	9	—	16	18	—	10	9	(10)	(8)	9	12	11	11	—
—	—	—	—	10	5	—	10	10	—	5	6	(4)	(7)	6	5	7	2	—
—	—	—	—	6	5	—	4	9	—	5	3	(5)	(6)	1	3	2	1	—
—	99	—	—	—	—	—	—	—	—	—	—	—	—	—	—	—	—	—
—	1	—	—	—	—	—	—	—	—	—	—	—	—	—	—	—	—	—
—	—	—	94	—	—	96	99	—	—	98	—	—	—	—	—	—	—	94^t
—	—	—	6	—	—	4	1	—	—	2	—	—	—	—	—	—	—	6^t
—	—	—	96	—	99	95	—	99	97	—	98	(96)	99	98	99	100	98	—
—	—	—	4	—	1	5	—	1	3	—	2	(4)	1	2	1	0	2	—
—	—	—	—	82	93	—	93	93	—	92	95	(92)	(93)	94	94	97	95	—
—	—	—	—	18	7	—	7	7	—	9	5	(8)	(7)	6	6	3	5	—
—	—	—	77	—	—	77	—	—	—	—	—	—	—	77^t	—	77^t	—	83^t
—	—	—	23	—	—	23	—	—	—	—	—	—	—	23^t	—	23^t	—	17^t
—	74	—	56	—	—	—	—	—	—	—	—	—	—	—	—	—	—	—
—	25	—	38	—	—	—	—	—	—	—	—	—	—	—	—	—	—	—
—	2	—	7	—	—	—	—	—	—	—	—	—	—	—	—	—	—	—

Question wordings and variants

If your party nominated a generally well qualified man for president and he happened to be a Negro, would you vote for him?" See notes below for question variants in other years. In 1987 and 1997, the results include respondents aged 18–20, and the 1987 data are based on published data reported in the Gallup Monthly Report, June 1987.

    1. Yes

    2. No

  (Variants: Introductions to this item frequently refer to an upcoming election year or convention. This is the case in 1958 [reference to the 1960 election], 1959 [reference to the 1960 election], 1961 [reference to the 1964 election], and 1978 [reference to the 1980 convention]. In 1983, the question did not refer to either an election or a convention, but instead was asked as follows: "If your party nominated a generally well qualified man for president and he happened to be black, would you vote for him?" In 1984, the question wording was: "This year there has been much discussion about the qualifications of presidential candidates—their education, age, religion, race, and the like. If your party nominated a generally well qualified man for president, would you vote for him if he happened to be black?" In 1987, the 1983 question wording was used, but with reference to the 1988 conventions. Other groups (most notably Jews, Catholics, and women) have also been offered to respondents as potential presidential candidates. Blacks were the first group mentioned in 1958,

Table 5.1B (continued)

Question wordings and variants

1959, 1961, 1971, 1978, and 1984; the last group mentioned in 1963 and 1965; and the third of several groups mentioned in 1967 and 1969. In 1983 and 1997, only a question about a black presidential candidate was asked. In 1987, four groups were asked about, in the following order: Jews, atheists, blacks, and women. In 1997, the question wording was changed from "man" to "person.")

Black Candidate (NORC): "If your party nominated a (Negro/black/African American) for president, would you vote for him if he were qualified for the job?"
1. Yes
2. No

Laws against Intermarriage (NORC): "Do you think there should be laws against marriages between (Negroes/blacks/African Americans) and whites?"
1. Yes
2. No

Intermarriage (Gallup): (1994: In general) "Do you approve or disapprove of marriage between whites and nonwhites (1983–1997: between blacks and whites)?" For 1997, the results include respondents aged 18–20.
1. Approve
2. Disapprove

General Segregation (ISR): "Are you in favor of desegregation, strict segregation, or something in between?"
1. Desegregation
2. Strict segregation
3. Something in between

a. This is one exception in which the inclusion of the oversample does change the results by more than a few percentage points in 1964. Specifically, the distribution without the oversample included is 73 percent "desegregation"; 21 percent "something in between"; and 6 percent "strict segregation."

t. Data collected through telephone survey rather than personal interview.

willing to modify their right to residential choice when the question strongly encouraged such modification. (This is based on comparing the 1976 ISR version with the nearest NORC year of 1980.)

With question wording held constant, however, complete rejection of the NORC statement against equal treatment rose from 66 percent in 1980 to 86 percent in 1996. Thus there is increasing willingness on the part of blacks to oppose *enforced* segregation strongly even in the face of a question that appears loaded to support it.[8] Moreover, the 86 percent in 1996 should be compared with the much smaller 65 percent of whites who reject the principle of segregated housing in the same year.

Only a single recently asked question in Table 5.1 deals explicitly with integration rather than with equal treatment, though the integration is at a much more personal level than occurs in questions about schools or neighborhoods: this is the Gallup question on approval or disapproval of marriage between blacks and whites. As Figure 5.1

indicates, black approval of intermarriage is substantially higher than white approval (83 percent to 67 percent in 1997), but whereas white approval has shown much the same rise over many years as for most other principle items, black approval showed essentially no change over most of the past two decades, and the reliability of the increase in 1997 remains uncertain until replicated. We can also note that approval of intermarriage is significantly greater among younger and more educated blacks (data not shown), suggesting that in future years approval may rise for the black population as a whole—though if *only* age and education were affecting responses we should already have seen some increase in the level of black approval of intermarriage as older cohorts disappeared and the level of education rose.[9]

Another question on racial intermarriage in Table 5.1 does show a clear trend over time among blacks: black opposition to laws against intermarriage has moved from 82 percent in 1980 to the mid-90 percent level in recent years. From the perspective of whites, such a change could be interpreted as increasing support for integration. But again, from the perspective of black respondents, it is better seen as tapping a demand for equal treatment—in this case, an end to enforced segregation—rather than a desire for integration.

Two other questions that do deal more directly with integration are of limited value because neither has been asked in recent years. The

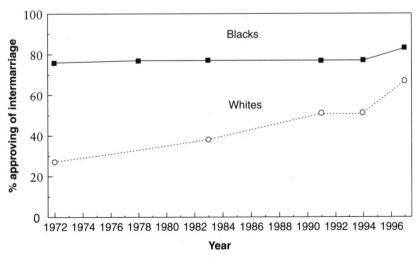

Figure 5.1. Approval of intermarriage, by race (Gallup).

Same Schools item showed no loss through 1985 of near unanimous black support for integration. It would be useful if NORC repeated the question for black respondents today, when there is new talk about emphasizing the quality of schooling rather than school integration.[10] The General Segregation item, which showed movement by whites toward support for "something in between" segregation and desegregation, presents somewhat similar movement for blacks during the 1970s, whether for the contextual reason discussed earlier or for some other reason not evident to us; however, no data exist beyond 1978.

To summarize, our discussion of black responses to survey questions about principles has made us sensitive to the important distinction between equal treatment and integration that could be largely ignored when dealing with white responses. The items in Table 5.1 that address equal treatment show generally high and increasing support. Because of the scarcity of relevant data, however, we know very little about recent changes in black attitudes toward racial integration as a general principle. There has been little or no increase in black approval for intermarriage, but this is a rather specialized and hypothetical topic for most people and does not in itself have clear implications for integration in other areas of life. When we move to questions on social distance, we will have some additional evidence on black attitudes toward integration, and specifically toward school integration.

Implementation of Principles

In Chapter 3 we found that white Americans show more support for principles of equal treatment and integration than for government implementation of the same principles. It is useful to make a similar comparison for blacks in order to determine whether a difference appears here also. The available data do not provide an ideal comparison, but with regard to issues of equal treatment, the most appropriate recent parallel is between NORC's Residential Choice question (Table 5.1B) and NORC's Open Housing question (Table 5.2). The comparison requires that we first collapse the four-point scale of the former into an agree-disagree dichotomy in order to match the dichotomous Open Housing question. If this is done, 97 percent of the black sample opposed residential segregation in principle in 1996, whereas 84 percent said they would vote for an open housing law. There is a difference in earlier years as well, though at times it is very small, as shown in

Figure 5.2 (p. 251). Thus there is some evidence for blacks of the same kind of separation of principle and implementation of principle that we found for whites, although the size of the gap remains somewhat larger for whites (19 percent versus 13 percent for blacks in 1996).

We do not have equally good comparisons at similar time points for questions that focus more directly on the principles and implementation of integration. But we note that for Federal School Intervention, which does deal explicitly with school integration, the proportion of blacks supporting government action in the 1990s is far from a ceiling (57 percent support in 1994) and has decreased substantially over the past two decades, though the major alternative chosen is the one indicating "no interest" in the issue rather than outright opposition to government implementation. Moreover, since their responses on the question about the principle of school integration (Same Schools) had approached 100 percent support in earlier years (and 99 percent in the recent telephone survey), blacks here also show something of the same gap between support for abstract principles and support for implementation of principles that whites show.

Support among blacks for busing is also far from unanimous, with some 40 percent indicating opposition in recent years on the NORC question. Two decades ago, the 1976 Detroit Area Study asked a sample of metropolitan Detroit residents a question on attitudes toward busing—not one of the busing questions presented in Table 5.2, but a question close enough to be of value for our present purpose. It was followed by a simple open-ended question: "Can you tell me why you feel this way?" The most frequently given reason for black opposition to busing was the belief that school quality is the paramount issue and that it can be achieved in better ways than through busing. Second in frequency was concern about the inconvenience and related problems said to be created by busing. These two reasons together accounted for just over half of all the explanations given by the 50 percent of blacks who opposed busing at that point in time (and for 35 percent of the explanations of white opponents). Very few of the black explanations for opposing busing dealt explicitly with racial reasons or with black-white conflict over busing. It seems likely that the same kinds of explanations would be offered today by the 41 percent of black respondents who opposed busing in the 1996 NORC Survey.

Finally, there is a highly significant decline on the Federal Job Inter-

Table 5.2 Implementation questions (black respondents)

Question	Year of survey												
	64	66	68	69	70	71	72	73	74	75	76	77	78
Federal School Intervention (ISR)													
% Govt see to it	82	79	90	—	86	—	82	—	76	—	70	—	64
Govt. stay out	8	10	7	—	7	—	12	—	14	—	12	—	12
No interest	11	12	4	—	8	—	6	—	10	—	18	—	24
Busing (ISR)													
% Bus (1–3)	—	—	—	—	—	—	39	—	33	—	44	—	—
Neutral (4)	—	—	—	—	—	—	8	—	11	—	13	—	—
In n'hood (5–7)	—	—	—	—	—	—	48	—	44	—	33	—	—
Not thought	—	—	—	—	—	—	6	—	12	—	11	—	—
Busing (NORC)													
% Favor	—	—	—	—	—	—	55	—	63	48	53	48	53
Oppose	—	—	—	—	—	—	45	—	37	52	47	52	47
Accommodations Intervention (ISR)													
% Gov't see to it	89	—	93	—	93	—	92	—	91	—	—	—	—
Gov't stay out	5	—	3	—	3	—	4	—	3	—	—	—	—
No interest	7	—	4	—	5	—	5	—	7	—	—	—	—
Open Housing (NORC)													
% Owner cannot refuse	—	—	—	—	—	—	—	—	—	—	—	—	71
Owner can decide	—	—	—	—	—	—	—	—	—	—	—	—	29
Federal Job Intervention (ISR)													
% Gov't see to it	92	—	86	—	—	—	85	—	81	—	—	—	—
Gov't stay out	4	—	9	—	—	—	8	—	8	—	—	—	—
No interest	4	—	5	—	—	—	7	—	11	—	—	—	—

Question wordings and variants

Federal School Intervention (ISR): "Some people say that the government in Washington should see to it that white and black (1972: Negro) children go (1964–1978: are allowed to go) to the same schools. Others claim this is not the government's business. Have you been concerned (1986, 1990: interested) enough about (in) this question to favor one side over the other? [If yes] Do you think the government in Washington should see to it that white and black children go to the same schools, or stay out of this area, as it is none of the government's business?" Data for 1974 are from an ISR Omnibus Survey; all other years are from the NES.

1. Government should see to it
2. Government should stay out
3. No interest

Note: See Chapter 3, p. 128 for important variations in the wording of this question.

Busing (ISR): "There is much discussion about the best way to deal with racial problems. Some people think achieving racial integration of schools is so important that it justifies busing children to schools out of their own neighborhoods. Others think letting children go to their neighborhood schools is so important that they oppose busing. Where would you place yourself on this scale, or haven't you thought much about this?" (Show card with 7-point scale)

							Year of survey										
79	80	81	82	83	84	85	86	87	88	89	90	91	92	93	94	95	96
—	—	—	—	—	—	—	63	—	—	—	63	—	59	—	57	—	—
—	—	—	—	—	—	—	8	—	—	—	15	—	16	—	13	—	—
—	—	—	—	—	—	—	28	—	—	—	22	—	25	—	31	—	—
—	38	—	—	—	(24)	—	—	—	—	—	—	—	—	—	—	—	—
—	12	—	—	—	(14)	—	—	—	—	—	—	—	—	—	—	—	—
—	38	—	—	—	(51)	—	—	—	—	—	—	—	—	—	—	—	—
—	12	—	—	—	(12)	—	—	—	—	—	—	—	—	—	—	—	—
—	—	—	55	56	—	57	62	—	58	(54)	61	63	—	59	60	—	59
—	—	—	45	44	—	43	38	—	42	(46)	39	37	—	41	40	—	41
—	—	—	—	—	—	—	—	—	—	—	—	—	—	—	—	(72')	—
—	—	—	—	—	—	—	—	—	—	—	—	—	—	—	—	(2')	—
—	—	—	—	—	—	—	—	—	—	—	—	—	—	—	—	(26')	—
—	71	—	—	75	79	—	80	82	90	88	85	82	—	85	80	—	84
—	29	—	—	25	21	—	20	18	10	12	15	18	—	15	20	—	16
—	—	—	—	—	—	—	79	—	71	—	—	—	73	—	—	—	64
—	—	—	—	—	—	—	7	—	5	—	—	—	8	—	—	—	6
—	—	—	—	—	—	—	15	—	24	—	—	—	20	—	—	—	30

Question wordings and variants

1. Bus to achieve integration
2.
3.
4.
5.
6.
7. Keep children in neighborhood schools
0. Not thought about this

Busing (NORC): "In general, do you favor or oppose the busing of (Negro/black/African American) and white school children from one school district to another?"

1. Favor
2. Oppose

Accommodations Intervention (ISR): "As you may know, Congress passed a bill that says that black people should have the right to go to any hotel or restaurant they can afford, just like anybody else. Some people feel that this is something the government in Washington should support. Others feel that the government should

Table 5.2 (continued)

Question wordings and variants

stay out of this matter. Have you been interested enough in this to favor one side over another? [If yes] Should the government support the right of black people to go to any hotel or restaurant they can afford, or should it stay out of this matter?" In 1974, this question was asked on an ISR Omnibus Survey; data from 1964–1972 are from the National Election Studies. For 1995, these data come from an add-on to the October and November Survey of Consumer Attitudes conducted by the Survey Research Center at ISR. Although the results for 1995 include only those respondents in an RDD sample ($n = 47$ cases), it should be noted that the full sample ($n = 88$), which includes a sample of re-contact respondents, yields an identical distribution.

  1. Government should see to it
  2. Government should stay out
  3. No interest

(**Variant:** in 1964 replaced "anybody else" with "white people.")

Open Housing (NORC): "Suppose there is a community-wide vote on the general housing issue. There are two possible laws to vote on. One law says that a homeowner can decide for himself who to sell his house to, even if he prefers not to sell to (Negroes/blacks/African Americans). The second law says that a homeowner cannot refuse to sell to someone because of their race or color. Which law would you vote for?"

  1. Homeowner can decide
  2. Homeowner cannot refuse to sell

Federal Job Intervention (ISR): "Some people feel that if black people are not getting fair treatment in jobs, the government in Washington ought to see to it that they do. Others feel that this is not the federal government's business. Have you had enough interest in this question to favor one side over the other? [If yes] How do you feel? Should the government in Washington see to it that black people get fair treatment in jobs or (1964, 1968, 1972: should the government in Washington leave these matters to the states and local communities) is this not the federal government's business?" Data for 1974 are from an ISR Omnibus survey; in all other years data are from the NES.

  1. Government should see to it
  2. Government should stay out
  3. No Interest

t. Data collected through telephone survey rather than personal interview.

vention question in black support for government action to see "that black people get fair treatment in jobs," with the shift in responses again going not to opposition to government action but rather to "no interest" in the issue. The decline is sharp and almost monotonic over three decades: from 92 percent in 1964 to 64 percent in 1996. As discussed in Chapter 3, we regard the phrase "fair treatment" as ambiguous and quite likely to have shifted in meaning over time from implying "non-discrimination" in hiring and promotion to suggesting a form of "preferential treatment." Whether this shift accounts for some of the decline in support by blacks is unclear—since the decline is similar on the Federal School Intervention question, more must be involved than the phrase "fair treatment"—but what is evident is that blacks are now far from unanimous in expressing support for govern-

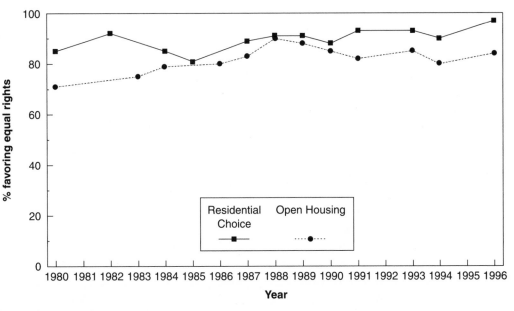

Figure 5.2. Comparing black responses to principle of residential choice (NORC) and implementation through open housing (NORC).

ment intervention on this implementation question. Moreover, unlike school integration, where controversies over busing and possible harm to black children may be a factor in discouraging black parents, employment involves only adults, is more impersonal than schooling, and presumably is a sphere where there is close to 100 percent support by blacks for the principle of equal treatment.

These results for our black sample suggest that characterizing the principle-implementation gap as a straightforward sign of hypocrisy on the part of whites may be too simple. The gap probably does imply less commitment to the enforcement of equal rights and integration than is evident when dealing only with abstract principles, but this reduced commitment seems to occur to some extent for blacks as well as for whites. It would be very helpful if open-ended questions were available to explain why some blacks oppose open housing laws (16 percent in 1996) and why they give other dissenting answers to implementation questions. In data not shown here, we find some evidence that it is less educated blacks who both oppose open housing and agree with constraints on residential choice as a principle, a type of association with years of schooling that we return to at the end of this chapter. But we need to learn much more about black attitudes toward government implementation, rather than assuming those attitudes to be obvious in direction and meaning.

Questions about Social Distance

The most useful questions available for assessing black attitudes toward more concrete issues of integration are the three NORC items in Table 5.3 about willingness to send a black child to schools with different proportions of white children. The questions have been asked regularly of blacks since 1978, and we presented the results earlier for whites in Table 3.3.[11] As Figure 5.3 (p. 257) shows, there is some lessening of willingness to send a child into an integrated situation as the proportion of white children increases, but the change is much less sharp for blacks than it was for whites (compare with Figure 3.12). Even where whites would be in the majority, at least three-quarters of black respondents claim to have no objection to such a white-black ratio.

Trends over time are not very clear in Figure 5.3. There is a suggestion that enthusiasm for integrated schooling may have peaked in the mid-1980s. At each level of integration, the percentages indicating no objection in 1985 and 1986 are higher than in the past several years, and other analysis indicates that this tends to be somewhat more true at higher than at lower educational levels. There is a good deal of unevenness in these trends, however, and it is possible that what looks like a slight decline in support for integrated schooling is entirely the result of sampling and other forms of error. The most we can say at this point is that the questions merit close watching in the future to see if there is a clear loss of black support for concrete integration in schooling.

The questions in Table 5.3 on preferences for different degrees of neighborhood integration and on inviting a white person to dinner could also be useful in charting black views of integration, but the lack of recent time points makes them of less value at present. The only other question in the table for which there is recent evidence asks whether black respondents would protest the exclusion of a white person from a social club. More than four out of five black respondents said they would make such a protest when the question was last asked in 1994, a significantly higher proportion than was shown for the parallel question asked of whites about the exclusion of a black person

(Table 3.3). There is no clear trend over time for this question, and the question was not included in the 1996 survey.

Explanations of Inequality

Black acceptance of various explanations for black disadvantage in jobs, income, and housing are shown in Table 5.4A (pp. 258–259). These can be compared with earlier percentages for whites in Table 3.4A. Here we focus on two explanations, one from an NORC question and the other from an ISR question, which when taken together bring out the contrasting beliefs that black and white Americans hold about the causes of continued racial inequality, economically and probably in other respects as well.

As Figure 5.4 (p. 263) shows, blacks emphasize discrimination as a cause of black economic disadvantage to a much greater extent than do whites: a difference of 32 percentage points on the NORC question in 1996.[12] (The difference is not quite as great, 21 percentage points, for the partially similar ISR question concerning discrimination, but since it also brings in "generations of slavery," its focus is on the past, not the present, and it thus provides a less adequate view of the racial gap in perceptions of life in America today.) At the same time, as Figure 5.5 (p. 264) shows, there is a large and perhaps increasing difference between blacks and whites in their agreement with the ISR question on low motivation as an explanation for racial inequality: "if blacks would only try harder they could be just as well off as whites." In 1994, the black-white difference in acceptance of this statement was 33 percent (75 minus 42). (The NORC version of the motivation question shows a somewhat smaller gap, but one that is still large: 24 percent more whites subscribe to the explanation than blacks in 1994; the difference shrinks to 11 percent in 1996, but again the change may not be reliable.) Thus blacks and whites point in different directions when accounting for black disadvantage: blacks see the main source as white discrimination, whereas whites see the main source as lack of motivation by blacks.[13]

The other explanations for black disadvantage show much smaller differences. For example, by 1994 there is no discrepancy between blacks and whites in their level of agreement with the "low ability" explanation. Similarly, blacks and whites are not far apart in stressing the need for more educational opportunities (9 percent higher for blacks than whites). Despite these areas of fairly close agreement, it is

Table 5.3 Social distance questions (black respondents)

Question	Year of survey										
	70	71	72	73	74	75	76	77	78	79	80
Few (NORC)											
% No objection	—	—	—	—	—	—	—	—	97	—	—
Objection	—	—	—	—	—	—	—	—	3	—	—
Half (NORC)											
% No objection	—	—	—	—	—	—	—	—	92	—	—
Objection	—	—	—	—	—	—	—	—	8	—	—
Majority (NORC)											
% No objection	—	—	—	—	—	—	—	—	86	—	—
Objection	—	—	—	—	—	—	—	—	14	—	—
Neighborhood Preference A (ISR-Personal)											
% Mixed/makes no difference	—	—	81	—	—	—	78	—	—	—	—
Mostly black	—	—	10	—	—	—	12	—	—	—	—
All black	—	—	9	—	—	—	10	—	—	—	—
Neighborhood Preference B (ISR-Telephone)											
% Mixed/makes no difference	—	—	—	—	—	—	95	—	—	—	—
Mostly black	—	—	—	—	—	—	1	—	—	—	—
All black	—	—	—	—	—	—	3	—	—	—	—
White Dinner Guest (NORC)											
% Not at all	—	—	—	—	—	—	—	—	—	—	96
Mildly	—	—	—	—	—	—	—	—	—	—	2
Strongly	—	—	—	—	—	—	—	—	—	—	3
Club Change Rules (NORC)											
% Yes would	—	—	—	—	—	—	—	—	—	—	—
No wouldn't	—	—	—	—	—	—	—	—	—	—	—

Question wordings and variants

Few (NORC): "Would you, yourself, have any objection to sending your children to a school where a few of the children are white?"

    1. Yes

    2. No

Half (NORC): [If No or DK to FEW] "Where half of the children are white?" Note that percentage "Yes" includes those who objected to Few.

    1. Yes

    2. No

Majority (NORC): [If No or DK to HALF] "Where more than half of the children are white?" Note that percentage "Yes" includes those who objected to Few and Half.

    1. Yes

    2. No

	Year of survey												
81	82	83	84	85	86	87	88	89	90	91	93	94	96
—	95	97	—	99	99	—	98	(97)	96	96	96	95	96
—	5	3	—	1	1	—	2	(3)	4	4	5	5	4
—	91	96	—	97	97	—	95	(93)	91	93	94	94	92
—	10	4	—	3	4	—	5	(7)	9	7	6	6	8
—	80	85	—	91	92	—	88	(81)	74	78	80	84	83
—	20	15	—	9	8	—	12	(19)	26	22	20	16	17
—	—	—	—	—	—	—	—	—	—	—	—	—	—
—	—	—	—	—	—	—	—	—	—	—	—	—	—
—	—	—	—	—	—	—	—	—	—	—	—	—	—
(92)	—	—	—	—	—	—	—	—	—	—	—	—	—
(5)	—	—	—	—	—	—	—	—	—	—	—	—	—
(3)	—	—	—	—	—	—	—	—	—	—	—	—	—
—	93	—	96	(97)	—	—	—	—	—	—	—	—	—
—	6	—	3	(1)	—	—	—	—	—	—	—	—	—
—	1	—	1	(1)	—	—	—	—	—	—	—	—	—
—	—	—	—	81	85	—	80	(85)	(85)	87	86	(70)	—
—	—	—	—	19	15	—	20	(15)	(15)	13	14	(30)	—

Question wordings and variants

Neighborhood Preference A (ISR-Personal): "Would you personally prefer to live in a neighborhood with all black people, mostly black people, mostly whites, or a neighborhood that's mixed half and half?"

    1. All black

    2. Mostly black

    3. Mostly whites

    4. Mixed

    5. No difference (volunteered)

(**Variant:** in 1976, the question read; "Would you personally prefer to live in a neighborhood that is all black, mostly black, about half white and half black, or mostly white?")

Neighborhood Preference B (ISR-Telephone): "Would you personally prefer to live in a neighborhood with mostly whites, mostly blacks, or a neighborhood that is mixed half and half? [If Mostly whites] Would you

Table 5.3 (continued)

Question wordings and variants

prefer a mostly white neighborhood or an all-white neighborhood? [If Mostly blacks] Would you prefer a mostly black neighborhood or an all-black neighborhood?"
   1. All black
   2. Mostly black
   3. Mixed
   4. Mostly white
   5. All white
   6. No difference (volunteered)

White Dinner Guest (NORC): "How strongly would you object if a member of your family wanted to bring a white friend home to dinner? Would you object strongly, mildly, or not at all?"
   1. Strongly
   2. Mildly
   3. Not at all

Club Change Rules (NORC): "If you and your friends belonged to a social club that would not let whites join, would you try to change the rules so that whites could join?"
   1. Yes (including volunteered response "wouldn't belong to club")
   2. No

evident that black and white Americans perceive and define the most important causes of racial inequality in American from quite different vantage points.[14]

Table 5.4B provides further data on black beliefs about the existence of specific types of discrimination—in employment, housing, and treatment by police—which can be compared with parallel data for whites (Table 3.4B). There are large differences between the amounts of racial discrimination that blacks perceive and the amounts that whites perceive. Figure 5.6 (p. 265) illustrates this gap using the question about whether the police treat blacks fairly.[15] Not only are the differences quite wide, but black beliefs in unfair treatment have risen over time, whereas white beliefs seem to have leveled off. Whether white beliefs will have shifted upward more recently because of subsequent national attention on Los Angeles police officers identified with racism, we cannot tell. Of course, black beliefs may have changed as well. In either event, graphs using the questions about discrimination in housing and jobs tell much the same story as Figure 5.6 about racial differences in perceptions of discrimination.

In sum, certain crucial beliefs that whites and blacks have about the causes of black disadvantage differ sharply, and this obviously has equally discrepant implications for what the two groups feel is the best way to reduce black disadvantage. Moreover, we should note that black

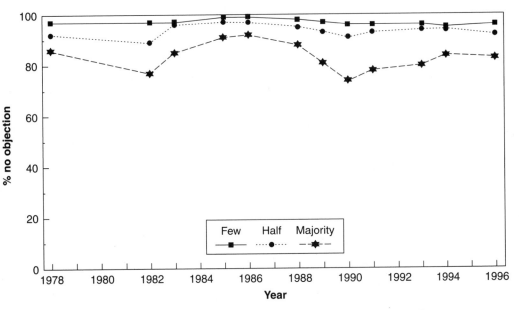

Figure 5.3. Percentages not objecting to schools with different proportions of white children (NORC).

perceptions of discrimination by the police, in housing, in managerial jobs, and in jobs generally are all significantly associated with education. For example, the table below shows the percentages by educational level who say that the police treat blacks unfairly.

0–8 years	9–11 years	12 years	13–15 years	16 years	17+ years
54%	68%	73%	76%	88%	90%
(63)	(111)	(288)	(118)	(103)	(50)

Clearly, the higher the education, the greater the perception of police unfairness.[16] This should be borne in mind by those who expect blacks who move into the middle class to be less concerned about racial discrimination than blacks who are not as successful. Just the opposite appears to be the case.

Affirmative Action

There are large racial differences with regard to support for both government expenditures to help blacks and preferential treatment in

Table 5.4A Explanations for Inequality (black respondents)

Question	Year of survey									
	63	68	72	77	78	80	81	82	83	84
Inequality due to:										
Discrimination (NORC)										
% Yes	—	—	—	—	—	—	—	—	—	—
No	—	—	—	—	—	—	—	—	—	—
Less Ability (NORC)										
% No	—	—	—	—	—	—	—	—	—	—
Yes	—	—	—	—	—	—	—	—	—	—
No Chance for Education (NORC)										
% Yes	—	—	—	—	—	—	—	—	—	—
No	—	—	—	—	—	—	—	—	—	—
No Motivation (NORC)										
% No	—	—	—	—	—	—	—	—	—	—
Yes	—	—	—	—	—	—	—	—	—	—
Blacks Should Try Harder(ISR)[a]										
% Disagree strongly	—	—	(26)	—	—	—	—	—	—	—
Disagree somewhat	—	—	(25)	—	—	—	—	—	—	—
Neither agree/disagree	—	—	(n/a)	—	—	—	—	—	—	—
Agree somewhat	—	—	(32)	—	—	—	—	—	—	—
Agree strongly	—	—	(17)	—	—	—	—	—	—	—
No Special Favors (ISR)										
% Disagree strongly	—	—	—	—	—	—	—	—	—	—
Disagree somewhat	—	—	—	—	—	—	—	—	—	—
Neither agree/disagree	—	—	—	—	—	—	—	—	—	—
Agree somewhat	—	—	—	—	—	—	—	—	—	—
Agree strongly	—	—	—	—	—	—	—	—	—	—
Generations of Slavery/Discrimination (ISR)[a]										
% Agree strongly	—	—	(50)	—	—	—	—	—	—	—
Agree somewhat	—	—	(35)	—	—	—	—	—	—	—
Neither agree/disagree	—	—	(n/a)	—	—	—	—	—	—	—
Disagree somewhat	—	—	(8)	—	—	—	—	—	—	—
Disagree strongly	—	—	(7)	—	—	—	—	—	—	—
Who to Blame (Gallup)[b]										
% White people	57/91	45/80	—	—	—	—	—	—	—	—
Blacks themselves	6/9	11/20	—	—	—	—	—	—	—	—
Both (vol.)	29/na	na/na	—	—	—	—	—	—	—	—
Neither (vol.)	na/na	na/na	—	—	—	—	—	—	—	—
No opinion (vol.)	9/na	44/na	—	—	—	—	—	—	—	—

					Year of survey						
85	86	87	88	89	90	91	92	93	94	95	96
79	75	—	81	(75)	71	83	—	83	81	—	66
21	25	—	20	(25)	29	17	—	17	19	—	34
82	82	—	92	(81)	87	90	—	80	90	—	89
18	18	—	8	(19)	13	10	—	20	10	—	11
74	67	—	69	(65)	70	62	—	72	63	—	54
26	33	—	31	(35)	30	38	—	28	37	—	46
65	61	—	68	(66)	58	52	—	63	70	—	59
35	39	—	33	(34)	42	48	—	38	31	—	41
—	34/38	—	27/31	—	32/36	—	28/31	—	22/25	—	—
—	23/25	—	25/29	—	18/21	—	24/27	—	30/34	—	—
—	9/na	—	12/na	—	11/na	—	10/na	—	12/na	—	—
—	21/23	—	21/24	—	25/28	—	22/25	—	18/21	—	—
—	13/15	—	14/16	—	14/16	—	15/17	—	18/21	—	—
—	26	—	19	—	26	—	25	—	11[c]	—	[c]
—	18	—	14	—	25	—	17	—	24	—	[c]
—	11	—	15	—	10	—	10	—	16	—	[c]
—	26	—	24	—	25	—	31	—	30	—	[c]
—	18	—	28	—	14	—	17	—	19	—	[c]
—	46/49	—	43/48	—	45/48	—	45/47	—	37/39	—	—
—	30/32	—	28/31	—	25/26	—	32/33	—	31/33	—	—
—	7/na	—	10/na	—	7/na	—	5/na	—	7/na	—	—
—	11/12	—	13/14	—	14/15	—	11/12	—	15/17	—	—
—	7/7	—	7/7	—	10/10	—	8/8	—	10/11	—	—
—	—	—	—	20[t]/37[t]	—	11[t]/31[t]	17[t]/37[t]	—	—	14[t]/25[t]	—
—	—	—	—	35[t]/63[t]	—	25[t]/69[t]	30[t]/63[t]	—	—	41[t]/75[t]	—
—	—	—	—	25[t]/na	—	41[t]/na	32[t]/na	—	—	30[t]/na	—
—	—	—	—	9[t]/na	—	10[t]/na	7[t]/na	—	—	6[t]/na	—
—	—	—	—	12[t]/na	—	13[t]/na	14[t]/na	—	—	8[t]/na	—

Table 5.4B Perceptions of discrimination (black respondents)

Question	Year of survey						
	63	70	78	80	81	83	84
Good Chance Jobs (Gallup)							
% Not as good a chance	77	—	64	—	—	—	—
As good/same chance	23	—	36	—	—	—	—
Discriminated in Housing (ABC/WP)							
% Yes	—	—	—	—	46[r]	—	—
No	—	—	—	—	54[r]	—	—
Discriminated in Managerial Jobs (ABC/WP)							
% Yes	—	—	—	—	68[r]	—	—
No	—	—	—	—	32[r]	—	—
Police Treat Fairly (ABC/WP)							
% Disagree	—	—	—	—	69[r]	—	—
Agree	—	—	—	—	31[r]	—	—

Question wordings and variants

Inequality due to Discrimination (NORC): "On the average, (Negroes/blacks/African Americans) have worse jobs, income, and housing than white people. Do you think these differences are . . . mainly due to discrimination?"
    1. Yes
    2. No

Inequality due to Less Ability (NORC): "Do you think these differences are . . . because most (Negroes/blacks/African Americans) have less in-born ability to learn?"
    1. Yes
    2. No

Inequality due to No Chance for Education (NORC): "Do you think these differences are . . . because most (Negroes/blacks/African Americans) don't have the chance for education that it takes to rise out of poverty?"
    1. Yes
    2. No

Inequality due to No Motivation (NORC): "Do you think these differences are . . . because most (Negroes/blacks/African Americans) just don't have the motivation or will power to pull themselves up out of poverty?"
    1. Yes
    2. No

Blacks Should Try Harder (ISR): (1986, 1990: "In past studies we have asked people why they think white people seem to get more of the good things in life in America—such as better jobs and more money—than black people do. These are some of the reasons given by both blacks and whites. Please tell me whether you agree or disagree with each reason as to why white people seem to get more of the good things in life.) (1988, 1992: Now, looking at the respondent booklet for your choices, here are several more statements.) It's really a matter of some people not trying hard enough; if blacks would only try harder they could be just as well off as whites." (Show card)
    1. Agree strongly
    2. Agree somewhat
    3. Neither agree nor disagree
    4. Disagree somewhat
    5. Disagree strongly

					Year of survey					
85	87	88	89	90	91	92	93	94	95	97
—	—	—	55[t]	59[t]	63[t]	—	(71[t])	—	64[t]	53[t]
—	—	—	45[t]	41[t]	37[t]	—	(29[t])	—	37[t]	47[t]
—	—	—	54[t]	—	—	—	—	—	—	—
—	—	—	46[t]	—	—	—	—	—	—	—
—	—	—	68[t]	—	—	—	—	—	—	—
—	—	—	32[t]	—	—	—	—	—	—	—
—	—	—	79[t]	—	—	88[t]	—	—	—	—
—	—	—	21[t]	—	—	12[t]	—	—	—	—

Question wordings and variants

No Special Favors (ISR): (Same introductions as Blacks Should Try Harder) "Irish, Italians, Jewish, and many other minorities overcame prejudice and worked their way up. Blacks should do the same without any special favors." (Show card)

1. Agree strongly
2. Agree somewhat
3. Neither agree nor disagree
4. Disagree somewhat
5. Disagree strongly

Generations of Slavery/Discrimination (ISR): (Same introductions as Blacks Should Try Harder) "Generations of slavery and discrimination have created conditions that make it difficult for blacks to work their way out of the lower class." (Show card)

1. Agree strongly
2. Agree somewhat
3. Neither agree nor disagree
4. Disagree somewhat
5. Disagree strongly

Who to Blame (Gallup): "Who do you think is more to blame for the present conditions in which blacks 1968: Negroes) find themselves—white people or blacks (1968: Negroes) themselves?" In 1995, the results include respondents aged 18–20, and are based on published data reported by the Gallup organization.

1. White people
2. Blacks themselves
3. Both (volunteered)
4. Neither (volunteered)
5. No opinion (volunteered)

(**1963 Variant:** "Who do you think is more to blame for the present position of the Negro race in American fe—Negroes or white people?")

Good Chance Jobs (Gallup): (1989–1991: "For the next few questions I'd like you to think about your own ommunity. 1995: I have a few questions about race relations in this country. First, . . .) In general, do you ink blacks (1963 and 1978: Negroes) have as good a chance as white people in your community to get any

Table 5.4A & B (continued)

Question wordings and variants

---

kind of job for which they are qualified, or don't you think they have as good a chance?" In 1997, the results include respondents aged 18–20.

 1. As good a chance
 2. Not as good a chance
 3. Volunteered: same ("same" coded separately only in 1963.)

Discriminated in Housing (ABC/WP): "In your area, would you say blacks generally are discriminated against or not in getting decent housing?"

 1. Yes, discriminated against
 2. No, not discriminated against

Discriminated in Managerial Jobs (ABC/WP): "In your area, would you say blacks generally are discriminated against or not in getting managerial jobs?"

 1. Yes, discriminated against
 2. No, not discriminated against

Police Treat Fairly (ABC/WP): "I am going to read you a few statements, and for each I'd like you to tell me whether you tend to agree or disagree with it, or if, perhaps, you have no opinion about the statement. These days police in most cities treat blacks as fairly as they treat whites." In 1992, this survey was conducted immediately following the riots that occurred after the Rodney King verdict was announced in Los Angeles.

 1. Agree
 2. Disagree
 3. No opinion

 a. In 1972, this question was asked without the "neither agree nor disagree" option presented to the respondent. Thus the response options for 1972 are not comparable to the response options for the 1986–1994 data. For comparison purposes, we have presented the 1986–1994 data in two ways. First, we present the data with the middle alternative included. Second we present the numbers excluding those respondents who indicated "neither agree nor disagree." For trend purposes, the second numbers presented for 1986–1994 may be compared with the 1972 results, if one is willing to make the assumption that if the respondents who selected the middle alternative in 1986–1994 were not given this option, they would have been distributed proportionally across the remaining response options.

 b. Across time, Gallup has been inconsistent in its coding of various "volunteered" responses to this question, which in some years have been substantial. Sometimes specific volunteered responses (e.g., "both" or "neither") are coded separately from "don't know," and in other years they are indistinguishable from each other. It should be noted, however, that in all years, these options were strictly volunteered by the respondents; they were not offered as explicit choices to them. Because of these inconsistencies in coding, the data are presented in two ways. The first set of figures provides all response options that were coded for a given year; thus it includes the various "volunteered" responses. The second set of figures excludes the volunteered responses, showing results only for the two explicitly offered options.

 c. The No Special Favors question was included in the NORC General Social Survey in 1994, with the following percentages: 25 (Disagree strongly), 17, 10, 27, 22 (Agree strongly). It was repeated in 1996, with these percentages: 15, 18, 14, 25, 29.

 t. Data were collected by telephone survey as opposed to personal interview.

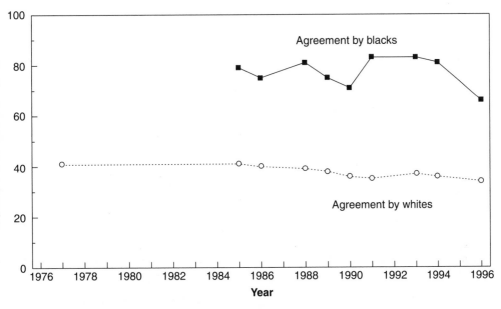

Figure 5.4. Discrimination as primary cause of black economic disadvantage (NORC).

favor of blacks. For example, to an NORC question about whether too little, too much, or the right amount of government money is being spent on blacks, the alternative "too little" is chosen by more than 80 percent of black Americans in most years, but by some 30 percent or less of white Americans in most years—a 50 percent difference. Some of the other questions in Table 5.5, when compared with Table 3.5, show smaller differences, yet in every case there is a decided gap between blacks and whites in their willingness to see government money used to improve the condition of blacks in the United States.

Much the same gulf in attitudes occurs with questions on preferential treatment, as shown in Figure 5.7 (p. 271). The gap between blacks and whites remains substantial at all times, though there appears to be some decrease in black support for such policies in the area of employment. Basically, blacks provide substantial (though by no means unanimous) support for policies of preferential treatment, whereas there is very little support among whites. Since preferential treatment involves policy decisions by elected officials, it is easy to see how it can become a divisive political issue, not only in terms of ideology but by accentuating further racial division as well.

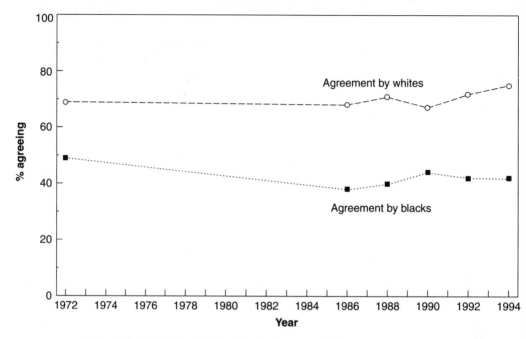

Figure 5.5. Blacks Should Try Harder, by race (ISR).

Although black belief in the importance of discrimination is positively related to educational attainment, support for preferential treatment in employment is negatively related to education, with most opposition found among those with at least some college experience. This is consistent with Dawson's (1994) finding that higher income and education among blacks are significantly associated with opposition to policies aimed at income redistribution, much as one would expect to be the case among whites (see also Tuch and Sigelman, forthcoming). The issue of preferential treatment in admission to colleges is somewhat different, and there is little variation across educational levels for blacks.

Black-White Differences on Other Questions

The miscellaneous questions shown in Table 5.6 may be of more interest for black-white comparisons than they were when considered for whites alone. Thus, if the ISR thermometer scale could be used earlier to assess the affective warmth or coldness of whites toward

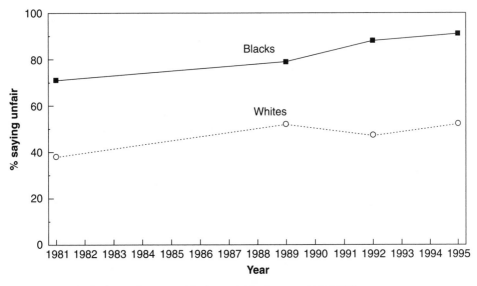

Figure 5.6. Beliefs that police treat blacks unfairly, by race (ABC/WP).

blacks, then we should note that the thermometer ratings that blacks give to whites in Table 5.6 are always noticeably higher than the ratings that whites give to blacks in Table 3.6 (for example, 73 points as against 61 points in 1994). Furthermore, black ratings of whites have risen significantly over the three decades that they have been queried, providing evidence against speculations about an increase in antiwhite attitudes.

These conclusions must be treated with considerable skepticism, however. As we reported in Chapter 2 (Table 2.4), blacks state considerably more warmth toward whites when their interviewer is white than when she is black. In 1994, when the interviewer was black, the average rating of whites was only 55.8, considerably below the 73 points cited above, and thus also below the 61-point rating of blacks by whites. Depending upon the race of the interviewer, we will draw exactly opposite conclusions about black thermometer ratings of whites, leaving the entire issue moot, to say the least.[17] (The same problem occurs for thermometer ratings by whites, but since so few are interviewed by blacks, the effect of race of interviewer is much less severe for white respondents.) This is a dramatic illustration of the importance of reporting race of interviewer as an essential variable with any data set. Even when this is done, the problem remains substantial

Table 5.5A Affirmative action questions—government expenditure (black respondents)

Question	Year of survey									
	70	72	73	74	75	76	77	78	80	81
A. Government expenditures										
Spending on Blacks (NORC)										
% Too little	—	—	83	84	85	82	80	84	80	—
About right	—	—	14	17	14	15	20	15	18	—
Too much	—	—	3	0	1	3	0	1	2	—
Help Blacks (NORC)										
% Gov't help (1–2)	—	—	—	—	67	—	—	—	—	—
Agree with both (3)	—	—	—	—	16	—	—	—	—	—
No special treatment (4–5)	—	—	—	—	17	—	—	—	—	—
Federal Spending (ISR)										
% Increased	—	—	—	—	—	—	—	—	—	—
Same	—	—	—	—	—	—	—	—	—	—
Decreased/vol: cut out	—	—	—	—	—	—	—	—	—	—
Aid to Minorities (ISR)										
% Gov't help (1–3)	78	73	—	76	—	64	—	57	a	—
Mid-point (4)	11	11	—	10	—	14	—	13	a	—
Help themselves (5–7)	5	9	—	7	—	12	—	16	a	—
Not thought	6	6	—	7	—	11	—	14	a	—
Aid to Blacks (ISR)										
% Gov't help (1–3)	—	—	—	—	—	—	—	—	—	—
Mid-point (4)	—	—	—	—	—	—	—	—	—	—
Help themselves (5–7)	—	—	—	—	—	—	—	—	—	—
Not thought	—	—	—	—	—	—	—	—	—	—

unless randomization is used and the effect of the variable is brought directly into the design of the study as well as the analysis.[18]

We suspect that the effect of race of interviewer is particularly strong with thermometer ratings because the question itself is so general ("warmth" or "coldness" toward an entire group), and the use of a huge response scale (zero to one hundred) means that respondents have little basis for deciding what a number on the scale represents beyond the intuitive notion of fifty as the middle. This apparently does not prevent the scale from correlating well with other questions—many of which also are likely to have been affected in the same direction by the race of the interviewer—but it means that comparisons of the type we wish to make here between ratings by blacks and whites become difficult, if not impossible. Likewise, attempts to look at changes of

					Year of survey								
2	83	84	85	86	87	88	89	90	91	92	93	94	96
0	80	(71)	(70)	(79)	80	(81)	(82)	(82)	82	—	(84)	81	84
9	20	(29)	(30)	(18)	18	(19)	(15)	(15)	16	—	(13)	16	15
1	0	(0)	(0)	(3)	2	(0)	(3)	(3)	2	—	(4)	3	1
-	58	54	—	56	54	58	53	54	61	—	53	51	48
-	30	38	—	33	29	31	30	36	33	—	33	39	35
-	12	8	—	11	17	11	17	10	5	—	14	11	16
-	—	71	—	74	—	69	—	72	—	70	—	—	—
-	—	26	—	22	—	29	—	27	—	28	—	—	—
-	—	3	—	3	—	2	—	1	—	2	—	—	—
9	—	50	—	42	—	53	—	—	—	—	—	—	—
1	—	23	—	25	—	20	—	—	—	—	—	—	—
5	—	15	—	22	—	19	—	—	—	—	—	—	—
6	—	12	—	11	—	8	—	—	—	—	—	—	—
-	—	—	—	42	—	40	—	49	—	39	—	39	45
-	—	—	—	21	—	23	—	21	—	22	—	29	21
-	—	—	—	32	—	25	—	24	—	29	—	25	23
-	—	—	—	5	—	12	—	6	—	11	—	7	11

ratings over time are compromised unless we know the proportions of blacks interviewed by blacks and by whites at each time point.

Other Miscellaneous Items

The picture that blacks have of white attitudes and actions on race also appears to have become more positive, or at least less negative, on the Gallup question called "Better Break." Blacks are less likely in recent years to see whites as trying to "keep blacks down," somewhat more likely to say that whites "want to see blacks get a better break," but also more likely to say that whites don't care either way. (Whites in Table 3.6 see themselves predominantly as wanting to give blacks a better break.) However, it is important to note that something on the

Table 5.5B Affirmative action questions—preferential treatment (black respondents)

| | Year of survey | | | | | | | |
Question	77	78	79	80	81	82	83	84
B. Preferential treatment								
Preference in Admissions (ISR)								
% Favor strongly	—	—	—	—	—	—	—	—
Favor not strongly	—	—	—	—	—	—	—	—
Oppose not strongly	—	—	—	—	—	—	—	—
Oppose strongly	—	—	—	—	—	—	—	—
Pref. Hiring/Promotion (ISR)								
% Favor strongly	—	—	—	—	—	—	—	—
Favor not strongly	—	—	—	—	—	—	—	—
Oppose not strongly	—	—	—	—	—	—	—	—
Oppose strongly	—	—	—	—	—	—	—	—
Pref. Hiring/Promotion (CBS/NYT)								
% Yes	—	—	—	—	—	—	—	—
No	—	—	—	—	—	—	—	—
Depends/DK (vol.)	—	—	—	—	—	—	—	—

Question wordings and variants

Spending on Blacks (NORC): "We are faced with many problems in this country, none of which can be solved easily or inexpensively. I'm going to name some of these problems, and for each one I'd like you to tell me whether you think we're spending too much money on it, too little money, or about the right amount . . . Improving the conditions of blacks. Are we spending too much, too little, or about the right amount on improving the conditions of blacks?" Improving the conditions of blacks is eighth in the list of problems, following such things as improving and protecting the environment, halting the rising crime rate, and improving the nation's education system. (*Note:* This item is one exception to the general finding that including or excluding the oversamples of black respondents does not substantially change the results. For 1987, the results with the oversample excluded differ appreciably from those shown above. Specifically, excluding the oversample yields a total of 57 cases, with the following distribution: 70% too little; 26% about right; 4% too much.)

    1. Too much
    2. Too little
    3. About the right amount

Help Blacks (NORC): "Some people think that (Negroes/blacks/African Americans) have been discriminated against for so long that the government has a special obligation to help improve their living standards. Others believe that the government should not be giving special treatment to (Negroes/blacks/African Americans). Where would you place yourself on this scale, or haven't you made up your mind on this?" (SHOW CARD)

    1. I strongly agree the government is obligated to help blacks
    2.
    3. I agree with both answers
    4.
    5. I strongly agree that government shouldn't give special treatment
    0. Don't know

Federal Spending (ISR): "If you had a say in making up the federal budget this year, for which (1986–1992) of the following) programs would you like to see spending increased and for which would you like to see spending decreased . . . Should federal spending on programs that assist blacks be increased, decreased, or kept

					Year of survey							
85	86	87	88	89	90	91	92	93	94	95	96
—	63	—	68	—	64	—	64	—	—	—	—
—	17	—	14	—	8	—	12	—	—	—	—
—	8	—	4	—	13	—	8	—	—	—	—
—	13	—	14	—	15	—	16	—	—	—	—
—	49	—	55	—	63	—	47	—	37	—	49
—	19	—	9	—	11	—	11	—	11	—	10
—	13	—	14	—	14	—	15	—	22	—	13
—	20	—	22	—	12	—	27	—	31	—	29
73[t]	—	75[t]	—	—	54[t]	52[t]	73[t]	63[t]	—	63[t]	—
16[t]	—	20[t]	—	—	25[t]	26[t]	14[t]	25[t]	—	28[t]	—
12[t]	—	5[t]	—	—	21[t]	22[t]	13[t]	13[t]	—	10[t]	—

Question wordings and variants

about the same?" In 1988 and 1992, volunteered "cut out entirely" answers were accepted by interviewers, and coded separately. In Table 5.5A, this small group of respondents are included in the "Decreased" category.

    1. Increased
    2. Decreased
    3. Same
    4. Volunteered: "cut out entirely" (1988 and 1992)

(**Variant:** In 1984, the question was asked as follows: "If you had a say in making up the federal budget this year, which programs would you like to see increased and which reduced . . . Should federal spending on assistance to blacks be increased, decreased, or kept about the same?")

Aid to Minorities (ISR): "Some people feel that the government in Washington should make every possible effort to improve the social and economic position of blacks (1970: Negroes) and other minority groups. Others feel that the government should not make any special effort (1972–1988: To help minorities because they should help themselves) (1970: But they should be expected to help themselves). Where would you place yourself on this scale, or haven't you thought much about this?" (Show card with seven-point scale)

    1. Government should help minority groups (1988: minorities)
    2.
    3.
    4.
    5.
    6.
    7. Minority groups (1988: minorities) should help themselves
    0. Haven't thought much about this

Aid to Blacks (ISR): "Some people feel that the government in Washington should make every possible effort to improve the social and economic position of blacks. Others feel that the government should not make any

Table 5.5A & B (continued)

Question wordings and variants

special effort to help blacks because they should help themselves. Where would you place yourself on this scale, or haven't you thought much about this?" (Show card with seven-point scale)

1. Government should help blacks
2.
3.
4.
5.
6.
7. Blacks should help themselves
0. Haven't thought much about this

(**Note:** In 1986 and 1988, a split-ballot design was used to phase out the use of the "Aid to Minorities" version of this question, and to phase in the use of the "Aid to Blacks" version of the question. Thus both versions were used in 1986 and 1988. Beginning in 1990, however, only the "Aid to Blacks" form of the question was asked.)

Preference in Admissions (ISR): "Some people say that because of past discrimination, it is sometimes necessary for colleges and universities to reserve openings for black students. Others oppose quotas because they say quotas give blacks advantages they haven't earned. What about your opinion—are you for or against quotas to admit black students? (If for) Do you favor quotas *strongly* or *not strongly*? (If against) Do you oppose quotas *strongly* or *not strongly*?"

1. Favor strongly
2. Favor not strongly
3. Oppose not strongly
4. Oppose strongly

Preference in Hiring/Promotion (ISR): "Some people say that because of past discrimination, blacks should be given preference in hiring and promotion. Others say that such preference in hiring and promotion of black is wrong because it gives blacks advantages they haven't earned. What about your opinion—are you *for* or *against* preferential hiring and promotion of blacks? (If for) Do you favor preference in hiring and promotion *strongly* or *not strongly*? (If against) Do you oppose preference in hiring and promotion *strongly* or *not strongly*?"

1. Favor strongly
2. Favor not strongly
3. Oppose not strongly
4. Oppose strongly

Preference in Hiring/Promotion (CBS/NYT): "Do you believe that where there has been job discrimination against blacks in the past, preference in hiring or promotion should be given to blacks today?" In 1987, volunteered "depends" responses were not reported separately from DK. In all other years, "depends" was coded as a separate category.

1. Yes
2. No
3. Depends/don't know (volunteered)

(**1991 Variant:** "Do you believe that where there has been job discrimination against blacks in the past, preference in hiring should be given to blacks today?")

a. In 1980 the phrase "even if it means giving them preferential treatment in jobs" was added to the first sentence. It is quite probable that this change in wording altered the meaning of this question for respondents, and therefore we do not include the 1980 data in our trend analysis. For interested readers, however, 42 percent supported government aid to minorities, 21 percent thought minorities should help themselves, and 16 percent hadn't thought much about the issue.

t. Data were collected through telephone survey rather than personal interview.

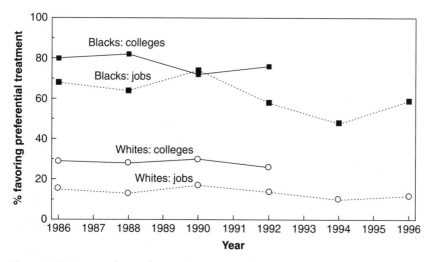

Figure 5.7. Support for preferential treatment, by race (ISR).

order of a quarter of the black population in recent years still chooses the alternative stating that most whites "want to keep blacks down." The relation of answers to education is clear-cut: more-educated blacks are more likely to select the "don't care" alternative, whereas less educated blacks are more likely to select the "better break" alternative; neither of these educational groupings leans disproportionately toward the "keep down" alternative.[19]

A question on the pace of civil rights activity also shows an important degree of racial difference, as presented in Figure 5.8 (p. 275). Nearly half the black sample in 1992 chose "too slowly" as a response to the ISR Civil Rights Push question, whereas the figure for whites is only 13 percent, though both groups have shown some increase in the "too slowly" response over time. Particularly important is the fact that "too slowly" is chosen especially by more-educated black respondents, as shown below for aggregated data from 1986 through 1992:[20]

0–11 years	12 years	13+ years
33%	41%	52%
(233)	(259)	(253)

Thus it is middle-class blacks who express the most impatience with the pace of civil rights activity.

Table 5.6 Miscellaneous questions (black respondents)

Question	Year of survey										
	64	65	66	68	69	70	72	73	74	75	76
Thermometer Rating of Blacks (ISR)											
Mean of 100-pt scale	90	—	86	90	—	85	88	—	86	—	86
Thermometer Rating of Whites (ISR)											
Mean of 100-pt scale	66	—	72	68	—	64	64	—	74	—	67
Ku Klux Klan Rating (Gallup)											
% Highly unfavorable (-4, -5)	—	88	—	—	—	93	—	84	—	—	—
Unfavorable (-1, -2, -3)	—	7	—	—	—	4	—	12	—	—	—
Civil Rights Push (ISR)											
% Too slowly	27	—	22	30	—	38	31	—	32	—	39
About right	64	—	55	62	—	55	58	—	61	—	55
Too fast	9	—	23	8	—	7	11	—	7	—	6
Black Push (NORC)											
% Disagree strongly	—	—	—	—	—	—	—	—	—	—	—
Disagree slightly	—	—	—	—	—	—	—	—	—	—	—
Agree slightly	—	—	—	—	—	—	—	—	—	—	—
Agree strongly	—	—	—	—	—	—	—	—	—	—	—
Riots (ISR)											
% Solve (1–3)	—	—	—	[a]	—	[a]	(74)	—	69	—	64
Mid-point (4)	—	—	—	[a]	—	[a]	(4)	—	12	—	7
Use force (5–7)	—	—	—	[a]	—	[a]	(13)	—	11	—	5
Not thought	—	—	—	[a]	—	[a]	(9)	—	9	—	24
Better Break (Gallup)											
% Keep down	—	—	—	—	48	—	—	—	—	—	—
Whites don't care	—	—	—	—	29	—	—	—	—	—	—
Blacks get break	—	—	—	—	22	—	—	—	—	—	—

Question wordings and variants

Thermometer Rating of Blacks (ISR):[b] "There are many groups in America that try to get the government the American people to see things more their way. We would like to get your feelings toward some of these groups. Blacks. Where would you put them on the thermometer?" (*Note:* This is the one exception to the general practice of including black oversamples in the NES analysis. For the thermometer ratings of both bla[c] and whites, the black oversamples for 1964, 1968, and 1970 were *not* included in the analysis.)

Response: Mean of a 100-point scale

Thermometer Rating of Whites (ISR):[b] "There are many groups in America that try to get the government the American people to see things more their way. We would like to get your feelings toward some of these groups. Whites. Where would you put them on the thermometer?" (See note for Thermometer Rating of Bla[c] above.)

Response: Mean of a 100-point scale

Ku Klux Klan Rating (Gallup): "How far up the scale or how far down the scale would you rate the following organizations: Ku Klux Klan?"

1. Highly favorable (4,5)
2. Favorable (1,2,3)

	Year of survey														
9	80	81	82	83	84	85	86	88	89	90	91	92	94	95	96
-	89	—	76	—	78	—	80	81	—	82	—	86	81	—	82
-	77	—	67	—	71	—	—	68	—	—	—	70	73	—	74
)	—	—	—	—	—	—	—	—	—	—	—	—	—	—	—
5	—	—	—	—	—	—	—	—	—	—	—	—	—	—	—
-	44	—	—	—	(51)	—	46	44	—	34	—	44	—	—	—
-	50	—	—	—	(43)	—	48	50	—	53	—	49	—	—	—
-	6	—	—	—	(7)	—	6	6	—	13	—	6	—	—	—
-	34	—	54	—	38	(30)	—	—	—	—	—	—	48	—	53
-	20	—	15	—	23	(24)	—	—	—	—	—	—	20	—	12
-	22	—	15	—	26	(24)	—	—	—	—	—	—	22	—	15
-	25	—	16	—	13	(23)	—	—	—	—	—	—	10	—	21
	—	—	—	—	—	—	—	—	—	—	—	59	—	—	—
	—	—	—	—	—	—	—	—	—	—	—	11	—	—	
	—	—	—	—	—	—	—	—	—	—	—	13	—	—	—
	—	—	—	—	—	—	—	—	—	—	—	18	—	—	—
-	—	36	—	28	31	—	—	30[t]	24[t]	—	21[t]	27[t]	—	29[t]	—
-	—	35	—	33	36	—	—	34[t]	40[t]	—	40[t]	41[t]	—	44[t]	—
-	—	28	—	40	32	—	—	37[t]	36[t]	—	39[t]	32[t]	—	27[t]	—

Question wordings and variants

3. Unfavorable (-1,-2,-3)
4. Highly unfavorable (-4,-5)

(Note: The Ku Klux Klan was the first organization to be rated in 1970 and 1979, the fourth in 1965, and ɛ third in 1973. The YMCA, CORE, and the FBI were first, second, and third, respectively, in 1965; CORE d the FBI were first and second, respectively, in 1973.) Note that percentages for scale ratings of 1 to 5 are t shown in Table 5.6 but can be obtained by subtraction.

Civil Rights Push (ISR): "Some say that the civil rights people have been trying to push too fast. Others feel ɛy haven't pushed fast enough. How about you: Do you think that civil rights leaders are trying to push *too* ɬ, are going *too slowly*, or are they moving at *about* the *right* speed?"

1. Too fast
2. Too slowly
3. About the right speed

Black Push (NORC): "Here are some opinions other people have expressed in connection with ɛgro/black)–white relations. Which statement on the card comes closest to how you, yourself, feel? ɛgroes/blacks/African Americans) shouldn't push themselves where they're not wanted." (*Note:* This is an ɛeption to the general finding that including and excluding the black oversamples does not alter appreciably

Table 5.6 (continued)

Question wordings and variants

the results. Specifically, without the oversample, there are 145 cases, and the distribution is as follows: 62% disagree strongly; 14% disagree slightly; 12% agree slightly; and 12% agree strongly.)

    1. Agree strongly
    2. Agree slightly
    3. Disagree slightly
    4. Disagree strongly

    Riots (ISR): "There is much discussion about the best way to deal with the problem of urban unrest and rioting. Some say it is more important to use all available force to maintain law and order—no matter what the results. Others say it is more important to correct the problems of poverty and unemployment that give rise to the disturbances. (1992: And, of course, other people have opinions in between.) Where would you place yourself on this scale, or haven't you thought much about this?" (Show card with seven-point scale)

    1. Solve problems of poverty and unemployment
    2.
    3.
    4.
    5.
    6.
    7. Use all available force
    0. Not thought much about this

    Better Break (Gallup): "On the whole, do you think most white people want to see blacks get a better break, or do they want to keep blacks down, or don't you think they care either way?" In 1981, 1983, and 1991, the results include respondents aged 18–20, and are based on published figures reported in the Gallup Monthly Report, June 1992. Data for 1995 are from a telephone survey conducted for the *New York Times,* and reported in the Roper Center's *Public Perspective,* vol. 7 (2), 1996, p. 22. Because of this, respondents aged 18–20 are included in the 1995 results

    1. Better break
    2. Keep blacks down
    3. Don't care either way

    a. In 1968 and 1970 the Riots question was asked *without* the interest filter, and for that reason we have not included those time points in our trend analysis. For interested readers, however, 84 percent of the black respondents in 1968 and 79 percent of the black respondents in 1970 said that we should solve poverty and unemployment, and 6 percent in 1968 and 9 percent in 1970 supported the use of all available force to maintain law and order.

    b. The wording of the introduction is as shown here for 1964, 1966, and 1968. A small change occurred in 1970: the second sentence was replaced with "Please use the thermometer again—this time to indicate your feelings toward these groups or persons." More changes too cumbersome to report in detail (and unlikely to affect results) were made in the introduction to the thermometer rating at the remaining time points (1972–1996). Generally, respondents were asked to express their feelings toward a number of groups (an average of roughly 22 different groups or organizations across the 16 surveys involved), with blacks falling about 13th on average. The relative order of the ratings of blacks and whites was highly inconsistent across time: about 1/2 the time points, whites were rated before blacks, and the reverse was true in the other 1/2 of the time points. In two years, whites were not asked about at all, and in only one year were whites and blacks asked about contiguously. Other groups asked about most regularly were liberals, conservatives, Democrats, Republicans, big business, labor unions, and poor people. "Don't know" responses were automatically coded as 50 in 1964, 1966, 1968, and 1970, but were coded separately in later years; for all analyses we have rescored "don't know" to 50.

    t. Data were collected through telephone survey as opposed to personal interview.

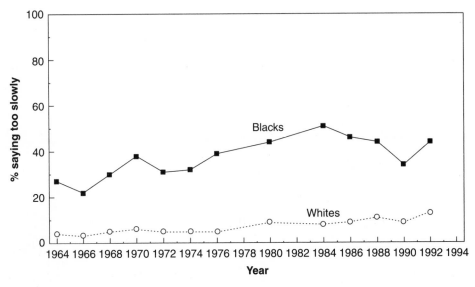

Figure 5.8. Proportions of blacks and whites saying that civil rights leaders are pushing too slowly (ISR).

Conclusions

The most important conclusion from this review of black attitudes concerns the large differences in the perspectives of blacks and whites about the causes of black disadvantage. Blacks emphasize continuing discrimination; whites stress low motivation on the part of blacks. This disagreement in perceptions of causality sets the stage for many other differences. Thus there is much greater support among blacks for various forms of strong affirmative action. Affirmative action may be seen by blacks partly as compensation for past discrimination, but it is also a way of counteracting the discrimination that they believe is still pervasive. We are not able with our data to separate the two components completely, but we can attempt to do so by comparing the two questions we have on discrimination as a cause of present black disadvantage: the ISR question that focuses on the past (Agree or disagree: "Generations of slavery and discrimination have created conditions that make it difficult for blacks to work their way out of the lower class"), and the NORC question that focuses on the present ("Do you think [blacks have worse jobs, income, and housing] mainly due to discrimination?" Contrast the black and white percentages agreeing to each of these explanations in 1994:[21]

Question	Blacks	Whites
ISR emphasis on past	72% agree	51% agree
NORC emphasis on present	81% agree	36% agree

Blacks emphasize *present* discrimination even more than they do past discrimination and slavery. Whites, however, give greater emphasis to the *past* than to the present, as well as mentioning both sources of disadvantage much less often than do blacks.

The two racial groups do come closer together in identifying lack of educational opportunities as a barrier for blacks, which suggests that this is one area where a policy might receive considerable support among *both* blacks and whites, especially if it is not defined as involving preferential treatment but rather involves a broader investment in education aimed at disadvantaged youth generally.[22]

We need to add one other qualification to the picture of quite different attitudes on the part of blacks and whites: blacks show some evidence of the same type of gap that whites reveal between support for principles of equal treatment and integration and support for government implementation of these principles. In particular, blacks have shown decreasing support over time for government intervention to increase both school integration and "fair treatment in jobs," though the shift has been not toward opposition to government action but instead toward responses claiming no interest in these issues. We do not understand the reasons for the decline in black support of implementation, especially in the face of little or no change in levels of support for preferential treatment, but they call for further analysis beyond what has been possible for this book.

For summary purposes, we have used multiple regression to identify the relation of education, age, and (as a control) year of survey to a number of the questions discussed above. Here we focus on education, a key variable because so much emphasis is often placed on the difference between blacks who have successfully used education to move toward a middle-class income and style of life, and others who have been less successful or clearly unsuccessful. Relative to the less educated, more-educated black Americans tend (to a statistically significant extent):

to be more supportive of racial intermarriage
to favor open housing laws

to believe that civil rights change has been too slow
to oppose preferential hiring
to reject low motivation as an explanation of black disadvantage
to believe there is discrimination in jobs, housing, and police
    treatment
to believe whites don't care about blacks

It is especially important to recognize that greater education heightens black support for equal treatment in the classic sense and for at least some aspects of integration. But it is equally important to see that education is associated with more, rather than less, belief in the continued prevalence and importance of racial discrimination.[23] Thus the assumption by some whites that racial problems in America are largely or entirely economic is off the mark. The perception of well-educated blacks that they—and blacks more generally—face racial discrimination in many areas of life is as profound a factor as purely economic disadvantage may be for other blacks.

Some reflection on the part of whites should make it evident why racial differences in perception are not limited to economic factors and, especially, why middle-class blacks are often even more negative about the present state of race relations than are lower-class blacks. Middle-class blacks are exposed to numerous forms of discrimination, for example, something as serious as being stopped by the police for minor or even no infractions of the law. Less serious perhaps, but equally or more pervasive, are insults and inconveniences such as the difficulty of obtaining a taxi or of not being served politely in a restaurant.[24] Moreover, given the existence of some continuing real discrimination, middle-class blacks have no way of knowing whether what seems to be unfair treatment (the taxi that speeds by, the poor seating in a restaurant) is, in fact, due to deliberate discrimination or to something more innocuous.[25] Thus the very real discrimination that continues to exist in the United States is almost certainly magnified because of the difficulty of separating one type of negative treatment from another. And the commitment that middle-class blacks have to equal treatment should make them even less prepared than other blacks to tolerate what appears to be racially based mistreatment.

Beyond personal experiences of the kinds just mentioned, middle-class blacks can seldom avoid identifying with the experiences and problems of lower-class blacks. In a society where racial identification is so pervasive, most middle-class blacks are likely to feel that no matter what their economic and professional achievements, they cannot entirely escape the stereotypes that pervade white (and black) perceptions of the black lower class. For this reason also, middle-class blacks will, almost inevitably, be extremely sensitive about stereotypes of all kinds. In sum, however important economic factors may be, American racial problems cannot be reduced to social class in a sense that is purely economic or even a matter of lifestyle. Attempts to do so are bound to misunderstand the situation that shapes perceptions by the black middle class in America.

Finally, we need to reiterate that our data on black attitudes have two weaknesses in addition to the obvious lack of questions on certain topics. One weakness is the fact that in most national surveys black subsamples are small and therefore lack precision for particular time points, making detailed analysis difficult. Also important is the real possibility of systematic error due to inconsistency in matching race of interviewer and race of respondent in the surveys that we draw on. The considerable effect of race of interviewer on black responses to many types of racial questions has been well documented for a number of years, and it is unfortunate that major survey organizations like ISR and NORC are unable either to do some systematic matching of interviewer and respondent by race, or to include some random assignment by race of interviewer. Yet given the enormous practical difficulties and expense of accomplishing this at the national level, one can understand why it is virtually never done, especially in face-to-face surveys.[26] Less understandable, however, is the failure to include in *every* data set a variable that identifies the race of a respondent's interviewer. It is likely that the levels of black responses to survey questions and perhaps also trends over time have been seriously affected by this important source of variation.

Theoretical Interpretations
of Changes in White
Racial Attitudes

A number of social scientists have attempted to interpret the nature
and direction of trends in white racial attitudes. The interpretations are
often linked by a concern, sometimes direct and sometimes indirect,
with the gap between attitudes toward matters of principle and attitudes toward specific policy issues, or indeed between attitudes of any
kind and behavior outside the survey interview. In this chapter we
review critically several of these interpretations, focusing on those that
have come to represent distinct vantage points from which data on
racial attitudes have been viewed. We make no attempt to cover all of
this literature—which is vast and constantly increasing—but rather to
single out a small number of theoretical positions that have become
important as social scientists try to understand the changes in racial
attitudes over the past half century. We also introduce some experimental results relevant to arguments that have developed between different
interpretations of the available survey data.

As we consider various interpretations, it is useful to bear in mind
exactly which trend data were available to earlier interpreters at particular points in time. Table 6.1 indicates in what year a second set of
data became available that was at least four years past the initial
inclusion of a question in a national survey—that is, the first point at
which a *trend* could be established for the question. The choice of a
four-year minimum is necessarily arbitrary, but we judge it to be the
shortest interval between two points for a durable trend to be noted.

It can be seen that NORC trend data on questions dealing mainly
with principles of racial equality became available first (1956), and that
Gallup trend data on social distance preferences appeared some seven
years later (1963). ISR data on trends in government implementation

Table 6.1 Years at which trend data became available on white racial attitudes

Year	Question
1956	Same Schools (NORC) (3.1)
	Segregated Transportation (NORC) (3.1)
	Same Block (NORC) (3.1)
	Intelligence (NORC) (see p. 353, n. 37)
1963	Equal Jobs (NORC) (3.1)
	Black Candidate (Gallup) (3.1)
	Few (Gallup) (3.3)
	Half (Gallup) (3.3)
	Majority (Gallup) (3.3)
	Next Door (Gallup) (3.3)
	Great Numbers (Gallup) (3.3)
1968	Residential Choice (NORC) (3.1)
	Residential Choice (ISR) (3.1)
	Laws against Intermarriage (NORC) (3.1)
	General Segregation (ISR) (3.1)
	Federal Job Intervention (ISR) (3.2)
	Federal School Intervention (ISR) (3.2)
	Accommodations Intervention (ISR) (3.2)
	Thermometer Rating of Blacks/Whites (ISR) (3.6)
	Civil Rights Push (ISR) (3.6)
	Black Push (NORC) (3.6)
	Who to Blame (Gallup) (3.4)
1970	Same Accommodations (NORC) (3.1)
	Black Dinner Guest (NORC) (3.3)
	Ku Klux Klan (NORC) (3.6)
1972	Intermarriage (Gallup) (3.1)
1974	Aid to Minorities (ISR) (3.5)
1976	Busing (ISR) (3.2)
	Busing (NORC) (3.2)
	Riots (ISR) (3.6)
	Neighborhood Preference (ISR) (3.3)
1977	Black Candidate (NORC) (3.1)
	Spending on Blacks (NORC) (3.5)
	Few (NORC) (3.3)
	Half (NORC) (3.3)
	Majority (NORC) (3.3)
1978	Open Housing (NORC) (3.2)
	Good Chance Jobs (Gallup) (3.4)

Table 6.1 (continued)

Year	Question
1983	Help Blacks (NORC) (3.5)
1985	Club Change Rules (NORC) (3.3) Inequality Due to Discrimination (NORC) (3.4) Inequality Due to Less Ability (NORC) (3.4) Inequality Due to No Chance Education (NORC) (3.4) Inequality Due to No Motivation (NORC) (3.4)
1986	Blacks Should Try Harder (ISR) (3.4) Generations of Slavery/Discrimination (ISR) (3.4)
1988	Better Break (Gallup) (3.6) Federal Spending (ISR) (3.5)
1989	Discrimination in Housing (ABC/WP) (3.4) Discrimination in Managerial Jobs (ABC/WP) (3.4) Police Treat Fairly (ABC/WP) (3.4)
1990	No Special Favors (ISR) (3.4) Preference in Admissions (ISR) (3.5) Preference Hiring/Promotion (ISR) (3.5) Preference Hiring/Promotion (CBS/NYT) (3.5) Aid to Blacks (ISR) (3.5)

Note: Date given is the first year in which a question had been replicated at least four years beyond its initial administration. Numbers in parentheses indicate tables in Chapter 3 that provide full dates, question wording, and national trends.

of principles became available only in 1968, though different versions of some implementation-type questions had been asked earlier. Trend questions on government financial aid to black communities became available in the mid-1970s, having been initiated in the years following the urban riots and the *Report of the National Advisory Commission on Civil Disorders* (1968). Trends in explanations for black disadvantage appeared a good deal later (1985 for NORC, 1986 for ISR), and trends in attitudes toward preferential treatment policies in the data we rely on here are quite recent (1990 for ISR and CBS/NYT).[1]

This general link between types of questions and dates was in good part a reflection of the underlying changes that surveys were attempting to measure: the basic principles of integration and equal treatment were still very much at issue in the 1940s and 1950s, whereas in subsequent years the implementation of these principles through government action emerged as the pressing problem. Still later came increasing recognition that neither civil rights protests nor civil rights legislation mandating equal treatment had succeeded in solving racial problems in the United States. The focus shifted to general questions about affirmative action in the form of government aid to blacks and then to explanations of continuing black disadvantage. Last came questions on preferential treatment, as it became a salient political issue.

There is one important qualification to this history, with its emphasis on abstract principles as the starting point: a trend question about personal acceptance of integration of one's neighborhood was begun by NORC in 1942, and other questions we have labeled as dealing with "social distance" were introduced by Gallup in the late 1950s. Thus if "implementation" is thought of in terms of personal acceptance of some degree of integration, such trends began early and to a considerable extent moved in the same way as did questions about abstract principles.

Some of the writings we will discuss provide a relatively optimistic perspective on trends over the past half century, and others a more pessimistic view. The differences seem to be partly a function of the particular items that were available for analysis at a given point. That was more true in earlier years than at present, but the difficulties of using data from more than one organization at a time still tends to confine analyses to a single conveniently available data set, such as NORC's General Social Survey or ISR's National Election Study, which, despite their excellence, sometimes provide a more limited perspective than is desirable. One notes, for example, the frequency with which many analyses take 1972 as a baseline date: this might suggest to an unwitting reader that 1972 was a major turning point in American history, whereas it happens simply to be the first year in which the General Social Survey was carried out.

Early Optimism: The *Scientific American* Series

The earliest of the post–World War II reports on trends in white racial attitudes appeared in *Scientific American* in four articles by social scientists associated with NORC: Hyman and Sheatsley 1956; Hyman and Sheatsley 1964; Greeley and Sheatsley 1971; and Taylor, Sheatsley, and Greeley 1978.[2] The four reports relied for baseline data on NORC surveys carried out during the 1940s and 1950s, which provided the only evidence on trends available when the first of the reports was published.

The 1956 *Scientific American* article focuses on three questions concerning the integration of schools, transportation, and neighborhoods, as shown at the top of Table 6.1. Consistent with the national trends for these questions that we sketched in Chapter 3, Hyman and Sheatsley identify large positive shifts on all three items between 1942 and 1956. They also draw on a question about racial differences in intelligence (see Chapter 3, note 37), pointing out the substantial rise between 1942 and 1956 in white belief in black-white equality in intelligence, and suggest that this rise provided an important basis for the general shift toward acceptance of integration. In addition, they find positive associations between integrationist sentiments on the three main questions and both younger age and higher education, which they interpret to mean that a new and better-educated generation will give increased support to integration—a form of the "continuous socialization" model that we discussed in Chapter 4. Their conclusions about change are perhaps best summarized as follows:

> the long-term trend is steadily in the direction of integration. It has moved far in 15 years, and it may be accelerating. Certainly there is no evidence that it will soon, if ever, reverse itself, for it is supported by revolutionary changes in ancient beliefs about Negroes and by the continued influx of better educated and more tolerant young people into the effective adult public. (Hyman and Sheatsley 1956:39)

The second *Scientific American* report in 1964 by the same authors focuses on the same four items. By this time equalitarian responses on the Intelligence question had leveled off, but responses to the other three questions continued to move strongly in an integrationist direction, and the associations with education (positive) and age (negative) continued to hold. The article also provides evidence that personal acceptance of integration often followed government actions that created integrated situations, as when Southern attitudes changed in a more liberal direction soon after schools in a Southern community were desegregated. In general, despite the leveling off for the Intelligence item and some signs that the youngest (twenty-one to twenty-four) age group among Southerners might no longer be a leading force for integration in that region, the authors' conclusions remain optimistic:

> the unbroken trend of the past 20 years, and particularly its acceleration in the past decade of intensified controversy, suggests that integration will not be easily halted. In the minds and hearts of the

majority of Americans the principle of integration seems already to have won. The issues that remain are how soon and in what ways the principle is to be implemented. (Hyman and Sheatsley 1964:23)

Note that the authors clearly recognize a distinction between principle and the implementation of principle. But because their results related largely to the former, the distinction may well have been lost on many readers.

In the 1971 *Scientific American* report—which appeared after the urban riots of the late 1960s—Greeley and Sheatsley open by summarizing the trend since 1942 as "distinctly and strongly toward increasing approval of integration." This conclusion is based on the Same Schools and Segregated Transportation items employed in the previous reports, together with five newer questions for which NORC trend data had become available: Same Accommodations, Black Dinner Guest, Residential Choice, Laws against Intermarriage, and Black Push (see Table 6.1 for dates and references to tables in Chapter 3 that give wordings and trends for these questions). (Nothing is said in this or the fourth report concerning the Intelligence and Same Block questions, neither of which had been asked in 1970, the most recent time point on which the authors relied.) All but the question about attitudes toward blacks "pushing themselves where they're not wanted" (Black Push) show increased support for integration during this period. Moreover, younger age and higher education continue to be associated with more integrationist answers; even the possible reversal for young white Southerners noted in 1964 is not evident in the 1970 data.

In stating conclusions, Greeley and Sheatsley (1971) appear to be somewhat ambivalent about the meaning of the continued strong positive shift indicated by their data. On the one hand, they write of the results as suggesting that the trend for attitudes toward integrated education (Same Schools) was proceeding so rapidly that in just a few years (1977 is the date they project) "desegregating schools [will have] ceased to be a significant issue." On the other hand, they also emphasize that "a change of attitude does not necessarily predict a change in behavior," and speak of the shifts "as creating an environment for effective social reform," rather than as being reform itself. In a follow-up article three years later, Greeley and Sheatsley (1974) also include data on the overwhelming white resistance to busing, and they note again the distinction between principle and practice, though without altering substantially their emphasis on progress toward acceptance of integration.

The last of the *Scientific American* reports, by Taylor, Sheatsley, and Greeley (1978), continues to record change in an integrationist direction, with the special additional note that the two-year period 1970–1972 saw an unexpected leap forward in racial tolerance. This conclusion is based on trend data through 1976 for five of the seven items employed in the 1971 report.[3] Younger age and higher education continue to be related to pro-integration responses, and region is identified as having taken on special importance, since the "liberal leap" of 1970–1972 appears to have occurred mainly in the South.[4]

In sum, the picture presented by these four reports is one of almost unvarying movement in an equalitarian and integrationist direction. Although qualifications concerning both implementation issues and actual behavior are introduced in each article, the thrust of the quantitative results is clearly toward progress in white support for integration in all major areas under inquiry. As in many other spheres of life, there was also a tendency to expect a trend once identified to continue in the same direction and in a more or less linear form.

The four *Scientific American* reports served as a major source of early data on trends in white racial attitudes during a period of great national change in terms of court decisions, executive and legislative actions, the remarkable mobilization of the civil rights movement during the late 1950s and early 1960s, and outbursts of collective disturbance across the land in the middle and late 1960s. The main message of the reports was that despite much talk about "white backlash" against both government actions on civil rights and black protests, there was virtually constant movement toward acceptance of basic principles of racial integration. And since the younger and better-educated generation was particularly sympathetic to integrationist goals, underlying demographic and social currents also favored integrationist trends.

As might be expected given our heavy use of the same NORC data, we agree with many of the major findings and conclusions of the *Scientific American* reports. There has indeed been a great deal of change in white racial attitudes, and the varying amount of actual change by area of life (with the most change in the least personal areas, such as public transportation) fits fairly well the ordering of integrationist sentiment in the NORC data. Yet a reader of our previous chapters will not have come away from them with the same sense of nearly unambiguous positive movement in racial attitudes. Nor do we think that most observers of the American scene over the past five decades will have perceived as much actual racial change as was anticipated by the early NORC survey data—for example, in terms of effective integration of schools (see the recent report by Orfield et al. 1997).

How can we reconcile these two pictures? The obvious answer is that the *Scientific American* reports draw almost entirely on questions that do in fact show remarkably steady positive change, primarily questions about general principles of equal treatment and about issues of social distance closely linked to general principles like the 1954 Supreme Court decision on school desegregation. But they do not include any government implementation or other more complex questions that have played an increasingly important role in the analysis of racial attitudes in recent years. Only the Intelligence question, which was dropped after the second report—and dropped entirely from NORC surveys after 1968—and the Black Push question, which both the *Scientific American* authors and we consider too ambiguous to deserve much emphasis, challenged the strong positive trends shown by the other items. Thus these authors were not faced with compelling survey evidence that might have prompted them to qualify more strongly their claims of progress toward integration.

With the benefit of hindsight, it appears that the items used in the *Scientific American* reports were too restricted in form and content to give an adequate picture of racial attitudes, especially in recent years. Yet it would be wrong to attribute the restriction to serious misjudgment on the part of these or other investigators, though we should try to learn from that experience. The baseline questions used by NORC in the 1940s dealt with fundamental issues and were hardly platitudinous for their time. It was both natural and desirable to replicate them in later years in order to measure change. And once such a set of items was established for replication, it no doubt tended to occupy the questionnaire space available for studying racial issues and therefore to limit the number of new items that could be entertained. Only in the 1970s did NORC introduce new trend questions that presented a somewhat different picture of racial change, and these questions (for example, Open Housing, Busing, Spending on Blacks, and the Few, Half, Majority series) were not referred to in the 1978 *Scientific American* report, perhaps because they were not part of the basic set that had been tracked in the previous articles.

What happened in these reports is probably best thought of in terms of the sociology of knowledge (Merton 1957) as applied to the construction of survey questionnaires. The main available set of distinctively different survey items, those concerning implementation of principles, were initiated by ISR National Election Studies, which were designed specifically to investigate the political process and were therefore naturally concerned with what "the government" should or should not do. Moreover, these items are not intrinsically better than, but rather different from, those in the NORC set. Questions asked in surveys are inevitably products of the social context in which their creators work.

In sum, the *Scientific American* reports are accurate and important in what they say, but they also leave out a great deal that can now be seen to be significant in the evolution of racial attitudes and behavior in America. Largely omitted are the struggles over how to implement principles and over the proportions of blacks "acceptable" to whites (and, of course, of whites acceptable to blacks) in particular life settings. Also largely omitted are questions dealing with beliefs about the causes of black disadvantage, about the extent to which discrimination is thought to exist, and about emerging issues under the rubric of affirmative action. In addition, average differences in social class between blacks and whites are not considered, and indeed in the case of the Same Block item were explicitly ruled out by the wording of the question (see Table 3.3).

The problems caused by these omissions can be illustrated by a consideration of the basic item employed in the *Scientific American* reports to tap attitudes toward the integration of schools: "Do you think white students and black students should go to the same schools, or to separate schools?" This is a good question as far as it goes, straightforward in phrasing and not obviously loaded in any direction. And it clearly captured an important trend in white American attitudes over the forty years it was asked by NORC, moving from 32 percent choice of the first alternative when initially asked in 1942 to 93 percent when it was finally dropped by NORC in 1985. Yet the question cannot capture the degree to which the *proportions* of black and white children matter in school integration, not to mention perceived problems due to differences in social class or to other factors ignored by the general phrasing. But it is evident from other questions that proportions *do* make an important difference to many respondents in surveys. Faced with the question's dichotomous choice, such people are likely to select the integrationist alternative, since they probably have no preference for segregated schooling in an *absolute* sense, but this choice does not indicate a commitment to all kinds and degrees of integration. Thus the question does not encourage or even allow people to indicate the considerations underlying real-life attitudes and behavior. Instead, it assumes a complete commitment to one of two abstractions called "integration" and "segregation." The choice is too simple for most respondents in more recent years, and thus in the end it may be the question—if used alone—and not the answer that is misleading. A single dichotomous item simply cannot capture the complexities of attitudes toward school integration once absolute segregation has been rejected.[5]

Despite the problems we have discussed, the *Scientific American* reports, and the NORC data on which they are based, are of great importance for recording fundamental changes in the values of white Americans. The data indicate that there is no longer an attempt by any significant number of Americans to justify segregation in principle, and that this evolution occurred steadily not only through the 1970s but indeed to the present day. Moreover, as we have seen, the change extends even to questions on racial intermarriage, though this and closely related symbols of complete integration have not moved as far as have attitudes in more public spheres of life. Without the NORC trend data on principles we would have a much more impoverished and inaccurate picture of trends in white racial attitudes and behavior. Behavior as well as attitudes must be emphasized, for the appointment and election of black Americans to high government positions, as well as many other indications of the crumbling of symbols of absolute segregation, could have come about only as part of this major change in modal white values. How seriously to take other changes in both attitude and behavior is the challenge raised by other social scientists whose work we now consider.

Reactions against the Early Optimism

In part as a reaction to the *Scientific American* optimism about progress toward integration, a number of social scientists developed much gloomier pictures of the course of race relations in America. We provide brief accounts of two of the more prominent of these, one advanced by Mary Jackman, the other by David Sears, Donald Kinder, and their colleagues. Both work within the framework of surveys of racial attitudes, and each assumes that a careful use of such attitude data can lead to valid conclusions. In this respect they differ from critics of the *Scientific American* conclusions who believe that attitude data based on surveys cannot be trusted to provide an accurate picture of white racial attitudes or behavior, a type of criticism that we will consider at a later point.

The Persistence of Domination

Mary Jackman has set forth a perspective on American race relations that is completely at odds with the views reflected in the *Scientific American* series. Jackman's fundamental thesis is that the primary goal of white Americans is to maintain economic, political, and cultural dominance over blacks. Her explicit focus has often been on the role of education in intergroup attitudes, but her writings have clear implications for how to interpret changes in white racial attitudes like those reported in the *Scientific American* series, as well as in the principles and social distance sections of our Chapter 3.

An early important empirical effort by Jackman (1978) contrasted what she called "general" and "applied" measures of tolerance. She used two standard ISR items as measures of general or abstract support for integration: General Segregation (our Table 3.1) and Residential Choice (Table 3.1). Two other ISR items were used as measures of applied or policy-relevant support for integration: Federal Job Intervention (our Table 3.2) and Federal School Intervention (Table 3.2). Her distinction is similar to the one we drew in Chapter 3 between questions concerning principles and questions about the implementation of principles, and indeed Jackman was one of the first to emphasize that distinction in the context of racial attitudes.

When she finds that education is positively related to endorsement of the integrationist alternatives on the two general or principle items, but is unrelated or more weakly related to similar endorsement on the two implementation items, Jackman concludes that "increasing years of education leads to a greater familiarity with the appropriate democratic position on racial integration," but not to greater commitment to that position as indicated by support for policies aimed at achieving integration (1978:322). She claims not that more educated respondents deliberately lie to interviewers, but rather that they have a superficial adherence to principles and no greater tendency than the less educated to call on these principles when real-life issues are at stake. (See Stember [1961] for an earlier analysis challenging the assumption that education reduces prejudice.)[6]

The implication of Jackman's argument for our analysis of change over time is evident: if responses to principle questions are essentially superficial, then the massive shifts recorded on such items between 1942 and the present have little importance, since some implementation items (for example, Federal School Intervention, Table 3.2) do not show a similar kind of change. Moreover, the increasing support over time for integration in principle has always been in the direction of the position held initially by more educated respondents, and thus the increase might be seen as merely a process whereby democratic slogans were first learned by the more educated and then passed on to the less educated. In sum, just as the association of principle items with education would be much less important than it at first appears, so their change over time would also cease to point to important shifts in white racial attitudes and behavior.

In terms of her own 1978 argument, Jackman's conclusions can be questioned in two respects. First, on at least one government implementation item (Open Housing) there are fairly strong positive trends over time, as well as a clear association with education (see pp. 134–136 above). Evidently, under some circumstances there is increasing white support for government intervention in the enforcement of equal treatment, at least as reflected in attitude data.

Second, Jackman's early assumption that white respondents who endorse school or residential integration in the abstract but oppose government implementation lack real commitment to integration can also be seen as inconsistent with results for questions on personal social distance, as reported in our Chapter 3. We see no reason not to give considerable credence to rising support for integration in the sense of some black families moving into previously white neighborhoods (Figure 3.13), of very high levels of support for "a few" black children in previously all-white schools (Figure 3.12), and even of a fair amount of support for schools with half the students black (Figure 3.12). Jackman (1981a) seems to consider these results unimportant, and in her later writings she treats them as merely token concessions intended to sweeten and camouflage domination: the "velvet glove." But in one sense they are more about real-life involvement with integration than are general questions about government implementation. In any case, they provide a picture different from *either* principle or implementation questions. Unless one treats the responses as completely misleading—a claim we will consider later, but one not made by Jackman—they indicate real change in areas of life of considerable importance in terms of practical support for integration.

In her next major publication on race, Jackman and Muha (1984), and then in her 1994 book *The Velvet Glove,* Jackman offers a different interpretation of the relation of education to intergroup attitudes, though she maintains the basic assumption that whites are primarily motivated to retain dominance over blacks. Both the article and the book draw on data Jackman collected herself in a 1975 survey, and they cover gender and social class attitudes as well as racial attitudes. Although it is interesting to treat race, gender, and social class attitudes together, generalizations that attempt to cover all three areas may miss important conclusions that apply to one area but not to the others. Thus we shall be concerned here only with her results bearing on race.

Jackman and Muha find in their data that education does not in general produce "liberation from intergroup negativism" (1984:751), though they qualify this somewhat with regard specifically to racial attitudes. Our examination of their main table suggests that such a qualification is needed. Of the fifteen racial attitude questions that they consider, almost all show significant positive relations with education, in a number of cases essentially monotonic relations.[7] For example, and of special interest given our own results with an Open Housing question (Table 3.2), Jackman and Muha report a nearly linear and significant relation between education and a question about whether the federal government should "make sure that blacks can buy any house on the market that they can afford" (p. 767). Yet it is also true that the relation of education to general principle statements in her table appears to be a good deal stronger than the relation of education to specific policy questions. Thus, in *relative* terms, the data are consistent with the basic argument that Jackman made in 1978 about the difference between general and applied attitude questions.

Despite what we see as some continuing support for her 1978 position, in this 1984 article and more fully in her 1994 book, Jackman does not pursue the distinction between "general" and "applied" questions. Instead, her new stress is on a distinction between "individual rights" and "equal rights" as the primary strategy by which white Americans seek to maintain dominance over black Americans. She believes that the paternalistic strategy of treating blacks as an inferior category of beings lost its legitimacy in recent years as a result of black resistance, and that in order to discourage collective thinking and collective action on the part of blacks, whites now emphasize individual rights and individual achievement as the touchstone of success in the United States. In doing so, white Americans ignore the disadvantaged starting point that blacks face as a group. Education enters the picture because it is those with more schooling who are most skilled in promulgating an ideology of individualism. She also claims that minor symbolic concessions are made—such as instances of token integration—that are intended to mollify the subordinate group but do nothing to alter the basic power dynamic between blacks and whites.

Although Jackman's recent writing does not focus on attitude change as such, it does speak to it indirectly. What the *Scientific American* authors saw as genuine change in white attitudes over the past half century, Jackman regards as no more than a superficial shift in ideological tactics that is used to defend white interests more effectively. Thus an emphasis on "individualism" is seen by Jackman as merely a way of avoiding the essential problem—that of inequality of resources between whites and blacks.

One result from our earlier analysis does seem to us to support an important point that Jackman has emphasized throughout her writing: our finding in Figure 3.10 that evidence of a very strong commitment to the principle of equal treatment (in this case, equal treatment in housing choice) is congruent with the relevant policy position (support for an open housing law). By the simple step of measuring *strength* of commitment to principle, we are able—at least in this one case—to estimate closely the level of support for implementation of that principle. This suggests the value of obtaining additional measures of attitude strength in research on racial attitudes (Schuman and Presser 1981, Chapter 10). Admittedly, even such findings might not alter Jackman's belief that white Americans demand domination over black Americans, so strong is that conviction throughout her writings, but the results could help bridge the important distinction that she has emphasized between questions about principles and questions about policies that implement principles.

Symbolic Racism and Racial Resentment

At about the same time that Jackman was developing her thesis of "superficial tolerance," a somewhat different challenge to the optimistic picture presented by the *Scientific American* series was formulated by David Sears and his colleagues (Sears, Hensler, and Speer 1979; Kinder and Sears 1981; Sears 1988), and more recently by Kinder and Sanders (1996). It differs in important ways from Jackman's argument, connecting more directly to traditional analyses of racial and ethnic prejudice, rather than to Jackman's neo-Marxist thesis of domination (see Taylor and Pettigrew [1992] for a brief authoritative discussion and references regarding "prejudice"). However, like Jackman, Sears and his coauthors are skeptical about the significance of white attitudes that appear liberal with regard to principles of equal treatment and yet do not extend to support for policies aimed at creating fuller racial equality.[8] They have developed the concept of "symbolic racism" to address this disjunction.

According to Sears and his colleagues, symbolic racism is a new form of racial attitude, composed of a blend of antiblack affect and belief in traditional American values of individualism and self-reliance. The word "symbolic" is used to imply that these new white attitudes are based not on self-interest (for example, having one's own children involved in court-ordered busing), but rather on a more general sense that blacks are violating American values of individualism through their persistent demands for special treatment like affirmative action. Antiblack affect is regarded as coming largely from childhood, though its exact origin is left somewhat indeterminate. Much of the impetus for research on symbolic racism came from attempts to understand specific policy and voting preferences that appeared to the authors to be hostile to progress toward racial equality, and an important contribution of the research was to challenge with considerable success the common assumption that such white attitudes reflect immediate material interests in a simple and direct way.

The term "symbolic racism" has been both a blessing and a problem for Sears and his colleagues. The word "symbolic" has a mysterious ring to it that attracted a good deal of attention from the start, and the term quickly made its way into the literature on racial attitudes. Yet the meaning of the term is hardly clear from the words, and it has been defined and operationalized in complex and varying ways, giving rise to a good deal of controversy over both meaning and measurement. One of the problems with the concept itself is that neither of its components—antiblack affect and reliance on individualism—seems particularly new (Bobo 1988:104–105). Antiblack affect has obviously been a part of white American racial attitudes for a very long time, and, according to Sears (1988), it has been regularly operationalized in ISR election studies by a straightforward scale of favorable-unfavorable feelings about blacks (the thermometer scale discussed at several earlier points in our book). Likewise, emphasis on individualism and self-reliance is certainly implied in traditional white beliefs, notably the long-term negative stereotypes of blacks as "happy-go-lucky, lazy, sexual, dirty, musical, childish, and so on" (Sears 1988:72). Although Sears emphasizes that it is the *blending* of affect and values that is unique, it is difficult to understand why that blending should be regarded as requiring a new label (see Bobo 1988).[9]

In their own writing, Kinder and Sanders (1996) acknowledge the importance of earlier work on symbolic racism, but then set aside the term in favor of words they consider to be more descriptive and less subject to misunderstanding: "racial resentment." As a measure of racial resentment they develop a set of questions that ask whites in various ways whether black disadvantage is due mainly to lack of "trying" or mainly to external obstacles like discrimination—what we earlier termed "explanations for inequality." Operationalized in this manner, racial resentment is highly related to three pairs of major policy issues that we have also discussed: government implementation of equal opportunity in employment and integration in schools; federal spending and other efforts to improve the conditions of blacks; and compensatory preferential treatment for blacks in jobs and college admission.[10] Thus, following the earlier symbolic racism goal, they seek to explain policy stands by means of a general attitude, racial resentment, which they consider a new or subtle form of prejudice.

As with symbolic racism, it is not entirely clear why it is necessary to claim that "racial resentment" is something new. Kinder and Sanders do describe persuasively how what is called prejudice today differs in two important respects from what would have been found half a century ago. First, negative attitudes toward blacks are usually accompanied at present by white claims to support equal treatment of all people regardless of race. Second, such negative attitudes today are seldom undergirded by assertions of white biological superiority to blacks. However, the first of these changes from the past was the clear emphasis of the early *Scientific American* articles and is now widely recognized, and the second was also evident by the late 1960s (Campbell and Schuman 1968) and developed in depth by Apostle et al. (1983) and Kluegel and Smith (1986).

Apart from these differences, which are recognized in most assessments of racial prejudice today, racial resentment would seem to be something new only if it performed in unique ways not captured by other approaches. Yet Kinder and Sanders (1996) show in their analysis that their measure of racial resentment is "closely related" to simple questions inviting traditional stereotypes of blacks as lazy, unintelligent, and violent (1996:113–114 and Appendix B).[11] The fact that blatant stereotypes can be asked of the general population and produce much the same correlations with policy issues as their own measure suggests that the authors have produced essentially another set of items for assessing traditional prejudice, though one shorn of open defense of discrimination on a biological basis. Indeed, one of Kinder and Sanders's more interesting findings is that racial resentment (and presumably a measure based on stereotypes as well) is much like the classic Adorno et al. (1950) E and F scales in that it is related to a range of dissimilar issues such as attitudes toward abortion and gay rights, thus capturing a broad and largely illiberal world view today, much as did those pioneer efforts in the 1940s. (Similar results indicating that negative stereotypes are readily expressed by substantial proportions of whites and that they reveal at least a moderate relation to authoritarian-type measures are reported by Sniderman and Piazza [1993].)[12]

Kinder and Sanders make other valuable contributions. They replicate with careful analysis the earlier symbolic racism finding that public attitudes on policy issues such as preferential treatment show very little relation to beliefs by whites that they are being *personally* disadvantaged by affirmative action. The assumption that self-interest is at the root of wider opposition to busing and affirmative action has been taken for granted in much public debate, but the accumulation of evidence against that assumption is now substantial.[13] Kinder and Sanders also present evidence that when self-interest is defined in terms of one's race, rather than oneself, it does relate to policy positions. Circularity is again a danger here, since both sets of items are framed in terms of whites versus blacks. This is not to discount the importance of group interest and competition, as emphasized for more than a decade by Bobo (1983; 1988; Bobo and Hutchings 1996), but rather to note that it runs through all the attitude items that are being intercorrelated.[14]

Despite their different starting points and some important differences in ideological emphasis, Jackman, Sears, and Kinder and Sanders consider white antipathy toward blacks a major factor in preventing full racial equality. And they treat changes in attitudes toward principles of equal treatment as of little relevance to the most pressing racial policy issues today. In response, other writers have argued that the primary motivation of white opposition on policy issues is not racial hostility but rather a positive commitment to larger American ideals. The ongoing debate points to two basic theoretical questions:

1. Is emphasis by whites on the value of individual accomplishment a traditional and genuine way to allow everyone to achieve equally on his or her merits, or is it primarily a subterfuge for avoiding attention to the collective needs of the black minority, a minority that has been prevented from acquiring the material and psychological resources that would allow it to compete on an equal playing field?

2. Is opposition to government action based on genuine resistance to government intrusion—resistance not limited to racial issues but involving a broad rejection of government (and especially federal) activism—or is it mainly a way of preventing effective steps toward full integration and full racial equality?

The two questions are connected in that individualism is said to underlie both, but the first focuses directly on values and the second on attitudes toward the government. A good deal of the recent theoretical writing on race in America addresses one or both of these questions, as do Kinder and Sanders in other parts of their book that we call on below. There also remains the important question of what to make of the very substantial liberalization in some types of white attitudes that we and others have reported.

Counter-reactions: The New Optimists

Individualism and Equalitarianism

Lipset and Schneider (1978) and more recently Lipset (1996) have argued forcefully that "individualism" is a genuine and strongly held value that motivates many whites who oppose attempts to improve the status of blacks by means of preferential treatment. Lipset and Schneider review a wide range of survey results (though not mainly trend data) and conclude that "on the central issues involving racial discrimination . . . the American consensus is powerfully *against dis-*

crimination . . . The consensus breaks down, however, when *compulsory integration* is involved . . . Many whites deeply resent efforts to force racial integration on them, not because they oppose racial equality, but because they feel it violates their individual freedom" (Lipset and Schneider 1978:44).

Lipset and Schneider see the basic conflict as one "between two values that are at the core of the American creed: individualism and egalitarianism" (1978:43). They assert that "most Americans favor equal rights and equal opportunity" (p. 38), and they report that there is also considerable white support for "compensatory treatment" for blacks, such as special educational programs. They conclude, however, that white public opinion is strongly opposed to preferential treatment in the form of quotas or similar steps in school or work situations. Their view that this is a logically defensible combination in terms of national values provides a sharp contrast to characterizations of the role of individualism as a defense against minority group advancement, as Jackman argues.

In order to investigate this issue more rigorously and with recent data, we carried out a split-sample experiment in a 1995 ISR survey (October–November Survey Research Center Monthly): half the respondents were asked a question about preferential hiring and promotion that we discussed in Chapter 3 (see Table 3.5B for results over time):

> Some people say that because of past discrimination, blacks should be given preference in hiring and promotion. Others say that such preference in hiring and promotion of blacks is wrong because it gives blacks advantages they haven't earned. What about your opinion—are you *for* or *against* preferential hiring and promotion of blacks?
> (IF FOR) Do you favor preference in hiring and promotion strongly or not strongly?
> (IF OPPOSE) Do you oppose preference in hiring and promotion strongly or not strongly?

The other half were asked the following reworded question about a less extreme form of affirmative action that calls for remedial training:

> Some people say that because of past discrimination, blacks should be given special job training. Others say that special job training for blacks is wrong because it gives blacks advantages they haven't

earned. What about your opinion—are you *for* or *against* special job training for blacks?

(IF FOR) Do you favor such special job training strongly or not strongly?

(IF OPPOSE) Do you oppose such special job training strongly or not strongly?

The results are partly consistent with the earlier conclusion reported by Lipset and Schneider:

Response	Preferential hiring and promotion	Preference in job training
Favor strongly	8%	19%
Favor not strongly	6	13
Oppose not strongly	26	30
Oppose strongly	60	38
Total	100	100
N	(355)	(354)

White respondents are clearly much more likely to support affirmative action in the form of special job training than in the form of preference for actual hiring and promotion. However, even special job training receives much less than majority support, and thus these results present an important difference from Lipset and Schneider's claim. Since this was an original experiment, we do not have trend data for the question about special training. What the present data do make clear is that when speaking of support for "affirmative action," it is always important to specify exactly which kind of affirmative action policy is intended.

Yet considering the broad range of questions we have dealt with in this book, white hostility to affirmative action is unlikely to represent simply a defense of individualistic values. Indeed, Lipset and Schneider present evidence elsewhere in their article that most white support for executive actions and judicial decisions that challenged discrimination and segregation during the 1950s and 1960s was provided by Northern white liberals, with Southern whites as the targets, and with most other Northern whites as onlookers. The support diminished considerably when the focus shifted to *de facto* segregation in the North. And we have found considerable white opposition to straightforward government implementation of principles of equal treatment, as well as reluctance at a personal level to be involved in integration where blacks would be in the majority. More than individualism is needed to explain such data.

Following earlier work by Sears (1988) and others, Kinder and Sanders (1996) approached the issue by making use of a set of six questions in the National Election Study that attempt to measure economic individualism without mentioning race; for example, "Any person who is willing to work hard has a good chance at succeeding." Whatever the limitations of the items, it was reasonable to expect that those high on economic individualism would be those most likely to oppose government actions to help blacks. However, controlling for social background factors, they found very little evidence of such a relationship. Thus despite the fact that white opposition to government action is usually justified in terms of the importance and efficacy of the individual work ethic, there seems little sign that strong adherence to that value at the level of individual differences is connected to policy positions such as opposition to preferential treatment.[15]

Kinder and Sanders (1996) do find that equalitarian beliefs are related as predicted to support for government help in ending discrimination and in spending funds to improve the conditions of blacks, though not, it should be noted, to questions specifically on preferential treatment of blacks. The distinction between preferential treatment and other policy questions provides evidence of the construct validity of the equalitarian measure, and also evidence that preferential treatment introduces policy issues different from those that have been bound up with the civil rights movement over much of its history.

Opposition to Government Intrusion

As we and others have found repeatedly, support for principles of equal treatment is often accompanied by opposition to government implementation of such principles. Whereas some writers see this as evidence that white support of the principles is superficial, other writers regard opposition to government implementation as a genuine political force that motivates many white Americans who otherwise do support the goal of equal treatment. For example, the main criticism offered of Jackman's (1978) analysis of general versus applied tolerance was that it ignored the fact that the "applied" survey questions confound attitudes toward integration with attitudes toward government intervention more generally (Kuklinski and Parent 1981; Margolis and Haque 1981). Thus more educated respondents might have a genuine commitment to integration but be so opposed to intrusion by the federal government that they will not endorse concrete steps toward integration on the two items Jackman employed. Jackman answered this criticism initially by showing that a negative attitude toward federal power or coercion as such is not strongly related either to education or to the implementation items she employed (Jackman 1981a, 1981b).

However, the argument that many white Americans are negative toward government enforcement of equal treatment because of a more general rejection of government—especially federal—coercion, continues to be offered by critics of both Jackman and Sears, most strenuously by Sniderman and Piazza in their book *The Scar of Race* (1993). Sniderman and Piazza first propose that there are three distinct "policy agendas" (equal treatment, social welfare, and race-conscious affirmative action) into which different racial attitudes fit. This is a proposal that is consistent with our own division of racial attitude items into several different types that vary in terms of levels and trends over time, though they rely on product-moment correlations to make the distinctions. They then argue that "prejudice" or bigotry of a traditional kind (which they operationalize at one point by the number of negative stereotypes held about blacks, and at another point by agreement with anti-Semitic stereotypes) plays some role in producing opposition to each type of policy, especially for less educated whites. But they also hold that nonracial principles are even more important, with somewhat different principles relevant to different policy agendas. For example, using the NORC Open Housing item (our Table 3.2) to represent the "equal treatment agenda," they maintain that especially among the more educated, the nonracial principle is "whether the power of law should be employed to assure equal treatment" (p. 127), that is, intervening "in decisions which people would ordinarily take to be their own business" (p. 125).

The entire history of race in America shows, however, that one cannot make such a neat separation between support for equal treatment and other principles, for they have always been in conflict. To take one of the most obvious examples, sit-ins at lunchcounters in 1960 directly challenged the privacy rights of proprietors to include race as a reason for denying service. The decision in the early 1960s may have been difficult but the outcome has been clear and has become widely accepted: ownership of a business does not now carry with it the right to discriminate on the basis of race. Moreover, we can recognize that a person who defends discrimination on the basis of the principle of private ownership, even if sincerely rather than simply as a disguise for racial prejudice, is evidently willing to give more support to that principle than to the principle of equal treatment. And it is no surprise that, as shown earlier (Figure 3.10), the choice of which principle to support—owners' rights or equal treatment—is closely connected to how strongly one feels about the principle of equal treatment itself.[16]

As with the nature of "individualism," so with the issue of government coercion: it is possible to focus on much the same evidence and interpret it in entirely opposite ways. Since opposition to government enforcement of equal treatment could be due *either* to the means or to the ends, means and ends are confounded and very difficult to disentangle. Moreover, both could be involved in varying degrees for different individuals. Social scientists who differ in their interpretations tend to talk past one another, each side quite confident of its correctness.

Some Experimental Evidence on Government Coercion. We have tried to take some modest steps toward disentangling this issue, though we certainly cannot claim to have resolved it completely. We used the Open Housing item (Table 3.2) as our focus, since it seemed a clear and well-balanced question, though given the differences among implementation questions in trends, more than one such item certainly needs to be investigated. It appeared to us possible that the relatively positive and increasing level of support for open housing (Table 3.2 and Figure 3.10) has been due to its focus on voting for a local referendum, rather than on having a federal law sent down from Washington. Therefore, we administered the original local referendum form of the Open Housing question to a random half of a national sample in 1985. We asked the other half of the sample a reworded version in which the local referendum was changed to a federal law to be decided by Congress.

Local referendum item: Suppose there is a community-wide vote on the general housing issue. There are two possible laws to vote on. One law says that a homeowner can decide for himself who to sell his house to, even if he prefers not to sell to blacks. The second law says that a homeowner cannot refuse to sell to someone because of their race or color. Which law would you vote for?

Federal law: Suppose your representative in Congress is about to vote on the general housing issue. There are two possible federal laws to vote on. One law says that a homeowner can decide for himself who to sell his house to, even if he prefers not to sell to blacks. The second law says that a homeowner cannot refuse to sell to someone because of their race or color. Which law would you want your representative to vote for?

Thus the two forms of the question vary experimentally the *means* by which an open housing law would take effect, while the substance of the law itself remains constant.

In addition, as a way of measuring generalized attitudes toward government coercion, whether local or federal, we preceded both versions of the Open Housing item with an entirely unrelated Gallup question carefully chosen to focus on the issue of government enforcement per se: "Would you favor or oppose a law that would fine a person $25 if he or she did not wear a seat belt when riding in an automobile?" On the one hand, a seat-belt law seems as remote as any issue could be from matters of race. On the other hand, it asks about a topic where the goal (safety) is not really in dispute: use of seat belts. Thus opposition can be expected to be based almost entirely on the fact that the government is mandating such behavior. Indeed, this was exactly the point made by the director of a successful 1986 campaign to repeal the Nebraska mandatory seat-belt law: "All through our campaign, we encouraged people to go ahead and wear seat belts, but we feel education is a more healthy way to go about it. Rather than mandate—educate." (*New York Times,* December 1, 1986, p. A14). In our survey, the seat-belt item was asked prior to any of the racial items in order to avoid deliberate attempts at consistency after answering racial questions. The split-sample experiment, preceded by the seat-belt question, was carried out originally in 1985 and replicated in 1995.

The 1985 results showed that the local referendum yielded slightly more support (6 percent) than the federal law version, a difference just barely significant at the conventional .05 level. This suggested that the source of the law—local or federal—contributes in a small way to levels of support for open housing.[17] However, on replication in 1995, the difference in levels of support was even smaller (2 percent) and no longer reliable. Thus we do not find much evidence that opposition to government coercion is centered on compulsion from Washington. If such opposition does play a role, it is only a very small role in accounting for the extent to which white Americans oppose open housing laws. (See also Olzak, Shanahan, and West 1994.)

What of the connection between opposition to open housing and opposition to mandatory seat-belt laws? Here the evidence of a connection was stronger in 1985 (Schuman and Bobo 1988), and the results below from 1995 provide a consistent replication:

	Favor seat belt law	Oppose seat belt law
Oppose open housing law	36%	49%
Favor open housing law	64	51
Total	100	100
N	(476)	(274)

Those who oppose seat-belt laws are 13 percent more likely to oppose open housing laws than are those who favor seat-belt laws. The association is highly reliable ($p < .001$), but it cannot be claimed to be very large in magnitude (tau-b = .13), despite the fact that the distributions on the two questions are similar enough to allow a much stronger relationship. In particular, more than a third of the people who have no objection to a seat-belt law nevertheless oppose an open housing law, which suggests that these people are against open housing as such and not because it is coercive. (The substantial proportion that opposes seat-belt laws but favors open housing evidently believes strongly enough in equal treatment to override any concerns about government intrusion.)[18]

We do not consider the open housing experiment and its relation to seat-belt laws to be definitive. Perhaps we have failed to capture adequately the abstract opposition to government coercion. Certainly there is such opposition, as indicated by the fact that more than a third (36 percent) of the population in 1995 opposed a mandatory seat-belt law, despite its goal of saving lives and reducing insurance costs for everyone. But for the present we believe that the case is not yet proven that resistance to government implementation of the principles of equal treatment and integration is due primarily to a broader reluctance to have enforcement by government. On the basis of current evidence, opposition to government implementation of equal treatment and integration appears to be based much more on lack of strong commitment to those goals than on the role of the government itself.[19]

Furthermore, there are many examples where individuals and groups that are critical of government intervention in one area are enthusiastic supporters of such intervention in a different area closer to their own interests or predilections. And of course, when the principle of opposition to government coercion fits nicely one's substantive goals, the two can come together quickly, as occurred when Barry Goldwater's vote against the 1964 Civil Rights Act and his attacks on the federal government during the 1964 election provided the Republican Party's first major entry into the white South (Carmines and Stimson 1989).

Discounting Positive Responses Entirely

Neither Jackman nor Sears and his colleagues claim that pro-integration responses to questions about principles are meaningless, but they (especially Jackman) do not give much weight to such responses unless they are accompanied by support for government implementation and indeed for affirmative action. Thus it seems only a small step to discounting entirely positive answers to survey questions, such as those dealing with broad principles of integration or nondiscrimination, and treating the responses as merely lip service to equalitarian values. From this perspective, the massive shifts shown in Table 3.1 become merely slopes of hypocrisy, glaring examples of the gap between verbal responses to surveys and both true thoughts and actual deeds.

There is certainly plenty of evidence to make one suspicious of survey responses on racial issues. Race-of-interviewer studies have shown that white respondents give more pro-integration responses to black than to white interviewers, with the differences sometimes very large, as reviewed in Chapter 2. This suggests that such responses are highly situational in nature or might even represent deliberate falsifications for the benefit of the black interviewers. In either case, the findings make the validity of responses to white interviewers uncertain as well, for such professional interviewers may also be perceived by white respondents to represent values different from their own. In Chapter 2 we provided further evidence inviting just such an interpretation: first, differences by white interviewing staffs based on their regional origin, and second, variations between interviews and self-administered mail surveys.

More direct evidence of the need to use care in interpreting responses to survey questionnaires comes from an occasional investigation of discrepancies between attitudes and behavior. Silverman (1974) sent some incoming white college students a supposedly genuine inquiry from their college about having a black roommate, and sent a comparable group a purportedly "scientific" survey on the same subject. The students were significantly more likely to appear favorable toward having a black roommate on the "scientific" questionnaire than on the supposedly real inquiry, but the number of students is not reported and the nature of the scale used makes it possible that only a small proportion of students were responsible for the discrepancies. Also difficult to interpret are a series of "bogus pipeline experiments" that show whites giving more antiblack answers when under the impression that they are connected to a "lie detector" than under more ordinary conditions (for example, Allen 1975). The results are ambiguous if one assumes that white Americans are often ambivalent and insecure in their racial views, as some social psychologists argue (Poskocil 1977; Katz 1981), and that the pressure to "tell the truth" makes them feel that they should reveal whatever negative thoughts they may have.

Still another source of evidence on what might be called "covert racism" comes from the literature on unobtrusive research, where race has been introduced as a variable in studies of helping, nonverbal behavior, and the like. A review by Crosby, Bromley, and Saxe concluded that "discriminatory behavior is more prevalent in the body of unobtrusive studies than we might expect on the basis of survey data" (1980:557). However, the authors do not test this conclusion directly, since few of the investigations they review gathered *any* survey data at all. Even more important, as we have seen in previous chapters, the degree to which negative sentiments toward blacks are revealed in surveys depends largely on the specific questions asked. It is a serious mistake to summarize all "survey data" as implying that negative attitudes are rare.[20]

Other explorations of white behavior in relation to attitude responses appear in a series of interesting and imaginative studies of "aversive racism" by Gaertner and Dovidio (1986), where the assumption is that some whites have accepted equalitarian norms but continue to feel negative toward blacks. This perspective argues that whites behave differently in interracial situations depending upon whether clear-cut equalitarian norms are or are not present to dictate certain behaviors. These studies make use of convenience samples, often college students, and thus are difficult to place in the context of the national white population. In addition, frequently the experimental conditions are themselves ambiguous in implication. Although these studies show that whites behave differently in different situations, exactly what the difference means is seldom clear-cut. (See also our reinterpretation of one experiment, pp. 3–4.)

It seems to us highly likely that at least some number of white responses to survey questions today are affected by social pressure to give racially liberal answers. It does not take elaborate experimentation, such as is increasingly being undertaken, to show that most whites (and most blacks) in America—including no doubt the present writers and the experimenters themselves—are not without ambivalent feelings on matters of race. However, this assertion in and of itself is substantively important, for it means, as pointed out at the beginning of this book, that norms in the United States have changed radically over the past half century. Antiblack speech and action that were once entirely acceptable are now almost completely taboo in the public arena and perhaps even in that special semipublic setting known as the survey interview. It is striking to recall that the first and classic demonstration of attitude-behavior discrepancy (LaPiere 1934) showed verbal responses to a questionnaire to be discriminatory and actual behavior to be equalitarian. That our concern today is with exactly the opposite problem indicates how great has been the change from the 1930s to the 1990s. The same radical shift is equally evident in many other ways, such as in the difference between the blatantly racist job advertisements of the 1930s and those that today proclaim a commitment to "equal opportunity." We are dealing with a fundamental transformation of social norms and with the issue of what this transformation means at the individual level. It would be as simplistic to regard such a sweeping change as mere "lip service" as to take at face value all pro-integration responses given in surveys. Because this is such a large and difficult issue, we defer further discussion of it to our concluding chapter.

We have shown in this book that the great majority of white respondents to surveys give some responses of an equalitarian nature. But by the same token, a high proportion of the *same* white respondents give answers to racial questions that are anything but equalitarian in implication (for example, some two-thirds of whites in 1994 claiming that blacks are disadvantaged only because they do not really try to get ahead). Thus though some feelings and points of view may well be hidden from investigators, there is no shortage of evidence in ordinary surveys that many white Americans are highly ambivalent on matters of race.[21]

Conclusions

Each of the theoretical approaches considered in this chapter contributes to what has become a kind of dialectic in the attempt to understand changes in white racial attitudes.

The *Scientific American* reports provide the fullest record of major shifts in white attitudes between the early 1940s and the present. During that period, most white Americans ceased to defend segregation in public spheres of life and came to accept, at least in principle, the idea that race should make no difference when it comes to buying a house, gaining employment, or enrolling in a school. But because the survey items used did not address difficult issues of implementation, nor other issues such as the meaning of integration in terms of racial proportions, the *Scientific American* articles could not represent adequately all important trends in racial attitudes.

Partly in reaction to the picture of a nearly continuous liberalizing trend presented in the *Scientific American* reports, a number of social scientists expressed skepticism about the purportedly large changes in adherence to principles of equal treatment. Some went so far as to challenge the truthfulness of answers given in survey interviews, suggesting that instead of revealing their genuine feelings, respondents merely say what they think interviewers want to hear. Doubtless some such deception does occur. It is implausible to assume, however, that a high proportion of whites are unwilling to express reservations about various steps toward integration, especially where responses (as reported in Chapter 3) are obviously quite sensitive to the type of issue presented and the degree of integration proposed.

One way of conceptualizing the difference between direct expression of attitudes in surveys and expression through other forms of behavior (including responses that vary by race of interviewer, as described in Chapter 2) is to see them as different points on a continuum, much as we saw responses to different questions in Chapter 3 (for example, Figures 3.5 and 3.6). Although the levels of support differ for different questions about principles of integration (school integration versus intermarriage), they tend to show similar trends over time. Is the same thing true when we add a focus on behavior as a further point on the continuum? For this purpose, the one-shot convenience sample used by many researchers to investigate interracial behavior is quite inadequate. What is needed is some way of sampling behavior over time in the general population and comparing it with similar samples of survey responses—we give one such example in our concluding chapter. A different but also useful approach would be to do over-time studies of race-of-interviewer effects, since these involve a kind of manipulation of behavior within the interview setting, and there are earlier baseline time points waiting to be built upon.

A different type of critique of the *Scientific American* emphasis on liberalizing trends has been offered by two other important theoretical approaches. Both Jackman and Sears and his colleagues acknowledge as real the changes reported in the *Scientific American* articles, but regard the changes as too superficial to have much impact on the significant racial issues of today. White Americans may have come to believe in equal treatment or in integration or in economic progress for blacks, but the beliefs are said to be largely fine-sounding abstractions that do not substantially influence other attitudes or behavior. According to Jackman, unless an individual subscribes to the implementation of principles through government action, the principles themselves lack real meaning. Sears takes a less extreme position on this point, but also seems to regard commitment to concrete implementation as the touchstone of important change.

Both Jackman and Sears and his colleagues have identified compelling reasons not to rely exclusively on the kinds of questions that formed the basis of the *Scientific American* articles. At the same time, their interpretations may be guided too completely by the assumption that anyone who claims to be unprejudiced at the level of principle must confirm this by subscribing fully to virtually all forms of implementation and affirmative action. This dichotomous view of social life seems unrealistic. It does not fit the wide variation that we find across questions about government enforcement of principles of equal treatment, and it fits even less well variations across a set of social distance questions about personal willingness to be involved in integrated situations. It is also inconsistent with the variation our data show in black attitudes toward implementation. (See also Kluegel and Bobo 1993).

Lipset's approach is close to the *Scientific American* reports in emphasizing the degree to which Americans have come to believe in equal treatment of blacks and whites, but he is mainly concerned with distinguishing nondiscrimination and voluntary integration from strong affirmative action steps and enforced integration. He sees the distinction as involving basic conflicts in values, primarily between "individualism" and "equalitarianism." Both Lipset and Sears regard individualism as an important American value, but Lipset sees it as a legitimate basis for opposing some forms of government implementation, without implying antiblack sentiments, whereas Sears sees individualism as a conservative value, at least when it is merged with antiblack attitudes to create "symbolic racism." A problem with both views, but especially Lipset's, is the absence to date of any evidence that measures of individualistic values per se are much related to racial attitudes.

One other theoretical approach, exemplified by Sniderman and Piazza, attempts to explain differences between principle and implementation items by identifying a general rejection by many whites of government intervention, quite apart from racial issues. There is some evidence for the antigovernment explanation when considering the difference in *levels* of support between principles and implementation questions. However, we think it more useful to emphasize the reluctance of many people to accept constraints of *any* kind on behavior in cases where commitment to the goals of equal treatment or of integration are weak. We also believe that Sniderman and Piazza urge too simple a separation of prejudice from nonracial political beliefs.

As our book entered the final stage of production, it was possible to read a new book by Sniderman and Carmines (1997), *Reaching Beyond Race*, though it was too late to consider the book in detail here. The authors draw on a number of survey-based experiments to argue that affirmative action in the form of preferential treatment has little support in America, that it tends to divide even many who call themselves "liberal" on a liberal-conservative scale, and that a large part of the opposition to race-conscious policies is based on high moral principles rather than on any form of prejudice. Although the authors occasionally state that they are surprised by their results and conclusions, there will be few such surprises for those who have read Sniderman and Piazza (1993).

Most of the social scientists we have discussed have developed clear positions on the nature and source of racial attitudes, and the positions tend to be repeated with reanalyses of old data or new analyses of fresh data. Many of the analyses are hampered by the difficulty of drawing clear conclusions from what are essentially correlations among a range of attitude measures. The problem is, first, that the attitudes exist at much the same level in the heads of respondents, and it is virtually impossible to establish firm causal priority such that attitude A can be said with great confidence to be a cause of attitude B, rather than B of A, or both A and B of a third attitude C. Second, the various attitude items often overlap in meaning, so that there is a serious danger of circularity at the measurement level when two supposedly different concepts are correlated. Third, both of the preceding problems may be compounded by change over time, as item meanings shift, as well as by other kinds of complications such as the impact of race of interviewer.

For further progress beyond what are now familiar positions, these problems need to be brought to the fore, rather than passed over quickly on the way to data analysis and conclusions. Experimental work can help in this task by examining differences in the way questions are asked, though it is seldom the panacea that advocates of its increasing use (including we ourselves) sometimes suggest.[22] Likewise, qualitative explorations of what questions and answers mean to respondents can help in pointing to ambiguities and alternative meanings not readily visible to the academic investigator. All of these approaches are likely to be of value, and in addition it is useful to recognize that there is still much to learn about white and black racial attitudes, rather than assuming that we already know the main answers and that it is only a matter of marshaling evidence to persuade the unenlightened.

7

The Complexity of
Race Relations[1]

Seek simplicity and distrust it.
—*A. N. Whitehead*

Color and other racial identifications are such powerful ascriptive markers that nobody can fully escape them, regardless of their pursuits or achievements in life. The late Secretary of Commerce Ronald Brown kept in his desk a news photograph from a Midwestern paper that had been sent to him by Colin Powell. The picture was of Mr. Brown, but the caption identified him as General Powell. Attached to the clipping was a handwritten note from Powell: "Ron, they *still* can't tell us apart" (*New York Times*, April 4, 1996, p. A10). Such perceived similarities in appearance, and the complementary distinction between whites and blacks, are fundamental in the United States, as they are to varying degrees in other parts of the world.[2]

There is no evidence that this virtually absolute differentiation of the American population has been reduced by the changes of the last half century, though it has no doubt been further complicated by the increase in several Asian, Hispanic, and other minorities. Indeed, the black-white division may even have deepened in some respects as a result of the growth of black consciousness and the use of racial enumeration as a way of monitoring progress in civil rights. Americans are not much more color-blind today than they ever were, and despite some growth in the rate of racial intermarriage (Harrison and Bennett 1995), a melting-pot solution to racial differences in the United States is not likely to occur in the foreseeable future.

What *has* changed over the past half century is the normative definition of appropriate relations between blacks and whites. Whereas discrimination against, and enforced segregation of, black Americans were taken for granted by most white Americans as recently as the World War II years, today the norm holds that black Americans deserve the same treatment and respect as whites, and in addition that racial integration in all public spheres of life is a desirable goal. Questions like the ones discussed under principles of equal treatment in Chapter 3 (Table 3.1) reflect this normative change, with aggregate responses having moved in many cases along almost the entire percentage scale within little more than a generation. How far back in time the development of the new norm goes, and what led to both the initial and the continuing movement of whites toward acceptance of the principle of equal treatment are interesting questions, but available survey data do not allow us to answer them very well.[3] In any case, the more pressing problem here is the meaning for the present of this great normative shift and its implications for the future.

Do the changes in individual attitudes that flow from the larger normative shift mean anything outside the survey interview? It is difficult to believe that they do not, for the evidence is all around us of important and pervasive changes in the relations between blacks and whites in the United States. Beyond the total elimination of a vast structure of legal segregation throughout the South and Southwest and within the U.S. armed forces, there is an abundance of *non*survey evidence of genuine change in white actions toward blacks. Black Americans today hold a wide range of high elected and appointed political positions, and not by any means only in areas with black majorities. African Americans are also prominent in television and film, in major universities and colleges, and to a greater or lesser degree in many other public spheres of life.[4] In most of these spheres they are still greatly underrepresented in proportion to their numbers in the total population, and the large black lower class is almost totally excluded from participation in this change. But these crucial qualifications do not alter the fact that actual change in public life over the past half century has been very substantial. Only because so much of the population of the United States—both black and white—is now too young to have any memory of race relations circa 1940 or even 1960 can there be any doubt about the magnitude of the change.

The tendency to look for exact consistency between attitudes and behavior also misses a useful distinction that can be made between literal consistency and correlational consistency (Schuman and Johnson 1976). The former asks whether people do what they say they will do; the latter asks whether people are ordered or ranked in the same way along both attitude and behavioral dimensions. In the case of trends

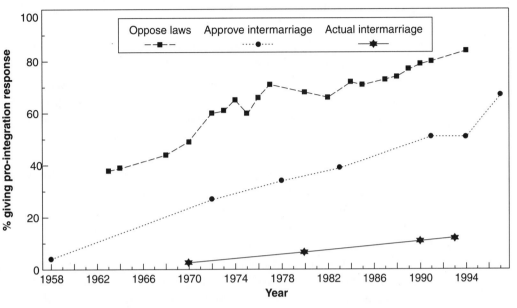

Figure 7.1. Comparison of actual intermarriage rates with attitudes toward laws against intermarriage and attitudes toward approval of intermarriage.

over time, correlational consistency implies only that wherever there is a liberalizing trend in attitudes, there should also be a similar liberalizing trend in behavior. However, the two trends may differ in the "level" of response reached at any particular point in time, because performing a behavior may be more "difficult" than expressing an attitude in an interview—an important point made by Donald Campbell (1963) when interpreting the apparent attitude-behavior inconsistency shown in LaPiere's (1934) classic study. It is not easy to test this idea—and we doubt that it holds in every sphere of life—but a supportive instance is shown in Figure 7.1. This figure repeats Figure 3.6, which showed trends on two intermarriage items that have different thresholds for expressing liberal racial attitudes, but here adds a third indicator of actual intermarriages in the United States. The behavior, represented by recent intermarriage rates, displays much the same upward trend as the attitude question on approval of intermarriage and the attitude question opposing laws banning intermarriage. All three measures move in an upward direction, though each remains at a quite different level.[5]

In other words, attitude measures can be seen as tapping broad currents of social change, though of course imperfectly, and if they show correlational consistency we should be able at the same time to see similar trends in directly relevant behaviors. Thus, at the other extreme of intimacy from intermarriage, we hardly need systematic observation to conclude that behavioral trends with regard to desegregation of public accommodations have followed the same generally upward path as have responses to relevant attitude questions. Less obviously and less sharply, desegregation of employment opportunities has also occurred in substantial if still incomplete ways, though in this case the only directly relevant attitude question had almost reached a ceiling twenty-five years ago (the Equal Jobs question in Table 3.1). Even in the seemingly intractable area of housing, Farley (1996:329) states that "the Census of 1990 reports that most suburbs had at least a few black . . . residents, often more than token numbers." This provides some evidence of correlational consistency with our several attitude questions in the area of housing. Farley also notes that residential segregation is decreasing especially in the fast-growing cities of the West. In this connection, as another example of correlational consistency, our best measure of attitudes toward residential integration (the NORC Residential Choice question in Table 3.1) shows significantly more white receptiveness toward integration in the West than in the East.[6]

Yet even where behavior is consistent correlationally with attitudes, one can still ask whether changes in either survey responses *or* public behavior represent a true inner transformation by white Americans. Or are the changes a kind of veneer that conceals continued profound racism on the part of most or all white Americans? This is a complex question: in the language of social science, it asks whether the new norm has been internalized. One legitimate response is to insist that the change in public norms is important in itself, especially as it is reflected in white actions. If a white president appoints a black general to the position of chief of staff of the armed forces, or if a substantial part of a white electorate votes for a black gubernatorial or congressional candidate, we may never know whether they do so because in their hearts they are genuinely nondiscriminatory, or because they have temporarily put aside their deep racism to make that particular decision. But all of us conform to norms that we may or may not have internalized deeply, yet that guide our actions in ways that are of considerable consequence for our relations with others. Myrdal spoke of the American Dilemma as being "in the heart of the American," but what he surely meant was that it was located in the values and norms of our society, and that most Americans are capable of feeling pressure from these values and norms—if not out of personal guilt, then from social shaming when they are blatantly violated. We should not over-psychologize the problem of conformity to social norms, as though each of us has either internalized a norm completely or chosen to ignore it completely.

Another approach to the same issue is to acknowledge that white persons who respond to a survey question on the principle of school integration by saying "blacks and whites should go to the same schools" doubtless run the full gamut from those deeply committed to that idea to those who feel quite otherwise but are embarrassed to admit it to an interviewer. However, most Americans, black as well as white, probably fall somewhere in the middle: they feel some genuine belief in the norm but also have other beliefs and preferences that put them in conflict on the issue. It is clear from the combination of questions we have examined that many white respondents do feel conflict about school integration and similar issues, and that their responses in support of integration in principle are unlikely to be translated directly and completely into action. It is therefore important to try to understand—and to measure—the sources of these conflicts.

One such source, as pointed out earlier, is the fact that questions like the one about blacks and whites going to the same schools are too simple, asking in dichotomous form about "segregation" versus "integration," without defining these abstractions or allowing consideration of either the amount or the form of integration. The questions we reviewed on white willingness to be personally involved in integration, as well as other survey data (Levine 1971; Rothbart 1976; Smith 1981; Farley et al. 1994), make it quite clear that whites are much more positive toward a situation with a white majority and a black minority than toward one defined as fifty-fifty or certainly one with a black majority. Given the history of white dominance in this country and the persistence of color as a significant dividing line, this is not a surprising finding; nor is it out of keeping with the way majority ethnic groups behave in other countries, including black African countries. These propensities are at least as much a matter of power and control and of fear of being controlled by others as they are of "prejudice" as a separate and self-contained psychological state.

One sign of this fact of political life about intergroup relations in America is the ability of a black candidate frequently to obtain more white votes when blacks are clearly in the minority than when blacks approach a majority (Hacker 1995). White voting in the latter instances tends to be determined not so much by attitudes toward the race of the candidate as by the perceived balance of power between blacks and whites as groups. For a similar reason, Colin Powell has appeared attractive as a presidential candidate to many white Americans in part because he did not ever suggest that he represented or would represent blacks as a collective political force.

Resistance to government intervention in support of black employment, school integration, or open housing is probably at least partly due to the same perceived conflict between blacks and whites as competing groups, which in turn is based on the way in which physical appearance shapes personal identification of individuals with one group or the other and its political positions. The identification can range from a relatively innocuous form, much like boosting one's hometown sports team, all the way to the most extreme forms of ethnocentrism. Thus many questions about government intervention can be understood as implying large-scale group change, and they suggest a degree of integration that many whites are reluctant to accept, at least at this point in time.

Norms, Preferences, and Personal Conflicts

As we consider the implications of attitudes based on norms, it is useful to get some sense of their generality and of the distinction that many people make between larger societal norms and those attitudes that reflect personal preferences or more local norms. As Myrdal (1944) clearly recognized, a great deal of social behavior is a compromise between the two. We summarize below a series of experimental investigations subsequent to the earlier edition of this book that show both the power and limitations of norms of equal treatment and the importance of distinguishing them from personal preferences. The experiments focused on issues of residential discrimination, but would apply in other spheres as well.[7]

Individual vs. Group Rights

The first experiment was developed to test the intuitively attractive notion that there would be more support for the right of a single black family to move into an all-white neighborhood than there is for a broad

Table 7.1 Experiment contrasting Open Housing law and single black family[a]

Open Housing			Single black family		
Suppose there is a community-wide vote on the general housing issue. There are two possible laws to vote on. One law says that a homeowner can decide for himself who to sell his house to, even if he prefers not to sell to blacks. The second law says that a homeowner cannot refuse to sell to someone because of their race or color. Which law would you vote for?[b]			Suppose a black family plans to move into a house in an all-white neighborhood, and some people in the neighborhood want to stop them from moving in. Do you think the government should enforce the black family's right to live wherever they can afford to or that it should be left entirely up to the white neighborhood residents to decide?		
1. Second law: no discrimination	61%	57%	1. Government should enforce	80%	52%
2. First law: homeowners decide	39	37	2. Leave it up to white neighbors	20	13
3. (*Volunteered*): neither	—	1	3. (*Volunteered*): "People should be able to live wherever they want, *but* the government should not be involved"	—	23
4. Other	—	5	4. Other	—	11
5. Don't know	—	1	5. Don't know	—	1
Total	100	100		100	100
N	(145)	(155)		(97)	(149)

a. Data from November 1986, white respondents only. For each question, percentages in first column are only for respondents who chose one of the two offered alternatives, omitting other respondents; percentages in second column include all respondents.

b. Results for the two laws are presented in reverse order to allow easier comparison with the results for the single black family question.

open housing law, which at that point in time (1986) showed an approximately 50-50 division of opinion by whites. First, the focus on a single black family points up forcefully the implications of the norm of equal treatment for real individuals. Second, by keeping the focus on a single family, there should be somewhat less concern about rapid transformation of a neighborhood from entirely or largely white to majority black, as might be implied by an open housing law. However, the initial results of the experiment were unexpected and led in surprising directions.

Half of a national telephone sample was randomly assigned to answer the Open Housing question discussed earlier in Chapter 3 (Table 3.2), and half was assigned to answer a specially written question about a single black family. Moreover, unlike the typical survey interview, we explicitly instructed interviewers to allow and immediately record any volunteered answer that did not fit the alternatives offered to respondents. This change in procedure proved instructive. The wordings and results for the two questions are shown in Table 7.1.

If only the explicitly offered dichotomous answers to the questions are considered—comparison of columns 1 and 3—there is, as predicted, a great deal more support for government enforcement of the rights of a single black family than for a general open housing law. Of those making a clear choice, 80 percent express support for government enforcement of the rights of a single black family, as against only 61 percent who support a general open housing law, a difference that is highly significant statistically. Taken by itself, this finding indicates that when the focus is on an individual or an individual family, the norm of equal treatment has greater efficacy than when a more general racial transformation is proposed.

A comparison of columns 2 and 4 reveals, however, that a large proportion of respondents (35 percent) who were asked the question about the single black family avoided choosing either of the alternatives offered, whereas only a tiny fraction (7 percent) failed to give a direct answer to the question about open housing laws. Most of those who volunteered their own response to the single family question claimed to favor the right of a black family to live wherever it wished *but* also opposed any use of government power to enforce that right. Such answers, quite overt rather than concealed, show respondents who are trying to conform to the norm of equal treatment yet avoid committing themselves to government enforcement of that norm. The responses emphasize the conflict in the minds of about a quarter of the white population between support of a principle and support of its implementation through government action.

If we now compare the distributions of the two questions in terms of those who support government enforcement vs. all others (outright opposition plus "other" responses), we see that there is no difference in support for implementation: 57 percent support an open housing law and 52 percent support government enforcement of a single black family's right, a difference that is small and not statistically significant. Thus the variation in the question about the single black family suggests the same general difference that we found in Chapter 3 between levels of support for principles of equal treatment and levels of support for government implementation of those principles. We saw earlier in Chapter 6 that some of this resistance to government enforcement of equal rights can be accounted for by a general rejection of government coercion, as in the case of opposing mandatory seat-belt laws, but it is quite likely that much of it is tied to weaker support for the principle of integration.

Our results thus far indicate that when blacks are involved, a substantial portion of the white population either opposes residential integration or tries to have it both ways by supporting the goal but not the means to equal treatment. Is this a sign of the special barriers erected against African Americans? A series of further experiments indicates that the implications are different than they initially appeared. We first considered the possibility that white American "racism" applies to *all* nonwhite groups. We repeated the previous experiment with a new variation: half of a national sample was asked the question about a single black family; the other half was asked the same question about another nonwhite group, a single Japanese-American family, on the assumption that white resistance would be somewhat less in this case (see Table 7.2). To our surprise, there was no difference approaching statistical significance between the two distributions (enforcement vs. all nonenforcement responses combined), and the trend is in the direction of greater support for enforcement in the case of the black family.

Next, in order to allow for the possibility that white opposition to enforcement of equal rights may have roots in a still broader ethnocentrism (Adorno et al. 1950), a further experiment was carried out. A "Jewish family" was substituted for a "Japanese-American family" and a "Christian neighborhood" was substituted for a "white neighborhood." The comparison was again with the parallel question about a single black family and a white neighborhood.[8] And again we discovered that there was no significant difference between the two questions: no greater willingness to enforce equal treatment for the Jewish family than for the black family.

Finally, we carried out a still more extreme experiment that reversed the issue posed between Jews and non-Jews. This time the question about the single black family was compared with a parallel question about enforcing the right of a single Christian family to move into a

Table 7.2 Enforcement for single black family vs. enforcement for Japanese-American family[a]

Black		Japanese-American	
Suppose a black family plans to move into a house in an all-white neighborhood, and some people in the neighborhood want to stop them from moving in. Do you think the government should enforce the black family's right to live wherever they can afford to *or* that it should be left entirely up to the white neighborhood residents to decide?		Suppose a Japanese-American family plans to move into a house in an all-white neighborhood, and some people in the neighborhood want to stop them from moving in. Do you think the government should enforce the Japanese-American family's right to live wherever they can afford to *or* that it should be left entirely up to the white neighborhood residents to decide?	
1. Government enforcement	60%	1. Government enforcement	57%
2. Leave it up to white neighbors	12	2. Leave it up to white neighbors	18
3. Other (volunteered)	27	3. Other (volunteered)	24
4. Don't know	1	4. Don't know	1
Total	100		100
N	(157)		(155)

a. Data are from September 1986, white respondents only.

previously all-Jewish neighborhood. The basic finding remained the same: the distribution of answers to the two questions does not differ significantly, and in fact the trend is toward more support for the black family than for the presumably white, Christian family.

In sum, there is little evidence from this series of experiments that opposition to enforcement of a single black family's right to move into a white neighborhood represents simply a form of antiblack sentiment. On the contrary, there is evidence that it reflects a more general resistance to government enforcement of equal treatment in residential integration, though not necessarily rejection of the desirability of equal treatment. This conclusion fits our impressions based on occasional monitoring of the actual interviews and also the impressions of the interviewers themselves. Opposition to government enforcement in this area of life takes on the force of a principle for many respondents, regardless of the group involved and regardless of what may seem a contradiction inherent in statements by many of these same people that all individuals should be allowed to live where they wish.[9]

Table 7.3 Mind a black family vs. mind a Japanese-American family[a]

A. "Same income and education" phrase omitted

Mind	Black family	Japanese-American family
A lot, a little	20%	10%
Not at all	71	88
Depends (volunteered)	10	2
Total	100	100
(N)	(143)	(154)

B. "Same income and education" phrase included

Mind	Black family	Japanese-American family
A lot, a little	19%	3%
Not at all	79	92
Depends (volunteered)	3	5
Total	100	100
(N)	(143)	(146)

a. If a (black/Japanese-American) family (with the same income and education as you) moved next door to you, would you mind it a lot, a little, or not at all? (Data are from July 1987, white respondents only.)

Norms vs. Preferences

Given the patterns of actual segregation in the United States, it is difficult to believe that there is the same resistance on the part of whites to Japanese-American or Jewish families moving into a previously white, non-Jewish neighborhood as there is to blacks (Farley and Frey 1994; see also Thomas Wilson 1996). How can we explain that fact if the same degree of adherence to the norm of equal treatment is found regardless of the ethnic group involved? A further experiment casts some light on this question.

The new experiment shifted attention from "rights" to "preferences," as shown in Table 7.3. This time half the respondents were asked if they would "mind a lot, a little, or not at all" if a black family moved next door, and the other half was asked a parallel question about a Japanese-American family's moving next door. (The word "mind" was intended to emphasize personal preference rather than a general norm.) Moreover, the experiment was carried out twice, once with the addition of a phrase stating that the family moving next door would have "the same income and education" as the respondent, and a second time without that phrase.

As can be seen in Table 7.3, there is noticeably (and significantly) less personal objection to a Japanese-American family's moving next door than to a black family's, and this is true regardless of whether or not the income and education of the new neighbors are equated to the respondent's income and education. Thus our earlier finding that acceptance of equal treatment and support for government enforcement do not vary by racial or ethnic group is indeed restricted to these normative issues, since personal preferences *do* vary by the race of the group mentioned. The distinction here is reminiscent of one made in Chapter 1 between attitudes based on norms and attitudes based on personal preferences, though that is not meant to be an absolute distinction: insofar as attitudes based on norms are deeply internalized, they become personal, while at the same time even the most personal attitudes are almost always shaped by the larger culture (that is, by norms).

One final observation is possible when we compare the two different experiments shown in Table 7.3, one of which equated the potential neighbor with the respondent in terms of income and education, and one of which did not. For both minorities, there is less objection when equating is done as part of the question than when it is not. One might have expected equating to have had a smaller effect for Japanese Americans, on the assumption that they are generally perceived as well-off in terms of both education and income, but for Japanese Americans also, explicit equating makes a difference in residential preferences. (The volunteered responses classified under the category "Depends" typically asserted that "it depends on what the people are like.")

This series of experiments indicates something of the complexity of the forces that are likely to operate in real situations when neighborhood integration becomes a concrete issue. The norm of equal treatment is one such force and we believe that it has some efficacy, but obviously it is not the only factor influencing the outcome. Perceptions of social class differences clearly play a role, so that the potential similarity of a new black (or Japanese American or any other) neighbor in these terms is likely to influence concrete behavior on the part of those already making up the neighborhood. Still an additional element derives from the level of personal preference, and it is important to recognize that some whites who do not seem to distinguish among different groups when considering government enforcement of the norm of equal treatment do make such distinctions when answering in terms of their own preferences.[10] Thus it is not, or not only, a matter of respondents' concealing preferences, but of their overtly making a distinction between their preferences and what they think they ought to do in a situation. Finally, we should add a further important complication that we deliberately eliminated in these experiments: the proportion of blacks likely to move into a previously white neighborhood makes a considerable difference to white respondents (Farley et al. 1978; Farley et al. 1994).

In real life, all the above elements come into play. Moreover, the balance among them is likely to be greatly affected by the positions taken by community leaders, as well as by external laws and government actions, whether wanted or not. Our survey data can help identify the elements that enter the picture, as they have done in these experiments, but they cannot lead to simple predictions about outcomes. If the experiments are repeated over time, however, it should be possible to measure changes in the balance of the forces.

Of course, neighborhood integration, or indeed an even broader perspective on racial integration, omits other major issues of race in America. Not even mentioned in the evidence just reviewed are the social and economic obstacles faced by a substantial proportion of the black population, obstacles that may have little to do directly with issues of integration. Most relevant here from our earlier chapters and from writings by other social scientists are findings about white explanations for black disadvantage (see Kluegel and Smith 1986). It is particularly important to recall that racial discrimination is not seen by whites as the major factor in racial inequalities, despite the evidence of continuing discrimination that we cited in Chapter 1. Furthermore, there are signs that whites increasingly believe that discrimination has virtually disappeared in the United States, or has now been reversed and favors African Americans. This leads to even more emphasis on the attribution of all problems to failures of black motivation and effort. Only with regard to making greater investment in education does there seem to be much white support for further intervention to improve the standard of living and opportunities for blacks at the bottom of the socioeconomic ladder. Since the majority of blacks do believe that discrimination is still a major factor in American racial relations, both the causes and the solutions for racial problems in the United States are perceived from quite different perspectives by most members of the two racial groups.

Epilogue: History and Social Psychology

This book has been about the recorded answers over time of national samples of Americans to some fifty questions about racial issues. For the survey analyst, the record takes the place of the historian's trail of documents as a source for understanding a period of history. The data and interpretations we have discussed are efforts to view from one vantage point the complex and changing meaning of race in America.

When President Truman's Committee on Civil Rights reported in 1947, Jim Crow laws were still alive and constituted in many places an unchallenged set of social rules. Black Americans were second-class citizens, mostly impoverished, poorly educated, and widely disdained by the white majority. The prosperity and social dislocation brought about by World War II, the importance of the black labor force to the war effort, the growing influence of black urban voters within the Democratic coalition, the heightened impatience of black leaders (driven in part by their increasingly urban, educated, and politicized constituencies), and the need of the United States as the self-proclaimed leader of the Free World to rid itself of racial bigotry, were some of the factors that placed a challenge to Jim Crow high on the national agenda. Other evidence suggests that this was also part of a larger ideological transformation that affected attitudes toward other minorities as well (for example, toward Jews, and eventually toward women and other disadvantaged groups).

Many of those who tried to understand America's glaring racial discrimination in the postwar era emphasized prejudice as the core of the problem. Prejudice, in turn, was regarded primarily as the product of ignorance. From this standpoint, prejudice could be attacked by teaching tolerance and by facilitating contact between blacks and whites in ways not structured by Jim Crow. The emotional roots of white contempt for blacks depended upon the regular symbolic humbling of blacks through petty exclusions, separate and starkly unequal facilities, a demand for traditional deference, and even lynchings in parts of the country. If the government could intervene in these practices, both the symbolic and the concrete social relations required by Jim Crow would be weakened. Contact on new terms would gradually reduce the level of prejudice and set us on the path toward becoming a color-blind society.

In many ways, this analysis of the American racial dilemma bore fruit in the 1940s, 1950s, and early 1960s. The slow, steady decline of norms supporting prejudice is consistent with, for example, the strong educational differentials in response to racial principle items, the liberalizing impact of the cohort-replacement process, the positive changes in the attitudes of individuals, the nearly complete rejection of biological arguments for white racial superiority, and an increasing recognition of the importance of black-white relations to U.S. world leadership. It is understandable that one of the most forceful governmental statements opposing segregation came from nine white male Supreme Court justices in 1954—individuals likely to be sensitive to changes in both social norms and national needs insofar as they can be construed as relevant to law.

These shifts in public opinion seemed to support Myrdal's view that, at core, Americans maintained a value for equality (surely equality before the law). This value would break through more plainly as soon as the intellectual and emotional underpinnings of prejudice began to dissipate. Government played its role through court decisions (like the *Brown* ruling) and executive actions (like Truman's order to desegregate the armed forces). Prejudice seemed an enemy that could be overcome. Categorical inequalities overtly premised upon notions of innate inferiority fell as the government intervened, backed by public attitudes that not only increasingly rejected such views but were moving toward full endorsement of the principle of racial equality. This process was fueled by insistent and often integrated civil rights demonstrations, which not only focused national attention upon black grievances but served an educational purpose and pressed the government to act more urgently in racial matters.

There was a growing consensus to all of this, and in the late 1960s the government began to move beyond the paradigm of reducing prejudice through ending discrimination—though this goal had by no means been achieved—to the often implicit paradigm of increasing the economic and political standing of blacks; that is, to treating the race problem as a matter of social inequality as well as of prejudice. But during these same years, the civil rights movement was becoming not only more visible but also more variegated. In many of its important branches, it was no longer itself integrated. The thrust of the demand for change was decreasingly toward integration and increasingly toward redistribution. The sudden outburst and then decline of the riots and the Black Power Movement; the assassination of Martin Luther King, which silenced the most widely listened to voice for nonviolent racial change; and Richard Nixon's victory over Hubert Humphrey, the national white political figure most closely associated with civil rights legislation, were both symbols and partial causes of a halt, or at least a pause, in government action in favor of racial equality. The later election of more conservative presidents and legislatures placed further brakes on change.

Moreover, the issues shifted from removing an absolute color bar to eliminating the pervasive inequalities that the bar had furthered. There were no longer struggles over allowing *one* or *two* black students to enroll at a public university; instead, there were struggles over city-wide desegregation plans. Our data indicate that survey researchers were attentive, though not always quickly so, to these changing issues and social contexts. Questions on the implementation of racial principles were asked beginning around 1964. The results showed that enthusiasm for large-scale policy change was less strong than the support of broad principles of equal treatment. Still later, questions concerning the causes of black disadvantage and questions about strong forms of affirmative action issues were added, in both cases producing evidence that a large part of the white population was reluctant to go beyond supporting more general principles of equal treatment, and indeed was coming to think that those principles were already in effect throughout much of the society.

The changes of the past half century are seldom of transparent meaning for students of racial attitudes. Nonetheless, our examination of the attitudinal record—this venture in historical social psychology— points to some important considerations for those grappling with racial inequality today. To the extent that public attitudes are important, it is possible to bring societal pressure, indeed public shame, on any white American who clearly discriminates against blacks, provided that the discrimination can be brought to light, as in videotapes of police beatings, audiotapes of corporate obstruction of equal opportunity laws, or public remarks that impugn African Americans. The application of the term "racist" to a person or an organization is itself a severe sanction in most parts of the country. Such pressures will not always be successful, but they often are and they are not a trivial force. Moreover, there is willingness to go further and to elect black leaders, provided they offer assurance that their concern clearly includes whites equally with blacks.[11]

But beyond the enforcement of norms of equal treatment, there seems to be little public support for any but remedial forms of special training to help disadvantaged African Americans, or perhaps for broader programs that can be described in ways that do not emphasize race. It is not likely that affirmative action plans that call for clear forms of preferential treatment of blacks will survive for long outside a few insulated places (for example, academic departments in liberal universities), except where clear and recent discrimination has been documented. Exactly how the black underclass can escape from its present cycle of poverty, crime, and hopelessness is unclear, and this in turn adds to the alienation of the black middle class from white society.[12] There is no real sign that the larger white public is prepared to see norms of equal treatment reconceptualized to support substantial steps toward drastically reducing economic and social inequality in this country. It would be worth trying to present questions to the white population that succinctly point to the basic problem of disappearing employment opportunities for lower-class blacks in central cities: perhaps then there would be greater support for government efforts to create substitute training and jobs.

A final word about our own research. In terms of the data on which this book is based, we must recognize that not only do our attitude questions measure changes over time, but the changes themselves affect our surveys. We pointed out earlier that a question first asked in 1964 about federal intervention in the area of employment may have shifted somewhat in meaning over the years. It asked: "Should the government in Washington see to it that black people get fair treatment in jobs, or is this not the federal government's business?" When the question was first posed in the mid-1960s, "fair treatment" could be assumed to refer to "equal treatment," but by the 1990s "fair treatment" could be taken by some proportion of the population—both black and white—to mean affirmative action in the sense of compensatory preferential treatment. In this case, and in some others as well, surveys reflect change not only in terms of the movement of percentages across tables and graphs, but by the new meanings that questions take on for those who are asked to answer them.[13]

Locating Trend Data
on Racial Attitudes

When we began our study of racial attitudes, we were faced with the task of identifying both relevant questions and the precise number of times each question had been asked. For the first edition of this book, in the early 1980s, we drew on a number of excellent compendiums of survey questions that had already been published. Among the more general of these were Hadley Cantril's *Public Opinion, 1935–1946* (1951); Hastings and Southwick's *Survey Data for Trend Analysis* (1975), written as a guide to the Roper Center archives; and Hazel Erskine's various articles in the *Public Opinion Quarterly* during the 1960s. Collections specific to a single survey organization proved very helpful as well. We consulted the *Cumulative Codebooks* for the NORC General Social Surveys; *A Continuing Guide to the American National Election Surveys* (1980), compiled at ISR by the Center for Political Studies and the Inter-university Consortium for Political and Social Research; George Gallup's *Gallup Poll* (1972) and the monthly *Gallup Opinion Index;* Miller, Miller, and Schneider's *American National Election Studies Data Sourcebook* (1980); Converse, Dotson, Hoag, and McGee's *American Social Attitudes Data Sourcebook* (1980); and Martin, McDuffee, and Presser's *Sourcebook of Harris National Surveys* (1981).

For the 1985 edition, we also spent a considerable amount of time reviewing the actual questionnaires from ISR and NORC surveys, the two organizations whose interview schedules were accessible to us, and searching the scholarly literature for items or replications that might otherwise have escaped our notice. In addition, the Roper Center documented which racial attitude questions had been archived by Gallup since the publication of its 1975 guide, and the Harris Archive Retrieval System of the University of North Carolina used keywords to generate for us a list of race-related questions. By the early 1990s, the Roper Center's archival system was "on-line," so that we were able to search their compilation of survey data for ourselves, using relevant keywords. This resource provided valuable information about which survey questions on racial attitudes had been asked by a wide variety of survey organizations, including Gallup, CBS/NYT, ABC/WP, and many others. Piecing together the information from these searches, we were also able to identify questions that had been asked more than once by any given organization.

Search Strategy and Selection Criteria

1985 Edition

The search for the 1985 edition of the book resulted in approximately 120 questions that had been asked of cross-section samples of white American adults more than once. This original pool was reduced in a number of ways, beginning with consolidating items that were very slight variations of the same question. For example, the Gallup Candidate item was initially represented by four slightly different questions, each asked in a different year. The wording varied only in the introductory sentences (see note to Table 3.1), however, and since it did not appear likely that these changes systematically influenced answers to the main questions, we combined all the items into a single time series. (All important variants of our chosen questions are described in the notes to Tables 3.1 through 3.6.) A second decision, not to use data from the Harris organization because of various problems we encountered in our attempt, further reduced the initial list of 120 questions. Finally, we decided to try to limit our selection only to items that had been asked at least three times over a period of ten or more years and that gauged individual racial attitudes along a positive-negative dimension.[1] These criteria eliminated questions asked over too brief a time span and questions that dealt with more objective factors, such as the actual racial composition of schools, neighborhoods, and friends. The latter decision was made reluctantly, but it was necessary to keep the magnitude of our analysis within practical limits.

1997 Edition

The available pool of racial attitude questions, as well as the number of different survey organizations asking them, had increased considerably by the early 1990s, and our search for questions for this edition was necessarily more targeted and somewhat less exhaustive. Our first concern, of course, was to update the trends for the original set of questions. We found that twenty-eight of the original thirty-six entries had more recent time points than 1983, the endpoint of the first edition of our book.

In addition to updating the old, we were interested in identifying new questions, particularly those that would capture dimensions of racial attitudes that had become important more recently. Our search for additional items took two forms. First, we inspected the codebooks and reports from NORC's General Social Survey, ISR's National Election Studies, and Gallup's public polls. This search yielded sixteen new questions that roughly fit our selection criteria. Second, we used relevant keywords to search the Roper Center's Poll Service. The latter strategy resulted in a large number of potential items that had been asked more than once (approximately sixty questions). However, the majority of these items did not cover a ten-year time span, were asked at only two different time points, or were already included in our set of questions. On the basis of these criteria, this large pool of questions was reduced to just four additional items for inclusion in the 1997 edition.

Regrettably, a number of interesting questions had to be eliminated from our consideration on the basis of our selection criteria. It should be noted, however, that there were some special circumstances in which the criteria were relaxed, mainly for the purposes of including questions that represented a particular quite important topic that otherwise would not have been covered in our trend analysis. First, three questions about perceptions of discrimination (Discriminated in Housing, Discriminated in Managerial Jobs, and Police Treat Fairly), with time points in 1981 and 1989 by the ABC/WP, were included. But we augmented this brief time series with a replication of our own by including the items in an SRC Monthly Survey in August 1995. With this replication we were able to obtain a time series spanning fourteen years, with data points in three separate years.[2]

Second, several questions of interest were eliminated because they had not been replicated over a long enough period. Since these items were repeated in quick succession, their content seems particularly confounded with time period. In addition, some address concerns that no longer have much current meaning, for example, a Gallup item assessing public approval of the U.S. Supreme Court's ruling against segregated schools, asked for the last time in 1961. However, we have included four questions with time spans slightly shorter than our limit because each provides a useful perspective on very important aspects of current racial attitudes.[3] Despite the short time period covered, it should be noted that for each of these items we have data from at least three—and for some items, as many as seven—different time points.

Unstandardized Coefficients
for Variables from Regression
Models in Chapter 4

Questions	Constant	Period (year)	Civil rights movement cohort	Post–civil rights movement cohort	Reagan/Bush era cohort	Year x Post–civil rights cohort	Year x Reagan/Bush cohort
Principles							
Residential Choice (1 alt.)	1.95	.022*** (.001)	.239*** (.022)	.392*** (.020)	.502*** (.037)		
Laws against Intermarriage	−1.61	.022*** (.003)	.696*** (.048)	1.24*** (.051)	1.42*** (.121)		
Black Candidate	−.18	.024*** (.004)	.440*** (.099)	.840*** (.117)	.070 (1.05)	−.020* (.009)	
Same Schools	−.22	.04*** (.009)	.298** (.098)	.836*** (.115)			
Intermarriage	−3.42	.028* (.014)	.121 (.564)	2.93*** (.478)	1.72 (2.99)	−.069*** (.019)	
Implementation							
Federal School Intervention	1.75	−.006*** (.0001)	.042* (.018)	.116*** (.021)	.302*** (.035)		
Open Housing	−1.78	.043*** (.003)	.639*** (.044)	1.06*** (.041)	1.26*** (.084)		
Federal Job Intervention	1.84	−.000 (.001)	.097*** (.024)	.197*** (.028)	.233*** (.044)		
Busing (NORC)	−2.21	.050*** (.005)	.438*** (.105)	.896*** (.104)	2.89*** (.691)	−.019** (.007)	−.092* (.033)
Social distance							
Few (NORC)	1.15	.023*** (.005)	.248* (.100)	.395*** (.098)	.386 (.213)		
Half (NORC)	.45	.009** (.003)	.195*** (.049)	.356*** (.048)	.694*** (.106)		
Majority (NORC)	−.52	.002 (.002)	.043 (.044)	.138*** (.040)	.515*** (.077)		
Black Dinner Guests	2.12	.007*** (.002)	.042* (.016)	.128*** (.017)			
Club Change Rules	−1.84	.058*** (.007)	.687*** (.203)	1.36*** (.204)	1.94 (.996)	−.037** (.012)	

Year x civil rights movement cohort	Income	Female	High school graduate	Some college	College graduate or more	North	Adj. R^2 / model X^2
	.056*** (.008)	.041* (.016)	.208*** (.022)	.399*** (.025)	.628*** (.027)	.311*** (.017)	.17
	.187*** (.019)	−.034 (.038)	.698*** (.044)	1.37*** (.058)	2.30*** (.077)	1.12*** (.039)	4832***
	.162*** (.023)	.207*** (.045)	.315*** (.054)	.653*** (.069)	1.28*** (.086)	.803*** (.045)	1291***
	.175*** (.038)	.024 (.076)	.709*** (.088)	1.54*** (.145)	1.89*** (.176)	1.45*** (.075)	1016***
	.119*** (.035)	−.183** (.064)	.771*** (.113)	1.30*** (.127)	2.23*** (.131)	.959*** (.073)	1544***
	−.053*** (.009)	.069*** (.014)	−.010 (.018)	.012 (.022)	.160*** (.023)	.204*** (.015)	.02
	.007 (.017)	.186*** (.034)	−.048 (.047)	.145** (.053)	.401*** (.056)	.569*** (.036)	1980***
	−.038** (.013)	−.015 (.018)	−.065** (.024)	−.043 (.029)	.214*** (.030)	.135*** (.020)	.03
	−.191*** (.020)	.149*** (.039)	−.409*** (.054)	−.472*** (.063)	.072 (.063)	.468*** (.044)	997***
	.166*** (.037)	.311*** (.072)	.637*** (.088)	.930*** (.119)	1.25*** (.143)	.773*** (.072)	502***
	−.048* (.019)	.050 (.037)	.243*** (.048)	.406*** (.058)	.585*** (.063)	.371*** (.039)	418***
	−.131*** (.016)	−.114*** (.032)	−.022 (.044)	.134** (.051)	.314*** (.054)	.376*** (.035)	305***
	.025*** (.006)	.066*** (.013)	.107*** (.017)	.244*** (.020)	.358*** (.021)	.288*** (.014)	.10
	−.036 (.026)	.402*** (.050)	.057 (.069)	.397*** (.080)	.846*** (.086)	.635*** (.053)	863***

Questions	Constant	Period (year)	Civil rights movement cohort	Post–civil rights movement cohort	Reagan/Bush era cohort	Year x Post–civil rights cohort	Year x Reagan/Bush cohort
Explanations for inequality[a]							
Less Ability	.62	−.023*** (.005)	−.752*** (.080)	−1.07*** (.073)	−1.19*** (.126)		
No Motivation	1.77	−.008 (.005)	−.500*** (.065)	−.554*** (.057)	−.674*** (.084)		
Blacks Should Try Harder	4.07	.011*** (.002)	−.143*** (.041)	−.138*** (.036)	−.124** (.048)		
Generations of Slavery	3.70	−.030*** (.006)	−.141** (.051)	−.102* (.042)	−.062 (.055)		
Discrimination	−.80	−.002 (.006)	.344 (.178)	.854*** (.172)	1.66* (.659)	−.044*** (.010)	−.078* (.034)
No Special Favors	3.81	.027*** (.005)	−.270*** (.042)	−.288*** (.035)	−.281*** (.045)		
No Chance Education	−.91	.000 (.006)	.027 (.186)	.342 (.181)	.996 (.688)	−.022* (.010)	
Affirmative Action							
Preference in Hiring (ISR)	2.02	−.013** (.004)	.061 (.034)	.122*** (.028)	.186*** (.036)		
Spending on Blacks	1.71	.007*** (.001)	.096*** (.024)	.171*** (.026)	.736** (.273)	−.006** (.002)	−.029* (.014)
Aid to Minorities	2.98	.012** (.004)	.425*** (.096)	.671*** (.116)		−.029*** (.007)	
Aid to Blacks	3.37	−.016* (.008)	−.015 (.059)	.087 (.050)	.155* (.066)		
Federal Spending	2.07	−.006* (.003)	−.036 (.021)	−.300* (.125)	.070** (.026)	.011* (.005)	
Help Blacks	2.12	−.005* (.002)	−.040 (.031)	.040 (.027)	.170*** (.046)		
Preference in Hiring (CBS/NYT)	−.34	−.038*** (.011)	.042 (.099)	.231** (.082)	.274** (.102)		
Preference in Admissions	2.17	−.012 (.007)	.147** (.047)	.208*** (.039)	.316*** (.053)		

*p < .05
**p < .01
***p < .001

Note Standard errors are shown in parentheses. Coefficients for the interaction of each cohort category and year are included only when they attained significance beyond the .05 level. In addition, coefficients for the Reagan/Bush cohort could not be calculated for those questions that were not asked by NORC or ISR after the mid-1980s (Same Schools, Black Dinner Guest, and Aid to Minorities) because the youngest cohort did not yet contain enough cases.

Year x civil rights movement cohort	Income	Female	High school graduate	Some college	College graduate or more	North	Adj. R^2 / model X^2
	−.070* (.030)	−.329*** (.057)	−.330*** (.070)	−.832*** (.089)	−1.58*** (.110)	−.560*** (.058)	1078***
	.028 (.023)	−.240*** (.046)	−.082 (.068)	−.527*** (.075)	−1.08*** (.077)	−.487*** (.049)	730***
	.012 (.020)	−.143*** (.028)	−.244*** (.041)	−.544*** (.046)	−1.09*** (.048)	−.251*** (.030)	.12
	−.067** (.023)	.088** (.034)	−.092 (.051)	.095 (.056)	.504*** (.058)	.255*** (.036)	.04
	−.129*** (.023)	.232*** (.044)	−.230*** (.064)	−.052 (.072)	.265*** (.074)	.528*** (.048)	276***
	.050** (.019)	−.104*** (.028)	−.044 (.042)	−.286*** (.046)	−.803*** (.048)	−.183*** (.030)	.10
	.009 (.022)	.294*** (.043)	.160** (.062)	.466*** (.070)	1.18*** (.075)	.596*** (.046)	621**
	−.105*** (.016)	.071** (.022)	−.302*** (.034)	−.341*** (.037)	−.130*** (.038)	.063** (.024)	.04
−.005* (.002)	−.031*** (.006)	.081*** (.011)	.029 (.015)	.096*** (.018)	.258*** (.018)	.154*** (.012)	.04
−.024*** (.006)	−.139*** (.020)	.132*** (.028)	−.029 (.038)	.161*** (.045)	.568*** (.046)	.387*** (.030)	.04
	−.197*** (.028)	.224*** (.040)	−.077 (.059)	.155* (.065)	.581*** (.068)	.289*** (.042)	.04
	−.056*** (.010)	.046** (.014)	−.055* (.021)	−.027 (.024)	.101*** (.025)	.103*** (.016)	.02
	−.041*** (.011)	.077*** (.022)	−.097** (.031)	.016 (.035)	.364*** (.037)	.224*** (.023)	.03
	−.142*** (.035)	.149* (.064)	−.454*** (.108)	−.778*** (.118)	−.629*** (.119)	.199** (.068)	116***
	−.109*** (.022)	.162*** (.031)	−.290*** (.048)	−.326*** (.052)	−.088 (.054)	.185*** (.034)	.03

a. The response options for this category of questions were not ordered along a conservative to liberal dimension. Instead, the coding extends from disagreeing with the explanation to agreeing with it. Thus the order is sometimes in a liberal direction and sometimes in a conservative one depending upon the phrasing of the item itself. For No Special Favors, No Motivation, Blacks Should Try Harder, and Less Ability, the high number is the most conservative rather than the most liberal response.

Notes

1. Theoretical and Historical Perspectives

1. This theoretical introduction draws on Schuman's (1995) chapter "Attitudes, Beliefs, and Behavior," to which readers are referred if interested in a more extensive discussion of the nature and use of attitudes. See also Eagly and Chaiken's comprehensive book *The Psychology of Attitudes* (1993).

2. Of course, as will become clear, such trends occur only for some types of questions, and other types of questions show no movement at all over time, or even in one case a move away from support for integration. Interestingly, skepticism about the validity of attitude data is much less often expressed when trends go in the direction that agrees with a reader's own intuition of the truth.

3. What is true of norms about equal treatment is true of almost all norms. They produce both external constraint and internal force, with the mixture varying for different individuals (Parsons 1937). Even such "universal norms" as the incest taboo work partly by being accepted deeply by many people and partly by being enforced on others who have not fully internalized the norm. With regard to norms that influence racial attitudes, it is also useful to keep in mind that there are some white Americans today who are oblivious to or openly oppose equalitarian norms (for example, explicitly white racist groups), just as there were some in the early part of the twentieth century who did not express widely accepted racist norms calling for negative views of blacks.

4. Readers should also note that what sometimes looks like a discrepancy between individual attitude responses and later behavior is more correctly seen to be a discrepancy between individual behavior and what sociologists call "collective behavior." It is not often, for example, that mass uprisings—the urban riots in American cities in the 1960s, or the Solidarity movement in Poland in 1980—are predicted in advance on the basis of individual-level data. But in these instances there may be as much or more discrepancy between the preceding overt individual *behavior* and the collective outbursts as there is between the latter and individual *attitudes*.

5. Despite their bleak and deeply pessimistic predictions, Jefferson and Toc-

queville were convinced that slavery was a moral wrong fundamentally at odds with democratic principles. Both of these beliefs that a peaceful society in which blacks and whites were equals was unattainable and that black slavery was a doomed antidemocratic institution have sometimes made Jefferson and Tocqueville exemplars of moderate elite opinion in their times. Recent reassessments of Jefferson, including his failure to manumit his own slaves through his will, have led to a more negative view of him than traditionally taught. For one such current treatment, see Ellis (1997).

6. There were those at the time who objected to the *Plessy* ruling, including Justice John M. Harlan, who said in a strong dissenting opinion:

> The arbitrary separation of citizens, on the basis of race, while they are on a public highway, is a badge of servitude wholly inconsistent with the civil freedom and the equality before the law established by the Constitution. It cannot be justified upon any legal grounds. If evils will result from the commingling of the two races upon public highways established for the benefit of all, they will be infinitely less than those that will surely come from state legislation regulating the enjoyment of civil rights upon the basis of race. We boast of the freedom enjoyed by our people above all other peoples. But it is difficult to reconcile that boast with a state of law which, practically, puts the brand of servitude and degradation upon a large class of our fellow-citizens, our equals before the law. The thin disguise of "equal" accommodations for passengers in railroad coaches will not mislead anyone, nor atone for the wrong this day done. (p. 561)

7. Some authors contend that the use, or potential use, of blacks as strikebreakers and the general apprehension of whites regarding black competition for jobs were the main sources of racial animosity between black and white workers. See, for example, Bonacich (1972, 1976) and William J. Wilson (1980).

8. Meier and Rudwick say at a later point: "Black workers who joined the CIO unions did indeed benefit substantially. Not only were their wages and working conditions improved along with those of all union members, but racial differentials in wages paid for identical work, prevalent in the South, were wiped out, and black union officers, previously a rarity, became fairly common" (1976:329).

9. This figure is an average of segregation index scores for 107 cities reported in Taeuber and Taeuber (1965:35–36).

10. The letter became a major chapter in King's book *Why We Can't Wait* (1963).

11. Burstein (1985) has studied legislation on equal employment opportunity and concluded that the primary factor leading to its eventual passage in 1964 was the gradual liberalization of white racial attitudes toward blacks, supported by periods of intense public concern and by individuals in and out of Congress who had been developing laws.

12. The actual extent of intimidation and violence used against blacks generally, and civil rights activists more specifically, is not easily documented. Most of the incidents we note here drew considerable national attention, in no small

part because the violence was directed at whites as well as at blacks. But, as others have noted, these notorious cases involving whites "cannot convey the magnitude and the impact of repression during this era when many blacks were beaten, bombed, fired from jobs, or shot" (Morris 1984:30).

13. See Skrentny (1996) for a useful discussion of how the urban riots of the late 1960s stimulated a change from color-blind goals to color-conscious goals on the part of those in and out of government who believed that faster movement toward racial equality was essential.

14. The case of *United Steelworkers of America v. Weber* (99 S. CT. 2721 [1979]) established that preferential hiring programs were acceptable under Title VII of the Civil Rights Act of 1964. Claims that the act forbids any consideration of race in hiring practices were repudiated. Such an interpretation, the Court held, was tantamount to construing the act to prohibit voluntary efforts to make up for past and lingering discrimination. In *Fullilove v. Klutznick* the Court held that Congress had the authority to make race-conscious decisions. The case concerned a provision of the Public Works Employment Act of 1977 stipulating that 10 percent of all public works contracts must go to minority businesses. The Court upheld this provision. A little later, however, the Court ruled that affirmative action goals could *not* take precedence over seniority in making layoff decisions. The Court held that "bona-fide" seniority programs had a protected status under the 1964 act. In the most celebrated affirmative action case of the 1970s, *Regents of the University of California v. Bakke* (438 U.S. 265 [1978]), the Court ruled that the racial quota at the Medical School of the University of California at Davis, which set aside sixteen of one hundred slots for minority or disadvantaged students, was unconstitutional. The Court did not, however, reject all preferential treatment for minorities; it rejected only state-imposed rigid quotas that had the effect of discrimination against whites.

15. Bositis (forthcoming) provides a more skeptical view of what these reelections imply about white willingness to vote for a black congressional candidate.

2. Problems in Studying Changes in Racial Attitudes

1. One of the present authors (Schuman) served as a consultant to the development of Gallup's 1997 questionnaire.

2. As part of the preparatory work for Gunnar Myrdal's *American Dilemma,* several questions were included in a survey conducted for *Fortune* magazine by Roper in September 1939. These questions are quite similar in content, though not in precise wording, to some of our items. The questions and the distributions of responses across regions are reported in Horowitz (1944).

3. It is interesting to note that though many survey organizations (for example, NORC) have usually excluded from their samples those people who do not speak English well enough to respond to an interview, more recently some (for example, ISR) have translated their questionnaires into Spanish and employed Spanish-speaking interviewers.

4. For example, the proportion of Hispanic respondents in the NES from 1980

to 1994 ranged from 4 to 8 percent. More specifically, the number of Hispanics *not* included among our "white" samples (because they were identified as either "other" or "black") has also been quite small, ranging from a low of three respondents in 1982 to a high of forty in 1992.

5. The problems and issues are somewhat more complicated for the data from ABC/WP and from our own recent ISR telephone surveys. In both of these cases, race and ethnicity have been merged into a single question in which respondents are classified into black non-Hispanic, white non-Hispanic, Hispanic, American Indian, and Asian/Pacific Islander. It is thus not possible to distinguish among white and black Hispanics; consequently we are unable to define the samples in exactly the way we have for the main ISR election surveys.

6. The only exception to this exclusion of 18–20-year-olds is in a small number of Gallup and CBS/NYT time points where we had to rely solely on published figures, which included 18–20-year-olds in their samples. Such exceptions are noted in the tables. In addition, in a departure from the 1985 edition, we have included respondents who were reported by the survey organization as "missing data" on age, since we assume that the great majority of such respondents would fall into the twenty-one and over age bracket. It is worth stressing, however, that the practical significance of this decision is negligible.

7. NORC's 1994 and 1996 General Social Surveys were divided into six subsamples. Although the individual attitude questions we use always appear on at least two of the subsamples—thus providing at least one-third of the total number of cases for each item—cross-tabulations between any two items can be based on only one-sixth of the total cases, since both items may appear together on only one of the six subsamples. Along with losses due to missing data, such cross-tabulations can be based on no more than 500 cases for white respondents, and of course many fewer for black respondents. As indicated, this only affects cross-tabulations of attitudes, not cross-tabulations between an attitude item and a nonattitude variable such as year or education.

8. "Sampling error" refers to the variation in survey results that occurs when different samples are drawn by the same random method from a particular population. The variation of one sample's result from another's (or from the result that would be obtained if the entire population were enumerated) is due to chance and is termed sampling error. When random selection procedures are used, the amount of sampling error can be estimated from the survey data themselves. (Other important forms of error related to the survey process can also occur, such as the inability to interview a respondent who has been drawn into a sample; these are noted further below.) When sample statistics from two or more time points are being compared, each is subject to sampling error, and an apparent difference between them may also be due to chance. If on the basis of statistical testing one can reject chance as an explanation for such a difference, the difference is termed statistically significant; sometimes, the term "significant" is used alone with the same meaning. Whenever the entire country is sampled, as in most of our surveys, a clustering of cases by areas is employed, resulting in more sampling error than if every case had been drawn inde-

pendently. For an introductory discussion of sampling, including the problem of clustering (part of "design effects"), see Moser and Kalton (1971).

9. With full probability methods, every step in the selection of persons to be interviewed is strictly controlled and nothing is left to the discretion of the interviewer. ISR has always used full probability designs, and during 1975 and 1976 the NORC General Social Survey shifted to full probability sampling. With modified probability designs, blocks are selected by probability methods, but quotas are introduced at the block level to determine respondents. The interviewer does not list the composition of the household and does not apply a selection table, but administers the questionnaire to the first person who is at home and who fits a quota description, such as an employed woman or man under thirty-five years of age. All surveys conducted by NORC from the early 1950s to 1975, and regular face-to-face surveys by Gallup since the early 1950s, have relied upon modified probability designs or probability sampling with quotas, as it has sometimes been called. Available comparisons suggest that these differences in sampling design should ordinarily not have important effects on results (Stephenson 1979), though of course such discrepancies are undesirable from the standpoint of making comparisons across surveys.

10. Modified probability samples are also open to some bias of this type, and one organization, Gallup, has devised a weighting procedure that attempts to correct for this deficiency (Glenn 1975).

11. See Steeh (1981) and Groves (1989) for data on nonresponse generally, and Farley, Hatchett, and Schuman (1979) for one possible confounding of nonresponse with real attitude change.

12. A relevant example of nonresponse bias is reported by Schuman and Krysan (1996), where the nonresponse rate of supporters of David Duke is *lower* than that of their neighbors. More generally, people who have a greater interest in political issues are known to take part in surveys more readily than the broader population (Brehm 1993).

13. We have not attempted to weight our various samples to make them fit Census reports for each year. Such weighting can only be approximate in any case, since the missing part of the population may still differ from its substitute weighting. We have assumed that such variations from Census estimates of the true population will have little effect on trends over time, and much of our later analysis controls for the variables that would be included in any such weighting. We did compare recent NORC (GSS) and ISR (NES) results for four demographic variables with those reported by the 1993 Census. Our results are very close to Census data for region and for broad categories of age. For sex, the survey data overrepresent women by about 4 percent (somewhat more for NORC and somewhat less for ISR). For education, both surveys show about a 5 percent overestimate of those with at least some college years, with smaller underestimates of those with zero to eleven years of school and those with high school graduation. Thus, where education or gender is related to attitudes, our results will be slightly affected, though this probably does not extend to the shape of trends over time. (Smith [1991] reports that a compari-

son of relevant GSS and Current Population Survey data shows that except for sex, most inconsistencies are due either to question wording or to the need to weight the GSS for number of adults per household.) Gallup data came to us in weighted form, however, though wherever we have been able to compare weighted and unweighted results, the differences are small.

14. It is not always possible to maintain perfectly identical wording on items. For one thing, as in this example, references to "Negroes" changed to "blacks" in survey questions around 1972, and there is nothing we can do now to take account of this. In other cases, introductions to items vary somewhat from one survey to another. In still other cases, it is not the word but its meaning that may have changed, as we will point out later (pp. 136–137). In our work with these data we paid careful attention to variations in wording, and wherever such variations might possibly have an effect on results we try to note this for readers. We must also acknowledge that our assumption that the four-point scale used for the NORC version of the Residential Choice question can be collapsed to parallel the dichotomous ISR is plausible but by no means certain. (See note 15 of this chapter.)

15. The leveling off is clearer and smoother if the NORC four-point scale is dichotomized between "strongly agree" and the other three points. The percentages over time through 1982 become: 60, 69, 71, 78, 78, 78, 84, and 86. With logistic regression we explicitly tested for differences in trends between the two Residential Choice items. A series of models were estimated, ranging from a simple model hypothesizing no change over time for either question to one allowing for differences in curvilinear trends. The latter complex model provided the best fit. There was a significant difference ($p < .01$) in curvilinear trends. The NORC version leveled off, whereas the ISR version showed a somewhat steeper trend in later years ($X^2 = 85.22$, d.f.$= 82$, $p < .001$). Still another way to collapse the NORC scale is presented in Chapter 3 (Figure 3.10) and proves quite informative.

16. For interviews, question context and question order are the same. For self-administered questionnaires, context and order are separable, since respondents may read and be influenced by later questions before answering earlier ones (Schwarz and Hippler 1995). With the exception of a special experiment reported later in this chapter, our data come exclusively from interviews where the order of questions was controlled.

17. We did carry out one further context experiment on the Federal Job Intervention item, but in this case the experiment was methodologically motivated. Two of our main racial items, Accommodations Intervention and Federal Job Intervention (see Table 3.2), were included contiguously in Survey Research Center monthly surveys in a "split-ballot" design, with Accommodations Intervention asked first in a random portion of the interviews and Federal Job Intervention asked first in the remaining portion. The results indicate no context effect at all on the Accommodations Intervention item (55 percent endorsement on both forms), but for the Job Intervention question there is greater support (41 percent as against 29 percent; $p < .01$) when it appears after rather than before

the Accommodations Intervention item. We suspect that respondents who have agreed to federal intervention on the less controversial accommodations issue feel some pressure to agree to similar government action in the more sensitive area of jobs. It is also likely that the ambiguity of the phrase "fair treatment in jobs," which we discuss further in Chapter 3, contributes to variability in response in different contexts.

18. The classic empirical demonstration of the lack of importance of organization to the determination of results appears in Stouffer (1955), where the independent administration of the same questionnaire by two different organizations—Gallup and NORC—produced essentially the same final results. On the sensitivity of responses to real differences in question wording, see Davis (1976).

19. Groves (1989) points out certain limitations of these past experimental and nonexperimental studies, but the main reported effects of race of interviewer are so large and pervasive across so many investigations that it is extremely unlikely that they are due to any other confounding variable or process.

20. NORC is said to attempt to match race of interviewer and potential respondents at the segment level, but no information is available on how completely this is accomplished (personal communication from Tom W. Smith, 1995).

21. We have not attempted to control statistically for "clustering" within interviewers in these simple tabulations (Dijkstra 1983). However, we have examined the averages separately for each interviewer. All five of the black interviewers who interviewed whites obtained higher average ratings of blacks than did 133 of the 134 white interviewers—a striking difference. A similar systematic difference, though not quite as sharp, occurs when blacks are interviewed by whites: 46 of the 57 white interviewers obtained average ratings of whites that were higher than any of the average ratings obtained when the interviewer was black. We obtained essentially the same results as in Table 2.4 when using the aggregated 1986–1994 data in order to increase sample size. In addition, as one way of disentangling race-of-interviewer assignment from other confounding variables, we analyzed black ratings of whites by black educational levels, using only the data obtained by white interviewers, and found no relation at all. Nor was there clear evidence that black interviewers were assigned to black respondents having disproportionately low (or high) educational levels.

22. The 1976 experimental study included three other racial items that are not part of our trend data. All three show the same tendency for responses to be more positive (liberal) on the telephone, and for this tendency to be stronger for Southerners than for Northerners. In two of the four cases (including the Neighborhood Preference question), the three-way interaction of response by mode of administration by region is significant at the .05 level.

23. The sample was randomly divided across the three survey conditions. The three subsamples were comparable in response rates and on most demographic characteristics, with one exception being a higher educational level for the mail survey, which was then controlled through weighting and in the course of

multivariate analysis. Race of interviewer had been matched by design, and ten cases where this had not been possible were omitted from the analysis. For further details about the design, analysis, and results of the study, see Krysan (1995).

24. In a recent report of a survey on another sensitive issue—sexual behavior—Laumann et al. (1994) used the mode 2 method to attempt to provide greater privacy of response. They concluded that the lack of a difference from mode 1 results for their data indicated the absence of interviewer effects altogether. Exactly the opposite conclusion might be drawn in the light of Krysan's total results, as we will see.

3. Trends in White Racial Attitudes

1. Burstein (1985:18; personal communication) believes that the term "affirmative action" originated in the 1935 National Labor Relations Act and initially had to do with labor organizing, not at all with racial discrimination. It was then adapted for use in various bills prohibiting employment discrimination that were introduced in Congress starting in the 1940s. Finally, the phrase was borrowed from these bills and included in President Kennedy's 1961 Executive Order, with the meaning expanded to imply somewhat more proactive recruitment, though still clearly within the framework of nondiscrimination in hiring.

2. Graham (1990) and Skrentny (1996) provide valuable analyses of how the term "affirmative action" was transformed from an emphasis on creating equal opportunity in the 1961 Executive Order by President Kennedy to an emphasis during Lyndon Johnson's term on equal outcomes. The main impetus for the change was the sense of crisis produced by the urban riots of the late 1960s, though Skrentny's account shows how the change in elite thinking found support in other ways as well. The fact that survey questions on preferential treatment were not asked regularly in surveys until a much later time point is consistent with his thesis that the move from color-blind enforcement to a color-conscious emphasis occurred in ways that involved little open public debate.

3. Owing to space limitations, the six tables that present results by years (Tables 3.1 to 3.6) do not show years during which no survey data were collected. Thus the physical distance between two columns in a table may or may not correspond to the chronological difference between the two years; however, the years are identified clearly, and thus the omitted years are also clear.

4. We use the terms "nondiscrimination" and "equal treatment" as synonyms here and employ them interchangeably. In theory, the term "integration" is somewhat different from either, but for many of the principle questions it would be difficult to make such a distinction based on answers by white respondents, though we will do so in our choice of wording wherever practical. For black Americans there is a clear distinction between the two concepts, for blacks might insist, for example, on the right to "live wherever they can

afford" to live without necessarily wishing to live in an integrated residential area.

5. Note that within the table, the alternatives for a question are ordered from liberal to conservative, as these terms are generally used today when discussing race, but below the table the questions are shown as they were actually asked in surveys. The results we present are subject to limitations due to nonresponse and other factors discussed in Chapter 2. In addition, small amounts of "missing data" are omitted from percentaging in these tables, as explained in Chapter 2. However, where the percentage of spontaneously volunteered "don't know" responses is very high for an item, we will ordinarily note that fact. (Don't Know responses that result from an alternative offered as part of a question are always presented in the main tables, regardless of their size.) Data from a single question asked more than once within a single year by the same organization have been averaged and are presented as a single time point. For the approximate sample sizes on which the percentages in the main tables are based, see Chapter 2, as well as notes to the individual tables.

6. According to Page and Shapiro (1992:69), this "change of more than sixty percentage points is the largest for any policy preference question of any kind among the thousands we examined."

7. The line has been drawn using ordinary least squares regression, and the degree of linearity is indicated by a correlation coefficient of .98 calculated from the regression. The constraint imposed as responses move toward 100 percent tends to produce the slight dipping of points below the line in the 1980s, since it is impossible to exceed that ceiling, as will become clearer in Figure 3.2. Yet even though linearity does not provide the best formal description of the points, the fit in Figure 3.1 is remarkably good.

8. We note, however, that the *positive* change between 1970 and 1972 in support for school integration is unusually large, and corresponds to the "liberal leap" discussed further in Chapter 6, note 4. Why this occurred—during Richard Nixon's presidency!—is unclear.

9. Statements about variation over time and between categories (for example, Northerners vs. Southerners) have been tested for statistical significance when uncertain, although not where the size or regularity of the variation is so great as to make testing unnecessary.

10. Since education and age are negatively correlated, more-educated respondents also tend to be younger. In Chapter 4 we discuss educational effects with age controlled; *both* education and age have large effects for this and most other questions about principles.

11. This certainly does not mean that attempts to maintain segregation and discrimination have disappeared entirely from such public spheres of life, as shown by a 1994 federal court decision awarding more than fifty million dollars to black customers who sued the Denny's restaurant chain on grounds of discrimination (Feagin and Vera 1995).

12. The 1942 NORC questionnaire did include a question on the principle of residential segregation, but it was not repeated at later time points. However,

a question on personal acceptance of neighborhood integration was first asked in 1942 and repeated subsequently. See Table 3.3, including note b.

13. The decline in opposition to segregation (disagree strongly) between 1993 and 1994 reaches conventional statistical significance ($p < .05$), but there is enough unevenness in these trend data to warrant caution in drawing conclusions about recent change on the basis of the downturn in a single year. Note that there are seemingly similar reversals of the overall trend between 1976 and 1977 and between 1989 and 1990, yet in both cases the upward movement resumed in the next survey, as it does again in 1996. In addition to the difficulty of calculating design effects on significance levels for every variable, there are a number of other factors discussed in Chapter 2 that can contribute to unevenness in changes from one year to the next in all of the data we use. Only where there are good theoretical reasons (as with a dramatic event) or empirical cross-validation (as with the "liberal leap" referred to in note 8) should a change from one time point to another be given much credence until it is supported by still later time points.

14. As we note at several points, when respondents are forced to choose between just two extreme alternatives, as is the case with the ISR version of Residential Choice, their response should be considered to indicate a preferred leaning, not a literal embracing of the wording of either alternative. Such a dichotomous question format is obviously not well suited for revealing ambivalence. We shall see below when dealing with the implementation of residential desegregation that the more one-sided NORC question and four-point scale have distinct advantages.

15. The percentages shown for the 1997 Gallup Intermarriage item exclude don't know and similar nonsubstantive responses, which together total 9 percent—considerably higher than for most questions. If these are counted as disagree, as seems plausible, the total opposition would increase to 40 percent. In addition, Gallup measured race-of-interviewer effects in 1997, finding a 9 percent increment when interviewers were black. Thus, though there has definitely been a rise in verbal approval of intermarriage, it is probably not as high as Figure 3.6 suggests.

16. In the previous edition of this book we included under implementation a set of general questions about government spending to improve the lives of black Americans. These questions have now been moved to the section on affirmative action, since they deal not with government enforcement of nondiscrimination and integration as conceived in the early years of the civil rights movement, but rather with positive steps the government might take to improve the lives of black Americans. This change is consistent with critical points raised about our 1985 edition (Thernstrom 1986; Graham 1990).

17. Percentages for implementation questions in this and other figures in this section have been recalculated with "no interest" omitted, since most principle items did not include such an alternative. Full percentages including "no interest" are always given in our main tables whenever that alternative is an explicit part of the question. See also note 18 in this chapter.

18. There was also, after 1972, a sharp rise in "no interest" responses, which increased from 11 percent in the 1960s to more than 30 percent in the 1990s. This appears to result especially from a shift to the "no interest" alternative from the "government see to it" alternative (see Table 3.2). If all three alternatives are kept, the drop in the "government see to it" response is 16 percent. The trade-off between "government see to it" and "no interest" is somewhat similar to what occurred on the General Segregation item with its middle alternative.

19. The 1964 and 1994 subtables by year differ significantly ($p < .01$) from each other. "No interest" responses, which are given predominantly by the least educated, are omitted here.

20. Olzak, Shanahan, and West (1994) have argued that school desegregation itself, rather than federal busing orders as such, and the threat desegregation seemed to pose to white dominance were mainly responsible for antibusing activity.

21. The decline in support for federal school intervention was not entirely a white phenomenon; data to be presented in Chapter 5 show a somewhat similar trend among blacks, though not necessarily for exactly the same reason.

22. For a forceful statement that might well interpret the change on the Federal School Intervention item as simply a reflection of an underlying shift in the economic and political basis of racial domination, but not an alteration of racial domination itself, see Bobo, Kluegel, and Smith (1997).

23. None of this is clear from the National Election Study cumulative codebook, which is simply wrong about the actual wording in the questionnaires.

24. Mayer (1992:373) examined the full scale for the ISR item and showed that there was clear movement from the most extreme negative point (7) to the less extreme negative points (6, 5), though it did not cross onto the positive side of the scale, as is also evident from Table 3.2.

25. In recent years, opposition to busing is stronger (by about 10 percent) in the South than in the North, and there is a slight trend toward greater opposition by whites with middling education.

26. Rokeach and Rokeach (1989) drew on our initial data showing a decrease of the desegregation response to the General Segregation item in order to bolster a conclusion of their own about a decline in the ranking of the value of "equality" during the 1970s. See our response to what we consider an incorrect interpretation of our data (Schuman, Steeh, and Bobo 1990).

27. There are probably several explanations for acceptance of federal implementation with regard to public accommodations, although they are difficult to disentangle without experimentation. First, unlike all the other questions about federal intervention, this one begins by stating that "Congress passed a bill that says that black people have a right to go to any hotel or restaurant." Thus the basic intervention itself is said to be legitimized already, and it only remains to ask whether "the government in Washington" should support this legislation. See Sniderman and Piazza (1993:132–133) for later evidence on this point. Moreover, the phrasing of this question differs subtly from that of the jobs and

school intervention questions; it speaks of government "supporting" rather than "seeing to" a right. These kinds of variations in wording make comparisons across questions very difficult. A second explanation may be that the kind of interracial interaction implied by hotel and restaurant integration is so superficial that it poses little threat to whites, unlike the more profound interaction involved when jobs, schools, and neighborhoods are integrated. Finally, at least token desegregation in most hotels and restaurants is no longer a live issue. Endorsement of government action may be easier when it is no longer much needed, although our results from 1995 discussed below do not bear this out.

28. As Table 3.2 shows, the proportion of whites who said they had "no interest" in the issue doubled between 1964 and 1974 and moved even higher in recent years. The increase has been largely at the expense of the alternative "the government should stay out," but this may represent not a genuine loss of interest but a way of avoiding what might be considered an antiblack response. The question does show relations to education and region: support for government intervention is greatest for the higher educated and for Northerners, though the regional difference disappears in the most recent years and the education difference appears only for those with college degrees or beyond.

29. For 1975 and 1978, when the questions were asked by both organizations, the percentages used for Figure 3.12 are averages across the two organizations. For 1990 only, the Gallup results show much more acceptance of school integration than does NORC for the same year, a discrepancy that may result from Gallup's move to the telephone at that point. As indicated in Chapter 2, putting telephone and face-to-face results together as a single trend risks distortions. The 1990 Gallup sample is also much smaller than the NORC sample, and sampling error may be a factor as well. (Educational differences between the samples do not seem to account for the Gallup/NORC differences in 1990.) Therefore, in Figure 3.12, we rely on NORC data entirely from 1982 on, and thus all time points are based on face-to-face administration. Full results are shown in Table 3.3 separately for each organization.

30. In the experiment, a random half of a national telephone sample in January 1983 was given the Half question preceded by the Few question, while the remainder of the sample was given the Half question without any preceding racial item. Contrary to prediction, the Few/Half sequence produced a significantly ($p < .05$) *smaller* proportion of responses accepting integration than the Half question alone. The experiment was replicated in March of the same year and showed the same trend, though nonsignificantly. We are uncertain whether any question-order effect occurs, but if so, it lowers rather than raises the acceptance of integration in the sequence regularly used by Gallup and NORC, pointing to a contrast rather than a consistency effect.

31. The two questions were asked face-to-face prior to 1990, but in that year the survey changed to telephone. Moreover, it appears that interviewer instructions for handling ambivalent responses differed in 1990 and 1997 from earlier years. In the absence of other data, we include here the recent results, but

caution that they may be somewhat different than would have been obtained had there been no changes in method, specifically a larger "yes, might" category and smaller "no, not move."

32. The alternative "mostly black" was also included, but we have added the tiny number of people who made this choice (about one in each survey) to the "mixed" category.

33. We note in Table 3.3 the sharp increase in volunteered "makes no difference" responses at the 1994–1995 time point, but that finding calls for replication before a serious attempt at interpretation is warranted. Moreover, although volunteering "makes no difference" seems different in subtle ways from choosing "mixed," analysis by region and education does not yield different correlates for the two answers. Other exploratory analysis indicates that women and younger respondents tend to choose "mixed," men and older respondents to volunteer "no difference."

34. By beginning the question with the statement that blacks are disadvantaged, no room is allowed for whites who do not wish to accept that assumption. In Campell and Schuman's 1968 survey for the Kerner Commission, 4 percent of the sample volunteered disagreement with the assumption. The percentage would probably be higher now and would almost certainly be much higher if provided as an explicit alternative.

35. Three of these items are nearly the same as those developed by Apostle et al. (1983). The main addition of the latter study was to include a supernatural explanation. However, they also divided "discrimination" into emphasis on the effects of past discrimination and emphasis on current discrimination, a distinction we will see repeated in the difference between the NORC and ISR items that ask about discrimination.

36. Agreement to mutually exclusive statements also points to the presence of acquiescence response bias, which is especially common among less educated respondents (Campbell et al. 1960; Schuman, Bobo, and Krysan 1992). Thus in the present case, agreement with *both* the low ability and the discrimination explanations decreases as education rises: 35 percent for those with zero to eleven years of schooling, 27 percent for high school graduates, and 23 percent for those with at least some college. Moreover, agreement with *all four* explanations is inversely related to education, whereas *dis*agreement with all four is positively related to education.

37. An NORC question comparing black and white "intelligence" was discussed in the previous edition of this book (1985:123–125), and it showed a large increase in beliefs in equal intelligence (from 47 percent in 1942 to 80 percent in 1956), then an unexplained leveling off over the next decade, before the question was dropped after 1968, reportedly because it seemed to the investigators that even posing such a blunt question might seem racist. The rather similar question on in-born ability that is now being asked as part of the four items discussed here has produced a trend ranging from 74 percent denying differences in ability when it was first asked in 1977, thus not very different from the earlier plateau, to 90 percent in 1996. (Another approach to inquiring

about the same basic issue has been to avoid a dichotomous ability question altogether, and instead to obtain beliefs about variations in abilities among blacks and among whites and then compare what respondents say to the two types of questions. This approach yields somewhat more evidence of continued beliefs by whites of lower black intelligence, though the question wording is also somewhat different, as "in-born" is not used.) See Jackman (1994) and also our discussion of stereotypes in Chapter 6.

38. Kluegel and Bobo (1993) separate out the low-ability explanation as one reflecting traditional prejudice, as distinct from the individualistic emphasis of the explanation in terms of will power, but both might be seen as a result of prejudice in the sense of relieving whites of all responsibility. Kluegel (1990) shows, however, that a motivation explanation is much less highly correlated with traditional prejudice items such as Laws against Intermarriage than is the in-born ability explanation.

39. ISR unfortunately changed its method of handling residual "neither agree nor disagree" answers between their first time point in 1972 and all later time points: in 1972 such responses were coded only if volunteered, but in later years "neither agree nor disagree" was included as an explicit alternative to the questions. We know from other research that a change from volunteered to offered responses raises the percentage choosing the offered category, but there is also evidence that in most cases the ratio of substantive alternatives to each other is not significantly affected by this kind of change (Schuman and Presser 1981). Relying on this necessary, though undesirable, assumption, we show in Figure 3.16 the repercentaged total agreement (agree somewhat plus agree strongly) for all years, omitting "neither agree nor disagree" in the calculation.

40. This question about no special favors for blacks is partly about explanations for inequality, but also partly calls for a response about affirmative action ("Blacks should do the same without any special favors"), and this may account for the high level of agreement that blacks should do the same as other minorities and not expect special treatment. NORC's General Social Survey included the No Special Favors question in 1994 and 1996. The results are, from "disagree strongly": 3, 9, 10, 30, and 40 in 1994, and 4, 8, 11, 29, and 48 in 1996. Since the 1994 results differ quite significantly from the 1994 ISR results, we assume that the difference reflects survey differences of some type (perhaps context effects) and have not included either NORC year as part of the trends shown in Table 3.4A.

41. There are a number of differences in the wording of the ISR and NORC questions about motivation, and in addition the NORC item may be affected by its placement as the last of four explanations for black disadvantage. It is not possible to disentangle the sources of the variations in direction of the two items, but the overall trend should be clarified when future time points are obtained by both organizations.

42. The meanings of the two alternatives "white people" and "blacks themselves" are not specified as clearly in the Gallup question as they are in the NORC and

ISR sets of items, but presumably "blacks themselves" includes both the NORC low-ability and low-motivation beliefs, despite their different implications, whereas "white people" would include both past and present discrimination. Low education is not clearly implicated in either "white people" or "blacks themselves."

43. A complication in tracing trends for this Gallup question is that in addition to the two substantive choices of "white people" and "blacks themselves," only the residual code "no opinion" was reported in 1968, whereas in the later years the volunteered responses of "both" and "neither" are also reported. On the fairly plausible but not certain assumption that volunteered "no opinion" in the early years was made up largely of respondents who said or would have said "both" or "neither," one can treat the trend as extending over more than two decades, though obviously this is less desirable than if the coding of residual responses had been the same throughout. "Both" but not the small "neither" category was coded in every year but 1968, so omitting 1968 provides a more constant wording over time. Table 3.4 shows the full available responses for each year and a second set of repercentages for the two main alternatives only.

44. Gallup asked a question in 1963 about perceptions of job discrimination, and it also shows a very large change between that time point and the next one in 1978: a drop from 49 percent to only 18 percent who indicate a belief that blacks do not have as good a chance at employment as whites. Moreover, this Good Chance Jobs question is significantly and meaningfully related to the Who to Blame question: those who perceive job discrimination also tend to blame whites more than blacks for black disadvantage. (We consider the Good Chance question again in the next section. The survey containing both questions was administered during June 21–26, 1963, which was soon after the events of Birmingham that we describe in Chapter 1.)

45. The ABC/WP surveys included several other areas of discrimination as well, but we were able to replicate only the three shown in Table 3.4B in order to provide sufficient trends to present here. The SRC monthly survey took place in August 1994. Since both ABC/WP and our survey were by telephone, the method of interviewing is held constant, though there may be other differences between the two organizations that are less visible. Thus the linking of the two surveys still must be viewed with caution.

46. According to Farley et al. (1994), most blacks in the Detroit area actually prefer a mixed neighborhood, though one with at least half the houses occupied by blacks.

47. Sigelman and Welch (1991:77) found that the least-educated whites in a 1981 national sample were more likely to perceive discrimination against blacks than were the more educated. We did not find this with our questions, however.

48. Unfortunately, we do not have any trend questions on "set-asides" intended to help businesses having black ownership.

49. One of the ISR items appears in two slightly different wordings: Aid to Blacks and Aid to Minorities vary in whether the focus is entirely on blacks or on

"blacks and other minority groups." ISR moved from exclusive use of the Minorities wording between 1970 and 1984 to exclusive use of the Black wording from 1990 to the present. Fortunately, in 1986 and 1988 a split-sample experiment was employed to compare the two wordings. Exclusive focus on blacks lowers the percentage of support for government expenditures significantly, with differences of about 7.5 percent, as can be calculated in Table 3.5A ("government help" response). For the purpose of graphing the total series in Figure 3.19, we used the Black version from 1986 on, and also used the Minorities version for earlier years by adjusting the figures downward by 8 percent (rounding 7.5) for the years 1970 to 1984.

50. Since all four questions provide explicit middle alternatives at all time points (and most are substantial in size), we do not use repercentaging for Figure 3.19. Inclusion or exclusion of middle positions does not change results appreciably, since the proportions in the middle positions do not shift much over time.

51. We are not sure why the two one-sided items using lists, one by NORC and one by ISR, differ so much from each other. One possibility is that the NORC question wording stresses that the list contains problems that need to be solved, whereas the ISR item places somewhat more emphasis on budgetary constraints.

52. Sniderman and Piazza (1993) use a government expenditure question similar in content to those in Table 3.5A but do not offer a middle position to respondents. They find that a large proportion of respondents can be persuaded by a counterargument to change their initial response. This is not a remarkable finding if these respondents lacked a clear pro or con position to begin with but were not offered a way of indicating this by Sniderman and Piazza's questionnaire.

53. Bobo and Hutchings (1996) report a similar curvilinear relation to education, though in their case the dependent variable is white perceptions of threat from minorities.

54. The South-North difference is greater among the more-educated respondents, who are presumably those more likely to vote Republican in the South.

55. A further value of the scale interpreted in this way is to provide information on respondents who avoid choosing a substantive alternative to a question and instead take advantage of ISR filters like "both" or "not concerned enough . . . to favor one side over the other." In every case, these people are intermediate in their thermometer scores between those who give a liberal racial response and those who give a conservative response, though usually their scores are closer to the latter.

56. There is a very small positive association of the ratings with year ($r = .04$), which reaches statistical significance with these large yearly sample sizes, but it is so tiny as to be of little substantive importance. It occurs mainly because of a slight decrease in scores at the low end of the scale (zero to forty-nine) in recent years.

57. This does not mean that context is irrelevant to thermometer ratings. In 1970 ISR carried out a split-sample experiment, with half the sample asked to rate

whites first, then blacks, and half the sample asked to provide ratings in the opposite order. Black ratings went up significantly (from 55.9 to 61.2) when they followed white ratings, whereas white ratings appeared not to be influenced by question order (77.3 and 78.5). This is exactly the opposite of what we find for change over time—white ratings being the ones that change, black ratings the ones that are stable.

58. Scores on the thermometer measure of blacks are positively related to education and slightly higher for Northerners than for Southerners. If we use the difference between white and black scores as our indicator, then the relations to both education and region become a good bit stronger.

4. Sources of Change in White Racial Attitudes

1. There are other demographic changes that may affect the overall attitudes of a population. The drastic loss of young adults during a widespread war may shift the age distribution, causing a sort of cohort replacement in reverse. Also, large-scale immigration, by increasing the proportion of ethnic minorities, could result in increased public support for programs that affect their well-being. We have avoided this latter possibility to some extent by looking separately at whites and blacks and by eliminating other identified ethnic groups such as Asians and American Indians. We have not been able, however, to adjust for the effects of an expanding Hispanic population, since surveys have only recently begun to collect data that would allow us to determine Hispanic origin accurately (see Chapter 2, pp. 71–72).

2. Mayer (1992:178–185) presents a strong case that age effects play little if any role in accounting for attitude change, though he suggests that in some instances age may be a stabilizing factor when there is little overall change despite evidence of cohort effects. Neither his examples nor his reasoning about such stabilizing apply to racial attitudes.

3. To create the four cohorts, we first calculated the year each respondent became eighteen (birth year plus eighteen). Respondents were then grouped according to the following definitions:

> Pre–civil rights movement cohort: those who became eighteen in 1953 or before
> Civil rights movement cohort: those who became eighteen between 1954 and 1965
> Post–civil rights movement cohort: those who became eighteen between 1966 and 1980
> Reagan-Bush cohort: those who became eighteen between 1981 and 1995.

4. Thus no measurements for this cohort exist before 1970.

5. There are usually at least eighty cases in this youngest cohort for items asked by NORC from 1988 to 1990. Spending on Blacks is the only question where the number of cases in these years falls as low as fifty (owing to NORC's use of split-samples in recent years). In ISR surveys this cohort contains at least

one hundred cases by 1986 except for Aid to Minorities, Preference in Admissions, and Preference in Hiring and Promotion, where split-ballot wording experiments substantially reduced the sample size.

6. We are talking here about aggregate conversion for the cohort as a whole. Without panel data we cannot make assumptions about how individual respondents may have altered their opinions. For example, suppose two sample surveys conducted in different years showed the same fifty-fifty distribution of responses to an identical question. Several different kinds of conversion at the individual level could produce this similarity, but our two cross-sections can only tell us whether or not the same proportion of people were for and against the issue at time 1 and time 2. With panel data on the same individuals at both time points, we would be able to calculate how many respondents had actually changed their opinion. Even with a fifty-fifty distribution, which indicates no conversion over time, some, all, or none of the individuals could have switched positions.

7. Again see Davis (1992), who provides evidence for a similar assumption.

8. Because many respondents refuse to reveal their family income to survey interviewers, we have recoded all cases with missing data to the mean for the respondents answering the question.

9. Using region as a background variable does bring up the issue of controlling for migration effects on interregional differences in racial attitudes. Several findings support our decision not to do so. First, the amount of this kind of migration does not appear to be substantial, at least not in our NORC sample of adults, with only 7 percent of the residents in the combined cross-sections living in the other region when they were sixteen years old. It is quite likely that this percentage has varied over time, becoming much larger during the 1980s and 1990s than it was in the 1970s. However, in a study similar to ours, whether migrants were included or excluded made little difference to the analysis of period or cohort effects (Firebaugh and Davis 1988). Second, we recognize that some recent analysis indicates that region may be a surrogate for a number of compositional factors—such as urbanization and percentage black—that differ in their geographic distribution (Fossett and Kiecolt 1989; Quillian 1996), but we have not been able to test this possibility here.

10. For interested readers, we list all regression statistics in Appendix B.

11. Data from NORC's 1996 General Social Survey and ISR's 1996 National Election Study became available too late to be included in the analyses for this chapter, but it is unlikely that their inclusion would have altered our results appreciably. Other considerations, such as discrepancies in response categories (see the tables in Chapter 3), missing variables, or changes in the mode of administration, caused the elimination of most studies conducted by Gallup and ABC/*Washington Post* even where we were able to obtain individual-level data.

12. For the ISR questions, the relevant income category is the middle third of the distribution.

13. The predicted values or probabilities for any subset of the sample population can be calculated from the table of regression statistics in Appendix B. The statistics in the table represent the "pure" effects of each variable when all the other variables are set at zero. For the dummy variables, gender, region, education, and cohort (education and cohort having been conceived as four two-category variables), zero indicates males, Southerners, people who have less than a high school education, and those who are members of the oldest cohort—that is, the reference groups for the dummy variables. For the continuous variables of year and income, zero indicates the lowest value: for year, the year of the first measurement—for example, 1972 in Figure 4.1—and for income, the lowest income category. The constant or intercept of the regression (column 1) represents the predicted value of the dependent variable at the zero level for all independent variables, that is, the predicted value in the first year of the specific time series (1972 for most NORC data) for male Southerners with less than a high school education who belong to the pre–civil rights movement cohort and have the lowest income.

To obtain a value for a particular subgroup, coefficients can be added to the constant for each characteristic of the subgroup that is not already reflected in the constant. Thus for white Northern males with a high school diploma and an income in the second quartile of the income distribution, the predicted value for a person in the pre–civil rights movement cohort in the first year of the time series would be the sum of the following regression coefficients in Appendix B [constant + income + North + high school graduate]. In the case of the Residential Choice question shown in Figure 4.1, this leads to the value of 2.52 in the year 1972. For this same subgroup in the second year of the survey the formula would be the same except that the coefficient for year would be added to the equation. Subsequently in year "k" of the survey, the coefficient for year would be multiplied by (k − 1). If we had wanted to plot Southern females in the pre–civil rights movement cohort who have a college education and the highest level of income as our subgroup in year 3, the formula would be [constant + female + college graduate or more + 3(income) + 2(year)]. Note that the years intervening between survey measurements must be counted in determining the multiplier for year whether there is actual data for that year or not. For example, the series for the Gallup Intermarriage question has three actual time points: 1983, 1991, and 1994. Nineteen ninety-one would be year 9 in this time series, not year 2, and to calculate a predicted value for our subgroup you would need to multiply the regression coefficient for year by 8.

Finally, one further step is involved in plotting the estimates from the logistic regressions. The values predicted for various subgroups by the equation must be transformed into probabilities. The process is straightforward. The predicted result (logit) for a group must be changed to an odds ratio and then divided by (1 + odds ratio). For example, in the case of Laws against Intermarriage (Figure 4.2), the predicted logit for Northern males with a high school education and an income in the second quartile of the income distribution and who are also members of the pre–civil rights movement cohort in 1972 would be .395. (That is, the logit = constant + North + income + high school = −1.61 + 1.12 + .698 + .187.) The equation that transforms this statistic into a probability is:

$$\text{probability} = e^{.395} / (1 + e^{.395}) = 1.48 / (1 + 1.48) = .597.$$

Thus the predicted probability is approximately 60 percent that white, Northern males of average income and education would disapprove of laws against intermarriage in 1972. (See Demaris 1992:47–49 for a discussion of this step, and see Hanushek and Jackson [1977], especially pp. 198–200, for assumptions needed for logistic regression, assumptions we cannot always meet fully with our data.)

14. We realize that we have placed a constraint on the time trends by treating period (year) as a continuous variable rather than as a series of dummy variables. We felt that we could tolerate this assumption because the analyses of Chapter 3 did not reveal widespread curvilinearity.

15. Full question wordings, as well as overall percentages by year, can be found in Table 3.1. As we noted in Chapter 3, the Same Schools question shown in Figure 3.1 was dropped by NORC after 1985. We also do not discuss the Gallup Intermarriage question here because of the limited time span (1981–1993) for which we have full demographic data, but the regression coefficients are given in Appendix B.

16. The coefficients for the three cohorts included in Appendix B represent the differences between these cohorts and the cohort that constitutes the reference group, in this case the pre–civil rights movement cohort. To obtain the intercohort differences for other pairs of cohorts, one coefficient can be subtracted from another. Thus for NORC's Residential Choice item, the civil rights movement cohort has a mean that is .239 higher than the mean for the pre–civil rights cohort. The mean for the post–civil rights cohort is .153 (.392 − .239) more positive than the mean for the preceding civil rights cohort, and the Reagan-Bush cohort has a mean that is .110 (.502 − .392) higher than its predecessor. The shrinkage in these differences over cohorts (.239, .153, .110) can be seen in Figure 4.1.

17. The question wordings can be found in Table 3.2.

18. In this chapter, we analyze Federal School Intervention and Federal Job Intervention using all the alternatives shown in Table 3.2, including the "no interest" response as a middle alternative, thus producing a three-point scale. Our conclusions would be much the same had the variable consisted of only two categories.

19. Inclusion of data for 1996 on the NORC Busing question fails to yield a significant coefficient for the intracohort trend, and this further confirms our sense that the apparent decline in Figure 4.5 may not be reliable.

20. Generational forgetting conceived as a broad process has usually been thought of as working the other way, that is, to promote illiberal tendencies among young adults because they did not live through the years of the civil rights movement and thus cannot remember the injustices that spawned it.

21. The overall data and question wordings can be found in Table 3.3. Although Gallup asked Few, Half, and Majority black schools over a relatively long period (see Table 3.3), we do not attempt to analyze these questions here since recent data are sparse. In addition, our data for the neighborhood integration questions, Next Door and Great Numbers, extend for only two years; as we stated earlier, series with only two time points will not sustain the kind of analysis we are attempting.

22. The Reagan-Bush cohort was not included in this analysis because it consisted of fewer than one hundred members in 1985, the last year NORC asked about having a black dinner guest.

23. A significant interaction ($p < .01$) between year, the post–civil rights movement cohort, and approval of changing the rules provides statistical evidence of this convergence.

24. The full text for the questions can be found in Table 3.4.

25. No Motivation (NORC) and Blacks Should Try Harder (ISR) involve essentially the same premise—that blacks as individuals lack the necessary components of an effective work ethic, will power and effort, and yet the two questions do not share a common intracohort pattern. We discussed this anomaly in Chapter 3, p. 163.

26. The interactions with year for both the Reagan-Bush and the post–civil rights movement cohorts are highly significant ($p < .001$).

27. Full question wordings are given in Table 3.5.

28. Interaction effects among year, cohort, and attitude are significant beyond the .05 level in the regression analyses for these items.

29. Thomas Wilson (1996) has examined cohort effects on attitudes about social distance and stereotypes with questions asked of national samples only once, in the 1990 General Social Survey. Consequently, there are no time series of similarly worded items to consider. He concludes that his youngest cohort (born 1961–1972) was not more liberal than its immediate predecessor. Unfortunately, all of his questions differ from ours, and his cohort definitions also differ, making comparisons difficult. Some of our results are quite similar to his, but our data do not allow such an unequivocal conclusion about the youngest cohort.

30. We should note again that our approach, which was taken deliberately because of our theoretical goals, may have underestimated total cohort effects. One reason that Stouffer (1955) anticipated future liberalization of attitudes toward civil liberties was his confidence about an increase in education of the American population from the vantage point of the mid-1950s. See also the specific examples of underestimation given by Firebaugh and Davis (1988:269).

31. See Appendix B for coefficients for these analyses.

32. The relations we find here are more reliable than those we reported in a previous article (Steeh and Schuman 1992): ten of the twelve questions are significant beyond the .001 level and one is significant beyond .01. (See Appendix B.) This may be the result of including in the present analysis the years beyond 1990, of extending the sample population to include all ages, or of both.

33. The graphed statistics are the opinions of white male Northerners who have a high school education, but this time we control cohort by choosing to plot values for the civil rights movement cohort only. Here, income is allowed to vary. Other combinations of these variables would produce exactly the same picture, just located higher or lower on the attitude item scale.

34. In Appendix B, for three of the implementation questions the only education coefficients that are significant beyond the .001 level are those for college graduates.

35. Note that these are *differences* among the coefficients for adjacent educational categories, as found in Appendix B, rather than the coefficients themselves. For example, for the Spending on Blacks item, the first number in column 1, +.030, is the difference between the education effect for those with a high school education and those with less than a high school education; the second number, +.068, is the difference between those with some college and those with a high school diploma; and the third number, +.159, represents the difference between those with some college and those with a college degree.

36. For all of these questions, $p < .001$. See Appendix B.

37. For this figure we have equalized the control variables so that we can clearly see the effect of gender on racial attitudes. The statistics in the graph represent the opinions of white Northerners who belong to the civil rights movement cohort, have a high school education, and have an income level in the second quartile of the income distribution (the middle third for Aid to Blacks); other combinations of these variables would present the same picture except for being placed higher or lower in relation to the vertical axis showing item scores.

5. Trends in Black Racial Attitudes

1. For example, immediately after O. J. Simpson was found not guilty of murder in a criminal trial in October 1995, Gallup reported that 78 percent of blacks but only 42 percent of whites agreed with the verdict. At the end of the subsequent civil trial in which Simpson was found responsible for murder, only 26 percent of blacks but 74 percent of whites agreed with the verdict (both sets of figures are from the Gallup Poll News Service, February 7, 1997). Although not as well documented, the size, tenor, and effects of the Million Man March in October 1995 clearly came as a great surprise to most white Americans.

2. Although the problem is potentially serious for all questions, it may be more so for ISR than for NORC data. NORC evidently tries to match on race at the segment level (Tom Smith, personal communication, 1995), so most blacks are probably questioned by black interviewers, though this also suggests that blacks living in more integrated areas are more likely than those living in mostly black areas to have been interviewed by whites. ISR may make a similar attempt to match at the segment level, but in the 1986 through 1994 surveys, where we have data available on race of interviewer, the majority of blacks had been interviewed by whites. We lack information on most Gallup and ABC/WP polls, but have some information on our CBS/NYT surveys, though in these

telephone interviews other factors, such as characterizations of respondents based on their voices, complicate inferences about the effects of race of interviewer. Fortunately, for three trend questions asked by Gallup in 1997 we do have a measure of race-of-interviewer effects, as well as a large sample size. We will draw on these recent data at appropriate points. More generally, across all items, race-of-interviewer effects are expected to occur primarily on questions that deal with distrust and antipathy between the races, though some seemingly nonracial political issues have also shown effects (Schuman and Hatchett 1974). See also the discussion of validity in Chapter 2, p. 90.

3. Myrdal (1944:xlvii) stated: "Although the Negro problem is a moral issue both to Negroes and to whites in America, we shall in this book have to give *primary* attention to what goes on in the minds of white Americans . . . All our attempts to reach scientific explanations of why the Negroes are what they are and why they live as they do have regularly led to determinants on the white side of the race line. In the practical and political struggles of effecting changes, the views and attitudes of the white Americans are likewise strategic. The Negro's entire life, and, consequently, also his opinions on the Negro problem, are, in the main, to be considered as secondary reactions to more primary pressures from the side of the dominant majority."

4. On design effects, see Chapter 2, note 8. For the GSS, sample sizes of blacks across the years (omitting ages younger than twenty-one) ranged from 123 to 518, with a median of 167. For ISR's National Election Studies, black samples have ranged from 134 to 422, with a median of 229. For the Gallup years for which we had access to raw data, the range has been 51 to 398, with a median of 184, except that the 1997 Gallup black sample is very large (1,269 cases). We ordinarily do not include results based on fewer than 50 cases in tables, and results based on 50 to 99 cases are indicated by parentheses. It is also likely that black samples for surveys suffer from the same problem of undercount that the Census has faced. For example, the sex ratio for blacks in both NORC and ISR surveys shows a higher proportion of females than do the white samples, and it is doubtful that all the difference can be accounted for by such factors as differential mortality by sex among blacks. The black sample in the 1996 General Social Survey is further attenuated by the placement of different racial questions on different questionnaire forms. This especially limits use of cross-tabulation because the base N then becomes too small to work with (for example, for cross-tabulating the Residential Choice and Open Housing questions, there are only 53 cases, even though 384 blacks are included in the total sample).

5. In particular, the National Black Election Panel Study, directed by James S. Jackson, Patricia Gurin, and Shirley Hatchett. See Gurin, Hatchett, and Jackson (1989) for more details, and the reanalysis by Dawson (1994). See also Tate (1993) for a useful analysis of recent black voting. A number of earlier studies of black attitudes are cited below.

6. For other comparative results on black and white attitudes, see Sigelman and Welch (1991), who draw on a wide range of data for their analysis.

7. A further comment is needed for the two questions in Table 5.1 about voting for a *black* presidential candidate. For blacks, an affirmative response to the questions would not seem relevant to *either* equal treatment or integration, and the questions have been included in Table 5.1 only for completeness. However, quite unexpectedly the 1997 time point for Gallup, which allows a test of race-of-interviewer effects, shows that black respondents give significantly fewer "yes" answers to black than to white interviewers—a puzzling result.

8. It would be especially helpful in this case to be able to look at answers separately for blacks interviewed by blacks versus those interviewed by whites: the NORC version of the question stresses the rights of white people, making it a particularly difficult question for black respondents to answer when the interviewer is white.

9. In the 1997 Gallup data, age has an effect on approval of intermarriage (younger more approving), but education none at all. Race of interviewer does not show an effect on intermarriage responses for blacks, unlike the finding for white respondents (Chapter 3, note 15).

10. The Same Schools question was repeated in 1995 by Princeton Survey Research Associates, with 99 percent choosing the "same schools" response, as shown in Table 5.1. This was a telephone survey, and we are hesitant to treat the results as indistinguishable from those obtained by NORC's face-to-face survey, though in this case it is unlikely that they would be very different.

11. When the question was administered to whites, the respondents were asked about different proportions of black children. Blacks, by contrast, were asked about different proportions of white children.

12. We suspect that the sharp drop for blacks between 1994 and 1996 is at least partly due to random error (that is, some combination of sampling error and changes in race-of-interviewer composition). It is difficult to think of any real occurrence between 1994 and 1996 that could account for such a drop, and a temporary decline nearly as large occurred once before. In any case, it will be important to check this further in the next GSS survey.

13. As noted in Chapter 3, note 40, the ISR No Favor question has recently been included in NORC's General Social Survey. For blacks, the GSS percentages are, from "strongly agree": 22, 27, 10, 17, and 25 in 1994, and 29, 25, 14, 18, and 15 in 1996.

14. The finding that low ability is not stressed by either blacks or whites, but that both emphasize the importance of education, testifies to the belief of both groups that inequality in outcomes can be attributed to differences in past educational opportunities. (A similar observation is made by Sigelman and Welch 1991:92.) Investments in education presumably should have wide support from both whites and blacks.

15. The 1995 time point for blacks is based on only thirty-three cases, below the minimum we employ for our main tables, but it is included here to allow a rough comparison with the white data.

16. The table aggregates black respondents from the three years we have available using ABC/WP data (1981, 1989, 1992). The relation of education to perceptions of police unfairness is maintained when year, age, and gender are controlled using multiple regression. (Sigelman and Welch 1991, chapter 4, report somewhat different findings from their data: that education is positively related to perceptions of discrimination against oneself, but not to discrimination against blacks more generally.)

17. See also the extensive analysis by Anderson, Silver, and Abramson (1988b) of race-of-interviewer effects on earlier thermometer-scale data for blacks.

18. Statistical controlling can be used when randomization is impractical, but it is important that there have been a fair number of interviewers of both races and that their assignment has not been too tightly bound to geographic location, since location is likely to be substantially correlated with the extent of residential integration, as well as with socioeconomic levels. See Anderson et al. (1988b) for an example of statistical controlling when analyzing race-of-interviewer effects.

19. Again, this is a question that has shown race-of-interviewer effects, so the picture of whites held by blacks would quite likely be less positive if only black interviewers had been used (Schuman and Hatchett 1974). (The Better Break question was unfortunately not included in the 1997 Gallup Poll.)

20. The aggregation is used in order to provide reasonably large subsample sizes by education. It is not possible with the ISR codes to separate out education beyond the college-graduate level, as done earlier on p. 157, and other refinements in the education variable do not change the picture shown in the table here.

21. The percentages are taken from Tables 3.4A and 5.4A. For the ISR question, "agree strongly" and "agree somewhat" are combined, after repercentaging with "neither agree nor disagree" responses omitted. We use 1994 as the last year for which we have data from both surveys.

22. Bobo and Kluegel (1993) report more white support for an income-targeted than a race-targeted approach. A report by Sigelman (forthcoming) is more pessimistic. However, this is an area where political leadership could probably accomplish a great deal.

23. See also Bobo and Suh (1995) for evidence that greater education is related to increased reports of employment discrimination among blacks, and Bobo and Hutchings (1996) for evidence that alienation increases with income among blacks.

24. Useful discussions of why middle-class experience does not lead to less black concern with prejudice and discrimination appear in Willie (1978) and Feagin (1991). Hochschild (1995) provides an extensive consideration of class differences among blacks in what she refers to as belief in the "American Dream." Our conclusions are generally consistent with hers, though she provides more interpretation than we have here. Her book includes both socioeconomic and attitude data, along with other, more qualitative kinds of information.

25. The main conclusion of one study of discrimination in Manhattan restaurants was the virtual impossibility in many circumstances of determining when poor service was intentional and when it had nothing to do with the race of the customers (Schuman et al. 1983).

26. Survey organizations might attempt to define two or three subsamples for randomization within the larger sample, for example, one in a middle-sized Northern urban area and one in a rural Southern area. This would provide some handle on race-of-interviewer effects, even though generalization to the entire country would be less certain.

6. Theoretical Interpretations of Changes in White Racial Attitudes

1. Although beliefs about the extent of discrimination in specific areas such as housing, managerial positions, and police treatment (Table 3.4B) were first asked about as early as 1963, we were not able to locate any replications meeting our four-year minimum until 1989, more than a quarter of a century later.

2. Three other publications were based on these same data: Sheatsley 1966; Schwartz 1967; Greeley and Sheatsley 1974. Schwartz also discusses a number of questions asked by other organizations, but most of these are from single time points, not part of a trend series.

3. The remaining two items, Segregated Transportation and Same Accommodations, were dropped because of having earlier reached ceilings. Of the items originally used in 1956, only the Same Schools question remains in the 1978 analysis.

4. We were uncertain as to whether this "liberal leap" in the South would show up beyond the NORC surveys relied upon by Taylor, Sheatsley, and Greeley. Examination of Gallup and ISR data for approximately 1970–1972 does indicate that change was almost always appreciably greater in the South than in the North during that period. Why that happened remains a mystery.

5. Beginning in 1972, NORC included in its General Social Survey the Few, Half, Majority series on acceptance of varying proportions of black children in schools; the responses clearly show that integration is not perceived as an all-or-nothing choice. But these items do not figure in any of the *Scientific American* reports. Indeed, in 1958 Gallup had begun the same series of questions on amounts of school integration and also similar questions on residential integration, and these were available well before the second *Scientific American* article was written. As pointed out in Chapter 2, the focus of most investigators on the data gathered by their own organization can prevent them from seeing issues that other data show to be important.

6. An earlier article by Jackman (1973) complements her argument, though from a different angle and using anti-Semitism rather than antiblack attitudes as the

substantive focus. She argues that the apparent evidence that low education is associated with prejudice is due to acquiescence response bias. If low education is not a source of prejudice and high education is at best a superficial measure of tolerance, then respondents' education—emphasized in the *Scientific American* series and in many other writings on racial and ethnic attitudes (including our Chapters 3 and 4)—ceases to provide a useful explanation of variations in racial attitudes.

7. Jackman and Muha (1984) present their results in two forms, neither of which is entirely satisfactory if one is concerned about the impact of education per se. On the one hand, they report results (using regression coefficients) for education alone as a predictor, though it would be desirable to control for region, age, and income. On the other hand, their second set of results includes these controls but also others that are less appropriate: Duncan socioeconomic scores, which have a built-in association with education that should not be removed, and subjective social class identification, which is basically an attitude and thus should not be controlled as a variable antecedent to other attitudes. (A more useful approach would have been to present a series of models so that the effect of each control variable could be examined separately from the others.) On balance, their first set of results seems more informative, though with the recognition that education may be slightly confounded with age or income or both, as discussed at the end of our Chapter 4.

8. Sears seems to see the change in white acceptance of principles of equal treatment as more genuine and more meaningful than does Jackman, yet his focus is similar to hers in taking as more critical today such racial policies as busing and strong forms of affirmative action.

9. Bobo himself has proposed a different new term, "laissez-faire racism," which "involves persistent negative stereotyping of African Americans, a tendency to blame blacks themselves for the black-white gap in socioeconomic standing, and resistance to meaningful policy efforts to ameliorate America's racist social conditions and institutions" (Bobo, Kluegel, and Smith, 1997).

10. The six items appear in our earlier tables: Federal Job Intervention and Federal School Intervention (Table 3.2), Federal Spending and Aid to Blacks (Table 3.5A), Preferential Admissions and Preferential Hiring/Promotion (Table 3.5B).

11. This is a fortunate finding because there is some circularity in the association between the resentment measure and the policy items. The two types of questions are similar in meaning and at times even in wording, for example, agreement with the "resentment" assertion that "if blacks would only try harder they could be just as well off as whites" is close to the choice on a policy item that "the government should not make any special effort to help blacks because they should help themselves." But showing that traditional stereotypes tap much the same concept reassures one that more than circularity of wording is involved. (Kinder and Sanders use deviations of beliefs about blacks from beliefs about whites, a seemingly more subtle measure than simple stereotypes. However, the simpler and the more subtle measures correlate highly [mid-.80s

for lazy and violent], and in a study by Wilson [1996] both measures are reported to have yielded the same results in an analysis of cohort and region effects.)

12. Sniderman and Piazza (1993) show that stereotyping blacks as "not trying" performs better as a predictor of policy positions than does a measure that combines such stereotypes with others of a more traditional type (for example, innate difference). As Kluegel (1990) has emphasized in his analysis, it becomes important to distinguish the unique sources and effects of the "not trying" type of attribution, as distinct from other kinds of stereotypes.

13. An important qualification to this conclusion is the finding by Green and Cowden (1992) that antibusing activists do show self-interest motivation. And of course lawsuits against affirmative action, as in the *Bakke* case, have largely hinged on the personal interests of whites who claim to have been discriminated against.

14. See also Quillian (1996) who follows Pettigrew (1959) in emphasizing percent black as an important factor in negative white attitudes, specifically in accounting for North-South differences.

15. There is now a good deal of research yielding similar conclusions: Kluegel and Smith (1986), Feldman (1988), Sears (1988), Bobo (1991), Sniderman and Piazza (1993). It is puzzling that so little relation is found, and it would be worth exploring individualism measures further, allowing for nonlinearity and interactions with other variables, especially a measure of authoritarianism. Given their own results, it is also puzzling that Kinder and Sanders (1996) continue to say that racial resentment, like symbolic racism, "is thought to be the conjunction of whites' feelings toward blacks and their support for American values, especially secularized versions of the Protestant Ethic" (p. 293).

16. The Sniderman and Piazza book (1993) includes other useful results, some of which we draw on elsewhere, but it also presents a number of difficulties for the serious reader. Only product-moment correlations are employed, without showing the underlying distributions that constrain such a summary statistic. At times even the needed correlations are not given numerically, but only summarized in vague verbal terms (see, for example, p. 92). Causal models are stated among attitude variables where there is no temporal sequence, and the authors' own ordering can seem quite arbitrary. More generally, the analysis appears selective in terms of which items are used and how they are analyzed in different parts of the book. Some additional evidence and background information is presented in Sniderman, Brody, and Tetlock (1991), but the two sources are not coordinated.

17. See Schuman and Bobo (1988) for more details on the analysis of the data from the 1985 investigation. (Because of the results of the 1995 replication, our conclusions here differ somewhat from those in the earlier article.)

18. The relation of the seat-belt question to open housing turns out to be more complex than the bivariate association just shown. When we take account of the two different forms of the Open Housing question—local referendum and

federal legislation—the relation of opposition to seat belts is considerably stronger at the federal level, as shown below using the 1995 results:

Percentage opposing open housing, by seat-belt law and local vs. federal version of question

Attitude toward seat-belt law	Local referendum	Federal law
Favors belt law	38% (226)	34% (243)
Opposes belt law	43% (138)	55% (132)

Note: Base Ns are shown in parentheses.

When a local referendum is at issue, the seat-belt law produces only a 5 percent difference in opposition to open housing, whereas when a federal law is at issue the difference is 21 percent. This interaction appears to be reliable in 1995 ($p = .05$), as it was also in 1985. But it is difficult to interpret. Taken at face value, the result suggests that opposition to government coercion as such plays a strong role when federal open housing laws are the focus. Yet when the focus shifts to the local referendum level, the reduction in concern about government coercion does *not* lead, as we expected, to an appreciable increase in acceptance of open housing laws. It is possible that the stronger relation at the federal level is largely a question-order effect, due to a desire to oppose a federal law after having stated opposition to a seat-belt law. In any case, the direct effect of the seat-belt item on the local referendum is very slight, so that we cannot conclude that opposition to government coercion as such is an important factor in opposing open housing at the local level. Similar results were obtained in 1985, as reported in Schuman and Bobo (1988).

19. Kinder and Sanders (1996) report correlational evidence that support for limited government is related to opposition to government help for blacks. Their items in this case seem in danger of being related in circular fashion to their policy items, especially if question order had an effect on answers. Our single experimental test involving the issue of seat belts seems to us to provide a stronger test of the hypothesis that opposition to government coercion is an important factor in opposition to open housing laws. However, this is clearly an issue where further focused research is needed.

20. Another problem with many of the experiments reviewed by Crosby, Bromley, and Saxe (1980) is the ambiguity of the behavior reported. For example, the fact that whites sit farther away from blacks than from other whites has possible interpretations other than covert racism.

21. This is even more true when some subtlety is employed in assessing questionnaire data. Thus Dovidio and Fazio (1992) report studies showing that white college samples did not rate blacks differently from whites when presented with negative characteristics, but did rate whites higher than blacks on positive characteristics. Similar results are reported by Rothbart and John (1993).

22. Sniderman and his colleagues tend to treat randomized experiments as more

definitive than they can ever be, for example, claiming in one case that a single experiment of theirs produced results that "explode the notion that whites will say what they believe they are supposed to say about matters of race" (Sniderman and Piazza 1993:172). What Campbell and Stanley (1966) called "external validity" in experimentation always involves difficult issues of interpreting what experimental stimuli mean and what they imply beyond the experimental situation itself. Survey-based experiments, when well carried out, address problems of internal validity and of generalizing to a larger population of people, but their conceptual interpretation is not necessarily any more self-evident than are the meanings of ordinary survey questions and answers, as indeed a long history of conflicting interpretations of laboratory experiments in social psychology has shown. In the next chapter, two sets of experiments on open housing are presented that lead to different conclusions because of the different ways in which the experimental questions were worded, and we suspect that still other variations might cause us to alter our general conclusions further.

7. Conclusion: The Complexity of Race Relations

1. Since each of our chapters has one or more summary sections, we do not provide a further detailed summary here. Readers interested in an overview of the main empirical findings of the book can refer to the following concluding sections of the three primary substantive chapters: Chapter 3, pp. 191–195; Chapter 4, pp. 228–229, 235–237; and Chapter 5, pp. 275–278. These summaries do not cover important theoretical and methodological issues that are discussed in Chapters 1, 2, and 6, nor other issues raised elsewhere in the book, but they will provide a general sense of the main substantive conclusions of the work.
2. Rigid categorization can be enforced even where the physical signs of race lead in an opposite direction, as in the occasional case of someone who seems white in appearance but either elects or is forced to be viewed as black. One striking account can be found in an autobiography by Williams (1995) with the subtitle *The True Story of a White Boy Who Discovered He Was Black.* The clear contrast of racial identity with the "symbolic ethnicity" of many white Americans is discussed by Waters (1990).
3. The normative change was clearly a broad one that extended to other minorities besides blacks (see, for example, Stember et al. 1966).
4. Ironically, one recent commentator considers the success of some blacks and the portrayal of friendly black-white relations in the media to be dangerous, since they allow the white population to ignore the tremendous obstacles faced by the larger black lower class (DeMott 1995).
5. The intermarriage rates used in the figure come from Besharov and Sullivan (1996). We expect the item on opposing laws to come close to unanimity in the foreseeable future. Approval of intermarriage is likely to take much longer to approach 100 percent agreement, but also seems headed in that direction. We would not expect the intermarriage rate ever to reach such a level; rather, we would expect it to continue rising to some equilibrium point, so in that

sense there is a more basic difference between the two types of questions we have available here and the actual phenomenon of intermarriage.

6. Using multiple regression, $p = .01$, with education controlled. Black receptiveness shows much the same trend—95 percent in the West compared with 86 percent in the East disagreeing strongly with segregation—but the small samples of nineteen and forty-four cases, respectively, do not yield significance. The General Social Survey regions of New England, Middle Atlantic, and East North Central were coded as East; West North Central, Mountain, and Pacific were coded as West; and all Southern regions were omitted. An important qualification to our conclusion is that we do not know what will happen if the black population in the West increases appreciably. Massey and Denton (1993) might expect the pattern in that case to become more similar to the East, as would Quillian (1996).

7. The experiments were first reported in Schuman and Bobo (1988), which includes some additional analysis.

8. All Jewish respondents were omitted from this comparison and from the one described below.

9. Despite these results, which are important in themselves, we suspect that our hypothesis about the difference between application of the norm of equal treatment to a single person and application to a large group is likely to prove correct, and that our original way of operationalizing that distinction was not adequate, perhaps because the Open Housing question itself is already written with something of a focus on individuals.

10. We do not actually ask the same white individuals both types of questions, but since the two samples were drawn to represent the same population of individuals, one can reasonably draw this inference.

11. Of course, there are individuals and groups, mostly well outside the American mainstream, that continue to be openly racist in words and actions. But despite the individual tragedies that such virulent racism can produce—as in the random assassination of a black couple in 1995 by two army paratroopers—one should not give extreme deviance a larger social significance than it deserves. One can see this even more clearly in the case of another group: Jews represent a minority that has been highly successful and highly assimilated in almost all respects, yet one that is still the target of hostility and occasional violence from scattered extremist groups. Sometimes such hostility occurs because of progress toward incorporating a racial or ethnic minority into the larger society, which becomes a threat to those who feel themselves estranged from what they see the society becoming (Green et al. 1996).

12. A short but sensitive description of this complex of problems is found in Anderson's (1990) ethnographic account of one such area in Philadelphia, and of course there are other larger-scale research efforts such as William Wilson (1996).

13. We also increasingly feel that questions asked on racial issues have lacked useful variation in format. More scales like that for the NORC Residential Choice question (Table 3.1) would be of value, and more attention should be paid

experimentally to what happens when middle alternative and no opinion options are offered. Scattered throughout this book are hints that a good deal can be learned about the *strength* of racial attitudes by such variations, as distinct from simple dichotomous questions and also from the multi-item indexes sometimes made up of such questions.

Appendix A: Locating Trend Data on Racial Attitudes

1. This reflects a change from the 1985 edition, where the stated criteria were two, not three, separate time points. In actuality, the 1985 edition did not include any items with fewer than three time points. In light of the importance of having at least three time points when studying trends, we made the decision to make that our stated criterion for this edition.

2. In 1981 and 1989, ABC/WP devoted an entire survey to racial issues. A number of interesting items included in the survey would have been relevant for this book, but because of the short time span covered and the limited time points, they were deemed inappropriate for inclusion. Unfortunately, a lack of funds prohibited more widespread replications like those used for the perceptions of discrimination items. In the future, however, if ABC/WP continues to replicate these items, they will be a valuable source of time series data.

3. Same Accommodations, No Special Favors, Federal Spending, Preference in Admissions, and both ISR and CBS/NYT's Preference in Hiring and Promotion questions.

References

Aberbach, Joel D., and Jack L. Walker. 1970. "The Meanings of Black Power: A Comparison of White and Black Interpretations of a Political Slogan." *American Political Science Review* 64:367–388.

Adorno, T. W., E. Frenkel-Brunswik, D. J. Levinson, and R. N. Sanford. 1950. *The Authoritarian Personality*. New York: Harper.

Ajzen, Icek, and Martin Fishbein. 1977. "Attitude-Behavior Relations: A Theoretical Analysis and Review of Empirical Research." *Psychological Bulletin* 84:888–918.

Allen, Bem P. 1975. "Social Distance and Admiration Reactions of 'Unprejudiced' Whites." *Journal of Personality* 43:709–726.

Allport, Gordon W. 1954. *The Nature of Prejudice*. Garden City: Doubleday Anchor Books.

Anderson, Barbara A., Brian D. Silver, and Paul R. Abramson. 1988a. "The Effects of the Interviewer on Measures of Electoral Participation by Blacks in SRC National Election Studies." *Public Opinion Quarterly* 52:53–83.

——— 1988b. "The Effects of the Race of the Interviewer on Race-Related Attitudes of Black Respondents in SRC/CPS National Election Studies." *Public Opinion Quarterly* 52:289–324.

Anderson, Elijah. 1990. *Streetwise: Race, Class, and Change in an Urban Community*. Chicago: University of Chicago Press.

Apostle, Richard A., Charles Y. Glock, Thomas Piazza, and Marijena Suelzle. 1983. *The Anatomy of Racial Attitudes*. Berkeley: University of California Press.

Ashmore, Harry S. 1982. *Hearts and Minds: The Anatomy of Racism from Roosevelt to Reagan*. New York: McGraw-Hill.

Baxter, Sandra, and Majorie Lansing. 1983. *Women and Politics*. Ann Arbor: University of Michigan Press.

Begley, Thomas M., and Henry Alker. 1982. "Anti-busing Protest: Attitudes and Actions." *Social Psychology Quarterly* 45:187–197.

Berman, William C. 1970. *The Politics of Civil Rights in the Truman Administration*. Columbus, Ohio: Ohio State University Press.

Berry, Mary Frances. 1994. *Black Resistance, White Law*. New York: Allen Lane, The Penguin Press.

Besharov, Douglas J., and Timothy S. Sullivan. 1996. "One Flesh." *The New Democrat*, July–August 1996, pp. 19–21.

Bobo, Lawrence. 1983. "Whites' Opposition to Busing: Symbolic Racism or Realistic Group Conflict?" *Journal of Personality and Social Psychology* 45:1196–1210.

——— 1988. "Group Conflict, Prejudice, and the Paradox of Contemporary Racial Attitudes." In Phyllis A. Katz and Dalmas A. Taylor (eds.), *Eliminating Racism: Profiles in Controversy*, pp. 85–114. New York: Plenum.

——— 1991. "Social Responsibility, Individualism, and Redistributive Policies." *Sociological Forum* 6:71–92.

Bobo, Lawrence, and Vincent L. Hutchings. 1996. "Perceptions of Racial Group Competition: Extending Blumer's Theory of Group Position to a Multiracial Social Context." *American Sociological Review* 61:951–972.

Bobo, Lawrence, and James R. Kluegel. 1993. "Opposition to Race Targeting: Self-Interest, Stratification Ideology, or Racial Attitudes?" *American Sociological Review* 58:443–464.

Bobo, Lawrence, James R. Kluegel, and Ryan A. Smith. 1997. "Laissez Faire Racism: The Crystallization of a 'Kinder, Gentler' Anti-Black Ideology." In Steven A. Tuch and Jack K. Martin (eds.), *Racial Attitudes in the 1990s: Continuity and Change*. Greenwood, Conn.: Praeger, pp. 15–44.

Bobo, Lawrence, and Susan A. Suh. 1995. "Surveying Racial Discrimination: Analyses from a Multiethnic Labor Market." Russell Sage Foundation Working Paper no. 75.

Bogardus, Emory S. 1928. *Immigration and Race Attitudes*. Boston: D. C. Heath.

Bogart, Leo (ed.). 1969. *Social Research and the Desegregation of the U.S. Army*. Chicago: Markham.

Bonacich, Edna. 1972. "A Theory of Ethnic Antagonism: The Split Labor Market." *American Sociological Review* 37:547–559.

——— 1976. "Advanced Capitalism and Black/White Race Relations in the United States: A Split Labor Market Interpretation." *American Sociological Review* 41:34–51.

Bositis, David A. Forthcoming. "The Future of Majority-Minority Districts and Black and Hispanic Legislative Representation." In D. A. Bositis (ed.), *A New Framework for Redistricting: The Prospects for Minority Representation Post-Miller*. Washington, D.C.: Joint Center for Political and Economic Studies.

Bound, John, and Richard B. Freeman. 1992. "What Went Wrong? The Erosion of Relative Earnings and Employment among Young Black Men in the 1980s." *Quarterly Journal of Economics* 107:201–232.

Brannon, Robert, Gary Cyphers, Sharlene Hesse, Susan Hesselbart, Roberta Keane, Howard Schuman, Thomas Viccaro, and Diana Wright. 1973. "Attitude and Action: A Field Experiment Joined to a General Population Survey." *American Sociological Review* 38:625–636.

Brauer, Carl M. 1977. *John F. Kennedy and the Second Reconstruction.* New York: Columbia University Press.

Braungart, Richard G., and Margaret M. Braungart. 1990. "Political Generational Themes in the American Student Movements of the 1930s and 1960s." *Journal of Political and Military Sociology* 18:79–121.

Brehm, John. 1993. *The Phantom Respondents: Opinion Surveys and Political Representation.* Ann Arbor: University of Michigan Press.

Brink, William, and Louis Harris. 1964. *The Negro Revolution in America.* New York: Simon and Schuster.

Burstein, Paul. 1985. *Discrimination, Jobs, and Politics: The Struggle for Equal Employment Opportunity in the United States since the New Deal.* Chicago: University of Chicago Press.

Campbell, Angus, Philip E. Converse, Warren E. Miller, and Donald E. Stokes. 1960. *The American Voter.* New York: Wiley.

Campbell, Angus. 1971. *White Attitudes toward Black People.* Ann Arbor: Institute for Social Research.

Campbell, Angus, and Howard Schuman. 1968. "Racial Attitudes in Fifteen American Cities." In *Supplemental Studies for the National Advisory Commission on Civil Disorders.* Washington, D.C.: U.S. Government Printing Office.

Campbell, Donald T. 1963. "Social Attitudes and Other Acquired Behavioral Dispositions." In S. Koch (ed.), *Psychology: A Study of a Science,* vol. 6, pp. 94–172. New York: McGraw-Hill.

Campbell, Donald T., and Julian C. Stanley. 1966. *Experimental and Quasi-Experimental Designs for Research.* Chicago: Rand-McNalley.

Cantril, Hadley. 1951. *Public Opinion: 1935–1946.* Princeton, N.J.: Princeton University Press.

Caplan, Nathan S. 1970. "The New Ghetto Man: A Review of Recent Empirical Studies." *Journal of Social Issues* 26:59–73.

Caplan, Nathan S., and Jeffery M. Paige. 1968. "A Study of Ghetto Rioters." *Scientific American* 219:15–21.

Carmichael, Stokely, and Charles V. Hamilton. 1967. *Black Power.* New York: Vintage.

Carmines, Edward G., and James A. Stimson. 1989. *Issue Evolution: Race and the Transformation of American Politics.* Princeton: Princeton University Press.

Congressional Quarterly. 1970. Moynihan Memo. In *Civil Rights: Progress Report 1970,* pp. 23–24. Washington, D.C.: Congressional Quarterly, Inc.

———— 1972. "Presidential Messages and Statements: School Busing." In *Congressional Almanac* 28, pp. 50A–53A. Washington, D.C.: Congressional Quarterly, Inc.

Converse, Philip E., Jean D. Dotson, Wendy J. Hoag, and William H. McGee III. 1980. *American Social Attitudes Data Sourcebook, 1947–1978.* Cambridge, Mass.: Harvard University Press.

Cose, Ellis. 1993. *The Rage of a Privileged Class.* New York: Harper-Collins.

Cotter, Patrick R., Jeffrey Cohen, and Philop B. Coulter. 1982. "Race-of-Interviewer Effects in Telephone Interviews." *Public Opinion Quarterly* 46:278–284.

Crano, William D. 1997. "Vested Interest, Symbolic Politics, and Attitude-Behavior Consistency." *Journal of Personality and Social Psychology* 72:485–491.

Crosby, Faye, Stephanie Bromley, and Leonard Saxe. 1980. "Recent Unobtrusive Studies of Black and White Discrimination and Prejudice: A Literature Review." *Psychological Bulletin* 87:546–563.

Dalfiume, Richard M. 1969. *Desegregation of the U.S. Armed Forces: Fighting on Two Fronts, 1939–1953*. Columbia: University of Missouri Press.

Danigelis, Nicholas L., and Stephen J. Cutler. 1989. "Old Dogs and New Tricks: Cohort Changes in Racial Attitudes." Unpublished paper.

—— 1991. "Cohort Trends in Attitudes about Law and Order: Who's Leading the Conservative Wave?" *Public Opinion Quarterly* 55:24–29.

Davis, James A. 1975. "Communism, Conformity, Cohorts, and Categories: American Tolerance in 1954 and 1972–73." *American Journal of Sociology* 81:491–513.

—— 1976. "Analyzing Contingency Tables with Linear Flow Graphs." In *Sociological Methodology*. San Francisco: Jossey Bass.

—— 1992. "Changeable Weather in a Cooling Climate Atop the Liberal Plateau: Conversion and Replacement in Forty-two General Social Survey Items, 1972–1989." *Public Opinion Quarterly* 56:261–306.

—— 1996. "Patterns of Attitude Change in the USA: 1972–1994." In Bridget Taylor and Katarina Thomson (eds.), *Understanding Change in Social Attitudes* pp. 151–179. Aldershot, U.K.: Dartmouth Publishing.

Davis, James A., and Tom W. Smith. 1996. *General Social Surveys, 1972–1996*. Chicago: National Opinion Research Center.

Dawson, Michael C. 1994. *Behind the Mule: Race and Class in African-American Politics*. Princeton: Princeton University Press.

Demaris, Alfred. 1992. *Logit Modeling: Practical Applications*. Newbury Park, Calif.: Sage Publications.

DeMott, Benjamin. 1995. *The Trouble with Friendship: Why Americans Can't Think Straight about Race*. New York: The Atlantic Monthly Press.

Dentler, Robert A. 1995. "The Political Sociology of the African American Situation: Gunnar Myrdal's Era and Today." *Daedalus* 124:15–36.

Devine, Patricia G., and Andrew J. Elliot. 1995. "Are Racial Stereotypes *Really* Fading? The Princeton Trilogy Revisited." *Personality and Social Psychology Bulletin* 21:1139–1150.

Dijkstra, Wil. 1983. "How Interviewer Variance Can Bias the Results of Research on Interviewer Effects." *Quality and Quantity* 17:179–187.

Dovidio, John F., and Russell H. Fazio. 1992. "New Technologies for the Direct and Indirect Assessment of Attitudes." In Judith M. Tanur (ed.), *Questions about Questions: Inquiries into the Cognitive Bases of Surveys*. New York: Russell Sage Foundation.

Dowden, Susan, and John Robinson. 1993. "Age and Cohort Differences in American Racial Attitudes: The Generational Replacement Hypothesis Revisited."

In Paul M. Sniderman, Philip E. Tetlock, and Edward G. Carmines (eds.), *Prejudice, Politics, and the American Dilemma,* pp. 86–103. Stanford: Stanford University Press.

Du Bois, W. E. B. 1961. *The Souls of Black Folk.* Greenwich, Conn.: Fawcett.

Eagly, Alice, and Shelly Chaiken. 1993. *The Psychology of Attitudes.* New York: Harcourt Brace.

Easterlin, Richard. 1980. *Birth and Fortune: The Impact of Numbers on Personal Welfare.* New York: Basic.

Elder, Glen H., Jr. 1974. *Children of the Great Depression.* Chicago: University of Chicago Press.

Ellis, Joseph J. 1997. *American Sphinx: The Character of Thomas Jefferson.* New York: Knopf.

Farley, Reynolds. 1968. "The Urbanization of Negroes in the United States." *Journal of Social History* 1:241–258.

——— 1984. *Blacks and Whites: Narrowing the Gap?* Cambridge, Mass.: Harvard University Press.

——— 1996. *The New American Reality: Who We Are, How We Got Here, Where We Are Going.* New York: Russell Sage Foundation.

Farley, Reynolds, and William H. Frey. 1994. "Changes in the Segregation of Whites from Blacks during the 1980s: Small Steps toward a More Integrated Society." *American Sociological Review* 59:23–45.

Farley, Reynolds, Shirley Hatchett, and Howard Schuman. 1979. "A Note on Changes in Black Racial Attitudes in Detroit: 1968–1976." *Social Indicators Research* 6:439–443.

Farley, Reynolds, Toni Richards, and Clarence Wurdock. 1980. "School Desegregation and White Flight: An Investigation of Competing Models and Their Discrepant Findings." *Sociology of Education* 53:123–139.

Farley, Reynolds, Howard Schuman, Suzanne Bianchi, Diane Colasanto, and Shirley Hatchett. 1978. "Chocolate City, Vanilla Suburbs: Will the Trend toward Racially Separate Communities Continue?" *Social Science Research* 7:319–344.

Farley, Reynolds, Charlotte Steeh, Maria Krysan, Tara Jackson, and Keith Reeves. 1994. "Stereotypes and Segregation: Neighborhoods in the Detroit Area." *American Journal of Sociology* 100:750–780.

Fazio, Russell H., and Mark P. Zanna. 1981. "Direct Experience and Attitude Behavior Consistency." In Leonard Berkowitz (ed.), *Advances in Social Psychology,* vol. 14. New York: Academic Press.

Feagin, Joe R. 1991. "The Continuing Significance of Race: Antiblack Discrimination in Public Places." *American Sociological Review* 56:101–116.

Feagin, Joe R., and Hernán Vera. 1995. *White Racism: The Basics.* New York: Routledge.

Feldman, Stanley. 1988. "Structure and Consistency in Public Opinion: The Role of Core Beliefs and Values." *American Journal of Political Science* 32:416–440.

Fields, James M., and Howard Schuman. 1976. "Public Beliefs about the Beliefs of the Public." *Public Opinion Quarterly* 40:427–448.

Fienberg, Stephen E., and William M. Mason. 1985. "Specification and Implementation of Age, Period, and Cohort Models." In William M. Mason and Stephen E. Fienberg (eds.), *Cohort Analysis in Social Research: Beyond the Identification Problem,* pp. 45–88. New York: Springer-Verlag.

Finkel, Steven E., Thomas M. Guterbock, and Marian J. Borg. 1991. "Race-of-Interviewer Effects in a Preelection Poll." *Public Opinion Quarterly* 55:313–330.

Firebaugh, Glenn, and Kevin Chen. 1995. "Vote Turnout of Nineteenth Amendment Women: The Enduring Effect of Disenfranchisement." *American Journal of Sociology* 100:972–996.

Firebaugh, Glenn, and Kenneth E. Davis. 1988. "Trends in Antiblack Prejudice, 1972–1984: Region and Cohort Effects." *American Journal of Sociology* 94:251–272.

Fossett, Mark A., and K. Jill Kiecolt. 1989. "The Relative Size of Minority Populations and White Racial Attitudes." *Social Science Quarterly* 70:820–835.

Franklin, John Hope, and Alfred A. Moss, Jr. 1994. *From Slavery to Freedom: A History of African Americans.* 7th ed. New York: Knopf.

Fredrickson, George M. 1971. *The Black Image in the White Mind: The Debate on Afro-Americans' Character and Destiny, 1817–1914.* New York: Harper and Row.

Gaertner, Samuel L., and John F. Dovidio. 1986. "The Aversive Form of Racism." In John F. Dovidio and Samuel L. Gaertner (eds.), *Prejudice, Discrimination, and Racism,* pp. 61–89. San Diego: Academic Press.

Gallup Poll Monthly. 1995. no. 359. August. Princeton.

Gallup, George H. 1972. *The Gallup Poll: Public Opinion, 1935–1971.* 3 vols. New York: Random House.

Garrow, David J. 1978. *Protest at Selma: Martin Luther King, Jr., and the Voting Rights Act of 1965.* New Haven: Yale University Press.

Gitlin, Todd. 1987. *The Sixties: Years of Hope, Days of Rage.* New York: Bantam Books.

Glazer, Nathan. 1975. *Affirmative Discrimination: Ethnic Inequality and Public Policy.* New York: Basic Books.

Glenn, Norval D. 1975. "Trend Studies with Available Survey Data: Opportunities and Pitfalls." In Jessie C. Southwick (ed.), *Survey Data for Trend Analysis.* Williamstown, Mass.: The Roper Public Opinion Research Center in cooperation with the Social Science Research Council.

———— 1976. "Cohort Analysts' Futile Quest: Statistical Attempts to Separate Age, Period and Cohort Effects." *American Sociological Review* 41:900–904.

———— 1989. "A Caution about Mechanical Solutions to the Identification Problem in Cohort Analysis: Comment on Sasaki and Suzuki." *American Journal of Sociology* 95:754–761.

Graham, Hugh Davis. 1990. *The Civil Rights Era.* New York: Oxford University Press.

Greeley, Andrew M., and Paul B. Sheatsley. 1971. "Attitudes toward Racial Integration." *Scientific American* 225:13–19.

———— 1974. "Attitudes toward Racial Integration." In Lee Rainwater (ed.), *Inequality and Justice*. Chicago: Aldine.

Green, Donald P., Robert P. Abelson, Margaret Garnett, John Glaser, Andrew Rich, and Amy Richmond. 1996. "Cultural Encroachment and Hate Crime: An Ecological Analysis of Crossburnings in North Carolina." Paper presented to the Annual Meeting of the American Criminal Justice Society, Boston.

Green, Donald P., and Jonathan A. Cowden. 1992. "Who Protests: Self-Interest and White Opposition to Busing." *Journal of Politics* 54:471–496.

Groves, Robert M. 1989. *Survey Errors and Survey Costs*. New York: John Wiley.

Groves, Robert M., Paul P. Biemer, Lars E. Lyberg, James T. Massey, William L. Nicholls II, and Joseph Waksberg. 1988. *Telephone Survey Methodology*. New York: Wiley.

Groves, Robert M., and Robert L. Kahn. 1979. *Surveys by Telephone: A National Comparison with Personal Interviews*. New York: Academic Press.

Gurin, Patricia, Shirley Hatchett, and James S. Jackson. 1989. *Hope and Independence: Black Response to Electoral and Party Politics*. New York: Russell Sage Foundation.

Hacker, Andrew. 1995. *Two Nations: Black and White, Separate, Hostile, Unequal*. New York: Ballantine Books.

Hanushek, Eric A., and John E. Jackson. 1977. *Statistical Methods for Social Scientists*. New York: Academic Press.

Harris, Robert J. 1960. *The Quest for Equality: The Constitution, Congress, and the Supreme Court*. Baton Rouge: Louisiana State University Press.

Harrison, Roderick J., and Claudette E. Bennett. 1995. "Racial and Ethnic Diversity." In Reynolds Farley (ed.), *State of the Union: America in the 1990s. Vol. 2: Social Trends*. New York: Russell Sage Foundation.

Hastings, Philip K., and Jessie C. Southwick. 1975. *Survey Data for Trend Analysis*. The Roper Public Opinion Research Center.

Hatchett, Shirley, and Howard Schuman. 1975–76. "White Respondents and Race-of-Interviewer Effects." *Public Opinion Quarterly* 39:523–528.

Hauser, Robert M. 1993. "The Decline in College Entry among African Americans: Findings in Search of Explanations." In P. M. Sniderman, P. E. Tetlock, and E. G. Carmines (eds.), *Prejudice, Politics, and the American Dilemma*, pp. 271–306. Stanford: Stanford University Press.

Hernstein, Richard J., and Charles Murray. 1994. *The Bell Curve: Intelligence and Class Structure in American Life*. New York: Free Press.

Hochschild, Jennifer L. 1995. *Facing Up to the American Dream: Race, Class and the Soul of the Nation*. Princeton: Princeton University Press

Holtz, Geoffrey T. 1995. *Welcome to the Jungle: The Why Behind Generation X*. New York: St. Martin's Press.

Horowitz, Eugene L. 1944. "Race Attitudes." In Otto Klineberg (ed.), *Characteristics of the American Negro*. New York: Harper and Row.

Hyman, Herbert H. 1954. *Interviewing in Social Research*. Chicago: University of Chicago Press.

Hyman, Herbert H., and Paul B. Sheatsley. 1956. "Attitudes toward Desegregation." *Scientific American* 195:35–39.

——— 1964. "Attitudes toward Desegregation." *Scientific American* 211:16–23.

Hyman, Herbert H., and Charles R. Wright. 1979. *Education's Lasting Influence on Values*. Chicago: University of Chicago Press.

Jackman, Mary R. 1973. "Education and Prejudice or Education and Response Set." *American Sociological Review* 38:327–339.

——— 1978. "General and Applied Tolerance: Does Education Increase Commitment to Racial Integration?" *American Journal of Political Science* 22:302–324.

——— 1981a. "Education and Policy Commitment to Racial Integration." *American Journal of Political Science* 25:256–269.

——— 1981b. "Reply: Issues in the Measurement of Commitment to Racial Integration." *Political Methodology* 7:160–172.

——— 1994. *The Velvet Glove: Paternalism and Conflict in Gender, Class, and Race*. Berkeley: University of California Press.

Jackman, Mary R., and Michael J. Muha. 1984. "Education and Intergroup Attitudes: Moral Enlightenment, Superficial Democratic Commitment, or Ideological Refinement?" *American Sociological Review* 49:751–769.

Jackson, William E. 1995. "Discrimination in Mortgage Lending Markets as Rational Economic Behavior: Theory, Evidence, and Public Policy." In M. E. Lashley and M. N. Jackson (eds.), *African Americans and the New Policy Consensus: Retreat of the Liberal State?* Pp. 157–178. Westport, Conn.: Greenwood Press.

Jamieson, Kathleen Hall. 1992. *Packaging the Presidency: A History and Criticism of Presidential Campaign Advertising*. Second edition. New York: Oxford University Press.

Jaynes, Gerald D., and Robin M. Williams, Jr. 1989. *A Common Destiny: Blacks and American Society*. Washington, D.C.: National Academy Press.

Jefferson, Thomas. 1972. *Notes on the State of Virginia*, ed. William Peden. New York: Norton (orig. pub. 1785).

Johnson, Lyndon B. 1965. "Forward." *Daedalus* 95:v.

Jordan, Winthrop D. 1968. *White over Black: American Attitudes toward the Negro, 1550–1812*. Baltimore: Penguin.

Katz, Irwin. 1981. *Stigma: A Social Psychological Analysis*. Hillsdale, N.J.: Erlbaum.

Katz, Irwin, Joyce Wackenhut, and R. Glen Hass. 1986. "Racial Ambivalence, Value Duality, and Behavior." In John F. Dovidio and Samuel L. Gaertner (eds.), *Prejudice, Discrimination, and Racism*, pp. 35–59. San Diego: Academic Press.

Kinder, Donald R., and Lynn M. Sanders. 1996. *Divided by Color: Racial Politics and Democratic Ideals*. Chicago: University of Chicago Press.

Kinder, Donald R., and David O. Sears. 1981. "Prejudice and Politics: Symbolic Racism versus Racial Threats to the Good Life." *Journal of Personality and Social Psychology* 40:414–431.

King, Martin Luther. 1963. *Why We Can't Wait.* New York: Times Mirror.
———— 1967. *Where Do We Go from Here: Chaos or Community?* New York: Bantam.

Kirschenman, Joleen, and Katherine M. Neckerman. 1991. "'We'd Love to Hire Them, But. . .': The Meaning of Race for Employers." In C. Jencks and P. E. Peterson (eds.), *The Urban Underclass,* pp. 203–234. Washington, D.C.: Brookings Institute Press.

Kluegel, James R. 1990. "Trends in Whites' Explanations of the Black-White Gap in Socioeconomic Status, 1977–1989." *American Sociological Review* 55:512–525.

Kluegel, James R., and Lawrence Bobo. 1993. "Dimensions of Whites' Beliefs about the Black-White Socioeconomic Gap." In Paul M. Sniderman, Philip E. Tetlock, and Edward G. Carmines (eds.), *Prejudice, Politics, and the American Dilemma,* pp. 127–147. Stanford: Stanford University Press.

Kluegel, James R., and Eliot R. Smith. 1986. *Beliefs about Inequality: Americans' Views of What Is and What Ought to Be.* New York: Aldine de Gruyter.

Kluger, Richard. 1975. *Simple Justice: The History of Brown v. Board of Education and Black America's Struggle for Equality.* New York: Random House.

Krosnick, Jon A., and Duane F. Alwin. 1989. "Aging and Susceptibility to Attitude Change." *Journal of Personality and Social Psychology* 57:416–425.

Krysan, Maria. 1995. *White Racial Attitudes: Does It Matter How We Ask?* Ph.D. dissertation, University of Michigan, Ann Arbor.

Kuklinski, James H., and Wayne Parent. 1981. "Race and Big Government: Contamination in Measuring Racial Attitudes." *Political Methodology,* Fall, pp. 131–159.

LaPiere, R. T. 1934. "Attitudes vs. Actions." *Social Forces* 13:230–237.

Latane, Bib, and John M. Darley. 1970. *The Unresponsive Bystander: Why Doesn't He Help?* New York: Appleton-Century-Crofts.

Laumann, Edward O., John A. Gagnon, Robert T. Michael, and Stuart Michaels. 1994. *The Social Organization of Sexuality: Sexual Practices in the United States.* Chicago: University of Chicago Press.

Lawson, Stephen F. 1976. *Black Ballots: Voting Rights in the South, 1944–1969.* New York: Columbia University Press.

Lenski, G. E., and J. C. Leggett. 1960. "Caste, Class, and Deference in the Research Interview." *American Journal of Sociology* 65:463–467.

Leuchtenburg, William E. 1991. "The Conversion of Harry Truman." *American Heritage,* November, pp.55–68.

Levine, Robert A. 1971. "The Silent Majority: Neither Simple nor Simple Minded." *Public Opinion Quarterly* 35:571–577.

Levitan, Sar A., and Robert Taggart. 1976. *The Promise of Greatness.* Cambridge, Mass.: Harvard University Press.

Lipset, Seymour Martin. 1996. *American Exceptionalism: A Double-Edged Sword.* New York: Norton.

Lipset, Seymour Martin, and William Schneider. 1978. "The Bakke Case: How

Would It Be Decided at the Bar of Public Opinion?" *Public Opinion*, March/April, pp. 38–44.

Mannheim, Karl. [1928] 1952. "The Problem of Generations." In Karl Mannheim, *Essays on the Sociology of Knowledge*, pp. 276–322. London: Routledge and Kegan Paul.

Marable, Manning. 1995. *Beyond Black and White: Transforming African American Politics*. New York: Verso.

Margolis, Michael, and Khondaker E. Haque. 1981. "Applied Tolerance or Fear of Government? An Alternative Interpretation of Jackman's Findings." *American Journal of Political Science* 25:241–255.

Martin, Elizabeth, Diane McDuffee, and Stanley Presser. 1981. *Sourcebook of Harris National Surveys: Related Questions, 1963–1976*. Chapel Hill, N.C.: Institute for Research in Social Science.

Marx, Gary T. 1967. *Protest and Prejudice*. New York: Harper and Row.

Massey, Douglas S., and Nancy A. Denton. 1993. *American Apartheid: Segregation and the Making of the Underclass*. Cambridge, Mass.: Harvard University Press.

Mayer, Jane, and Jill Abramson. 1994. *Strange Justice: The Selling of Clarence Thomas*. Boston: Houghton Mifflin.

Mayer, William G. 1992. *The Changing American Mind: How and Why American Public Opinion Changed between 1960 and 1988*. Ann Arbor: University of Michigan Press.

McAdam, Douglas. 1982. *Political Process and the Development of Black Insurgency, 1930–1970*. Chicago: University of Chicago Press.

McConahay, John B. 1986. "Modern Racism, Ambivalence, and the Modern Racism Scale." In John F. Dovidio and Samuel L. Gaertner (eds.), *Prejudice, Discrimination, and Racism*, pp. 91–125. San Diego: Academic Press.

Mead, Lawrence M. 1986. *Beyond Entitlement: The Social Obligations of Citizenship*. New York: Free Press.

Meier, August, and Elliott Rudwick. 1976. *From Plantation to Ghetto*. 3rd ed. New York: Hill and Wang.

Merton, Robert K. 1957. *Social Theory and Social Structure*. Glencoe, Ill.: Free Press.

Miller, Warren E., Arthur H. Miller, and Edward J. Schneider. 1980. *American National Election Studies Data Sourcebook, 1952–1978*. Cambridge, Mass.: Harvard University Press.

Morris, Aldon D. 1984. *The Origins of the Civil Rights Movement: Black Communities Organizing for Change*. New York: Free Press.

Moser, C. A., and G. Kalton. 1972. *Survey Methods in Social Investigation*. New York: Basic Books.

Murphy, Raymond J., and James M. Watson. 1967. *The Structure of Discontent: The Relationship between Social Structure, Grievance, and Support for the Los Angeles Riot*. Los Angeles: Institute of Government and Public Affairs.

Murray, Charles. 1984. *Losing Ground: American Social Policy, 1950–1980*. New York: Basic Books.

Myrdal, Gunnar. 1944. *An American Dilemma: The Negro Problem and Modern Democracy.* 2 vols. New York: Harper and Brothers.

Newman, Dorothy K., N. J. Amidei, B. L. Carter, D. Day, W. J. Kruvant, and J. S. Russell. 1978. *Protest, Politics, and Prosperity: Black Americans and White Institutions, 1940–75.* New York: Random House.

Oates, Stephen B. 1982. *Let the Trumpet Sound: The Life of Martin Luther King, Jr.* New York: Harper and Row.

Olzak, Susan, Suzanne Shanahan, and Elizabeth West. 1994. "School Desegregation, Interracial Exposure, and Antibusing Activity in Contemporary Urban America." *American Journal of Sociology* 100:196–241.

Orfield, Gary, Mark D. Bachmeier, David R. James, and Tamela Ietle. 1997. "Deepening Segregation in American Public Schools." Unpublished paper, Harvard Project on School Desegregation, Cambridge, Mass.

Page, Benjamin I., and Robert Y. Shapiro. 1992. *The Rational Public: Fifty Years of Trends in Americans' Policy Preferences.* Chicago: University of Chicago Press.

Paige, Jeffery M. 1970. "Changing Patterns of Anti-White Attitudes among Blacks." *Journal of Social Issues* 26:69–86.

Parsons, Talcott. 1937. *The Structure of Social Action.* New York: McGraw-Hill.

Pettigrew, Thomas F. 1959. "Regional Differences in Anti-Negro Prejudice." *Journal of Abnormal and Social Psychology* 59:28–36.

——— 1979. "Racial Change and Social Policy." *Annals of the American Academy of Political and Social Science* 441:114–131.

——— 1997. "Generalized Intergroup Contact Effects on Prejudice." *Personality and Social Psychology Bulletin* 23:173–185.

Poskocil, Art. 1977. "Encounters between Blacks and White Liberals: The Collision of Stereotypes." *Social Forces* 55:715–727.

Powell, Colin. 1995. *My American Journey.* New York: Random House.

Prothro, James W., and Charles M. Grigg. 1960. "Fundamental Principles of Democracy: Bases of Agreement and Disagreement." *Journal of Politics* 22:276–294.

Quillian, Lincoln. 1996. "Group Threat and Regional Change in Attitudes toward African-Americans." *American Journal of Sociology* 102:816–860.

Report of the National Advisory Commission on Civil Disorders. 1968. Washington, D.C.: U.S. Government Printing Office.

Roberts, Carl W., and Kurt Lang. 1985. "Generations and Ideological Change: Some Observations." *Public Opinion Quarterly* 49:460–473.

Rodgers, Harrell R. 1975. "On Integrating the Public Schools: An Empirical and Legal Assessment." In Harrell R. Rodgers (ed.), *Racism and Inequality: The Policy Alternatives,* pp. 125–160. San Francisco: Freeman.

Rodgers, Willard L. 1990. "Interpreting the Components of Time Trends." In Clifford C. Clogg (ed.), *Sociological Methodology 1990,* vol. 20. Cambridge: Basil Blackwell Ltd.

Rokeach, Milton, and Sandra J. Ball-Rokeach. 1989. "Stability and Change in American Value Priorities." *American Psychologist* 44:775–784.

Ross, L., D. Greene, and P. House. 1977. "The 'False Consensus Effect': An Egocentric Bias in Social Perception and Attribution Processes." *Journal of Experimental Social Psychology* 13:279–301.

Rothbart, Myron. 1976. "Achieving Racial Equality: An Analysis of Resistance to Social Reform." In Phyllis A. Katz (ed.), *Towards the Elimination of Racism.* New York: Pergamon Press.

Rothbart, Myron, and Oliver P. John. 1993. "Intergroup Relations and Stereotype Change: A Social-Cognitive Analysis and Some Longitudinal Findings." In Paul M. Sniderman, Philip E. Tetlock, and Edward G. Carmines (eds.), *Prejudice, Politics, and the American Dilemma,* pp. 32–59. Stanford: Stanford University Press.

Sanders, Lynn M. 1995. "What Is Whiteness? Race-of-Interviewer Effects When All the Interviewers Are Black." Paper given at the American Politics Workshop, The University of Chicago.

Scammon, R. M., and B. J. Wattenberg. 1973. "Black Progress and Liberal Rhetoric." *Commentary* 10:35–44.

Schaeffer, Nora Cate. 1980. "Evaluating Race-of-Interviewer Effects in a National Survey." *Sociological Methods & Research* 8:400–419.

Schuman, Howard. 1966. "The Random Probe: A Technique for Evaluating the Validity of Closed Questions." *American Sociological Review* 31:218–222.

——— 1969. "Free Will and Determinism in Public Beliefs about Race." *Trans-Action* 7:44–48.

———1995. "Attitudes, Beliefs, and Behavior." In K. Cook, G. A. Fine, and J. S. House (eds.), *Sociological Perspectives on Social Psychology,* pp. 68–89. Boston: Allyn & Bacon.

Schuman, Howard, and Lawrence Bobo. 1988. "Survey-based Experiments on White Racial Attitudes toward Residential Integration." *American Journal of Sociology* 94:273–299.

Schuman, Howard, Lawrence Bobo, and Maria Krysan. 1992. "Authoritarianism in the General Population: The Education Interaction Hypothesis." *Social Psychology Quarterly* 55:379–387.

Schuman, Howard, and Jean M. Converse. 1971. "The Effects of Black and White Interviewers on Black Responses in 1968." *Public Opinion Quarterly* 35:46–68.

Schuman, Howard, and Shirley Hatchett. 1974. *Black Racial Attitudes: Trends and Complexities.* Ann Arbor: Institute for Social Research.

Schuman, Howard, and Michael P. Johnson. 1976. "Attitudes and Behavior." *Annual Review of Sociology* 2:161–207.

Schuman, Howard, and Maria Krysan. 1996. "A Study of Far Right *Ressentiment* in America." *International Journal of Public Opinion* 8:10–30.

Schuman, Howard, and Jacob Ludwig. 1983. "The Norm of Even-Handedness in Surveys as in Life." *American Sociological Review* 48:112–120.

Schuman, Howard, and Stanley Presser. 1981. *Questions and Answers in Attitude Surveys: Experiments on Question Form, Wording, and Context.* New York: Academic Press.

Schuman, Howard, and Cheryl Rieger. 1992. "Historical Analogies, Generational Effects, and Attitudes toward War." *American Sociological Review* 57:315–326.

Schuman, Howard, and Jacqueline Scott. 1989. "Generations and Collective Memories." *American Sociological Review* 54:359–381.

Schuman, Howard, Eleanor Singer, Rebecca Donovan, and Claire Selltiz. 1983. "Discriminatory Behavior in New York Restaurants: 1950 and 1981." *Social Indicators Research* 13:69–83.

Schuman, Howard, Charlotte Steeh, and Lawrence Bobo. 1985. *Racial Attitudes in America: Trends and Interpretations*. Cambridge, Mass.: Harvard University Press.

Schuman, Howard, Charlotte Steeh, and Lawrence Bobo. 1990. "A Clarification." *The American Psychologist* 45:674–675.

Schwartz, Mildred A. 1967. *Trends in White Attitudes toward Negroes*. Chicago: National Opinion Research Center.

Schwarz, Norbert, and Hans-Jurgen Hippler. 1995. "Subsequent Questions May Influence Answers to Preceding Questions in Mail Surveys." *Public Opinion Quarterly* 59:93–97.

Sears, David O. 1983. "The Persistence of Early Political Predispositions: The Roles of Attitude Object and Life Stage." In Ladd Wheeler (ed.), *Review of Personality and Social Psychology,* vol. 4, pp. 79–116. Beverly Hills: Sage Publications.

—— 1988. "Symbolic Racism." In Phyllis A. Katz and Dalmas A. Taylor (eds.), *Eliminating Racism: Profiles in Controversy.* New York: Plenum Press.

—— 1997. "The Impact of Self-Interest on Attitudes—A Symbolic Politics Perspective on Differences between Survey and Experimental Findings: Comment on Crano (1997)." *Journal of Personality and Social Psychology* 72:492–496.

Sears, David O., and C. L. Funk. 1991. "The Role of Self-Interest in Social and Political Attitudes." *Advances in Experimental Social Psychology* 24:1–91.

Sears, David O., Carl P. Hensler, and Leslie K. Speer. 1979. "Whites' Opposition to 'Busing': Self-Interest or Symbolic Politics?" *American Political Science Review* 73:369–384.

Sears, David O., and Tom Jessor. 1996. "Whites' Racial Policy Attitudes: The Role of White Racism." *Social Science Quarterly* 77:751–759.

Sears, David O., and John B. McConahay. 1973. *The Polities of Violence.* Boston: Houghton Mifflin.

Shapiro, Robert Y., and Harpreet Mahajan. 1986. "Gender Differences in Policy Preferences: A Summary of Trends from the 1960s to the 1980s." *Public Opinion Quarterly* 50:42–61.

Sheatsley, Paul B. 1966. "White Attitudes toward the Negro." *Daedalus* 95:217–238.

Sidanius, Jim, Felicia Pratto, and Lawrence Bobo. 1996. "Racism, Conservatism, Affirmative Action, and Intellectual Sophistication: A Matter of Principled Conservatism or Group Dominance." *Journal of Personality and Social Psychology* 70:476–490.

Sigelman, Lee. Forthcoming. "The Public and Disadvantage-Based Affirmative Action: A Baseline Assessment." *Social Science Quarterly.*

Sigelman, Lee, Timothy Bledsoe, Susan Welch, and Michael Combs. 1996. "Making Contact? Black-White Social Interaction in an Urban Setting." *American Journal of Sociology* 101:1306–1332.

Sigelman, Lee, and Susan Welch. 1991. *Black Americans' Views of Racial Inequality: The Dream Deferred.* Cambridge: Cambridge University Press.

Silverman, B. I. 1974. "Consequences, Racial Discrimination, and the Principle of Belief Congruence." *Journal of Personality and Social Psychology* 22:259–268.

Sitkoff, Harvard. 1971. "Harry Truman and the Election of 1948: The Coming of Age of Civil Rights in American Politics." *Journal of Southern History* 37:597–616.

——— 1978. *A New Deal for Blacks: The Emergence of Civil Rights as a National Issue.* Vol. 1: *Depression Decade.* New York: Oxford University Press.

———1993. *The Struggle for Black Equality, 1954–1992.* Rev. ed. New York: Hill and Wang.

Skrentny, John David. 1996. *The Ironies of Affirmative Action.* Chicago: University of Chicago Press.

Smith, A. Wade. 1981. "Racial Tolerance as a Function of Group Position." *American Sociological Review* 46:558–573.

——— 1985. "Cohorts, Education, and the Evolution of Tolerance." *Social Science Research* 14:205–225.

Smith, Tom W. 1980. "America's Most Important Problem: A Trend Analysis, 1946–1976." *Public Opinion Quarterly* 44:171.

——— 1984. "House Effects." In Charles Turner and Elizabeth Martin (eds.), *Surveying Subjective Phenomena,* vol. 1. New York: Russell Sage Foundation.

——— 1990. "Liberal and Conservative Trends in the United States Since World War II." *Public Opinion Quarterly* 54:479–507.

——— 1991. "A Comparison of the 1988 Current Population Survey to the 1987–1990 General Social Surveys." Unpublished NORC Report. February.

Sniderman, Paul M., Richard A. Brody, and Philip E. Tetlock. 1991. *Reasoning and Choice: Explorations in Political Psychology.* New York: Cambridge University Press.

Sniderman, Paul M., and Edward G. Carmines. 1997. *Reaching Beyond Race.* Cambridge, Mass.: Harvard University Press.

Sniderman, Paul M., and Thomas Piazza. 1993. *The Scar of Race.* Cambridge, Mass.: Harvard University Press.

Spilerman, Seymour. 1976. "Structural Characteristics of Cities and the Severity of Racial Disorders." *American Sociological Review* 41:771–793.

Steeh, Charlotte G. 1981. "Trends in Nonresponse Rates, 1952–1979." *Public Opinion Quarterly* 45:40–57.

Steeh, Charlotte, and Howard Schuman. 1992. "Young White Adults: Did Racial Attitudes Change in the 1980s?" *American Journal of Sociology* 98:340–367.

Steinberg, Stephen. 1995. *Turning Back: The Retreat from Racial Justice in American Thought and Policy.* Boston: Beacon Press.

Stember, Charles Herbert. 1961. *Education and Attitude Change.* New York: Institute of Human Relations Press.

Stember, Charles Herbert, et al. 1966. *Jews in the Mind of America.* New York: Basic Books.

Stephenson, C. Bruce. 1979. "Probability Sampling with Quotas: An Experiment." *Public Opinion Quarterly* 43:477–496.

Stimson, James A. 1991. *Public Opinion in America: Moods, Cycles, and Swings.* Boulder, Colo.: Westview Press.

Stoker, Laura. 1996. "Understanding Differences in Whites' Opinions across Racial Policies." *Social Science Quarterly.* 77:768–777.

Stouffer, S. A. 1955. *Communism, Conformity and Civil Liberties.* New York: Wiley.

Taeuber, Karl E., and Alma F. Taeuber. 1965. *Negroes in Cities: Residential Segregation and Neighborhood Change.* Chicago: Aldine.

Takaki, Ronald T. 1979. *Iron Cages: Race and Culture in Nineteenth-Century America.* Seattle: University of Washington Press.

Tate, Katherine. 1993. *From Protest to Politics: The New Black Voters in American Elections.* Cambridge, Mass.: Harvard University Press.

Taylor, D. Garth, Paul B. Sheatsley, and Andrew M. Greeley. 1978. Attitudes toward Racial Integration. *Scientific American* 238:42–51.

Taylor, Marylee C., and Thomas F. Pettigrew. 1992. "Prejudice." In Edgar F. Borgatta and Marie L. Borgatta (eds.), *Encyclopedia of Sociology,* vol. 3, pp. 1536–1541. New York: Macmillan.

Thernstrom, Abigail M. 1986. "How Much Racial Progress?" *The Public Interest* 85:96–100.

Tocqueville, Alexis de. 1945. *Democracy in America,* vol. 1. New York: Vintage (orig. pub. 1835).

Tomlinson, T. M. 1968. "The Development of a Riot Ideology among Urban Negroes." *American Behavioral Scientist* 11:27–31.

Tuch, Steven A., and Lee Sigelman. Forthcoming. "Race, Class, and Black-White Differences in Social Policy Views." In Barbara Norrander and Clyde Wilcox (eds.), *Understanding Public Opinion.* Washington, D.C.: CQ Press.

Turner, Margery Austin, Michael Fix, and Raymond J. Struyk. 1991. *Opportunities Denied, Opportunities Diminished: Racial Discrimination in Hiring.* Washington, D.C.: Urban Institute Press.

Tyler, Tom R., and Regina A. Schuller. 1991. "Aging and Attitude Change." *Journal of Personality and Social Psychology* 61:689–697.

U.S. Bureau of the Census. 1969. *Changing Characteristics of the Negro Population,* by Donald O. Price. A 1960 Census Monograph. Washington, D.C.: Government Printing Office.

——— 1979. *The Social and Economic Status of the Black Population in the United States: An Historical View, 1790–1978.* Current Population Reports, Special Studies Series, no. 80. Washington, D.C.: Government Printing Office.

—— 1980. *Social Indicators III*. Washington, D.C.: Government Printing Office.

U.S. National Advisory Commission on Civil Disorders. 1968. *Report*. Washington, D.C.: Government Printing Office.

U.S. President's Committee on Civil Rights. 1947. *To Secure These Rights*. New York: Simon and Schuster.

Useem, Bert. 1980. "Solidarity Breakdown Model and the Boston AntiBusing Movement." *American Sociological Review* 45:357–369.

Waldinger, Roger, and Tom Bailey. 1991. "The Continuing Significance of Race: Racial Conflict and Racial Discrimination in Construction." *Politics and Society* 19:291–323.

Waters, Mary C. 1990. *Ethnic Options: Choosing Identities in America*. Berkeley: University of California Press.

Weigel, Russell H., and Lee S. Newman. 1976. "Attitude-Behavior Correspondence by Broadening the Scope of the Behavioral Measure." *Journal of Personality and Social Psychology* 33:793–802.

Weil, Frederick D. 1985. "The Variable Effects of Education on Liberal Attitudes: A Comparative Historical Analysis of Anti-Semitism Using Public Opinion Survey Data." *American Sociological Review* 50:458–474.

—— 1987. "Cohorts, Regimes, and the Legitimation of Democracy: West Germany since 1945." *American Sociological Review* 52:308–316.

West, Cornell. 1996. "The Million Man March." *Dissent*, Winter, pp. 97–98.

Westie, Frank. 1965. "The American Dilemma: An Empirical Test." *American Sociological Review* 30:527–538.

Whalen, Jack, and Richard Flacks. 1989. *Beyond the Barricades: The Sixties Generation Grows Up*. Philadelphia: Temple University Press.

Wilkins, Roy. 1982. *Standing Fast: The Autobiography of Roy Wilkins*. New York: Viking.

Wilkinson, J. Harve, III. 1979. *From Brown to Bakke: The Supreme Court and School Integration: 1954–1978*. New York: Oxford University Press.

Williams, Gregory Howard. 1995. *Life on the Color Line: The True Story of a White Boy Who Discovered That He Was Black*. New York: Dutton.

Williams, J. A., Jr. 1964. "Interviewer-Respondent Interaction: A Study of Bias in the Information Interview." *Sociometry* 27:338–352.

Willie, Charles V. 1978. "The Inclining Significance of Race." *Society* 15, no. 5, pp. 10, 12–15.

Wilson, Barbara Foley. 1984. "Marriage's Melting Pot." *American Demographics*, July, pp. 34–45.

Wilson, Thomas C. 1986. "Interregional Migration and Racial Attitudes." *Social Forces* 65:177–186.

—— 1996. "Cohort and Prejudice: Whites' Attitudes toward Blacks, Hispanics, Jews, and Asians." *Public Opinion Quarterly* 60:253–274.

Wilson, William Julius. 1980. *The Declining Significance of Race*. 2nd ed. Chicago: University of Chicago Press.

—— 1987. *The Truly Disadvantaged: The Inner City, the Underclass, and Public Policy*. Chicago: University of Chicago Press.

———— 1996. *When Work Disappears: The World of the New Urban Poor.* New York: Knopf.

Wittenbrink, Bernd, Charles M. Judd, and Bernadette Park. 1997. "Evidence for Racial Prejudice at the Implicit Level and Its Relationship with Questionnaire Measures." *Journal of Personality and Social Psychology* 72:262–274.

Woodward, C. Vann. 1974. *The Strange Career of Jim Crow.* 3rd rev. ed. New York: Oxford University Press.

Yinger, John. 1996. *Closed Doors, Opportunities Lost: The Continuing Costs of Housing Discrimination.* New York: Russell Sage Foundation.

Zashin, Elliot. 1978. "The Progress of Black Americans in Civil Rights: The Past Two Decades Addressed." *Daedalus* 107:239–262.

General Index

ABC/*Washington Post* Poll, 60, 62, 72, 90, 158–159, 166–167, 260–261, 265, 281, 332–333
Aberbach, Joel D., 33, 239
Abramson, Jill, 41
Abramson, Paul R., 365nn17,18
Accommodations. *See* Public accommodations
Acquiescence bias, 95, 353n36
Adarand Construction v. Pena, 46
Addams, Jane, 20
Adorno, T. W., 295, 319
Affirmative action, 36, 38–40, 43, 45–46, 51–52, 55–56; questions about, 61, 101–102, 170–183, 194–195, 225–228, 257, 263–264, 266–270, 338–339
Afrocentrism, 48
Age, as variable, 73
Aging, and attitude changes, 197–199
Ajzen, Icek, 6
Alabama, 16, 22, 25–26, 28–29
Alker, Henry, 6
Allen, Bem P., 305
Alwin, Duane F., 198
Anderson, Barbara A., 88–90, 365nn17, 18
Anderson, Elijah, 42–43, 371n12
Annan, Kofi, 56
Apostle, Richard A., 154, 294, 353n35
Arkansas, 16, 23–24, 28
Ashmore, Harry S., 17, 19–20
Attitude conversion. See Period effects
Attitudes, 53, 56–57; defined, 1–2; and norms, 2–5, 311–312, 314–315; and behavior, 5–7, 312–314; and inner convictions, 7–8

Bailey, Tom, 47
Bakke decision. *See Regents of the University of California v. Bakke*
Barnett, Ross, 24
Baxter, Sandra, 205
Begley, Thomas M., 6
Behavior, 5–7, 312–314
Beliefs, 2
Beliefs about inequality, questions about, 61, 100–101, 153–170, 193–194, 219–225, 253, 256–262, 338–339
Bennett, Claudette E., 311
Bensonhurst racial incident, 44
Berman, William C., 19
Berry, Mary Frances, 44
Besharov, Douglas J., 370n5
Biological racism, 9–11
Birmingham, Ala.: demonstrations in, 25–27, 54, 197, 203; church bombing in, 30
Black disadvantage, belief questions about, 153–155, 161–166
Black English, 51, 56
Black Panthers, 33, 55
Black Power, 33–35, 55, 326
Black presidential candidate, principle questions about, 114
Bobo, Lawrence, 163, 220, 293–295, 303, 308, 351nn22,26, 353n36, 354n38, 356n53, 365nn22,23, 367n9, 368nn15,17, 369n18, 371n7
Bogardus, Emory S., 100
Bogart, Leo, 13
Bonacich, Edna, 342n7
Bond, Julian, 39
Bositis, David A., 343n15

Index of Survey Questions